Bertrand Russell's America
1945-1970

BERTRAND RUSSELL'S AMERICA
VOLUME II   1945-1970

A documented account by
Barry Feinberg & Ronald Kasrils

South End Press
Boston

Library of Congress number 82-061149
ISBN 0-89608-156-7 paper
ISBN 0-89608-157-5 cloth

Production by South End Press
Cover design by Lydia Sargent
Cover photo by Associated Press

SOUTH END PRESS 302 COLUMBUS AVE
BOSTON MA 02116

Table of Contents

Our Sources of Material And Assistance

Russell's writings on America began in earnest shortly before America's entry into World War I. His contributions to American periodicals commenced at that time and became extensive over the years. These writings which reflect the development of Russell's views on America, became more prolific in the 1950s and 1960s as the threat of nuclear war emerged and the crisis of the United States became more profound.

A further source of rich material reflecting Russell's interest in the United States is his collection of letters to and from Americans which, taken together with seven decades of American press coverage of Russell, and the epigrammatic accounts of his visits contained in his Autobiography, help give a detailed picture of Russell's relationship with the United States. Because of the enormous quantity of material, and in order to present it in an integrated and readable form, it has been necessary to produce this work in two volumes, covering the periods 1896-1945, and 1945-1970, respectively. Volume I was published in 1973. The end of World War II, when Russell returned to England after his six-year stay in the United States, provided a suitable dividing point, since the development and use of the atomic bomb foreshadowed a new era in his life. Volume II is in two parts: the first part presents in biographical and documentary form an account of Russell's involvement with the United States. The most representative of Russell's journalistic writings are highlighted throughout the narrative, and the full texts of the most important of these appear in the second part. This method of presentation was considered essential for continuity of narrative and ease of reference. Much of the correspondence is published here for the first time. Many of the letters have required considerable editing, so as to retain only those extracts which are of importance to the theme of this book. Except where otherwise stated and described all Russell's writings appearing in this volume have been unpublished and are reproduced with the joint permission of the Bertrand Russell Estate and the Bertrand Russell Archives at McMaster University, Hamilton, Ontario.

Special thanks are due to the late Edith, Countess Russell who encouraged us to complete and publish this book, and to the following individuals who helped in many and various ways during its preparation: Christopher Farley and Kenneth Coates of the Bertrand Russell Peace

Foundation, Anton Felton of the Bertrand Russell Estate, Kenneth Blackwell and his staff at the Bertrand Russell Archives, Professor Barrows Dunham, Ian Mordant, Bev Gosling, Lydia Sargent.

Thanks are also due Russell's publishers: George Allen and Unwin Ltd., Simon and Schuster, Monthly Review Press, O'Hare Books, *Cavalcade, News Review, The Listener, The Witchita Beacon, Evening Standard, Des Moines Sunday Register, New York Times Magazine, University of Chicago Law Review, New Republic, The Minority of One, Fact, Newsweek, Washington Post, Los Angeles Times, Ramparts, The Times, New Leader, Harper's Magazine, New York Times, Life, World Outlook, National Guardian, Tribune, Views, The Week, Le Monde, Morning Star, New York Herald Tribune, St. Louis Post Dispatch, Sunday Times, I.F. Stone's Weekly, New Statesman, Saturday Review, The Guardian.*

We are indebted to the following individuals or, where appropriate, their executors, extracts of whose letters appear in this book: Albert Einstein, Barrows Dunham, Corliss Lamont, Norman Thomas, Rudolf Carnap, Alice May Hilton, James Boggs, Julie Medlock, Howard Ozman, Upton Sinclair, Cedric Belfrage, Stephanie May, James Fulton, Cyrus Eaton, Linus Pauling, Rockwell Kent, Lewis Mumford, Muhammed Ali.

Introduction

A little over 22 years after Russell was judicially hounded out of his appointment as visiting Professor at the College of the City of New York, an American teenager wrote and asked him to comment on that notorious event which she had chosen as the subject of a school study project. "I became interested in this incident through my father," she explained, who was "one of the undergraduates deprived of becoming one of your students and has not stopped complaining to this day."[1]

In his reply of 6 August 1963, Russell described his treatment in New York as "a clear example of the danger of dogma and intolerance still widely prevalent in the United States." He also told her that he had "lost all income through the episode and was unable to gain employment in the United States for some time" but, he warned, "the consequence of dogma and fanatical cruelty then is nowhere near as grave as it is today when it shapes nuclear and foreign policy and threatens mankind with obliteration."

Russell's overriding concern to prevent a nuclear war and to oppose attitudes and actions which, he felt, helped bring it closer, is, in an American context, the central theme of this book. Like its preceeding volume, which covers the years 1896-1945[2] and includes a blow by blow account of the witch-hunting of Russell in New York in 1940, this volume tells the story of Russell's relationship with America largely through his own writing knit together with a biographical commentary.

Russell visited the United States on nine occasions, including a period of extended residence during World War II. He lectured at numerous colleges and held professorships at the universities of Harvard, Chicago and California. Apart from his impact as a philosopher, he came famous as a popularizer of socio-political ideas through public lectures and debates across the country. Russell's activities, including the publication of his numerous journalistic writings and books, brought him into close touch with the American public and with the forces shaping U.S. society. "He knew the United States as few Americans knew it since he had visited almost every part of it during his lecture tours" wrote Gerald Brenan, in his autobiography.[3] From England Russell kept abreast of developments in the U.S. through correspondence with many American friends.

"The hopes and fears of the world, probably for the next fifty years at least," he wrote in 1922, "depend upon the use which America makes of her vast power."[4] By 1924, he had become an outspoken critic of U.S. capitalism, and conducted an extensive socialist propaganda tour of the U.S. He was convinced that a socialist America was a necessary step towards solving the world's problems.

As Russell's association with America developed, and he became more intimate with problems facing the American people, so the scope of his activities widened. He found, in the land where human rights were idealised, gross inequalities in wealth and power, authoritarian interference with academic freedom and civil liberties, racism and the persecution of minorities. Russell recognized that radicalism in America was very weak; one of his main concerns, therefore, was to help promote liberal and tolerant attitudes. His emphasis on education as a powerful vehicle for reshaping society led him to express advanced views on the family and sexual morality which provoked great hostility towards him; and in the 1940s he found himself the subject of a fierce witch-hunt in which a coalition of his clerical and political opponents attempted to drive him from the country. But, Russell was also viewed as an outstanding symbol of reason and hope by wide sections of American opinion, including the peace and civil rights movements, students and academics, and was already in the early 1920s being described as "an inspiration to progressive forces in America."[5]

In 1945, however, Russell's view of American government policies had been conditioned by his dislike of communism and by his acceptance of the major war aims of the West. When the USSR rejected the U.S. proposal for atomic control, contained in the Baruch Plan, Russell recommended forcing the USSR to comply, by war if necessary. When in 1949, the USSR successfully tested an atomic bomb, Russell changed his view because it meant that "we cannot defeat Russia except by defeating ourselves."[6]

In later years Russell described his suggestion to threaten the USSR as "the worst thing I ever said—and I am sorry I did...it wasn't that I wanted war...but to preserve the peace of the world."[7]

The Cold War and the resulting erosion of civil liberties in the United States caused Russell to be increasingly apprehensive about America's future international role. His fears were reinforced by the McCarthy campaigns. His two lecture tours of the U.S. in 1950 and 1951 helped to convince him that world peace was threatened by fanatical anti-communism.

After the explosion of the first U.S. H-bomb in November 1952, Russell began to address himself increasingly to the problem of nuclear disarmament. He also campaigned on behalf of Morton Sobell and other victims of McCarthyism.

He pursued his major concerns with extraordinary energy. He was already under daily seige from an illimitable flow of mail from individuals and organizations the world over. He responded to almost all of it formulating his replies with care and concision. Most of his correspondents were American.

Russell's reputation and moral authority grew with his commitment to the cause of nuclear disarmament. This commitment left him with little time to consider any more long term political strategy and he confined himself increasingly to challenging through his own writings, the orthodoxy of the day. His outspoken views, succeeded, like no other foreign voice, in arousing Americans to the crisis of their society.

In 1958 his important, but now little known, correspondence with Khrushchev and John Foster Dulles on the subject of disarmament, caused a storm of controversy in the United States. Many Americans were hostile to Russell's views on the desirability of detente with the USSR. In response to one critic, who accused him of changing his position on dealing with the USSR, Russell commented "it has changed as circumstances have changed. To achieve a single purpose, sane men adapt their policies to circumstances. Those who do not are insane."[8] Equally angry reactions were provoked by his mediation between Kennedy and Khrushchev during the Cuban Crisis in 1962; but "the solution to the crisis," Russell confessed to one of the many Americans who praised his role, "made the week one of the most worthwhile of my entire life."[9]

But it was U.S. military actions in Vietnam which, more than any other factor, made him a vigorous opponent of United States policies. Russell believed that America's internal crisis—reflected in the revolt of Black Americans—taken together with its aggressive international policies, constituted the main threat to world peace.

When black ghettos in New York and other American cities erupted in the summer of 1964 Russell clearly indicated where his sympathies lay: "Were I in New York," he stated, "I should certainly be guilty of trying to overthrow the government of the State of New York."[10] So closely had Russell identified himself with the plight of Black Americans that the *Los Angeles Times*, after describing Russell as "a senile and garrulous old man," suggested that Martin Luther King "by his decision to use the prestige won in his campaign for civil rights for the purposes of conciliation in Vietnam" was "in danger of becoming the Bertrand Russell of the United States."[11]

When Martin Luther King was assassinated in 1968 Russell described his murder as "a foretaste of the violence erupting in America because the U.S. government cannot finance a full scale war in Vietnam and alleviate the misery of its most oppressed citizens."[12] Russell appealed to Black American soldiers in Vietnam to consider where their real struggle was. "Is it in Vietnam," he asked, "or is it in defence of your own people against oppression inside the United States."[13]

With the escalation of the Vietnam War Russell launched in 1967 a War Crimes Tribunal with the object of trying President Johnson and his government. An abusive press campaign was mounted against Russell. The *New York Times* described the Tribunal as a "pretence" and a "shoddy farce," "stage-managed" in Russell's name and that he had "turned into a full-time purveyor of political garbage indistinguishable from the routine products of the Soviet machine."[14] In contrast to the press, increasing numbers of Americans were demonstrating their opposition to the war. In a message to a "Rally to End the War in Vietnam Now" Russell assessed that Americans had allowed "corporate capitalism to identify its selfish and rapacious aims with the national interest of the American nation," and he warned: "American power challenges the aspirations of mankind."[15]

Shortly before his death on 2 February 1970 Russell urged "the people of America" to "repudiate their civil and military leaders." "If there is not a massive moral revulsion at what is being done in their names to the people of Vietnam," he wrote, "there may be little hope for the future of America."[16]

Footnotes

1. Dorothy Schneider to Russell 29 March 1963.
2. B. Feinberg and R. Kasrils, *Bertrand Russell's America* Vol. I, 1896-1945 (London, 1973, (Viking Press, New York, 1974).
3. *Personal Record*, (Jonathan Cape, London, 1974), pp. 264-5.
4. B. Feinberg and R. Kasrils, *Bertrand Russell's America* Vol. I, p. 220.
5. *Ibid.*, p. 91.
6. Interview in *National Guardian*, May 1956 (see below pp. 86-9).
7. *Ibid.*
8. Russell to Alfred Kohlberg, 8 March 1958.
9. See below, p. 158.
10. See below, p. 238.
11. See below, p. 240.
12. Statement published in *London Bulletin*, Summer 1968; see also below, p. 288.
13. See below, pp. 274-5.
14. See below, p. 282.
15. See below, p. 258.
16. See below, p. 291.

PART ONE
Bertrand Russell's America
1945-1970

1 The Atom Bomb

After six years in America, Bertrand Russell was pleased to get back to England in 1944, where he took up an appointment at Trinity College, Cambridge. He was accorded a great welcome and students thronged to his lectures; a response which was in marked contrast to the hostility he had endured so recently in America. Russell was greatly relieved to be free from acrimonious controversy and was able to relax in the more tolerant atmosphere of England. "I enjoyed once more the freedom of discussion that prevailed in England but not in America," he wrote, and added "In America, if a policeman addressed us, my young son burst into tears; and the same was true (*mutatis mutandis*) of university professors accused of speeding."[1] The need to constantly defend himself in America was a considerable strain and as a consequence Russell found that returning to England served to modify his outlook for, "the less fanatical attitude of English people diminished my own fanaticism, and I rejoiced in the feeling of home."[2]

Despite these strong feelings Russell regarded the United States as the best hope for a world based on freedom and tolerance. It is clear too that he felt Britain's liberal tradition could be effectively used as a positive influence on American society and U.S. policy. Russell was at pains to combat misunderstanding and prejudice between Britons and Americans—which was not entirely absent both at the public and private levels—and his expressed intention was to make his knowledge of America useful at home. In his wartime writings he had stressed his belief in the need for a special relationship between the United States and Great Britain, as the most acceptable way of securing world peace. Indeed so hopeful was he of the role the United States would play, despite the defects he had observed in American society, and the sharp criticisms he had voiced in an association of fifty years, that he was on record as stating:

Every country has its defects, but in relation to the world, I believe those of America to be less than those of any other country. I have considerable confidence that American influence will, on the whole, be exercised wisely and humanely....I think their hegemony will be kindly and tolerant to a greater degree than that of any European country would be, and whatever pangs I may feel as a patriot, I look to the Empire of America for the best hopes that our distracted world permits.

Russell was in an optimistic mood after his return to England and this outlook was enhanced by the advent to power in Britain of the Labour Government under Clement Atlee. Russell, who had been a socialist since the First World War, felt that the Labour Government would play an important role "in establishing an equilibrium" in war-torn Europe by dint of "its moral leadership and socialist example."[4] He expressed his hope to American readers in *Forward* of 29 September 1945, that democracy could be secured in Europe "wherever Anglo-American influence is sufficiently strong."[5]

Russell's hopeful outlook was dramatically offset by the dropping of two atomic bombs in August on a Japan already verging on defeat, which led him to say: "I have never, not even in 1940, felt the outlook as gloomy as now."[6]

The wartime alliance against Nazi Germany and its fascist allies was giving way to a period of intense distrust and uncertainty and a belief in the inevitability of war between America and the Soviet Union. Britain and America, especially under the Truman Administration, became preoccupied with containing communism in Europe. The global perspective of the United States stressed the decisive importance of Europe to the future course of world power. Already during the final phase of the war, the idea of using the atomic bomb as a diplomatic lever against the Soviet Union had gained ground.

The abolishment of war had become even more imperative in the age of atomic weapons, and Russell saw the need to find a way of cooperating with the Soviet Union in order to deal with the problem. In the *Forward* article he posed the problem as follows:

Russia's immense military strength as revealed by the war is held in check for the moment by the atomic bombs, but before long Russia, no doubt, will have as good (or bad) a bomb as that of the Americans, and as soon as this has happened it will be possible to have a really serious war. Such madness must be prevented if possible, but it is not easy to see how.[7]

4

His intense distrust of Stalin, and dislike of what he termed "Soviet communism," had led him to regard the United States as "the best hope" for the world. He therefore felt that the only way of preventing a third world war was to contain Soviet power, and that in this regard did not think peace could be permanently preserved by a "policy of appeasement such as we [Britain] pursued towards Germany until after Munich."[8]

Russell felt that America's monopoly of the bomb gave that country an opportunity "such as has never hitherto come to any nation throughout the whole history of the world"[9] to secure a permanent peace. He outlined this view during October 1945 in an article entitled "What America could do with the Atomic Bomb" in which he wrote:

At present, owing to the atomic bomb, it is clear that the United States would be the victor, and therefore war is unlikely while America retains this advantage. To tell Russia how to make atomic bombs would shorten the period of American supremacy and might therefore, contrary to everybody's intentions, hasten the advent of another world war. Whatever measures are to be taken to prevent another world war must be taken during the brief period of American supremacy, and must be enforced by a vigorous use of that supremacy, which should be used not to secure special advantages for the United States, but to compel the world to adopt a system making great war improbable.[10]

To Russell the issues confronting the world were so grave that the situation necessitated immediate and drastic action. Nuclear questions could only be resolved through international co-operation, and he therefore advocated the formation of a confederation of nations, or world government, under the leadership of the United States. The gravity of the situation justified an "element of compulsion" since "agreements could only be binding if the penalties for infringement were severe."[11] Russell argued that:

It would be utterly futile to negotiate a general treaty forbidding the use of atomic bombs, unless any power disregarding such a treaty knew that it would be met by a force of atomic bombs exceeding its own.[12]

In the face of an "irresistable" block, jointly controlling the atomic deterrant, the threat of war would become negligible "since not even Russia would dare to attack it."[13] Russell, who much later wrote that at the time he "thought Russia very likely to yield to the demands of the West,"[14] went on to urge the Americans to use "the new immense power for good or ill conferred by the atomic bomb...wisely, and with no undue shrinking from the responsibilities which this power confers."[15]

The gravity of the situation brought Russell to the House of Lords for the second time in his life, where on 28 November 1945 he repeated his warnings on the need to abolish war by finding a way of co-operating with the Soviet Union.[16] Russell reiterated his view that neither Britain nor America "must seek any advantage for ourselves" and outlined his hope "that the Russian Government can be made to see that the utilisation [of atomic warfare] would mean destruction to themselves as well as to everybody else." Russell argued that the deepening "attitude of suspicion" could only be overcome by "complete and utter frankness by stating [to the Russians]: 'There are things which we consider vital, but on other points we are quite willing that you should stand up for the things you consider vital. If there is any point which we both consider vital, let us try to find a compromise rather than that each side should annihilate the other, which would not be for the good of anybody.' "[17]

Russell felt that the compromise he had urged on the nuclear danger in his House of Lords speech was on offer in the Lilienthal and Baruch Proposal, which was put forward by the U.S. at the United Nations in April 1946. The Baruch Plan suggested that the United Nations should establish an International Atomic Development Authority and that the United States should bequeath to it the secret of which it was the sole possessor. Also proposed was the international inspection and dismantling of bomb piles. At the time Russell felt that the Baruch Plan had "very great merits and showed considerable generosity, when it is remembered that America still had an unbroken nuclear monopoly."[18] However he was later to write of this view: "I thought better of it (The Baruch Proposal) then, and of the American motives in making it, than I have since learned to think, but I still wish that the Russians had accepted it."[19]

According to Russell the Soviet Union found the Baruch Plan unacceptable for the following reasons:

It was Stalin's Russia, flushed with pride in the victory over the Germans, suspicious (not without reason) of the Western Powers, and aware that in the United Nations it could almost always be outvoted. The creation of a World Authority, which is an obvious necessity if the danger of Nuclear war is to be averted, has always been opposed by Russia as involving the stabilizing and perpetuating of economic and political systems which according to the Communist creed, are evil. If Russia is to be brought to accept any kind of International Authority, it will have to be one which does not give a definite superiority to non-Communist powers. This the Baruch Plan did not do.

Disappointed at this failure to achieve international agreement Russell expressed his fears for the future in a letter to Lucy Donnelly, whose friendship with Russell extended from his first visit to Bryn Mawr College in 1896:

> I go about with the feeling that within 20 years England will have ceased to exist. It makes everything hectic, like the approach of closing time at a party in a hotel—"We are for the night." A few bombs will destroy all our cities, and the rest will slowly die of hunger. In America, large sections of the rural middle-west and the desert south-west will probably survive. But not much of your America. Three cheers for Patagonia, the future centre of world culture.[21]

With the worsening of relations between the Soviet Union and the USA Russell "used every opportunity that presented itself to point out the dangers" of nuclear war.[22] In his article "The Prevention of Atomic War" written for *Plain Talk* and published in February 1947, and in a further speech to the House of Lords on 30 April 1947, he reiterated his strongly-held view that "if we are to preserve the peace of the world beyond the time when America ceases to have a monopoly of the bomb" control must be placed in the hands of an international authority "with a monopoly of serious armed force."[23] In the *Plain Talk* article Russell pointed out that "when I speak of an International Authority, I mean one that really governs, not...a pretentious sham like the United Nations under its present constitution." In order to obtain Soviet agreement in establishing such an authority Russell repeated his earlier argument that:

> If Russia does not agree to join in forming an international government, there will be war sooner or later; it is therefore wise to use any degree of pressure that may be necessary. But pressure should not be applied until every possible conciliatory approach has been tried and has failed. I have little doubt that such a policy, vigorously pursued, would in the end secure Russian acquiescence.

In his House of Lords speech Russell asked what was to be done "in view of the objections that Russia seems to have to any kind of international control?" In answer to his own question he stated:

Are we to do what I think would have to be done in that case (of concessions failing)—namely, to try to organise all the nations of the world which are in favour of international control into a somewhat tight alliance, giving them all the advantages that America at present possesses, and trying then to frighten Russia into joining that association, with all the privileges it would entail? Or are we to go on leaving Russia outside with the certainty that if we do so an atomic war will result?

Russell concluded his speech by declaring that the question arose "as to what degree of coercion it would be right and proper to apply" against the Soviet Union "in order to compel them to act in a way which, quite clearly, is as much to their interest as to ours."

It was at this time that the Emergency Committee of Atomic Scientists, formed in America in August 1946, was particulary active in its efforts to harness atomic energy for peaceful rather than war-like purposes and to educate the public accordingly. They, like Russell, believed that war could only be averted through the establishment of an international agency for the control of atomic energy. Like Russell, they had also pointed out that the Soviet Union would certainly be able to make an A-Bomb within a few years. However, there were significant differences in outlook between Russell and the scientists which were only overcome at a later stage.

Russell had produced a summary of his views on the nuclear issue entitled "Survival in the Atomic Age" which he submitted to Einstein, the leading physicist associated with the Atomic Scientists, for comment prior to publication.[24] Einstein wrote to Russell on 19 November 1947, suggesting certain alterations to Russell's article. Russell had criticized the Soviet Union's rejection of the Baruch Proposal on the grounds that "it is of course entirely obvious that apart from inspection [which the Soviet Government found intolerable] any scheme of international control is utterly futile."[25]

Einstein's view was:

The Lilienthal-Baruch proposal was a sensible and carefully worked out plan, which, as a first attempt at assurance against atomic attack certainly deserved better consideration on the part of Russia. On the other hand, it was very difficult for the Russians to agree to the plan. First of all, it assumed that the demands it envisaged should be met immediately, whereas the formulation of methods and delivery of bomb piles were to be postponed to a time deemed suitable in the judgment of the United States. Secondly, the Russians undoubtedly fear that inspection of such wide scope, and in general the presence in their country of so many "Westerners," would be a threat to Russia's inner balance.

As a consequence of the Soviet Union's rejection of the Baruch Plan Russell had stated:

However reluctantly, I have been driven to the conclusion that the Soviet Government foresees within a few years a situation in which it thinks it could win an atomic war. We may therefore expect its policy, if the West permits, to be one of temporizing until that time comes, while refusing steadfastly to agree to any plan which would make an atomic war impossible.[26]

Russell had gone on to assert that:

America should take the lead in organising a Grand Alliance of all those powers that are willing to consent to some such scheme as that set forth in the Lilienthal [Baruch] Report.

Einstein objected to these formulations on the following grounds:

We cannot concur [that]...Russia's refusal must be considered as motivated by her intention of undertaking an aggressive war at some later date. Publication of such a paragraph would necessarily increase the danger of a preventative war, which already haunts many people here. We should try as little as possible to assign a role of *leadership* to America, since a certain feeling of superiority has already spread in this country. If it should really be necessary to create a supra-national organization without Russia, it should not be an "alliance," but rather a kind of World Government with a centralized military power, not simply a realization of the Lilienthal Report.[27]

Apart from a few other minor points Einstein approved of the article, and hoped that Russell would make the suggested amendments. Russell replied to Einstein on 24 November 1947:

Thank you for your letter of November 19. I wish with all my heart that I could agree to the alterations you suggest. But your suggestions spring from an opinion different from mine, and if I agreed, the article would no longer say what I believe. I have no hope of reasonableness in the Soviet Government; I think that any hope of peace (and that a slender one) lies in frightening Russia. I favoured agreement before 1939, wrongly, as I now think; I do not want to repeat the same mistake. In particular, I only advocated "some such scheme" as that of the Lilienthal Report; I should be glad to see any emendation that did not make it ineffective, but inspection is essential. I did not say that Russia is proposing an aggressive war; what I said implied rather that Russia expects to have to wage a defensive war. The line of action is the same in either case. I think it essential that America should assume leadership; without a leader nothing gets done, and without U.S. leadership all minor Powers will be too frightened to do anything...

Generally, I think it useless to make any attempt whatever to conciliate Russia. The hope of achieving anything by this method seems to me "wishful thinking." I came to my present view of the Soviet Government when I went to Russia in 1920; all that has happened since has made me feel more certain that I was right.

The work of the Atomic Scientists of America seems to me most admirable and I am the more sorry that I cannot collaborate in this matter...

Russell has written that "throughout the forties and early fifties, my mind was in a state of confused agitation on the nuclear question.[28] It is obvious that during these years his views were more in line with the leaders of public opinion in America and Britain than at any other time in his public life, and he has stated that he had become *"persona grata* with the British Government because, though I was opposed to nuclear war, I was also anti-Communist."[29] This indeed was the period in which Russell's views on the Soviet Union were most hostile, summed up in his advocating that "the remedy" to a disastrous arms race "might be the threat of immediate war by the United States on Russia for the purpose of forcing nuclear disarmament upon her."[30] This approach, as well as the extent to which his thinking was influenced by "professional strategists," is indicated in a famous letter, dated 5 May 1948, to Dr. Walter Marseilles of Berkeley, California, with whose views of "compulsory inspection"of Soviet installations Russell agreed:

I have read your paper with great interest. I agree entirely with all the underlying assumptions. As soon as Russia rejected the Baruch proposals, I urged that all nations favouring international control of atomic energy should form an Alliance and threaten Russia with war unless Russia agreed to come in and permit inspection. Your proposal is, in effect, the same, for the compulsory inspection you advocate would be, legally an act of war, and would be so viewed by the Soviet Government.

During the past year, conversations with professional strategists have slightly modified my views. They say that in a few years we shall be in a better position, and that Russia will not yet have atomic bombs; that the economic recovery and military integration of Western Europe should be carried further before war begins; that at present neither air power nor atomic bombs could prevent Russia from over-running all W. Europe up to the Straits of Dover; and that the most dangerous period for us is the next two years. These views may or may not be correct, but at any rate they are those of the best experts.

There are some things of which Europeans are more vividly conscious than Americans. If Russia overruns W. Europe, the destruction will be such as no subsequent re-conquest can undo. Pratically the whole educated population will be sent to labour camps in N.E. Siberia or on the shores of the White Sea, where most will die of hardships and the survivors will be turned into animals. (Cf. what happened to Polish intellectuals). Atomic bombs, if used, will at first have to be dropped on W. Europe, since Russia will be out of reach. The Russians, even without atomic bombs, will be able to destroy all big towns in England, as the Germans would have done if the war had lasted a few months longer. I have no doubt that America would win in the end, but unless W. Europe can be preserved from invasion, it will be lost to civilisation for centuries.

Even at such a price, I think war would be worth while. Communism must be wiped out, and world government must be established. But if, by waiting, we could defend our present lines in Germany and Italy, it would be an immeasurable boon. I do not think the Russians will yield without war. I think all (including Stalin) are fatuous and ignorant. But I hope I am wrong about this.[31]

Russell had by now become very busy with international affairs—the government used him to lecture to the Armed Forces and at the time of the Berlin airlift he was sent to Berlin in a military capacity "to persuade the people of Berlin that it was worth while to resist Russian attempts to get the Allies out of Berlin."[32] He also travelled to Norway in October 1948 "in the hope of inducing Norwegians to join an alliance against Russia."[33] Russell's outlook and activity ensured for him a period of unprecedented respectability "in the eyes of the establishment," and according to him "it was felt that I...should be given the O.M." which he received in 1949.[34]

Russell's busy schedule left him very little free time and he apologized in a note to Lucy Donnelly for not having "time to write proper letters." Lucy maintained faithful communication and wrote him on 20 February 1948 with nostalgic reference to his wartime residence in America.

(Russell had earlier written to Edith Finch, his future wife and a colleague of Donnelly, commenting on her newly published biography of M. Carey Thomas, the former president of Bryn Mawr college.)[35]

Edith's great pleasure in your two letters I have shared. I am especially glad that you thought well of her book—whatever of MCT [M. Carey Thomas] herself. After living under two presidents who have succeeded at the College, I confess that my opinion of her has risen a good deal. The new ways on the Campus make it strange and *unheimlich* to me. O, for 'the Culture' of the '90s!...

The world all round now is a very grim one, as you say, and bitter to those of us who once lived in happier time. Here in America of course, we are among the fortunate ones, well fed, well housed and all the rest; but we do not grow wiser, more gruesome minded I fear. Everywhere it seems we can depend only on old affections and tried loyalties...

I have long wanted to write and hear from you again but seem away here to have nothing worth saying. Edith and I and other friends of course often talk of you and wish you back. Our neighborhood fell into dullness when you left. We drove out, Edith and I, one day in the autumn in a *pietas* to Little Datchett, now alas painted up in all colours and newly named "Stone Walls" on a sign at the gate.[36] But the wide Jeffersonian view was the same and very delightful. Are either of your elder children still in America? Conrad of course will have grown beyond my recognition. Will you not send me some word of them and of Peter.[37] I hope that he is better in health and able to get proper food...

Alas, that Edith and I are too poor to go to England this summer to breath its air again and to see our friends. How I wish it were not so....P.S. Barnes has been as quiet as a mouse these last years.

Lucy Donnelly's remark about Dr. Albert C. Barnes, whose controversial treatment of Russell in the early 1940s had caused a great deal of press interest, was confirmed by Barrows Dunham. Dunham had attended Russell's lectures at the Barnes Foundation and in renewing his acquaintance with Russell stated: "It may...interest you to know that Dr. Barnes has been singularly quiet since his defeat at your hands. I don't know whether this portends a new eruption or whether the volcano is at last extinct. The latter hypothesis seems, however, improbable."[38]

Russell was to receive only one more letter from Lucy Donnelly, for sadly she died that summer, while on holiday in Canada in the company of her close friend, Edith Finch. Writing to Russell on 8 May 1948, she remarked on the letters she had been receiving from him since 1902:

All that you wrote to me I seem to have treasured down to the merest notes. They are wonderfully-friendly, wise, kind letters, sympathetic almost beyond belief with my personal concerns and small Bryn Mawr affairs, while bringing in an invigorating breath from a larger freer world. A lifetime of gratitude I send back to you for them.[39]

Her words are eloquent testimony to Russell's deep concern for others and in a sense were expressive of his attempts to bring an "invigorating breath" into America itself. In this vein he continued with his efforts to build bridges of understanding between Britons and Americans. Britain's dependence on American aid had provoked feelings of resentment among people on both sides of the Atlantic, and in an article entitled "Don't Let's be Beastly to the Yankees"[40] Russell stressed the need for America and Britain to co-operate or be doomed. He sought to counter the "widespread hostility" to British socialism which existed "even amomg trade unionists" in the United States, and pointed out to the British the need to appreciate America's role and policies. "I have in mind especially Marshall Aid, the Atlantic Pact, and the offer to internationalise atomic energy," he wrote, and added "America, in my opinion, has proved to be the best of the Powers in the years since 1945."

Dealing with America's beneficial effect on Europe in the world of ideas—in an article entitled "Political and Cultural Influence of the USA"[41]—Russell wrote that the shift in world power, with the Soviet Union and the U.S. dominating the world, was bound to bring cultural changes of great importance. According to Russell:

The culture of America is closely akin to our own, and adaptation can be easy and painless. The culture of Russia, on the other hand, is profoundly alien....It is therefore the part of wisdom to facilitate co-operation with America, cultural, as well as political and economic... Our continued existence as free nations is only capable of being maintained by co-operation with America.

The explosion of the first Soviet atomic device in August 1949 confirmed Russell's earlier prediction as well as the views of many atomic physicists that America's monopoly of the bomb would be of short duration, leading to an entirely new situation. "Unfortunately," wrote Russell "the conviction that it was traitors, rather than Russian skill, which had deprived America of its monopoly, produced a general atmosphere of suspicion and gave rise to the reign of McCarthy and those who thought as he did."[42]

Footnotes

1. B. Russell, *Autobiography* (London, 1969), Vol. 3, p. 22; (New York, 1969), p. 13.

2. *Ibid.*

3. From "Some Impressions of America" in *Bertrand Russell's America* (London, 1973), (Viking Press, New York, 1974), Vol. I, p. 355.

4. From "What Should Be British Policy Towards Russia?" Reprinted as "Britain and Russia" in *Manchester Guardian* of 2 October 1945.

5. *Ibid.*

6. From letter to Dora Sanger of 2 September 1945 in *Bertrand Russell's America*, Vol. I, p. 208.

7. From "What Should Be British Policy Towards Russia?"

8. *Ibid.*

9. See below, pp. 311-14.

10. *Ibid.*

11. *Ibid.*

12. *Ibid.*

13. *Ibid.*

14. B. Russell, *Autobiography*, Vol. 3, p. 18; p. 7.

15. See below, pp. 311-14.

16. B. Russell, *Has Man A Future?* (London, 1961), pp. 22-8 (New York, 1962), pp. 19-25.

17. *Ibid.*

18. B. Russell, *Has Man A Future?*, p. 29; p.25.

19. B. Russell, *Autobiography*, Vol. 3, p. 17; p. 7.

20. B. Russell, *Has Man A Future?*, p. 29; p. 26.

21. B. Russell, *Autobiography*, Vol. 3, p. 42; pp. 42-3. The letter is dated 23 June 1946.

22. *Ibid.* p. 17; p. 7.

23. *Hansards* (Lords), Vol. 147, 30 April 1947, pp. 272-6.

24. Published as "Still Time for Good Sense" in *47 Magazine of the Year*, November 1947.

25. *Ibid.*

26. *Ibid.*

27. From his letter of 19 November 1947.

28. B. Russell, *Autobiography*, Vol. 3, p. 16; p. 6.

29. *Ibid.*, p. 20; p. 11.

30. *Ibid.*, p. 18; p. 7.

31. Published together with Russell's later views in *Saturday Review*, 16 October 1954. See also below, p. 63.

32. B. Russell *Autobiography*, Vol. 3, pp. 19-20; p. 10.

33. *Ibid.*, p. 21; p. 11.

34. *Ibid.*, p. 26; p. 18.

35. *Ibid.*, pp. 41-2; pp. 40-2.

36. A farmhouse in Malvern, near Philadelphia, where Russell and his family lived during 1941-2.

37. Patricia Russell née Spence, Russell's third wife.

38. From his letter of 29 November 1946.

39. B. Russell, *Autobiography*, Vol. 3, p. 43; p. 44.

40. See below, pp. 315-18.

41. See below, pp. 319-26.

42. B. Russell, *Has Man A Future?*, p. 30; p. 27.

2 American Lectures 1950

Russell travelled back to the U.S. in October 1950 to take up an invitation from Mount Holyoke College for Women in New England. He had undertaken to give a short course in philosophy to last until November 10. While at Mount Holyoke, Russell arranged with Irwin Edman, the Chair of the Philosophy department at Columbia University, to deliver the Matchette Foundation lectures at Colombia in mid-November. After completing the course at Mount Holyoke, Russell went briefly to Princeton to give a lecture and there renewed his contact with many friends, including Einstein, whom he had known during the latter days of his war-time stay in the U.S. It was while at Princeton that he learned he had been awarded the Nobel Prize for literature. This news immediately brought his presence in America to the notice of the press, and when he arrived in New York on November 14 he was welcomed as a celebrity.

Huge crowds gathered at the McMillin theater of Colombia University to hear his lectures, and two additional halls had to be wired up to accommodate the overflow of audience. Russell was pleased though somewhat surprised by this reception and found that his audience increased with each successive lecture. "I was astonished that, in New York, where I had been, so short a time before, spoken of with vicious obloquy, my lectures seemed to be popular and to draw crowds."[1] Russell averred that "the audience might have gathered to have a glimpse of so horrid a character, hoping for shocks and scandal and general rebelliousness.[2]

Julie Medlock, a New York literary agent who had been assigned by Columbia University to shepherd Russell in New York, and arrange for his publicity, described the scene at his lectures:

16

People were lined up 3 and 4 deep all the way around two blocks in the hope of getting in by some miracle, or at least hearing the piped voice, or catching a glimpse of Lord Russell in person. This crowd roundly cheered as we drove up... [A reporter accompanying Russell] viewed the assemblage with considerable astonishment, "Good Lord, Lord Russell," he said, "anybody would think it was JANE Russell they were here to see instead of just a philosopher."[3]

The subject of Russell's three lectures, over three successive days, was "The Impact of Science on Society," which had been originally given at Ruskin College, Oxford earlier that year and which were to form part of his book published later with that title.[4] The main theme of his lectures concerned the "increase of human power owing to scientific knowledge" and in this context he dealt with the need to establish a world government to ensure that scientific knowledge be used only for peaceful purposes.

Russell was given an enthusiastic reception by an audience which was on the whole young and liberal. As Edith Finch described the experience:

In spite of the crush and the heat and the enormous audience, there was absolute quiet all the time that B.R. spoke, save for an occasional roar of laughter or burst of applause. Not a shuffle nor a sneeze nor a whisper distracted attention from the words of the speaker. When he finished there was a moment or two's silence, then a prolonged great blast of approbation.[5]

"My audience was irreverent and so was I," Russell wrote in his later years. "I think this was the main basis of their liking of my lectures."[6] He also discussed the problem of moral values in a scientific society and, recalling his treatment in New York in 1940, Russell later commented: "I had the pleasant experience of being applauded on the very same remarks which had caused me to be ostracized on the earlier occasion."[7]

There was extensive and favorable press, radio and TV coverage of the lectures. Julie Medlock organized a packed press conference at her home in the course of which Russell commented on the Cold War and the consequent erosion of civil liberties in the U.S.

At the conclusion of his Columbia lectures Russell spent a short time with Edith Finch, who was living in New York, and then travelled on to Washington, D.C. to visit his daughter Kate, who had married Charles Tait, a State Department official. Before returning to London towards the end of November, Russell arranged for Julie Medlock to undertake further publicity work on his behalf and for her to come to London in January to discuss plans for the future.

From London Russell went to Stockholm to collect his Nobel Prize, but before doing so he wrote to his friends Rupert and Elizabeth Crawshay Williams on December 3:

> America was beastly—The Republicans are as wicked as they are stupid, which is saying a great deal. I told everybody I was finding it interesting to study the atmosphere of a police state, which didn't make me popular except with the young.[8]

On his return from Stockholm he wrote to Elizabeth Crawshay Williams on 2 January 1951 about the imminent arrival of Julie Medlock:

> A lady, who may be described as a whirlwind, is descending upon me from New York, Her name is "Public Interest Inc." She was appointed by Columbia University to look after my publicity in New York, and she has since devoted herself to schemes (on a 10% basis, like St. Paul) for making me vast numbers of dollars.[9]

"1950," Russell recalled, "seems to have marked the apogee of my respectability...I have always held that no one can be respectable without being wicked, but so blunted was my moral sense that I could not see in what way I had sinned. Honours and increased income which began with sales of my *History of Western Philosophy*[10] gave me a feeling of freedom and assurance..."[11]

It was at this time that American foreign policies were coming under increasing criticism from abroad. Since the explosion of the Soviet atomic bomb and the establishment of a Chinese revolutionary government, both events in September 1949, the Cold War had steadily intensified. At the beginning of 1950 Truman had announced special measures to facilitate the development of an American H-Bomb and thus embarked upon a full-fledged arms race. At the same time there was a hardening of American policies, especially in relation to China, and in June 1950 Truman ordered American armed forces to intervene in Korea.

Those Americans not caught up in the nationwide Cold War hysteria were becoming increasingly isolated. By early 1951 Senator Joseph McCarthy and his red-baiting apparatus held sway over a terrorized population. When Julie Medlock sent an article by Russell entitled, "Why America is Losing her Allies," to 1,850 U.S. newspapers, only the *Wichita Beacon*, a Kansas daily, took it up and published it on 5 February 1951, under an "Editors Note" which stated: "The Free World, outside America, is in an uproar of criticism over American foreign policy, which appears to be leading straight toward a war which could be avoided, according to Bertrand Russell."[12] In his article Russell challenged the legality of U.S.

and UN troops crossing the 38th parallel in Korea; he also argued that it was America's attitude to China in particular which "appears to the rest of the free world immoral." Russell believed that a "large part of the non-Communist world" would continue to view the U.S. as "the inheritor of British Imperialism, and as more of a warmonger than the Soviet Republic," unless the U.S., while remaining "firm against aggression," recognized "what is just in the claims of China to Formosa and to membership in the United Nations." Russell was also anxious to dispel the view that because Britain was in favor of negotiations with China she was "less hostile to communism" than the U.S.:

This is not the case. We differ from America not in the desire to combat communism, but in our estimate of the best way of doing so. We think that a method which alienates possible allies, and chooses a disputable issue, is not so wise as one which, after making all concessions that justice can demand, finds itself faced with an indubitable aggression against which the free world can be united without hesitation. It may be that no such aggression will occur; in that case, a great war can be avoided. But if it does occur, the chances of swift victory are very much greater than they are if the present policy of America is pursued.

In November 1950 Chinese forces had come to the assistance of the North Koreans and within weeks had succeeded in pushing American and UN troops back across the violated 38th parallel and advanced into South Korea. General MacArthur, the Commander in Chief of the American and UN forces, who advocated the use of nuclear weapons against China to save his forces from defeat, was severely criticized in the U.S., and in April 1951 Truman dismissed MacArthur and replaced him with General Ridgeway. Truman soon came under fire from the Republican Party for this action. Russell immediately issued a statement on the affair which, once again, was taken up by the *Wichita Beacon* on 18 April 1951. Only one other paper, *The Daily Compass*, published the statement on the same day, but in a slightly truncated form under the heading, "World Sighs with Relief at Firing of MacArthur: Bertrand Russell":

The dismissal of MacArthur has brought a sigh of relief to the whole non-Communist world, outside the United States, and at the same time a profound feeling of admiration for the courage of President Truman. This latter feeling is strongest in those who know America best. I do not think Americans realize at all how the matter looks to those outside America who are most anxious to preserve the free world from disaster. It seems to all of us that the forces of ignorance and stupidity in your country have banded together to impose a reign of terror, and to try to enforce a policy which must bring defeat on an international scale to the very policy in which President Truman's adversaries profess to believe.

We are astonished that men of certain political eminence can display such crass lack of information about the world, and such complete inability to adapt means to ends. We are outraged when we are told that our disagreements with Senator McCarthy are due to our being crypto-Communists, and when we find it hinted that any American who advocates a policy that has any chance of success against Russia must be in the pay of the Kremlin.

Many of us had supposed until now that Americans admired courage and guts, but we find that we were mistaken. Your President has displayed these qualities in the highest degree and receives little but abuse, while all the poltroons who say ditto to Senator McCarthy for fear of being smirched, are applauded as brave and vigorous men. It is difficult for any non-American who is either honest or intelligent to submit with any patience to the leadership in matters of policy of men who hold that it is right and proper for a general to mutiny against the constitutional powers to which he is legally subject.

Russell's attitude to U.S. involvement in Korea was in marked contrast to the position he adopted during the Vietnam War. He rejected the persistant allegations made by Professor Joseph Needham and others charging the U.S. with having used the Korean War as a proving ground for new biological and chemical weapons of mass destruction.[13] Later, as a result of U.S. behavior in Vietnam, he "had become convinced of the justice of these allegations," and in his *Autobiography* offered "Professor Needham and the others my sincere apologies for thinking these charges too extreme."[14] Russell, however, did associate himself with Lord Boyd Orr and other prominent members of the Peace Pledge Union in a letter to *The Times* of 8 July 1952 protesting at the "use of bombs containing napalm by the United Nations forces in Korea" against civilian targets.

Although Russell's main objective remained the avoidance of an atomic war and criticism of all tendencies which made such a war more likely, he was be no means conciliatory towards the USSR and communism, which he still regarded as a major threat to the "free world." He was concerned to defend the "free world" against what he saw as a common danger, but felt this could only be done by strengthening relations between Europe and the U.S., and in particular between Britain and the U.S. He returned to his theme of promoting Anglo-American understanding in an article published by *Look* magazine on 24 April 1951. *Look* featured Russell's portrait on its cover and gave great prominence to the article, but succeeded in distorting its content by changing the title from "What's

Wrong with Anglo-American Relations?" to the more provocative "What's Wrong with Americans?" In his article Russell was concerned to disabuse Americans of the idea that "because the Government of England is Socialist, it must be more friendly to the Russians than the American Government is." Russell criticized the "many American newspapers" which he believed had "deliberately misrepresented British affairs ever since the present Labour Government came into power." Russell dealt with what he regarded as common American prejudices about British socialism which he believed stemmed from the fact that "America in theory is dedicated to democratic equality, but is in practice dedicated to plutocratic inequality." He elaborated this view under a sub-title "England is More Democratic than America," inserted into the text by the *Look* editors:

When I read American novels, I find they are full of a kind of snobbery which was common in England about 100 years ago, but of which we should now be ashamed. I read about people born on the wrong side of the tracks; about rich people objecting to their daughters marrying outside their own class; about people who are despised because the crease in their trousers is inadequate. And all these things are taken for granted. Nobody seems to notice them as something inconsistent with the basic philosophy of democracy that is supposed to be accepted by all Americans. On the contrary, I have found repeatedly in recent years that Americans imagine England is less democratic than America because it allows less free play to capitalists. When I insist that England is more democratic than America, I am met either with anger or pitying contempt.

Russell continued:

While I am engaged in boasting of England, I may as well make a complete job of it. Consider for example, the atom bomb. I am not quite sure whether anyone ought to be proud of this. But if there is any pride involved, nine tenths of it should be European and only one tenth American. Very few Americans know that almost all the pioneer work on atomic structure was done at the Cavendish Laboratory in Cambridge, and I cannot think of a single American who contributed anything of any great importance at this stage. It was only after the really difficult work had been done that the Americans undertook the task of actually making the atom bomb.

But Russell argued that although England has "surpassed America in the power of discovering fundamental new ideas which may become the basis of future techniques," the U.S. was unsurpassed in its "capacity for ingenious utilisation of ideas and techniques." He concluded his article with the hope that the two countries would "co-operate without friction" by becoming "conscious more of each other's merits than of each other's faults." Such co-operation Russell believed, was essential "for the salvation not only of our own nations but of mankind."

Reaction to Russell's article was fast and furious. He was everywhere pilloried by the critics as anti-American and the letters columns of the subsequent issue of *Look* reflected the angry response anticipated by the editors when they appended a note to the article stating that "Russell's candid criticism might roil U.S. sensibilities."

Russell's concern about Anglo-American relations and his controversial insight into American society, based on his long association with that country, brought to him many requests from editors on both sides of the Atlantic for contributions to their journals. Russell welcomed all the opportunities allowed him in his effort to help reconcile the political and cultural differences between Britain and the U.S.

Russell saw that the moral codes governing the conduct of U.S. society were not without significance in their effect upon political life. In "Are These Moral Codes Out of Date?"[15] written for the London *Evening Standard* Russell criticized conventional sex ethics in the U.S., the "mental effects" of which he regarded as "very similar to those which were produced by prohibition." He felt that the code of morality in the U.S. was anachronistic and therefore incompatible with "a country which leads the world in mechanised technique." In a comment on the growing illiberalism in American political life Russell argued:

The attitude to sex in America is part of a more general attitude. Americans for the most part are unable to face reality except in a mood of cynicism. One finds this, for example, in politics. They have a set of ideal rules which they imagine that a virtuous politician would obey, but the rules are such as would cause any man to be out of politics in a week. Consequently, it is recognised that no politician can be virtuous according to the nominal code. It follows, so at least the average American concludes, that a politician cannot be justly blamed whatever crimes he may commit.

The intensification of the Cold War and the parallel growth of political intolerance in America, exemplified by the machinations of Senator Joseph McCarthy and his investigating committees, were making Russell increasingly apprehensive about America's future role in world affairs. While Russell remained firmly anti-Communist he was convinced that communism could only be effectively countered with liberal ideas and not with "fanaticism," which in the U.S. was "very common and very dangerous." "An anti-Communist," Russell maintained, "is a fanatic if he thinks it is worth while to make war in order to destroy communism."[16]

In a letter to Walter Graebner, the European Director of *Fortune* magazine, Russell inveighed against the fanatical attitudes which were promoting a "reign of terror" in American society. He wrote on 9 June 1951:

...Practically any Englishman when he goes to America is struck more forcibly by the absence of liberty than by any other feature of your civilisation. Political, economic and religious intolerance amaze an English visitor. Protestant women, who it is known cannot survive childbirth, have to die to please Catholics; the inquisition which is now common when a man seeks employment, not only under Government but in many private organisations, seems to us intolerable, especially as it is not content to investigate a man's political opinions, but also inquires into the virtue, or otherwise, of his private life. When, in 1940, I had to obtain a visa from an American Consul, he told me that he had been bombarded with messages and telegrams urging him to refuse me a visa on the ground that my opinions were somewhat of the Left. I said that they were not more so than those of the President. He replied with the utmost seriousness "Ah yes! But we couldn't keep him out because he was born in America." The kind of reign of terror which McCarthy has succeeded in establishing is infinitely shocking to an English mind. One has an impression only slightly exaggerated, that an American who thinks well of Acheson does not dare to say so until he has looked behind the door to make sure that no FBI man is listening. True, our own laxity has led to unfortunate cases, such as those of Fuchs and Pontecorvo, but your rigidity is leading able young scientists to avoid Government service, and this is likely to have very grave results if there is a war.

> "...The defects [in America] by which we are most impressed are not moral but intellectual. We know you are clever at technical matters, but in politics we think you rather stupid. I do not know of any other country where dislike of a rather small number of casualties would lead to advocacy of a policy leading straight to world war."

Russell, who had been asked by Graebner to give his views on the content of *Fortune*, commented further on some of the articles featured in the magazine:

One of the most interesting articles to me was the one called "Have We Any Friends." I will confess that some of the criticisms and statements which you quote from European intellectuals appeared to me monstrously unjust—even frivolous. Talk about bathrooms makes me sick. I should like everybody to have a bathroom and a refrigerator, and it is absurd for Europeans to boast of their lack in this respect. Nevertheless, I think that almost every cultivated European does sincerely believe that the European tradition contains something of value which so far is lacking in America. I may illustrate what I mean by a small fact. I have been a professor at various American universities and have enjoyed the hospitality for which your country is justly famous, but I found that when I was invited to dinner if my host wished to do me honour he invited me to meet business men rather than professors, on the ground that they stand higher in the social scale. This attitude is reflected in the difference between the administrative offices in Universities and the holes and corners in which the professors are housed. The offices of the administrations are large and airy and have luxurious carpets. The cubby holes of professors are very small and sparsely furnished, and obviously designed to make them realise their status as hired labour. I found the implied standard of values so universally accepted that hardly any professors felt themselves the equals of energetic, but uneducated executives.

I was very much interested by the discussion on the French attitude about a Third Force in the article "Individualism Comes of Age." I cannot see how capitalism can be regarded as the third force, for that would imply that there is some real difference between Communism and Fascism which, for my part, I fail to perceive. I think also that the worst features of American capitalism are more evident outside America than they are at home. American capitalism in its international dealings tends to ally itself everywhere with what is old and corrupt, since everything else appears to it to be tainted with communism.

One other point of criticism occurred to me. The writer of the article "Have We any Friends" seems to think that what Europeans object to in America is a lack of morals. This is by no means the case. On the contrary, we think you too much obsessed by morals. Such things as Prohibition and the Mann Act strike us as absurd. The defects by which we are most impressed are not moral but intellectual. We know you are very clever at technical matters, but in politics we think you rather stupid. I do not know of any other country where dislike of a rather small number of casualties would lead to advocacy of a policy leading straight to world war. Your immense power frightens us, and we feel as if a child had run away with a new and powerful car and was careering madly about the road to the danger of all its other occupants. It is especially MacArthur and McCarthy who make us feel that way, but Taft and Hoover seem to us only a shade less ignorant.

I have mentioned matters in which I feel critical, but there is a very large amount of material in the issue with which I am in agreement, and I very much admire the ability which has gone into producing it.

Despite Russell's unrelenting and trenchant criticism of many aspects of American social and political life there was a continuing demand for him to return to lecture in the U.S. When, in early May 1951, Columbia University Institute of Arts and Sciences invited him to address the opening of their autumn term, Russell, undeterred and, perhaps, even stimulated by mounting hostility from his political opponents in the U.S., accepted the invitation.

Footnotes

1. B. Russell, *Autobiography* (London, 1969), Vol. 3, p. 28; (New York, 1969), p. 22.
2. *Ibid.*
3. J. Medlock, "Bertrand Russell so Fondly Remembered", an unpublished memoir.
4. Included in his book under the same title, (London, 1952), (Columbia University Press, 1951).
5. From Edith Finch's notes to the authors, January 1975.
6. B. Russell, *Autobiography*, Vol. 3, p. 30; p. 24.
7. *Ibid.*
8. Quoted by R. Crawshay Williams, *Russell Remembered*, (Oxford University Press, 1970), p. 58.

9. *Ibid*, p. 68.
10. Published in 1945.
11. B. Russell, *Autobiography*, Vol. 3, p. 31; p. 26.
12. See below, pp. 327-8.
13. B. Russell, *Autobiography*, Vol. 3, p. 169; p. 243.
14. *Ibid*.
15. See below, pp. 329-31.
16. From "No Funk, No Frivolity, No Fanaticism", *The New York Times Magazine*, 6 May 1951.

3 American Lectures 1951

Encouraged by the success of his 1950 tour, Russell set about arranging, through Julie Medlock, an itinerary for a short three week lecture tour to follow his assignment at Columbia University. By the end of August 1951 Russell's tour program was finalized and he wrote to Julie Medlock on August 27:

You will, I know, remember that the British Government does not allow us one cent of American money, so that if you should by any chance fail to meet me at the airport, complete with dollars, I should not be able even to telephone you, but I should have to wait there until such a time as the personnel had organised a lecture on the spot, plus fee. I am glad the Forum will run to $300 for expenses. One can get quite a lot of drink for that sum. I hope you will manage to get on with the Ford Foundation. If you don't it will prove they are silly cases. I do not know John D. Rockefeller III. The only one I ever met was II. I never had the pleasure of meeting I, which accounts for my not having a dime.

No hotel reservations: I don't want to spend more than I must... If you can get Conrad Hilton of the Waldorf to give me a special price on condition of my saying that his is the best hotel ouside the Principality of Monaco, so much the better...

Julie Medlock announced Russell's tour plans to the press and Leonard Lyons' syndicated news column ran the following notice in early September:

Bertrand Russell is coming here next month for a series of lectures at universities throughout America. He will also participate in CBS

"Invitation to Learning" series. Two books were up for selection of the broadcast: John Stuart Mill's book "On Liberty" and George Bernard Shaw's "Back to Methuselah." The network notified Lord Russell that the final choice was Mill's book. "This may be short-sighted of you," replied the 79-year-old Nobel Prizewinner. "I am a godson of Mill, but I am also a rival of Methuselah."

Russell planned to arrive in New York on October 20 but due to mechanical trouble his plane was held up. When he finally arrived, 16 hours late, a crowd of reporters had gathered at the airport. Questioned about the reasons for his further delay through immigration Russell retorted: "I had to satisfy your authorities that I was not suffering from smallpox or communism."[1] Russell was quizzed about his opinions on a variety of topics. Asked for his views on political affairs in America he remarked:

Opposition to communism has got itself identified with opposition to change and now if anyone advocates change, he is immediately how-led down. You have got to leave room in the anti-Communist camp for people who want reform. That is not being done now.[2]

Russell's first engagement in New York was at a 3-day Forum organized by the *New York Herald Tribune* and held at the Waldorf Astoria Hotel. Russell, who had a suite at the hotel, was one of 50 illustrious participants who had been asked to "seek out the reasons for the present lack of balance between progress in science and the development of moral responsibility and to suggest means of bringing the two fields into equilibrium." Russell's contribution to the Forum was summarized in the *Herald Tribune* of October 24:

Lord Russell said men must learn to think of the human race as one family. He acknowledged that this mental change would be difficult. But the change could be brought about in a generation, if educators cooperated in bringing up the young as citizens of the world instead of as predatory warriors.

On the evening of October 24, Russell once again, as in 1950, faced a capacity audience at the McMillin Theater of Columbia University for his lecture on "The Future of Happiness." Russell argued that fear and envy were the twin causes of human unhappiness and in explaining these destructive impulses to his audience Russell, by innuendo, made reference to the workings of McCarthyism: "Suppose," he suggested, "somebody advances an opinion which, not being that of the majority of your social group, strikes you as subversive, you will feel instantly, if you are not on your guard against such feelings, that an opinion of this sort will let loose the floods of revolution, deprive you of your livelihood, and loosen all the bonds of morality by which society is held together."

Russell went on to demonstrate how effective fear could be in silencing opposition to injustice:

Suppose, for example, that you live in the Southern United States and that some negro has been condemned to death for a rape of which he was innocent; if you speak up for him you will be instantly regarded as subversive, and as one who has no proper horror of his crime. It will be useless to plead that you do not think that he committed the crime; this will be taken as only a further proof that you do not reprobate the crime as you should. There will be raised eyebrows, whispers, and at last a very widespread hostility. It may be that some of those who act in this hostile manner in their hearts agree with you, but fear will cause them to pretend that they do not.

Russell argued that one of the chief dangers in times of social crisis was the tendency for people to place an unquestioning trust in certain leaders:

Submission to leaders takes away the sense of individual responsibility and the habit of individual thought. If the chosen leader is not exceptionally high-minded, he will sooner or later betray his followers for the sake of his own interests, as happened almost invariably with Greek tyrants. And since his power is based upon a general diffused fear, he will probably do little to dissipate such fear, but will, on the contrary, encourage belief in threats from enemies. The result will be witch-hunts within, and wars without.

In Russell's view the future of happiness, the freedom from fear and envy, rested largely with educators:

The happy man, having been brought up in youth without the twin obsessions of sin and fear, will be free and generous and expansive, regarding other people, except where there is some definite reason to the contrary, as people with whom he cooperates rather than as competitors. He will not be constantly inhibiting impulses to friendliness for fear others should take advantage of him or should fail to respond... Having learned while he was young the economics and politics of cooperation, and the habit of regarding the human family as one, he will not instinctively think of foreign nations as enemies, and he will see war as the folly that it is.

Russell's New York itinerary was, to say the least, hectic. In the five

> "Most Americans think that if you wake up an Englishman in the middle of the night, he would speak American."

days before leaving for Boston to lecture at the Massachusetts Institute of Technology, and in the midst of his major engagements with the *New York Herald Tribune* Forum at Columbia he lectured to the Young Men's and Young Women's Hebrew Association, taped five broadcasts on "A Changing World" for CBS and was the guest of honor at several receptions including a Cosmopolitan Club party. Russell despite his 79 years was in an energetic and buoyant mood. When, at the end of one of his speeches, someone commented on his British accent he remarked "Americans think we talk that way out of affectation. Most Americans think that if you wake up an Englishman in the middle of the night, he would speak American.³"

News reports of his activities were extensive and mostly complimentary. Simon and Schuster, his publishers, sensing the popular impact of Russell's presence in New York remarked in a prepublication publicity blurb for his latest book *New Hopes for a Changing World*, "New York is alight this week wherever Russell's voice is heard, sweeping the cobwebs from our minds with the brilliance, lucidity, and wit which constitute his genius."

When Russell arrived on October 25 for his lecture at MIT he was given a standing ovation by the students in their vast and crowded amphitheater. He spoke on "Human Nature and Politics" and the success of the evening can be measured by the press reports which hailed him as "one of the world's most extravagant individualists" and praised "a wisdom that has distilled itself through one of the greatest periods of human development, one which has revived many minds which drew upon it for sustenance."⁴ They also paid tribute to Russell's integrity and the fact that hostility from many sources "has never deterred him from his convictions and he has always replied to his severest critics with patient and often humorous insight."⁵

Russell's next appointment was in Washington D.C. where he, together with Alistair Cooke, appeared on "Meet the Press." The confrontation was controversial and sometimes heated. Walter Winchell in his column the next day described the program as being "at its invective best when Bertrand Russell told the panel to go-to-hell in 24 words!"⁶

Two days later at the University of Virginia in Richmond, Russell provoked further controversy when he spoke on "Happy man in a happy world." His speech was a variation on the one he delivered to the Columbia Institute of Arts and Science, but a columnist enraged by Russell's criticism of religion and of the erosion of civil liberties in the U.S., denounced Russell as anti-American and, describing him as a "learned fool" and "a shady philosopher," attacked Russell for preaching "unconventional and Marx-

"Social revolution, to begin with, clearly does not include what happened in America in 1776, for that was good, whereas social revolution is bad...Perhaps we may define social revolution as any political movement anywhere which is displeasing to the Republican Party..."

ist opinions from a lecture platform in Richmond, where most people adhere to orthodox religious beliefs."[7]

It was clear, however, that Russell was not without admirers on that evening in Richmond. Howard Ozmon, now Professor of Education at Virginia Commonwealth University , attended the lecture as an undergraduate and recalls the event in a different light:

A friend...had driven 120 miles from Williamsburg to hear Russell that evening. We had both attended a rather bad Roman Catholic School, and our revolt against that kind of education, as well as concern with our own intellectual development (and certainly our intellectual motivation), were due in large measure to the man we were to see and hear that evening. We had read just about everything we could get our hands on by Russell since our freshman year in high school, and Russell seemed to reach us both intellectually and emotionally—though our parents and teachers never could...

We liked him too because he was a fighter. We were familiar with the attacks made on his views about free love, had heard him denounced from pulpits because of his views on religion, and knew how he had consistently argued against man's right to make war, despite social ostracism and imprisonment. Indeed, this frail gentleman from England had already turned us on, and no LSD trip could equal the excitement of hearing him in person... Russell's appearance on stage was an electric one, with his mane of flowing white hair and thin pipe clenched tightly between his teeth. He stood alone on the stage and spoke on the topic for only a short time. Then he invited questions. Many of the listeners had questions, half of them hostile and half of them friendly...

For an hour and a half he parried every question and answered on his own terms...It was obvious that he had come into the Bible Belt neither to excite nor to offend, but mostly to show that he did not have horns and a pitchfork (a point on which there had been considerable doubt).[8]

From Virginia Russell returned to Washington where after a short rest he flew to the midwest, where he was due to speak at Purdue University in Indiana and Oberlin College in Ohio. Russell was advised to keep off

31

> "Every honest man (honest men are only found in America)...knows that anybody whose second cousin once met a Communist at a party is likely to be infected..."

politics at Purdue, which as it turned out proved difficult in view of an article Russell had written for the October 30 edition of the *Manchester Guardian* attacking the Indiana educational system.[9] The article was picked up by Indiana newspapers on November 1, the morning of his arrival in Purdue.[10] Russell's article had been occasioned by a statement made by the Indiana State Superintendent of schools which had demanded that American youth should be taught that their government was the best in the world and to learn to "discredit definitions and descriptions used by foreign governments of such words as Social Revolution, Communism, Fascism, Totalitarianism, Police State, Dictatorship, Welfare State, Bureaucracy, Conservatives, Liberals, Capitalism, Socialism, Communal Enterprise, and Propaganda..."

The full statement had been sent to Russell in England by Harold Kastner, an Indiana school teacher. In his article Russell suggested alternative definitions for the words and terms, which, it was asserted, needed redefining from an American viewpoint:

> "Social revolution," to begin with, clearly does not include what happened in America in 1776, for that was good, whereas "social revolution" is bad... Perhaps we may define "social revolution" as any political movement anywhere which is displeasing to the Republican Party...
>
> Every honest man (honest men are only found in America) knows that Mr. Acheson is a Communist, that Mr. Atlee is a Communist, and that Communism is so catching that anybody whose second cousin once met a Communist at a party is likely to be infected...
>
> It is true that during the late war we thought that we were fighting to defeat "fascism," but we now learn that "fascism" is disliked by Moscow, and we conclude that it cannot be wholly vile...
>
> As we all know, America is not a "police state." It is true that Senator McCarthy's emissaries and his allies in the FBI are perpetually snooping, and that if by some misfortune you were to quote with approval some remark by Jefferson you would probably lose your job and perhaps find yourself behind bars. But this, of course, is done in defence of liberty.
>
> We all know that England is a "welfare state," and that this proves that England is only half-heartedly opposed to Moscow...
>
> The education authorities of the state in question will, I am sure, agree that the indoctrination which they advocate is not "propa-

ganda." It is not "propaganda" because it is teaching doctrines with which they agree.

In a letter to Harold Kastner of November 15 Russell hinted at the reception given him in Purdue and apologized for not taking up Kastner's invitation to visit him at his home because he was "only in Indiana just long enough to avoid getting lynched."

The following day Russell travelled to Ohio for his engagement at Oberlin College. Julie Medlock, who was in New York at the time, describes the events of that evening:

Late on the evening of Russell's scheduled lecture at Oberlin College, I had a telephone call from Dr. William Stevenson, Oberlin's President. In a worried voice he asked if by any chance I had had any word from Lord Russell. I said I had not, and asked what was the matter.

"It's past the opening hour for our lecture. The hall is packed to overflowing, although we're in the middle of the worst snowstorm of the season. And Lord Russell has not arrived—he is at least 5 hours late. We are getting quite worried for fear there may have been a road accident somewhere."

I reached for his travel schedule to check the arrangements. Yes...he was due at Oberlin hours earlier, coming by bus. What could have happened to the bus in the blizzard? President Stevenson said they had the State Police out looking for the bus. Meanwhile, the suspense was growing among the lecture audience, which refused to go home. He promised to keep me informed...

About 2 hours later the phone rang again. This time a jubilant President Stevenson reported "all's well that ends well." The State Police had located the bus which had gotten off the main road and lost its way in the storm. He reported that Lord Russell himself had now arrived, in high good humour despite being half frozen. He had been thawed out, with brandy, hot coffee and food; the patient audience had been fortified with coffee and doughnuts, and that hour, somewhat after midnight, the lecture was about to begin. Lord Russell had said to assure me that he was alright and felt quite up to going on with the planned lecture, and the audience too was taking it as a kind of lark. It was probably the latest college lecture on record, but both Lord Russell and audience were resilient, and all survived."[11]

Russell's final engagements before leaving America were at the Charleston Open Forum in West Virginia and the University of North Carolina in Greenshore at the conclusion of which he was totally exhausted. The constant travelling and socializing, which were a necessary accompaniment to his lectures, had depleted his energies and he was much relieved on November 9 to end what was to be his final visit to America. There is no doubt that despite the success of his tour which contrasted with the unrelenting hostility he encountered in the 1940s Russell remained as controversial as ever; indeed his outspoken criticism of American political affairs had served to arouse official indignation towards him more sharply than ever before. He had some consolation in knowing, however, that while in 1944 he had returned to England penniless, on this occasion, helped by the efforts of Julie Medlock and Public Interest Inc., he had earned more than $10,000.

Footnotes

1. Quoted in J. Medlock, "Bertrand Russell so Fondly Remembered", an unpublished memoir.

2. *Ibid.*

3. *Ibid.*

4. *Ibid.*

5. *Ibid.*

6. *Ibid.*

7. *Ibid.*

8. From "Bertrand Russell: Socrates of Our Age (1872-1970)" published in *Kappan*, Vol. 3, No. 3, November 1970.

9. See below, pp. 332-4.

10. Published as "Bertrand Russell Tweaks the State of Indiana", in the *Des Moines Sunday Register*, Iowa. See illustrations, p. 298.

11. J. Medlock, *op. cit.*

4 The Grip of Conformity

Julie Medlock's energetic promotion of Russell in America ensured that he was to be kept in the public eye long after he had returned to England. Two major articles by Russell appeared simultaneously in the *New York Times Magazine* and the *New York Herald Tribune Magazine* on 16 December 1951.

In the former article entitled "The Best Answer to Fanaticism—Liberalism" Russell continued his criticism of the McCarthyist assault on civil liberties and defended liberal attitudes which he felt were the essential antidote to the world's problems. In the course of his article Russell promulgated a set of ethical principles by which, given the prevailing mood of the times, he felt Americans should guide their thoughts and actions. Among the precepts which Russell advanced and codified in the form of "Ten Commandments" were:

> Have no respect for the authority of others, for there are always contrary authorities to be found. Do not fear to be eccentric in opinion, for every opinion now accepted was once eccentric. Find more pleasure in intelligent dissent that in passive agreement, for if you value intelligence, as you should, the former implies a deeper agreement than the latter.

In his other article, "The Narrow Line," Russell made a plea for new international policies which would work towards peace while avoiding open appeasement of the USSR. He argued against the view that the tensions in the world were "due to any inevitable conflict of interest" and asserted that "most of the conflicts of interest that exist are caused by irrational enmities." Russell was convinced that the harmony which existed between East and West during the war "would be equally true today

> "Have no respect for the authority of others, for there are always contrary authorities to be found. Do not fear to be eccentric in opinion, for every opinion now accepted was once eccentric. Find more pleasure in intelligent dissent than in passive agreement, for if you value intelligence, as you should, the former implies a deeper agreement than the latter."

if both sides would realise it" and that "the world could be filled with happiness if only East and West could believe that they are not concerned to compass each other's destruction." Russell believed that American contribution to peace could only come if positive ideals were substituted for "the somewhat arid cry of mere opposition to Communism."

Russell's views on American illiberalism roused an angry editorial comment from *The New Leader* on 24 December 1951, which took him to task not only on his criticism of the lack of tolerance in American society but also on his attitude to American foreign policy. The editorial, which reflected the extent to which some liberals were becoming affected by Cold War pressures, concluded with the hope that Russell "in his zeal to protect the flame of liberalism from internal enemies who would dim its glow, had not forgotten the external foes who could snuff it out altogether." *The New Leader* had initially been provoked by Russell's *Manchester Guardian* article attacking the Indiana education system,[1] in which, according to *The New Leader*, Russell had written "a vigorous indictment of what seemed to him to be an appalling growth of intellectual conformity and hysteria in America." The editor wrote to Russell asking his response to three questions which arose out of his successive articles:

1. Is it really the absence or prevalence of a capitalist economy that chiefly characterises the two worlds that lie east and west of the Elbe?
2. Is it true that the United States is in the grip of an intellectual and political conformity comparable to that in the Soviet Union?
3. Is the world today divided into two halves primarily because "persecution of opinion" makes it impossible for the two blocs to "understand each other?"

The New Leader felt that the issues raised by these questions were "becoming more and more acrimonious and could, in the long run, endanger the unity of the Atlantic democracies in the face of a common threat." Russell replied on 30 January 1952:

I am sorry to find myself in disagreement with *The New Leader*, having had a pleasant connection with it extending over many years. In your editorial you ask me certain questions to which I will endeavour to reply. First, you criticise my statement that "East of the Elbe it is absolutely certain that capitalism is tottering; west of the Elbe it is absolutely certain that capitalism is the salvation of mankind." I will admit that it would have been more accurate if, instead of "west of the Elbe," I had said "west of Land's End." But it is becoming increasingly difficult for western Europe to maintain its independence, and I think that if we are to get our daily bread (for which we pray to Washington, not to the Almighty) we shall have to abandon such socialistic measures as we have adopted. You ask "doesn't the issue of freedom vs. slavery, of democracy vs. totalitarianism enter into the equation at all." I reply, no. Not at all. That great champion of freedom, Franco, is being made welcome and it is hoped that we may all be induced to die for the sake of Chiang Kai Shek who did not prove himself exactly freedom-loving while he ruled China. Second, I will admit at once that intellectual and political conformity is demanded far more rigorously in Russia than in the United States, and on this ground I still think that a victory of the United States is to be desired if and when war breaks out. But I think the invasion of liberty in America is increasing and is already far more serious than is realised by those who live in New York. You suggest that attacks on liberty are confined to "irresponsibles." Do you include among irresponsibles State education authorities and Regents of State universities? Do you include Congress, which has sanctioned the decision that a man who seeks government employment is to be presumed guilty until he has proved his innocence? I learnt recently of a case of an American employee in Japan who was suddenly dismissed without any intimation as to the grounds of his dismissal except that he was considered unsatisfactory from a security point of view. No specific charge was formulated. At the end of a year, during which he had to spend every penny of his own property, it turned out that the sole evidence against him was that of a hotel porter in America who had a private animosity against him. When he had established this fact he was re-instated, but few people have either the means or the patience for such a procedure. Third, I certainly think that persecution of opinion is one of the main reasons why the two blocs cannot understand each other. You would, I am sure, admit that persecution of opinion in Russia is largely responsible, but persecution, or perhaps it would be better to say suppression, of unorthodox opinion in the West is a more potent factor than most people in the West realise. Are you aware that almost every American who has first-hand knowledge of China has been so smeared by the China Lobby as to make his knowledge of China useless? Are you aware that very few newspapers in the United States will publish what honest journalists wish to write about the Far East?

I want to say in conclusion that I am unalterably hostile to Soviet imperialism, to Soviet despotism, and to the whole Soviet system. But I am alarmed when I see the opinion gaining ground that the Soviet State can only be effectively combatted by imitation. I believe such an opinion to be very dangerous and in combatting it I feel that I am helping and not hindering the preservation of the world from dictatorship.

Russell's reply was published by *The New Leader* in its issue of March 3 under the dramatic title of "Is America in the Grip of Hysteria?" The editors featured the item prominently on the cover of their magazine and published with it a reply to Russell attempting to refute his arguments and concluding with a dire warning that "Anti-Americanism in England and Europe, and the xenophobic isolationism such sentiment provokes in America, serve not the cause of freedom and peace but the cause of the Kremlin."

In the meantime Russell's writings continued to find a sympathetic response in the U.S. The publication of *New Hopes for a Changing World* was reinforced by a great deal of press and radio attention. On January 14, the day of publication, Columbia Broadcasting put out the first of the five programs which Russell had taped with Dwight Cooke in October of the previous year; *Life* magazine included Russell in a portrait portfolio of "Famous Britons" by the photographer Alfred Eisenstaedt; and the national press in general gave prominence to favorable reviews of Russell's new book.

Back in England however Russell was engaged in a protracted and heated controversy through the correspondence columns of *The Manchester Guardian*. The argument was begun by William Henry Chamberlain, the American author and journalist, in a letter published under the heading "Bertrand Russell and the USA" on 8 January 1951:

The *Manchester Guardian Weekly* of November 1 reached me very late. But I still feel inclined to challenge two statements in Bertrand Russell's article "Democracy and the Teachers in the United States"—statements which seem to me inaccurate to the point of irresponsibility.[2] Let me cite them in Lord Russell's own words:

"In Germany under Hitler and in Russia under Stalin nobody ventured upon a political remark without first looking behind the door to make sure that no one was listening. When I last visited America I found the same state of things there.

If by some misfortune you were to quote with approval some remark by Jefferson you would probably lose your job and perhaps find yourself behind bars."

I lived for many years in the Soviet Union and for a shorter period in Nazi Germany and I am convinced that any attempt to equate occasional American lapses into bigotry, stupidity, and intolerance with the systematic terror of communism and nazism is quite unworthy of a scholar of Lord Russell's eminence. The mere fact that in America no one can be imprisoned except under due process of law, with all the familiar Anglo-Saxon safeguards for the rights of the accused, would eliminate at least 95 per cent of the standard terrorism of the totalitarian State.

Lord Russell seems especially unhappy in his suggestion that an approving quotation from Jefferson would entail danger to an individual's livelihood and liberty. Jefferson probably never stood higher in general American esteem. He is one of the patron saints of the Democratic party. And the opposition Republican party, which is opposed to centralization of power in Washington, is fully in accord with Jefferson's theses that the Government which governs least governs best. Two full-length new biographies of Jefferson have recently appeared; and it would certainly be surprising to learn that the authors or approving readers of these biographies are exposed to harassment and persecution.

If I may trespass further on your space, I should like to suggest that the whole tone of Lord Russell's article, apart from its gross exaggerations and misstatements of fact, reveals complete lack of appreciation of a dilemma that is no less real because it is unpleasant. The countries of North America and of Europe outside the Iron Curtain are faced with a form of aggression unknown in modern history, except for a short time during the Jacobin phase of the French Revolution. (It is interesting in this connection to re-read the speeches and writings of Pitt and Burke in 1793 and 1794 and consider how very topical they sound if "Soviet Union" is substituted for "France").

The very powerful military state which has greatly enlarged its boundaries and still more its sphere of political control since the war possesses a grip on the allegiance of Communists and Communist sympathisers throughout the world. Infiltration of these fifth columnists into positions where they can influence Government policy, betray strategic secrets, and influence public opinion in the interest of a hostile foreign power poses a threat and a problem with which traditional libertarian doctrine is scarcely prepared to deal.

I wonder whether even John Stuart Mill and Voltaire would not have recognised some exceptions to their sweeping theories of absolute tolerance in the case of those who proposed, on coming into power, to destroy for ever the possibility of the society of free and independent individual minds in which Mill and Voltaire believed. Especially when these persons were the advance guard of a foreign totalitarian despotism.

In conclusion I would suggest that men like Klaus Fuchs, Alan Nunn May, Bruno Pontecorvo, Alger Hiss, the figures in the Canadian spy case, and the many others who have taken part in the Communist conspiracy of subversion are a much more real threat to Western liberty that the exuberant Indiana school superintendent whom Lord Russell takes to task—with complete justice until he goes off into inexcusable exaggerations.

Russell's reply to Chamberlin was published on January 12:

Mr. William Henry Chamberlin, in your issue of January 8, takes me to task for some remarks of mine about America. I should like to suggest, to begin with, that, living in the safe haven of Harvard, he probably knows little of average America, and would feel as alien as I do if planted down in the Middle West.

I will concede at once that the reign of terror in America is far less severe than in Russia, but I will not concede that it is non-existent. Apart from legal penalties there are economic penalties which cause acute apprehension. And it is now the law that prospective federal employees must prove innocence; it is not necessary for the authorities to prove "guilt." Even legal penalties are to be feared: the Attorney General has prepared vast lists of persons to be interned whenever, in his opinion, such a course shall seem wise.

Mr. Chamberlin's remarks about Jefferson surprise me. He mentions, as if it were relevant, that Jefferson "never stood higher in general American esteem." Christ stands almost equally high, but everyone knows that it is dangerous to quote the Sermon on the Mount in war-time. As for Jefferson, I commend the following quotations:

"A little rebellion, now and then, is a good thing, and as necessary in the political world as storms in the physical... It is a medicine necessary for the sound health of Government" (Letter to James Madison, 30 January 1737. The rebellion concerned was in America, not in Europe.)

"What country can preserve its liberties, if its rulers are not warned from time to time, that this people preserve the spirit of resistance? Let them take arms...The tree of Liberty must be refreshed from time to time, with the blood of patriots and tyrants." (Letter to Colonel Smith, son-in-law of the second President, 13 November 1787).

"The late rebellion in Massachusetts has given more alarm than I think it should have done. Calculate that one rebellion in thirteen States in the course of eleven years, is but one for each State in a century and a half. No country should be so long without one." (letter to James Madison, 20 December 1787.) But for considerations of space I could multiply such quotations indefinitely.

> "...I cannot agree that the first step in a war for liberty should be the surrender of what you say you are fighting for."

Every alien wishing to visit America has to declare on oath his disagreement with such sentiments. And I think that if Mr. Chamberlin were to state (without mentioning that he is quoting Jefferson) that the United States ought to have rebellions oftener than once every 150 years he would secure the attention of the FBI even in Cambridge, Mass.

I am amazed by what he says about Pitt and Burke in 1793 and 1794, particularly coming, as it does, after praise of Jefferson, who vigorously disapproved of their attitude. Does Mr. Chamberlin regret that Pitt failed to catch and hang Tom Paine? I quite agree that Pitt, that sinister Tory, said things that sound topical now, if one places them in the mouth of an American Republican. For my part, I was brought up in childhood to execrate Pitt, and see no reason to change.

In conclusion, I cannot agree that the first step in a war for liberty should be the surrender of what you say say you are fighting for.

An anonymous American letter supporting Russell's argument appeared on February 11 under the pseudonym of "Science Doctor:"

Mr. Bertrand Russell's reply to Mr. Chamberlin, however poignant, may be even more convincing when read in conjunction with the following corroborative details:

In our University, and I can only conclude that the same is true for others, there are several resident FBI agents who interview department heads and their secretaries regularly about students who are prospective Government employees. They ask detailed questions about political opinions advanced by prospective candidates during their scholastic career. This is fairly well known and does not exactly encourage undergraduates to utter opinions critical of the United States Government.

What happens if one does utter such opinions may be illustrated by my own experience. I am employed by a leading university to do research in applied science. My work is unclassified, but the funds out of which I am paid come from a government agency. There must be many thousands of people working in universities under similar conditions. I was recently warned by the director of my institute that reports had come from the Washington office of the Government agency in question to say that I had, in a small circle, been heard to advance views critical of the United States Government. I was advised not to continue to make such remarks, because otherwise it might be difficult to continue my present employment. The remarks I did make were such as any thinking man might make who had no fear of speaking out his thoughts. I am neither a Communist nor even remotely a sympathizer or fellow-traveller. I made these remarks to at most three or four academic men, who, I thought, were my friends. This should illustrate the present atmosphere in the United States for your readers.

Here are the "economic penalites" Mr. Bertrand Russell writes about "which cause acute apprehension." Nobody is saying things are as bad as in Hitler's Germany or Soviet Russia. But they are bad enough. There is obviously an immense number of Government agents whose job it is to engage in political snooping. Every employee of an industrial or scientific organization, down to the last janitor, has to apply for security clearance if some classified work is going on on the premises. He has to list all organizations he ever belonged to and he will not be cleared if there happens to be one on the Attorney General's list. He never will be missed.

Just think how many men must be employed to scrutinize these forms and how dangerous the mere existence of such an apparatus can be. I must ask you to conceal my name and address.

The Manchester Guardian continued to receive and publish letters from various American academics challenging Russell's views. On February 26 Professor Eugene Bird from the History Department at the University of Oregon added his dissenting voice to the debate with Russell. Russell's reply was published on March 1:

The interesting letter which you published in your issue of February 26 from Professor Eugene H. Bird of the University of Oregon demands some reply. He has three accusations against me of (1) cultural snobbery (2) oversimplification (3) publishing criticism of America in English rather than American newspapers. His letter contains not one single fact concerning America except that he lives on the Pacific coast, and even that one fact does not seem to have registered since he has apparently never heard of the University of California.

I have noticed in all those Americans who take the same line as Professor Bird, a considerable shyness about facts. Those who champion the victims of oppression are quickly inundated with facts, and one is led to the conclusion that the orthodox succeed in not knowing the facts. I must repeat what I have said before, that I do not for a moment suggest that reign of terror in present-day America is any thing like as bad as the reign of terror in Nazi Germany or in Soviet Russia. But where I do perceive a very disquieting parallel is in the ignorance of the general public as to what is occurring. Most Americans professed indignant incredulity when the Germans said that they had not known what went on in Nazi concentration camps. Their own ignorance of what goes on in America should show that such Germans may have been quite sincere. Most of the cases of oppression that occur in America cannot be publicised since any victim who did so would be even more severely victimised.

It is only those who have private incomes who can let the world know what they have suffered. Take, for example, a letter which appeared in the *Saturday Review of Literature* on February 23 from Dr. Burnham P Beckwith, an economist who, after giving up a Federal position bringing him in $10,000 a year in order to write a book on price theory, was unable after writing the book to obtain re-employment because in the opinion of the authorities there is a reasonable doubt as to whether there is a reasonable doubt of his loyalty. Although he has never been a Communist or a fellow traveller he is henceforth barred not only from Government employment but from an academic post in the great majority of universities. He has not been informed of the ground on which he is suspect of being suspect and he has no method of redress. He is one of many thousands who are in this position, but most of them dare not mention their predicament.

Illiberality in America has reached proportions which are danger-ous not only to mankind but even to the United States. Practically every American who has any knowledge of China has become disqualified from giving any assistance to the Government by Senator McCarthy's irresponsible accusations. Professors of economics who are told that it is their duty to indoctrinate the young against communism are considered subversive if they know what the doctrines of communism are; only those who have not read Marx are considered competent to combat his doctrines by the policemen who have professors at their mercy. To object to this, I am told, is cultural snobbery. I suppose that, if I were not a culture snob, I should recognise at once that wisdom and virtue are only to be expected from ignorant hypocrites. Professor Bird takes me to task because I do not mention all the cases in which crimes have not been committed. There was a time when people made a fuss about the number of murders in Chicago, but it was not considered necessary to add that "of course there are many people in Chicago who are not murderers." When Dreyfus was sent to Devil's Island the world was shocked, and it was not considered that a Frenchman was giving an adequate defence if he said "Oh, but you ought to mention all the French Jews who are not in Devil's Island."

Professor Bird seems to think that when I protest against evils in America I do so because I am anti-American. This is not the case.

There are in America a great many men and women for whom I have profound respect, and when I protest against what is being done I do so for their sake. Those who inflict the terror and those who pretend that it does not exist are attempting to destroy what is best in America and what every friend of America must wish to preserve. I have in my day protested with equal vigour against evils in my own country, but not because I hated my own country. At the present time whatever hopes there may be for humanity have to be centred upon America since America alone has enough power to resist the Soviet Government. But for that very reason not only America but the whole free world is vitally concerned in preserving freedom in America.

Professor Bird takes me to task for writing about American evils in English rather than in American newspapers. The first and most obvious answer is that it is extremely difficult to get letters accepted by most American newspapers except such as I should consider intolerably pro-Russian. And when I do succeed in getting published in America, I am exposed to editorial distortions without my knowledge or consent. I wrote an article for *Look* which I called "What is Wrong with Anglo-American Relations.[2] It was a balanced article attributing faults to both sides. To my amazement it appeared under the title "What is Wrong with Americans," and owing to this change of title produced an effect totally different from what I had intended. I have no wish whatever to damage Anglo-American relations. On the contrary, I think good relations between America and Britain quite enormously important. But there cannot be good relations if America does things which shock British opinion and refuses to know that British opinion has been shocked. The shocking things that are done in America are known in every country of the Eastern hemisphere although most Americas remain unaware of them. It is no service to America to conceal the way that other countries feel about these things. I cannot remember any occasion since 1776 when Americans have concealed criticism of Britain. I do not blame them for this, but they should admit that liberty of criticism should be mutual.

In his covering note of February 27, enclosing a copy of his reply to Bird, Russell added privately:

I enclose a reply to your letter to the *Manchester Guardian* which I am sending to that paper, but I should like to add a few words to you privately. I am sorry to find that you and other Americans consider that one must be anti-American if one thinks that America in common with every other county is not wholly perfect. I married an American; both my grown-up children married Americans; and I lived in America for many years. Many of the people whom I like and admire most

44

are Americans. But every nation at times gets bad moods. I criticized my own country quite as severely as I have ever criticized yours. I have failed completely to understand why you accuse me of cultural snobbery. I think it regrettable when those who know about a subject are silenced merely on account of their knowledge and that is what is happening in America in regard to both communism and to China. I think it regrettable when ignorant and prejudiced policemen control the lives and fortunes of conscientious men of learning. If this is what you mean by cultural snobbery, I cannot pretend to be ashamed of it.

The debate ended at this point but the obvious interest it had aroused on both sides of the Atlantic encouraged NBC radio to organize and broadcast a "Round Table" discussion on the subject. The discussion was sponsored by the University of Chicago and published by them on June 22 under the title "Academic Freedom in America and Britain."

Footnotes

1. See above, p. 32.
2. See below, pp. 332-4.

5 Tributes from America

Russell's forthright views and public utterances on America ensured that his Richmond address in London was kept well plied with letters from American admirers as well as opponents. The year 1952, following as it did on his final lecture tour, was a bumper year for such correspondence, but despite his numerous commitments, Russell was at pains to reply. Harold Kastner from Indiana continued to keep Russell informed about the state of civil liberties in America. On February 6 he wrote to Russell complaining about Louis Fisher, the writer with whom he had had a rather bitter correspondence. Russell replied on February 20:

Thank you for the various things you have sent me. I am interested by your correspondence with Louis Fisher. I only once had contact with him and that was of a somewhat unfortunate kind. Just after the failure of the Cripps Mission to India, he and I had a broadcast discussion about India. At that time Gandhi (who is his God) thought the Japanese would win the war—the only case I know of in which his political acumen was at fault. Louis Fisher, who pretends to you that he is always charitable, told a pack of lies about the British which caused me to lose my temper. After the discussion was over he said to me "Lord Russell, I don't understand how you can think..." I interrupted and said, "No, I don't suppose you can." I was feeling at the time very sore because England was in grave danger and Americans who told lies against England increased the danger. Nevertheless, it is obvious that my behavior was indefensible and injudicious and not calculated to bring Louis Fisher around to my point of view. Those of us who feel that we belong to minorities which are more or less impotent almost inevitably become bitter and quarrelsome and querulous. So I have found it in my own case and so I expect you are finding it. I always find it difficult in situations of that sort to remember that it is more important to be persuasive than to say the things that give pleasure to oneself. I have the profoundest sympathy with you in your fight but I sometimes feel that you are in danger of falling into controversial errors of which I myself am constantly guilty. If I give you advice, it is like that of a man who urges total abstinence because he has a hangover. But the advice may be none the less sound. I do not want to see you getting into more trouble than public duty demands. And I should like you to remember that you have the sympathy of very many people who have not the courage to say what they feel.

During March 1952, a controversy arose about proposals to commercialize the BBC by admitting sponsored programs. Russell wrote to *The Times* and his letter was published on March 19:

It was my misfortune to be dependent on American radio in 1940 at the time of the fall of France. The most devastating news would be interrupted, just at the point where one's anxieties had reached their highest pitch, to assure one that So and So's pills would cure worry, or that more men smoked So and So's cigars than anybody else's. I used to find it difficult not to smash the machine in fury. The BBC is one of the most admirable of modern British institutions and it will be a disaster if, from commercial motives, it is vulgarized and degraded.

An American reader of *The Times* rushed immediately into a defense of American broadcasting and added in his letter to Russell, "I sympathize with you at not being able to obtain all the information you would have liked to receive at that time but doubtless you were enjoying other compensations at that time which we here were not." Russell replied on 5 April 1952:

I am interested by the letter of March 29 which you were so good as to send to me. I gather from the fact that you object to criticism of America by non-Americans that you have never in the course of your life made any unfavorable criticisms of England. This makes you unique among the inhabitants of your great country. I am charmed by your remark that in 1940 "doubtless you were enjoying other compensations at that time which we here were not." This is very true. I was enjoying the compensation of being treated throughout America as a criminal, of not being allowed to be a party to the suit against me, and of having the police of New York convened to be lectured by priests on the subject of my responsibility for the crime gang.

The publication of Russell's *New Hopes for a Changing World* earlier in the year and the publicity it had received in America contributed to the rash of letters which Russell was receiving. The book which had been advertised by its publishers as "A Frontal Attack on Defeatism" set out Russell's views on the prospects for the human race, given a more rational approach to the development of human and natural resources. Russell viewed nationalism as the "chief obstacle to the extension of social cohesion" and the "chief force making for the extermination of the human race."[1] He cited the American Republican party as an example of ardent nationalism and he criticised American newspapers for vilifying other nations and for using such phrases as "the yapping Yahoos of the British Socialist Government" which he felt was a clear example of "hatred overriding self-interest."[2] Donald G. Brennan, an American correspondent took issue with Russell over these statements and Russell in his reply of 28 April 1952 returned to his earlier theme of the desirability of Anglo American cooperation:

Thank you for your letter of March 26. I will admit at once that the two statements you quote are somewhat too sweeping. I ought to have confined them to the right wing of the Republican party. I do not find anything to object to in Eisenhower's views on international affairs, and if he becomes president, I think he will shape American policy wisely, but at the time of writing the contest between him and Taft remains undecided. There are some points in your letter for comment. In the first place I have never been a Marxian. My very first book, published in 1896[3] contained a vigorous attack on Marx and I have never since mentioned him except critically.

As to American opinion in general, I find that you in common with other people who live in Cambridge, Mass., are scarcely aware of opinion in less enlightened parts of America. The phrase which I quoted about yapping Yahoos was typical of most newspapers outside New York, Boston, and Washington. You seem to think that the point of view embodied in such phrases is no more influential in America than the point of view of Bevan in this country. In this I am afraid that you are quite mistaken. In travelling about America I have found that those who hold views similar to those which you express dare not give utterance to them except in the depths of the most inviolable privacy. I have found almost all the newspapers that I have seen in America spreading lies about the condition of England under the Socialist Government. I have found these lies believed by almost everybody. Kind friends have sent me food parcels under the impression that I am starving. When I inform people who think themselves enlightened

that British wage earners and their children have been better nour-
ished in recent years than ever before, I am thought to be engaging in
mendacious propaganda. My American friends, with few exceptions,
use "democracy" as synonymous with "capitalism" and when I say
that England is a democracy they refuse to admit it, not because of the
King and the House of Lords but because the undesirable activities of
plutocrats are somewhat curbed.

I have no wish to promote a conflict between British socialism and
American capitalism, but American capitalism has been promoting
such a conflict by dishonest and unscrupulous methods from which it
results that the British can only cooperate with America as slaves and
not as free men. If Anglo-American cooperation is to continue, as I
most profoundly hope that it will, it is essential that Americans
should tolerate an internal economic policy in this country which
they do not wish to see adopted in the United States.

I think if you were to live for sometime in any Middle Western state
or in California, you would realize that you have been living hitherto
in a little island of enlightenment by no means typical of your
country.

May 1952 was an important month for Russell. The weeks leading up
to his 80th birthday on May 18 were filled with requests to him for
contributions to the various media. The demands from America, prompted
as they were by Julie Medlock, were particularly heavy and Russell was
exhausted by the intensified activity. Julie Medlock recalls Russell
remarking: "I am utterly sick of being 80! I am looking forward to 10 years
of retirement, then, in 1962, great headlines: 'Bertrand Russell discovered
to be still alive, living contentedly in almshouse founded by his grand-
father.' "[4]

"It seemed impossible," Julie Medlock wrote, "for Russell to stay out
of the news. Even at the New York city funeral service for the popular
Hollywood actor, John Garfield, attended by 10,000 admirers of the actor
and countless celebrities, the press reported that 'the officiating Rabbi read
the 23rd Psalm, intoned the traditional Hebrew prayer for the dead, and
then delivered excerpts from Bertrand Russell's "Free Man's Worship." ' "[5]

Scheduled for May 18 was an NBC TV interview with Russell.
Arranged earlier in the year by Julie Medlock it was to be the first ever
American TV interview of its kind—a half hour portrait of a famous
individual. Also scheduled for the 18th was a tape recorded interview with
Russell in London for NBC radio. Advance publicity for these events was
provided fortuitously on May 12 when the *New York Times* reported under
the heading "Russell tape-record held up by Customs":

Bertrand Russell's fame for his frankness on such subjects as morals and sex led last night to his running afoul, by proxy, of the United States Customs. A tape-recorded interview, given in England by the 79 year old British philosopher and Nobel Prize winner, was held up by the customs for censorship on its arrival in New York International Airport, Idlewild, Queens, on a Trans-World Airlines plane from Europe.

The circumstances surrounding the episode were not immediately clear. At the NBC offices, a spokesman said that the tape recording was addressed to that office but that he did not know the contents. "All I know," the spokesman said, "is that somebody out at the airport mentioned Lord Russell and a Customs man was supposed to have said, "Isn't that the man who's for birth control, or against it?" or something like that, and then they said the recording couldn't be used until it had been reviewed.

The story became clearer when the *New York Post* published their version later that day, under the heading "Russell Spells S-E-X to Wary Customs Man."

Sex, which can't seem to be left out of things, got into the picture today again in a little imbroglio involving philosopher Bertrand Russell, who wasn't even there, and one Thomas Sullivan, a customs inspector at Idlewild Airport. It seems that Sullivan was on duty last night when a tape recorded interview with Russell arrived by plane consigned to the National Broadcasting Company.

Russell? Russell? Sullivan pondered as the flicker of memory roared into a flame and exploded.

"He's the fellow who wrote about sex, isn't he?"

The NBC men conceded that Lord Russell had upon occasion touched on that delicate subject.

"Then I'm afraid," Sullivan said, "that it'll have to be censored."

It was carefully explained to Sullivan that Russell who will be 80 on Sunday, was also a Nobel Prize winner, one of the world's most distinguished mathematicians, philosophers and writers, and that the recording was part of a birthday programme to be broadcast. Sullivan, unimpressed, finally released the tape to the NBC man—but only after he put a government seal on it which will have to be broken in the presence of the Customs censor.

The book Sullivan referred to—it is not known whether he had read it—is *Marriage and Morals* published in 1929. Sullivan did not exhibit any curiosity about another of Russell's books called *Principia Mathematica*—one of the cornerstones of modern mathematics.

The NBC interview with Russell on May 18 was an instantaneous success. The title of the program was "Eighty Years of Changing Beliefs and Unchanging Hopes" and in the course of half an hour Russell answered questions on his own life experiences and outlined his views on a wide range of social and political problems concluding with a hopeful prediction about mankind's future:

I believe most firmly, that through whatever pain and suffering, mankind will emerge....into some world that will be happier than any world that has existed in the past. I am firmly persuaded of that. What I don't know is how long it will take.[6]

Except for those most hostile to Russell, the critics were unanimous in their acclaim and the program was everywhere welcomed as an outstanding breakthrough for the TV media. *Variety* echoing the response of most major media reviewers hoped that it would be "the first of a series of programs showcasing men who have made some notable contribution to their chosen field and who have enriched mankind through their extraordinary talents or flair for living" but that "finding another Lord Russell won't be a simple task. For here was a perfect casting—a personality who projects on TV the same sort of exciting manner as a Toscanini." For *Variety*, one of the most outstanding and rewarding aspects of the interview "was Lord Russell's ability to reduce what might have been a formidable dissertation on a scholarly plane to a simple conversation within the realm of anyone's understanding."

Meanwhile Russell in London on his birthday was under siege from the press. *The New York Herald Tribune* correspondent, describing Russell as one of the noted philosophers of the century, reported him as saying:

On gloomy days I foresee a third world war in the near future, lasting for years and ending indecisively after unparalleled destruction— ending not in a real peace but in a grim determination on both sides to renew the fight as soon as possible and to continue this time until a definitive issue has been reached.

In the course of these struggles, I see Western Europe with its cities reduced to rubble and its countryside transformed into a radioactive desert. I see the total expulsion of all white men from Africa, and Asia rendered even poorer than at present, by internal strife. I see Latin American throwing off the yoke of the United States and reverting to barbarism. I see the United States shorn of power, surviving like the Byzantine Empire as the last fading glimmer of a more civilized age, endeavouring to survive behind a defensive wall and living on old ideas which the rest of the world will regard as archaic.

On his cheerful days, Lord Russell says he foresees "Russia and America gradually growing less suspicious of each other. Communism losing its fierceness and white men learning to acquiesce in equality for those of different pigmentation. I see science at last allowed to bring mankind the happiness it is capable of bringing. I do not know which of these two visions has the greater likelihood of being realized."

Life Magazine paid tribute to Russell on May 26 with an article entitled "A Great Mind is Still Annoying and Adorning Our Age":

The fame of philosophers seldom spreads beyond the confines of university campuses. But Russell's has, because for the last 40 years he has striven to think about complex current issues—politics, history, ethics, economics—and to convey his thoughts to those who longed for insight in language they could understand. And whatever Bertrand Russell has done, wherever he has gone there has usually been laughter.

When he was lecturing at the University of Chicago, he told President Robert Hutchins that one of the advantages of belonging to the British peerage was that you were treated well in jail.

While broadcasting on the BBC's Brains Trust program, he was challenged to demonstrate the conjugation of an irregular verb. "I am firm" was his answer. "You are obstinate. He is a pigheaded fool."

On the leaders of the utilitarians, who had worked out virtually everything for the new Utopia: "Bookish men...there was no rough-and-tumble in their lives, none of them would have known what to do with a horse dealer or a card-sharper, or even an ordinary drunkard."

In accepting the Nobel Prize, Russell denied that he had contributed anything particular to literature. "I feel like the intellectual but plain looking lady who was warmly complimented on her beauty."

To conclude an extraordinarily eventful month with Russell receiving more concentrated attention in America than perhaps at any other time in his life the press announced on May 28 the filing of a petition of divorce against Russell by Patricia, his third wife. The petition, which was undefended by Russell and gave no grounds, came after sixteen years of mostly unhappy marriage. American gossip columnists made the most of the situation even for a time linking his name with Julie Medlock. When Russell was apprised of this suggestion he sent a message to Julie Medlock commenting: "No one would think the worse of me, but they surely would think you rash." But as the divorce proceeding contradicted any claim of misconduct and as the British press treated the affair with due restraint, it soon ceased to be a topic for speculation.

Russell wrote several articles for American journals during this hectic period. "The Dangerous Days" (originally entitled "My Philosophy of Life") appeared in the May issue of *Glamour*: "Advice to those who want to attain 80," for the *NYTM* of May 18; "My first 80 years" for the *New York Post* of May 28 and "The American Way (A Briton says) is Dour" for the *NYTM* of June 15.[7] The last named article was lighthearted and amusing. In it Russell dealt with the crippling effect of a competitive existence and the resulting urge to conformity which he believed diminished the capacity of most Americans to give reign to their impulses and to enjoy life:

> When I try to understand what it is that prevents so many Americans from being as happy as one might expect it seems to me that there are two causes of which one goes much deeper than the other. The one that goes least deep is the necessity for subservience in some large organization. If you are an energetic man with strong views as to the right way of doing the job with which you are concerned, you find yourself invariably under the orders of some big man at the top who is elderly, weary and cynical. Whenever you have a bright idea, the boss puts a stopper on it. The more energetic you are and the more vision you have, the more you will suffer from the impossiblity of doing any of the things that you feel ought to be done. When you go home and moan to your wife, she tells you that you are a silly fellow and that if you became the proper sort of yes-man your income would soon be doubled. If you try divorce and remarriage it is very unlikely that there will be any change in this respect. And so you are condemned to gastric ulcers and premature old age.

Russell continued to write for American journals all through the summer. His more lighthearted articles proved extremely popular, were often reprinted and anthologized, and many Americans wrote commending him for them. Upton Sinclair, the socialist novelist whose work Russell admired and who stood by Russell during the City College of New York affair in 1941, wrote on August 15:

> Many years have passed since we last met. The occasion for my writing is the two articles which I have read, one in the *Atlantic* and one in the *Saturday Review*.[8] They seem to me extraordinarily wise and kind, and I am happy to find that I agree with every word of them. That

> "I am terrified about America. America is extraordinarily bellicose...they do not want war; but they expect it. The ordinary American thinks that there is going to be war with Russia, probably within a year...The Americans think that Western Europe is expendable. But if you are a Western European it is hard to see that point of view."

means a good deal to me and I hope it means something to you. Perhaps you have forgotten that you once joined in recommending me for the Nobel Prize.

I don't know if you have seen any of the things I have been writing of recent years. I am just finishing another "Lanny Budd" book after a three year interval. I am taking the liberty of having a little fun with you. My hero has a radio station, and I am opening the story with you as the speaker and quoting half a dozen sentences from your *Saturday Review* article. I am sure you won't mind this, it may have the effect of sending some of my readers to your books.[9]

I had a curious experience a year or so ago. I was having lunch in a cafe and I saw a man sitting at the counter and couldn't take my eyes off him. As I was going out I said to him "I wonder if anybody ever told you how much you look like Bertrand Russell." His answer was, "Who's Bertrand Russell?" I told him and suggested he look up a picture of you in the public library.

One of the few articles Russell wrote concerning America, but directed primarily at a British readership, was published in August by *European & Atlantic Digest* under the title of "Britain Can Lead Europe to Equality with America." Russell argued for a union of European countries, including Britain, "Which would have the closest possible relations with America—but as an equal." Russell felt that only in a united Europe could Britain remain independent of America while helping to influence its international policies in a positive way. Russell was apprehensive about the future of Western Europe which without unity would "continue to be merely a pawn between Russia and America" and he warned against the consequences of dependence on America:

> I am terrified about America, America is extraordinarily bellicose.... they do not want war; but they expect it. The ordinary American thinks that there is going to be a war with Russia, probably within a year. If you think that, you tend to bring war about. The Americans think that Western Europe is expendable. But if you are a Western European it is hard to see that point of view.

During August Russell received a letter from Mrs. Chase S. Osborn, wife of the one-time governor of Michigan. Mrs. Osborn wrote Russell on behalf of the Atlantic Union Committee which was concerned to establish a "Federal Convention of Democracies" to inform him that her organization was establishing a branch in Britain. Mrs. Osborn hoped for Russell's support and at the same time voiced disquiet about the weakening of Anglo-American relations which she felt was fostered by the "divisive genius of the Kremlin." Russell was interested to combat this view and replied on August 26:

As regards Anglo-American relations, a certain amount of strain is, I think, unavoidable. Forty years ago there was the same kind of strain between England and France. Anti-American feeling in England springs partly from the natural but indefensible envy of a formerly rich parent now living on a son's bounty. It has, however, other sources which are more serious. We think that, if America had not been so wedded to Chiang Kai-Shek, China might never have become Communist; or, if it did, might have preserved more independence of Russia. We have serious misgivings about Dulles's policy towards Japan, since we think it highly probable that, when the time is ripe, Japan will again proclaim itself the champion of Asia against the white man; or rather, against such white men as are not Russians. We think that Americans are too prone to view the conflict as a holy war against communism, rather than as a defensive reaction to Russian Imperialists. We cannot but notice that large and important sections of American opinion are bitterly anti-British and will stick at nothing to foment anti-British feeling. During the First World War I was put in prison for quoting from the Report of a Senatorial Committee certain facts about the employment of Federal troops to support employers in labour disputes.[10] This was done because the British Government considered good relations with America of paramount importance. No similar steps have ever been taken in America against those who abuse the British. In 1942, I was at a dinner party in Pennsylvania where a lady explained as something she knew through confidential information in Washington that the planes which attacked Pearl Harbor were British and that the whole thing was a dastardly British trick to turn America against the dear Japanese. None of the Americans present seemed to think this opinion preposterous....

Mrs. Chase Osborn wrote to Russell again on September 6 describing what she believed was the attitude of Americans to the socialist administration in Britain and advancing the tentative view that "until the Atlantic

Community achieves the framework of a community, with certain equalizations of burdens and benefits, these strains will increase."

Russell replied on September 15:

There is only one point in your letter that I feel calls for comment. It is where you say "a defence of Socialism in England by the statement that the majority of the population are better fed than at any time in British history would cause too many Americans to bristle: 'Yes, and they get glasses and false teeth free—at our expense!—while we have to pay for our own—at prices out of reach!' " It is a little difficult to know what English people are to do in order to remove American misunderstandings. Your newspapers have for many years been full of totally untrue statements to the effect that we were starving as a result of Socialism and you now tell me that if I say we are not starving, we shall be all the more hated on that account. It is true that the poorer classes in England are better fed than at any earlier time, but I do not see how the attitude you suggest in America can be justified until we have as many beefsteaks per head as you have. The argument that we get some money from America and ought therefore to starve quietly and humbly is a little wide of the mark. We should have no need whatever of American aid if you lowered your tariff and even if you did not increase it whenever some export of ours (other than whiskey) succeeds in surmounting it. As for the health service, that is totally irrelevant, since it is not financed by dollars and everybody who has taken the trouble to look into it (which hardly any American has) knows that it is a paying proposition from a national point of view since it renders hundreds of thousands of people efficient who were formerly inefficient from short sight, deafness, bad teeth or what not. It is impossible for English people not to get annoyed when they are lectured by ignoramuses for not sharing the ignorance of those who find fault with them. I am sure you do not share the sentiments that you report, and I hope you will do what you can to combat them.

On 4 November 1952, three days after a reported explosion of the first U.S. H-bomb at Eniwetok atoll in the Pacific, General Eisenhower, the Republican candidate, won an overwhelming victory over Adlai Stevenson in the American presidential election. Russell, who had hoped for (though not predicted) Stevenson to succeed in order to curb the activities of the McCarthyists, was bitterly disappointed. His marriage to Edith Finch on December 15 provided a happy interlude but the election result had made him basically pessimistic about the future.[11] After Eisenhower's inauguration on 20 January 1953, Russell indicated his mood in a letter to Julie Medlock of February 17:

My views about world politics are gloomy in the extreme. Eisenhower appears to be a complete nonentity, and American policy during his presidential term will, I fear, be completely governed first by Taft and Dulles and then by McCarthy. I do not know in what proportion to divide their conduct between wickedness and folly. It will, I fear, lead to World War before long. In that war I suppose that a very large proportion of the inhabitants of this country and Western Europe will perish, including my children and grandchildren. Nevertheless, most Americans consider it impertinent for Europeans to have views on American policy in which they have no stake but their lives.

In the same letter Russell, who did not underestimate the smear tactics of his opponents, asked Julie to pre-empt their inevitable "anti-American" accusation with the following statement:

Lord Russell admits that he is anti-McCarthy, and those who identify McCarthy with America will therefore think him anti-American. He is not anti-American in any other sense. For the last forty years he has been in the habit of severely criticising such British policies as he thought ill of, but is not on that account to be thought anti-British. Exactly the same applies when he criticises policies of certain sections in America.

Footnotes

1. Bertrand Russell, *New Hopes for a Changing World* (London, 1952) (New York, 1952) p. 69.
2. *Ibid.*, pp. 69-70.
3. *German Social Democracy.*
4. J Medlock, *op. cit.*
5. *Ibid.*
6. Transcript of NBC TV interview with Romney Wheeler.
7. See below, pp. 335-7.
8. "A Life of Disagreement", reprint of NBC TV interview, *Atlantic Monthly*, August 1952. "The Next Eighty Years", *Saturday Review*, 9 August 1952.
9. *The Return of Lanny Budd* was published in 1953 and included in its opening chapter a description of Russell as well as extracts from his article "The Next Eighty Years".
10. See *Bertrand Russell's America* (London, 1973) (Viking Press, New York, 1974), Vol. 1, p. 74.
11. See Illustrations, p. 299.

6 The Russell-Einstein Alliance

Because Russell was convinced that the relentless drive to reaction in America was militating against a peaceful solution of the world's problems he became increasingly sensitive to and critical of illiberal tendencies in that country. He devoted much time to studying the state of civil liberties in America. The current spate of Atom-spy cases on both sides of the Atlantic, particularly the case of Fuchs, whose confessions led to the trials of the Rosenbergs and Sobell, had served to intensify the McCarthyist campaigns in America. Although Russell at this stage did not challenge the validity of the trials or their judgments, he did perceive a direct connection between the trials and McCarthy's investigations. It was evident to Russell that the witch-hunting apparatus was beginning to permeate every facet of American social life. The American Committee for Cultural Freedom, which was an affiliate of the Congress for Cultural Freedom, an organization which he had agreed to sponsor in 1951, did not seem to be immune from these destructive processes. On 24 April 1953 Katherine Faulkner, a voluntary worker for the Emergency Civil Liberties Committee, an organization devoted to upholding the U.S. Constitution, wrote:

> In spite of many obstacles, such as lack of funds and being smeared as a Communist-front, we held a very interesting conference in January here in New York on the Bill of Rights which included forums on Academic Freedom, the Political Use of Fear, Freedom of the Arts and Loyalty and the Fifth Amendment. Dr. Alexander Meiklejohn, Senator William Langer of North Dakota and Professor Hugh H. Wilson of Princeton University were among the chief speakers.
>
> An organization calling itself the American Committee for Cultural Freedom was the instigator of the attacks against us and tried

by the best McCarthy tactics of smear and guilt-by-association to destroy us. Professor George Counts, chairman of the Committee, should know better but I understand that he was rabidly pro-Communist in the 1930s and is trying now to repudiate his past by projecting his guilt feelings onto a destructive level. I believe everyone has a right to change his mind and to think what he pleases, but certainly that does not entitle him to tell others what to think or to decide upon the degree of their anti-communism before they are acceptable. Many of us have been shocked to see your name listed as one of the Sponsors of this American Committee for Cultural Freedom. We have always looked to you as a free thinker in the finest tradition and cannot believe that you would knowingly support an organization which, accepting heresay as a basis for judgement, is helping to bring to pass in this country the very totalitarianism it fears.

Russell, whose name featured prominently on the letterhead of the American Committee for Cultural Freedom although has was in fact only associated with the international body, was upset by this information and wrote to the American Committee on May 16:

I have come to the conclusion that it is a mistake for me to be a sponsor of the American Committee for Cultural Freedom since at this distance I cannot know adequately what its actions are or whether they are such as I should wish to support. I shall be grateful therefore if you would take this letter as conveying my resignation.

The Committee was disturbed by Russell's decision and on May 26 David Bell, a member of their executive, wrote to Russell suggesting that his request arose out of a misunderstanding of his role in relation to the Committee:

The American Committee is autonomous...neither the Congress for Cultural Freedom nor its officers are wholly responsible or should be held responsible for the specific positions of the American Committee as we ourselves are not responsible and do not intervene in the affairs and policy positions of other national committees.

Bell offered, if Russell so wished, to rearrange the grouping of names on their letterhead so "as to indicate more clearly the separation of function." Bell's explanation was backed up on June 3 by a letter from Irving Kristol of the British Society for Cultural Freedom which stated:

As an honorary chairman of the Congress for Cultural Freedom you are a sponsor only of that organisation, and not of any of the national affiliates. However, as one who was until recently, an executive director of the American Committee, I am disturbed by your letter nonetheless. You seem to be under the impression that there have been actions by the Committee of which you might not approve. I am in a position to state quite definitely that your apprehensions are unfounded. I cannot think of a single action or statement by the American Committee which you would not wish wholeheartedly to support.

Russell, whose sole reason for complaint was the allegation by Katherine Faulkner of the Emergency Civil Liberties Committee and who knew of no other evidence to support her claim, took at that time no further action but remained an Honorary President of the International Congress for Cultural Freedom.

The tactics of McCarthysim were alienating an increasingly wide section of American opinion. But there were few individuals courageous enough to take a public stand against the investigations. Those arraigned before the Un-American Activities Committees were therefore under tremendous pressure to sacrifice their principles. The equivocal role of certain of the more liberal press only served to further isolate those subpoenaed. When, in a letter published in the *New York Times* of 12 June 1953, Albert Einstein suggested that intellectuals called before McCarthy's investigating committees should refuse to testify, the *New York Times* on June 13 took Einstein to task and accused him of taking an extremist position:

...it is one thing to fight the investigations because of the manner of their procedure and another to oppose the right of investigation...The situation which Professor Einstein rebels against certainly needs correction but the answer does not lie in defying the law.

Russell wrote the following letter to the *New York Times* on June 15:

In your issue of June 13 you have a leading article disagreeing with Einstein's view that teachers questioned by Senator McCarthy's emissaries should refuse to testify. You seem to maintain that one should always obey the law, however bad. I cannot think you have realised the implications of this position. Do you condemn the Christian martyrs who refused to sacrifice to the emperor? Do you condemn John Brown? Nay, more, I am compelled to suppose that you condemn George Washington, and hold that your country ought to return to allegiance to her Gracious Majesty Queen Elizabeth II. As a loyal Briton I of course applaud this view, but I fear it may not win much support in your country.[1]

He sent a copy of the letter to Einstein with a covering note on June 20 (the day after the execution of Julius and Ethel Rosenberg):

I am in whole-hearted agreement with your contention that teachers called before McCarthy's inquisitors should refuse to testify. When the *New York Times* had a leading article disagreeing with you about this I wrote a letter to it supporting you. But I am afraid they are not going to print it. I enclose a copy, of which, if you feel so disposed, you may make use in any way you like.[2]

Einstein replied on June 28:

With your fine letter to the *N.Y. Times* you have performed a good service for the good cause. The intellectuals here right down to the youngest students are completely overawed. Apart from you, hardly a single "prominent figure" has declared himself energetically for the fight against the mischief being wrought by the politicians. They feel so strong because they have successfully persuaded the masses that the Russians, and the Communists in this country, have endangered the fatherland. The further they carry this, the surer they feel of being re-elected by the misguided crowd. Linked with this is the fact that Eisenhower did not dare to reprieve the two Rosenbergs, even though he knows very well how much this execution has damaged America's image abroad.

I have read your latest publication, "Impact"[3] and "Satan..."[4] carefully and with great enjoyment. It is very commendable that you have placed your unique literary talent at the service of public enlightenment and education. I am convinced that the influence of your writings is great and lasting, so successfully have you resisted the temptation to win momentary triumphs through paradoxes and exaggerations.[5]

At the end of July Russell received news that Barrows Dunham, the philosopher who had stood by him in 1942-3 during his dispute with the Barnes Foundation, was called before an investigating committee in Washington and had refused to answer their questions.[6] As a result he was suspended from his professorship at Temple University and his dismissal or reinstatement was made subject to the decision of the Trustees of the University who had employed for the purpose a special legal counsel. Russell was informed that an intervention by him on behalf of Dunham might carry some weight in view of his record of activities on behalf of academic freedom. He therefore wrote to the University's President Robert L. Johnson on August 8:

> I learn with regret that my friend Professor Barrows Dunham is having trouble of a sort which I am convinced is entirely undeserved. I have known him for twelve and a half years and saw a good deal of him when we were both connected with the Barnes Foundation. I am quite sure that his opinions are in no way subversive, and I can hardly doubt that the university will support him. The cause of academic freedom is one of which the importance must be clear to everybody who understands the functions of universities, and it is clear that this cause will be furthered if the University stands by Professor Dunham. I hope you will not think me impertinent for adding my word in support of a friend and a cause, both of which I value.

Russell at the same time wrote a more general letter to *The Nation* which had earlier carried a report of the Dunham case. Russell's letter was published on 15 August 1953 under the title "Voice of Freedom":

> I am astonished that there is not more objection in America to the inquisition by your new Holy Office into the lives and opinions of American citizens and eminent aliens. The law which permits this inquisition is a bad one, and in my opinion everyone, whatever his opinion, ought to refuse to obey this law in order to promote its repeal. It is somewhat ironic that in America, which was once regarded as the land of liberty, the most resounding voice in favour of freedom should come from a German. I sincerely hope that Einstein's splendid lead will be widely followed.

Barrows Dunham, who had been sent copies of Russell's letters, wrote to him on September 5 expressing his "profound gratitude" and informing him about the progress of his case:

> There will probably be a decision next week. Whatever its character may turn out to be, I have no doubt of ultimate victory in this struggle. I hope you won't give Americans up as lost. The great liberal tradition is still strong, though it doesn't make many headlines; and I have learned very warmly, in the last six months, the friendliness of common folk.

Russell's intervention on behalf of Dunham proved to have no effect. On September 23 Dunham was dismissed from his position and accused of "intellectual arrogance."

The most significant event of 1953, an event which for Russell overshadowed even the death of Stalin in March and the Korean Armistice in July, was the announcement by the USSR of the successful detonation, in August, of their first thermo-nuclear device just nine months after the American test explosion. Shortly afterwards in an article entitled "The Danger to Mankind" Russell wrote "Never since human beings first existed have they been faced with so great a danger." The article was published in the January 1954 edition of the *Bulletin of Atomic Scientists* and in it, as well as in other articles that he wrote during this period, Russell argued for the "total prevention of large-scale wars" which he felt could be achieved only through the establishment of "one armed force possessed of a monopoly of the major weapons of war." Russell felt that without such a step "in the next fifty years, it seems hardly likely that man will survive." While Russell was repeating his earlier views on world government, views which had led him to support the Baruch proposals in 1947, there was a change of major significance in his outlook. Russell was rejecting his earlier view that an aggressive anti-Soviet policy, even considering a possible World War III, was the proper one for the USA to follow. Dr. Walter Marseilles, with whom Russell had corresponded in this regard in May 1948, brought this revision in Russell's thinking to the attention of the *Saturday Review*. The journal published Russell's original letter to Marseilles together with an explanation of why his views had changed.[7] "The main cause in my change of opinion is the shift which has occurred in the balance of forces." Russell dealt with the important international changes which had taken place since the late Forties, including the development of nuclear weapons, and continued:

> The situation now is that we cannot defeat Russia except by defeating ourselves. Those who still advocate war seem to me to be living in a fool's paradise. I must add, however, that I do not now, any more that at an earlier time, advocate either appeasement or a slackening in rearmament, since either might encourage the Communist powers in aggressive designs and would therefore make war more likely. The problem for statesmanship in the present situation, as I see it, is to avoid war without surrender on our side or the expectation of surrender on the other.
>
> I should not be wholly sincere if I did not admit that my opinions have undergone a change somewhat deeper than that warranted by strategic consideration. The awful prospect of the extermination of the human race, if not in the next war, then in the next but one or the next but two, is so sobering to any imagination which has seriously contemplated it as to demand very fundamental fresh thought on the whole subject, not only of international relations, but of human life and its capabilities...

Toward the end of January 1954 Russell spent several weeks in hospital following a serious operation. While still recovering, he was asked by the Emergency Civil Liberties Committee if he would contribute to their bulletin a short tribute "on Einstein and his continuing fight against tyranny."[8] The occasion for the tribute was to be Einstein's 75th birthday which the Emergency Civil Liberties Committee planned to celebrate with a conference on academic freedom at Princeton University. Russell agreed to the request and his contribution in the form of a letter was published in *Rights* during the first week of March. Upon publication Russell received a cable from the American Committee for Cultural Freedom. The cable concluded with the request for Russell to "please cable us collect" and was dated March 9:

Your name and greetings being used by Emergency Civil Liberties Committee in connection with meeting supposedly honoring Einstein's birthday. Group has discredited itself by refusing acknowledge suppression civil liberties academic freedom behind Iron Curtain. Einstein will not attend this meeting nor will Norman Thomas who has publicly strongly deplored this group's stand. Einstein's name being used to lend respectability to this Communist-line cause. J. Robert Oppenheimer will verify. We urge you publicly withdraw support from this undertaking which does no honor to Einstein's great name.

Russell replied on March 10:

I have received a telegram from you about a message of congratulation to Einstein which I gave to the Emergency Civil Liberties Committee. I do not see any reason why I should withdraw the message that I sent since it only expressed admiration for Einstein, which I would express to the devil himself if asked to do so. I cannot, at this distance, verify the accusations and counter-accusations which come to me across the Atlantic. Everybody knows that I am at least as hostile to communism as Senator McCarthy, and I should be very sorry to think that admiration for Einstein is now considered in America the mark of a fellow-traveller. I am not prepared to withdraw the congratulatory message unless I receive a personal request from Einstein to that effect.
P.S. It is impossible to cable collect from England to America.

Clark Foreman of the Emergency Civil Liberties Committee wrote Russell on March 17 to thank him for his contribution and commented on the role of the American Committee for Cultural Freedom:

I wonder if you know that despite your letter to Mrs. Faulkner of 16 May 1953, saying that you had resigned from the Committee for Cultural Freedom, they continue to carry your name on their letterhead as an honorary chairman of their international committee? The enclosed cutting from the *New York Times* on our conference will show you exactly the role of that Committee. They are so intent upon pointing out the beam in Russia's eye that they appear unwilling to admit the possibility of a mote in America's. Moreover, they strive to destroy any other organization which disagrees with them. The source of their funds is a mystery but there appears very good reason to believe that a part of them come from the State Department.

The Emergency Civil Liberties Committee is and has always been for civil liberties for everyone. We would like to see the whole world enjoy the benefits promised by our Bill of Rights, but we feel that there would be more chance of the rest of the world accepting that idea if they saw it working successfully in this country.

Russell's regard for Albert Einstein was not confined to the scientist's stand on issues of academic freedom and civil liberties in America. Einstein, like Russell, was profoundly interested and involved in world affairs and his viewpoint on major international problems often coincided with Russell's. Russell, when writing about his accord with Einstein, remarked: "He and I both opposed the First World War but considered the Second unavoidable. He and I were equally perturbed by the awful prospect of H-bomb warfare."[9] It was this mutual concern about the dangers of thermo-nuclear war that led Russell to write to Einstein on 11 February 1955:

In common with every other thinking person, I am profoundly disquieted by the armaments race in nuclear weapons. You have on various occasions given expression to feelings and opinions with which I am in close agreement. I think that eminent men of science ought to do something dramatic to bring home to the public and Governments the disasters that may occur. Do you think it would be possible to get, say six men of the very highest scientific repute, headed by yourself, to make a very solemn statement about the imperative necessity of avoiding war? These men should be so diverse in their politics that any statement signed by all of them would be obviously free from pro-Communist or anti-Communist bias. I have had a letter from Joliot-Curie which I found encouraging since the fact that he is a Communist and I am not did not prevent agreement on this matter. I expressed my own feelings in a broadcast of which I enclose a reprint. This has evoked a surprisingly favourable response in this country, but in other countries, other voices are needed. I do not know personally of any of the American atomic scientists, but I read their Bulletin monthly with interest and usually with agreement. I am sure that there are many of them who are anxious to find some way of preventing atomic disaster. Do you know of any way of securing effective action from any of these men?

There are certain points that seem to me important. First: it would be wholly futile to get an agreement prohibiting the H-bomb. Such an agreement would not be considered binding after war had broken out, and each side on the outbreak of war would set to work to manufacture as many bombs as possible. Second: it is important not to be side-tracked by the peaceful uses of atomic energy. These will become important when war ceases to be probable, but until then their importance is comparatively negligible. Three: in any attempt to avoid atomic war the strictest neutrality is to be observed. There must be no suggestion of seeking advantage for either side or of preferring either side. Everything must be said from the point of view of mankind, not of this or that group. For this reason, among others, if eminent scientists can be induced to make a pronouncement, it would be a good thing if some are known Communists and others known anti-Communists. Four: the thing to emphasize is that war may well mean the extinction of life on this planet. The Russian and American Governments do not think so. They should have no excuse for continued ignorance on the point. Five: although the H-bomb at the moment occupies the centre of attention, it does not exhaust the destructive possibilities of science, and it is probable that the dangers from bacteriological warfare may before long become just as great. This reinforces the general proposition that war and science can no longer co-exist.

Joliot-Curie apparently pins his faith to a large international conference of men of science. I do not think this is the best way to tackle the question. Such a conference would take a long time to organise. There would be difficulties about visas. When it met there would be discussions and disagreements which would prevent any clear and dramatic impression upon the public. I am convinced that a very small number of very eminent men can do much more, at any rate in the first instance.

My own belief is that there should be an appeal to neutral Powers. I should like to see one or more of the neutral Powers appointing small commissions of their own nationals to draw up a report as to the probable effects of war on neutrals as well as belligerents. I should like to see such a commission composed of say, six members: a nuclear physicist, a bacteriologist, a geneticist, an authority on air warfare, a man with experience of international relations derived from work in UNO, and a chairman who should be not a specialist but a man of wide culture. I should like their report to be published and presented to all the Governments of the world who should be invited to express their opinion on it. I should hope that in this way the impossibility of modern war might come to be generally acknowledged. Neutral nations are more likely to consider such a scheme favourably if they know that there is important support for it in countries which are not neutral. I should be very glad to know your opinion on these various matters.[10]

Russell had been tremendously encouraged by the very wide and sympathetic reception given to his "Man's Peril from the Hydrogen Bomb" which had been broadcast over the BBC on 23 December 1954, and he was not over optimistic in thinking that his views would find sympathetic echoes among men of science.[11] Einstein's response was immediate and enthusiastic and by April 1955 Russell had prepared a statement on the basis of which he succeeded, with Einstein's encouragement, in obtaining the signatures of an international group of eminent scientists including three Americans, Percy W. Bridgeman, Hermann J. Muller and Linus Pauling. The statement, warning of the dangers of nuclear war, concluded with a resolution to which scientists and the general public throughout the world were invited to subscribe:

In view of the fact that in any future world war nuclear weapons will certainly be employed, and that such weapons threaten the continued existence of mankind, we urge the Governments of the world to realize, and to acknowledge publicly, that their purposes cannot be furthered by a world war, and we urge them consequently, to find peaceful means for the settlement of all matters of dispute between them.[12]

Einstein, who had appended his signature to the statement on April 11, died just one week later and Russell, in an article entitled "The Greatness of Albert Einstein" published by the New Leader on May 30, paid tribute to Einstein's scientific work and his role in working for world peace in which activities "he has been completely self-effacing and only anxious to find ways of saving the human race from the misfortunes brought about by its own follies." Russell recalled Einstein's work on behalf of academic freedom in America:

After Congressional committees in America began their inquisitorial investigations into supposed subversive activities, Einstein wrote a well publicized letter urging that all men in academic posts should refuse to testify before these committees or before the almost equally tyrannical boards set up by some universities. His argument for this advice was that, under the Fifth Amendment, no man is obliged to answer if the answer will incriminate him, but that the purpose of this Amendment had been defeated by the inquisitors, since they held that refusal to answer may be taken as evidence of guilt. If Einstein's policy had been followed even in cases where it was absurd to presume guilt, academic freedom would have greatly profited. But, in the general *sauve qui peut*, none of the "innocent" listened to him.

On June 2, Corliss Lamont, an American radical, wrote to Russell and recalled how in 1924 Russell had come to his rescue when "as a student at Harvard I was trying to get the authorities to permit radical speakers to address the students."[13] Lamont congratulated Russell on the Einstein article but pointed out what he regarded as "a factual error in it." Lamont, who had himself "refused to answer the questions put by Senator McCarthy's committee" and was "under indictment for contempt of Congress" enclosed a copy of his letter to the *New Leader* of the same day:

...Russell calls attention to Einstein's suggestion that teachers should refuse to testify before Congressional committees conducting inquisitorial investigations and then says: "If Einstein's policy had been followed even in cases where it was absurd to presume guilt, academic freedom would have greatly profited. But in the general *sauve qui peut*, none of the "innocent" listened to him." Actually a number of teachers have followed Einstein's advice and declined on the grounds of the First Amendment, to answer improper questions put by Congressional committees. Those teachers included Dr. Lloyd Barenblatt, who taught at Vassar College; Dr. Horace Chandler Davis, who taught at the University of Michigan; Professor Wendell Furry of Harvard; Mr. Leon J. Kamin, formerly of Harvard; Mrs. Goldie E. Watson who taught in a Philadelphia public school; and myself. All of these persons have been cited and indicted for contempt of Congress, and will probably come to trial in the near future.

Russell replied on June 21:

Thank you for your letter of June 2. I think that in the passage about Einstein which you consider inaccurate you did not realize the meaning that I attached to the word "innocent" in quotes. I meant the quotes to indicate an ironical meaning—i.e. a complete lack of sympathy with liberal ideas. However, I am to blame for not having made this clear.

Russell had in the meantime been completing extensive preparations for the official release of the Scientists' Manifesto. The manifesto which became known as the Russell-Einstein declaration was presented to a special conference convened for the purpose in London on July 9. The full text of the statement was published in the *New York Times* on the following day. Messages of congratulation and support poured in from all over the world. Barrows Dunham who was still fighting against his indictment for contempt of Congress wrote on July 19:

> Do let me express to you my warm appreciation of the message which you and your eminent colleagues lately gave to the world. The lucidity of its statement and the cogency of its argument are alike irresistible. It is a good thing for us all to be thrown back at last upon the ultimate ground of our humanity. Any narrower view does indeed seem distorted and perhaps even corrupt. I am sure that most Americans agree with you on the question, whatever cautiousness they might want to use in expressing themselves.

Dunham wrote to Russell again on October 30:

> I thought you might like to know that, on October 19, in the Federal District Court of Washington, D.C., I was acquitted of the charge of contempt of Congress. It was quite a victory for civil liberties (and in particular for the Fifth Amendment). I need not tell you what it feels like to be a free man again. I would have thought my course of action worth while even if the decision had been different. To have it crowned with victory is wonderful indeed! Let me say that, during these months, I have felt much sustained and strengthened by the support you so generously gave me in my affairs with Temple University. I am very grateful. Mrs. Dunham joins me in cordial greetings.

Footnotes

1. Published 21 June 1953.
2. B. Russell, *Autobiography* Vol. 3, (London, 1969) pp. 58-9; (New York, 1969) p. 68.
3. *The Impact of Science on Society* (London, 1952) (New York, 1953).
4. *Satan in the Suburbs* (Bodley Head, London, 1953) (New York, 1953).
5. B. Russell, *Autobiography* Vol. 3, pp. 58-9; p. 68.
6. See *Bertrand Russell's America* Vol. 1, Chapter 13.
7. 16 October 1954.
8. Clark Foreman to Russell, 16 February 1954.
9. From the Preface to *Einstein on Peace* edited by Otto Nathan and Heinz Norden (Simon and Schuster, New York, 1960).
10. *Ibid.*, pp. 624.
11. *The Listener*, 30 December 1954.
12. The *New York Times*, 10 July 1955.
13. See *Bertrand Russell's America* Vol. I, pp. 96-8.

7 A Question of American Justice

The year 1955 had been a particularly busy one for Russell. While his main activities had centered upon preparations of the Scientists' Manifesto and the subsequent implementation of its proposals, he was also heavily involved with various personal matters including moving from Richmond to North Wales. He spoke at several important conferences which flowed from the Scientists' Manifesto. At one series of meetings, held in London, a delegation of three Soviet scientists made the first formal appearance of a Soviet delegation in the West since the war. Their participation and eventual agreement with the resolutions of the conference made Russell hopeful about the prospects for cooperation between East and West and for a major congress of Eastern and Western scientists which was planned for 1957. The need for such a meeting had become, in Russell's view, all the more urgent following on the lack of progress at the first round of disarmament talks between the great powers in Geneva. Russell and the consignatories to the Scientists' Manifesto had attempted to influence the proceedings of the Geneva meetings by putting their views before the heads of state concerned. Dulles, the American Secretary of State had hinted at the probably negative outcome of the talks in a reply to Russell of 10 November 1955.

...I am certain that all of the Western Delegations here are making every effort to turn the good words of the Head of State Conference into good deeds. I confess, however, that after Mr. Molotov's speech of November 8, I doubt whether the Soviets are equally sincere in their purpose.

Because Russell believed that cooperation between East and West on the question of nuclear disarmament would be seriously compromised by

71

the attacks on civil liberties in America, he continued to speak out against McCarthyism. When Mrs. Rose Sobell, the mother of Morton Sobell who had been convicted along with the Rosenbergs in 1951, visited Russell to secure his support on behalf of a campaign to release her son, who was sentenced to life imprisonment, Russell decided to add his voice to the campaign. He was later to write that "at the time of the Rosenberg's trial and death (one is tempted to say assassination)...I had paid, I am ashamed to say, only cursory attention to what was going on."[1] Russell was to discover that "eminent people in America had already taken up cudgels on his (Sobell's) behalf, but to no avail" and that "people both here and in the United States appeared to be ignorant of his plight and what had led up to it."[2] His study of the facts convinced him that the case was "monstrous" and he agreed to do all he could "to call people's attention to it."[3] Russell's first action was to write to the *Manchester Guardian* and his letter was published on 26 March 1956 under the heading "The Sobell Case":

I am writing to enlist your support in the case of Morton Sobell, an innocent man condemned as a result of political hysteria to thirty years in gaol and at present incarcerated in Alcatraz, the worst prison in the United States. He was sentenced as an accomplice of the Rosenbergs in espionage. I am ashamed to say that at the time of the Rosenbergs' trial I did not look into the evidence. I have now done so. I am almost certain that the Rosenbergs were innocent and quite certain that the evidence against them would not have been considered adequate if prejudice had not been involved. But the Rosenbergs are dead and nothing can be done for them now except to hold up their official murderers to obloquy. Sobell, however, is alive and it is not too late for the United States Government to make some reparation to him.

The facts in his case are briefly, as follows: He had a friend named Elitcher, who had been his best man. Elitcher had stated on oath that he had never been a Communist. The FBI discovered that in making this statement he had committed perjury. They let him know that he could escape punishment if he would denounce other people as accomplices in treasonable activities. He decided to save his own skin by denouncing his best friend, Sobell. While negotiations in this sense were going on between him and the FBI, Sobell and his wife and their two small children went to Mexico. Sobell toyed with the idea of not returning to the United States, but rejected it. His decision to return became known to the FBI which had determined to present him as a fugitive from justice. In order to be still able to present him in this light, they hired thugs who beat him into unconsciousness, hustled him and his wife and two children into fast cars, and drove them without stopping from Mexico City to the United States frontier. There they were handed over to an immigration officer, who falsely stamped their card of entry with the words "Deported from Mexico" although the Mexican Government had not been privy to the kidnapping and had expressed no intention of deporting them.

When Sobell was brought to trial these facts were not mentioned as his counsel considered that any criticism of the FBI however justified, would only increase the severity of his sentence, his condemnation being regarded by his counsel as certain in spite of lack of evidence. The judge instructed the jury that they could not find Sobell guilty unless they believed Elitcher. Elitcher, because he was useful in this trial, has never been indicted for his acknowledged perjury and, in spite of his being known to be a perjuror, every word that he said against Sobell was believed.

People express their scepticism when it is said that most Germans did not know of Nazi atrocities, but I am sure that the immense majority of Americans are quite ignorant of the atrocities committed by the FBI. They do not know of the standard technique of these defenders of what, with cynical effrontery, they still call "The Free World." The technique is one with which we have been made familiar in other police States such as Nazi Germany and Stalin's Russia. The police find a man whom they can prove to be guilty of some offence and they promise him immunity if he will manufacture evidence against people who could not otherwise be indicted. Perjury is especially useful as a lever because many people who have been Communist in their student days rashly hope that this can be concealed and swear that they were never Communists. After a sufficient number of secret interviews the FBI descends upon innocent people with a posse of terrified perjurors and in the general hysteria every word uttered by the perjurors is accepted as gospel truth.

I do not suppose for one moment that President Eisenhower is aware of this well-established technique. If he knew of it, he would not only feel the revulsion which all decent people must feel, but would realize that every such case which becomes known outside the United States turns hundreds of thousands of people, if not into Communists, at least towards neutralism and away from the policy of NATO. For this large reason of public policy, as well as from motives of humanity and justice, it is to be hoped that something will be done to curb the FBI. A beginning might be made by the release of Morton Sobell or, at least, by ordering a new trial of his case.

The reaction to Russell's letter was fierce and instantaneous. He has recalled how he was "inundated by angry letters from Americans and others denying my charges and asking irrately how I could be so bold as to call American justice into question."[4] There were a few letters of support mainly from London members of the campaign to free Sobell but as Russell pointed out, "no one in England, so far as I know, upheld my point of view publicly."[5] Some of the critical letters appeared in the *Manchester Guardian* of March 31. Wade N. Mack, an American member of St. Catherine's Society at Oxford University wrote:

The trial of the Rosenbergs was followed closely by everyone in the United States. When the trial was concluded and the verdict delivered, there was not one faction or group or section of the public, with the exception of the Communist Party, that did not believe that justice had been done.

Before we look at the "facts" of the Sobell case or discuss the "American Police State" let me mention the mission and the limitation of the Federal Bureau of Investigation. Briefly, it was formed to aid the Federal Government and the separate state, municipal and county law enforcement agencies (when they asked for help) in bringing to justice those criminals whose activities were interstate by nature. Further, it made available scientific aids to criminology which local agencies could not afford. In 1940 its field included the activities of those organizations which sought to destroy the United States from within, under the same scope and limitations.

Let me point out the specific limitations on members of the FBI.
1) They have no power of arrest whatever.
2) Their activities are restricted to the continental limits of the United States.
3) They do not prosecute for the State nor hold any special position in a trial. They are called to testify as any citizen.
4) They have no rights of search.
5) They may not initiate an investigation on their own.

They are not a police agency, but an investigating agency. I have never known a "thug" to work for them in any capacity. The agents must be, for the most part, university and law-school graduates. I have never known or heard of the FBI "beating up" anybody. But the facts of the recent letter not only implicate the FBI but also the United States Bureau of Immigration, the Mexican Government, and the Federal Court System, who were in a vast conspiracy to thwart justice.

Professor Bradford Perkins of the History Department at the University of California at Los Angeles wrote:

Firstly, as to the Sobell-Rosenberg case itself. I frankly admit that I have not read the entire record, as Lord Russell says he has. But I have followed the case closely and discussed it with lawyers of various political persuasions. None would agree that "official murder" had been committed, nor can it be claimed that Sobell was convicted on the evidence of Elitcher alone. That the sentences given in this case were harsh, not that the verdicts were wrong, is the utmost that I think informed non-Communist liberals in America would admit.

Secondly, as to the role of the FBI Lord Russell flits easily from unsubstantiated charges in this instance to a blanket indictment of the "well-established technique" very similar to "Nazi atrocities." I question the accuracy of the first and absolutely deny the phantasmagoria of the second. The FBI has been justly criticized on occasion, like all security services, but to compare it with the agents of "other Police states" is simply fantastic, and a charge which furthermore, by implication, asserts that the Supreme Court and the Presidents and officials of both Democratic and Republican Administrations have been false to their oaths to uphold the Constitution. This charge I flatly reject, even when Lord Russell palliates President Eisenhower's guilt by making it guilt by ignorance.

Lastly, as to the effect of the letter which you published. I cannot imagine that Lord Russell seriously believes that such a shrill and distorted protest can serve any useful purpose as far as Sobell is concerned. His letter can only please those who welcome Anglo-American discord.

Robert H. Rose from Whitchurch, Buckinghamshire wrote:

I count among my friends a substantial number of young men who are or have been agents for the Federal Bureau of Investigation and I can only say after fifteen years of intimate experience, that Lord Russell's allegations are not only without foundation but bordering on the hysterical.

It is curious that a man of his accomplishment can produce a letter full of unsupportable claims and opinions and then go on to demand action—his sort of action—from readers who have nothing more to go on than his reputation and the power of his hortatory histrionics. I suggest that he re-examine the facts, review his paucity of knowledge of the case, reconsider his emotional fervour, restrain his crusading zeal, and rewrite his letter.

The New York Times published a summary of Russell's letter in its issue of March 27 under the heading "Bertrand Russell Accuses the FBI of Atrocities, Doubts Rosenberg's Guilt." Corliss Lamont, who had earlier corresponded with Russell about his tribute to Einstein, wrote on March 29 citing his own experience of the FBI:

I was much interested in *The New York Times* story of March 27, giving a summary of your views of the Federal Bureau of Investigation. From my own experience I can assure you that you have not exaggerated the situation.

Ever since I said under oath before the McCarthy Committee in 1953 that I had never been a member of the Communist Party, the FBI has made strenuous efforts to obtain perjury evidence against me by sending around agents to question my friends. They kept one friend on the rack until three o'clock in the morning, trying to get him to say that I was a member of the Party.

FBI agents also came around to my apartment house and interviewed the Negro elevator man about me. They asked him, for example, whether he had ever heard me or my wife say anything against the U.S. Government. They also questioned the superintendent and a good friend who lives on the first floor. You can imagine the atmosphere of fear that such visitations create. Actually in my opinion FBI questionings of this sort are just as much designed to stir up fear as to elicit information.

Liberals and radicals throughout the USA are fearful that the FBI is tapping their phone, has installed a secret microphone in their living room or car, opens their mail or goes over the contents of their wastepaper basket. Because I have an independent income, I am not bothered by such possibilities as much as many other people. Even so, I am careful about using my own phone on confidential matters, as, for example, a call to my bankers, J.P. Morgan & Company, about my financial affairs. Some of my secretary's friends have requested her never to call them from my phone lest the FBI be listening in and then come after them as subversives.

Under separate cover I have taken the liberty of sending you a copy of my new book on civil liberties, *Freedom is as Freedom Does*. There is a good deal about the FBI in Chapter 7, "Police State in the Making."

Incidentally, I teach philosophy at Columbia University and as a Naturalist or Humanist find myself close to your own philosophical position in important respects.

Russell quoted a portion of Lamont's letter when he replied to his various critics in a letter published by the *Manchester Guardian* on April 5:

The letter from Professor Perkins which appeared in your issue of

March 31 demands an answer. It is possible to read through the whole of the official report of the judicial proceedings in the Sobell case without learning many of the most important facts. Some, however, can be learnt from the official report. Professor Perkins objects to my saying that Sobell was condemned on the evidence of Elitcher alone. As to this, Judge Irving Kaufman in his charge to the jury said: "If you do not believe the testimony of Max Elitcher as it pertains to Sobell, then you must acquit the defendant Sobell." Elitcher's motives for giving false testimony do not, of course, appear in the official report. But the interesting fact does appear there that the chief agent in the prosecution was McCarthy's now discredited henchman Cohn...

Mr. Wade N. Mack points out the limitations to the legal powers of the FBI. Has he never heard the ancient quip *Quis custodiet custodes*? He goes on to say that he has never known a thug to work for the FBI and has never known of the FBI beating up anybody. This, I do not deny: but I think he might remember Dr. Johnson's remark, "Sir, what you don't know would fill a very large book." Mr. Mack is mistaken in saying that I implicate the Mexican Government. On the contrary, it was not a party to the action against Sobell.

Mr. Corliss Lamont, of the well-known American banking family writes to me:

"I was much interested in the *New York Times* story of March 27, giving a summary of your views on the Federal Bureau of Investigation. From my own personal experience I can assure you that you have not exaggerated the situation...Liberals and Radicals throughout the USA are fearful that the FBI is tapping their phone, has installed a secret microphone in their living-room or car, opens their mail, or goes over the contents of their wastepaper basket."

Mr. Robert H. Rose seems to object to my quoting facts which have never reached the public and to accuse me of some secret source of knowledge. My sources of knowledge were all in published material. There is a very full account both of the Rosenberg case and of the Sobell case in a large book called *The Judgement of Julius and Ethel Rosenberg* by John Wexley, published by Cameron and Kahn, New York. Mr. Elmer Davis, the radio commentator, said after reading this: "Assuming that the record is here correctly cited (and I have no reason to suppose that it is not) I cannot believe the testimony of Elitcher and the Greenglasses, or much if any of that of Harry Gold." There is a brief summary in a leaflet called "The Facts in the Case of Morton Sobell" published by "The National Committee to Secure Justice for Morton Sobell." There is an informative pamphlet published by the same committee called "Atomic Scientist Harold Urey Asks Justice for Morton Sobell."

Dr. Harold Urey, who is a Nobel Prize man of by no means Left Wing opinion, said: "The integrity of justice as it is administered in the United States is at stake....Mr. Sobell was not properly tried and the verdict and sentence were not justified. Judge Patrick H. O'Brien, Detroit, Michigan, said: "In accordance with our inheritance as a liberty-loving nation I urge the immediate release of Morton Sobell." Perhaps when Mr. Rose has studied these documents he will admit that my letter was not full of unsupported claims.

In conclusion, I cannot do better than offer him the advice which he so kindly offers to me: "that he re-examine the facts, review his paucity of knowledge of the case, re-evaluate his emotional fervour, restrain his crusading zeal and rewrite his letter."

The New York Times summary of Russell's first letter of March 27 had provoked a strong reaction from the American Committee for Cultural Freedom. Their chairman, James T. Farrell wrote Russell on April 5 expressing his committee's "astonishment and profound dismay" at Russell's views on the Rosenberg case and on Morton Sobell. The letter, a copy of which was published in the *Manchester Guardian* of April 7 and also in the *NYT* and in several other papers, continued:

While we do not question your right to reach even what we consider a totally mistaken conclusion on the guilt of Morton Sobell and Ethel and Julius Rosenberg, we do most gravely question the propriety of any friend of cultural freedom, and in particular an officer of the Congress for Cultural Freedom, an organization of which we are an affiliate, in making false and irresponsible statements about the process of justice in the United States quoted from or attributed to you in this report.

There is no evidence whatever that the Federal Bureau of Investigation committed atrocities or employed thugs in the Rosenberg case. There is no support whatever for your charge that Sobell, an innocent man, was the victim of political hysteria. There is no ground whatever for your contention that either Sobell or the Rosenbergs were condemned on the word of perjurors, terrified or unterrified. May we bring to your attention at least one fact with which we believe you should have acquainted yourself before issuing this detailed indictment of the state of civil rights in the United States—that the American Civil Liberties Union, an organization (familiar to you for its valiant defense of your cause while you were in the United States) as firm in its defense of the civil rights of Communists as of democrats, made a thorough investigation of the apprehension and trial of Sobell and the Rosenbergs and publicized its conclusion that there had been no infringement of democratic freedom in their cases. (A copy of their statement is being sent to you under separate cover.)

On the basis of the long record of your probity and devotion to political truth, it is indeed shocking for us to have to recognize this extraordinary lapse from standards of objectivity and justice. Your remarks on American judicial procedure, the analogy you draw between the technique of the Federal Bureau of Investigation and the police methods of Nazi Germany or Stalin's Russia, constitute a major disservice to the cause of freedom and democracy in our troubled world, and a major service to the enemies we had supposed you engaged to combat.

Russell then wrote on April 10 to Stephen Spender, the poet, who was an executive member of the International Congress for Cultural Freedom, tendering his resignation from that body:

As you may be aware, the American Committee for Cultural Freedom is indignant with me for taking up the Rosenberg-Sobell case. As it is affiliated to the Congress for Cultural Freedom, I feel obliged to sever my connection with the latter. Some years ago I decided to resign because the American Committee appeared to me to be merely anti-Communist, but on that occasion I was over-persuaded. On this occasion, as I am the subject of criticism, there can be no question of my remaining connected with your body.

Spender replied to Russell on April 12:

Naturally, I feel very distressed at your decision. I have been away for nearly three weeks, and so I missed the correspondence in the *Manchester Guardian*. However, I did see the quotation from the letter of the American Committee to you, which was printed in *The Times*. When I read this, it struck me that, whatever the circumstances, they should not have written to the effect that your intervention in the Rosenberg-Sobell case was a blow directed against cultural freedom. For even supposing that you were wrong, nevertheless you are perfectly free to be mistaken, and I do not see what motive you could have for intervening except your love of freedom.

On the other hand, supposing they feel that they have mastered this case and are convinced the Rosenbergs were guilty, then I can understand their having a feeling of injury; though the injury would be to them in their endeavours, not to any "cause of freedom." They might of course feel slighted by the implication that members of the American Civil Liberties Union and many liberals and teachers in

America who had studied the testimony and believed the Rosenbergs to be guilty were being branded as indifferent to the truth.

Personally, I would be grateful if you would give some indication of the sources from which you derived your conclusions. I shall then study these, though as I do not have a legal mind nor a perfect confidence in my judgement about very complicated processes, I doubt whether I shall be able to attain the state of absolute certainty of any of the parties in this dispute.

In a further note on the same day from the offices of the magazine *Encounter*, which he edited, Spender informed Russell that his fellow members on the executive board of the Congress for Cultural Freedom "all appear to agree in deploring the letter of the American Committee to you." He also informed Russell that the executive board was to convene a special meeting in Paris on April 24 to "discuss this and our relations with the American Committee."

It was clear that Russell's membership and name were a great asset to the Congress for Cultural Freedom and they made every effort to dissuade him from his decision to resign. The Secretary General of the organization, Nicholas Nabakov, wrote to Russell on April 13 confirming the special meeting of the executive board and suggesting by way of conciliation that "all this has occurred not out of any basic divergence between you and ourselves over policy." He laid the blame squarely on the shoulders of the American Committee whose letter he said was sent to Russell, "without any prior consultation with the International Secretariat."

Russell replied to Spender on April 14 welcoming the attitude of the Executive Committee and referring Spender to the sources upon which his views on the Rosenberg-Sobell case were based, including *Was Justice Done? The Rosenberg Sobell Case* by Malcolm Sharp, which Russell was reviewing for the *University of Chicago Law Review*.[6] In his reply to Nabakov of April 17, Russell indicated that under certain circumstances he was prepared to reconsider his decision. Spender replied on April 19 re-affirming his personal criticism of the American Committee. He also commented on the bibliography of the case to which Russell had referred him:

I suppose I must read not only the testimony but also that of the higher courts—and as I say, I have no confidence in my power to form a judgement.

After the meeting of the Executive Committee in Paris, Spender wrote to Russell on April 30 informing him that they had written to the American Committee criticizing their action but for procedural reasons the letter

"Mankind is divided into two classes; those who object to infringements to civil liberties in Russia, but not in the U.S.; and those who object to them in the U.S., but not in Russia. There seems to be hardly anybody who objects to infringements of civil liberties (period)."

concerned would only be shown to Russell after the American Committee had had an opportunity of responding. Russell saw the letter towards the end of May when Nabakov visited him in Wales and he laid down to Nabakov certain conditions for withdrawing his intended resignation. Russell expected a public apology from the American Committee failing which it would be necessary for the Congress of Cultural Freedom to publicly disassociate itself from the action of the American Committee. Russell also wanted assurance that his name be removed from the letterhead of the American Committee.

On June 20, Nabakov wrote to Russell to inform him that "the American Committee is not disposed toward making a public apology." He acknowledged that the alternative course of action proposed by Russell seemed the only solution but that it was not for him to decide upon and would "have to be taken up by our Executive Board at its next meeting." He also informed Russell that he had "taken the necessary steps to see that your name is removed from the letterhead of the American Committee."

In the meantime the American Committee was taking steps of its own which they hoped in an indirect way might serve to justify their attack on Russell. Sidney Hook, the philosopher and author wrote to Russell under the letterhead of the philosophy department of New York University. Hook was a regular contributor to the columns of *The New Leader*. He was also a member of the board of directors of the American Committee. Hook's letter of June 5 referred to Russell quoting Lamont in his controversial letter to the *Manchester Guardian*.

One of the editors of the *New Leader* tells me that you have recently cited Corliss Lamont as an authority on the state of political freedom in the United States. Before accepting as true Lamont's report on anything which has political relevance, I believe you ought to know something about his political commitments. Although the enclosed article was written long ago, it is still substantially true.

The article which Hook enclosed dealt with Lamont's sympathy for the USSR during the period of Stalin's leadership. Russell replied to Hook on June 8:

81

Thank you for your letter and for the enclosed number of *The Modern Monthly*. I am not surprised by the facts about Corliss Lamont which you mention, though I profoundly disagree with the line which he took. As regards facts in America, I do not find him unreliable. Mankind is divided into two classes; those who object to infringements to civil liberties in Russia, but not in the U.S.; and those who object to them in the U.S., but not in Russia. There seems to be hardly anybody who objects to infringements of civil liberties (period). Corliss Lamont denied evils in Russia of which there was ample evidence; you deny evils in the U.S., of which there is equal evidence, except that they have not yet been publicly blazoned forth by Eisenhower. Have you, for example, examined with any care, the evidence that Sobell was kidnapped by the FBI and fraudulently represented as having been extradicted by the Mexican Government? Until you have looked into the evidence for such crimes, you have no right to criticize the American Communists for not looking into the evidence of Soviet crimes.

The fundamental fallacy which is committed by almost everyone is this: "A and B hate each other, therefore one is good and the other is bad." From the evidence of history, it seems much more likely that both are bad, but everybody vehemently rejects this hypothesis.

Critics of the American regime, one is told, can be ignored because they are all Communists or fellow-travellers. More shame to the Americans who are not. In like manner, one is told by the other side, that critics of Soviet Russia can be ignored because they are anti-Communist. Again I say, more shame to the Communists. I shall be expressing similar sentiments to Mr. Lamont.

Russell, who had been asked to write an introduction to the English edition of Lamont's new book, wrote to Lamont on June 8 inquiring about his views on the USSR:

The prospective English publishers of *Freedom is as Freedom Does* approached me with a request that I should do an introduction to the English edition of this book. I provisionally agreed, but there are some matters which I must discuss with you if I am to do it. You are very much more pro-Soviet than I am and you have, in the past, been pro-Stalin. This compels one to doubt whether you really care for civil liberties or only use it as a stick to beat anti-Communists with. I hope you will forgive me if I ask you some questions:
1) Do you accept Khrushchev's denunciation of Stalin?
2) Did you formerly admire Stalin or only think that, for the benefit of the Communist cause, it was necessary to profess admiration?

3) Were you ignorant of the misdeeds of the Stalinist regime which Khrushchev has denounced?

4) If you were, do you now acknowledge the better judgement of those—e.g. Dewey—who emphasized the facts which have recently been asserted by Khrushchev?

If I do the introduction that your publishers ask for, I shall have to make it clear that I consider the offences against civil liberties in Russia immeasurably worse than those in the U.S. There seem to be very few people who care for civil liberties both in the U.S. and in the USSR, and hardly any who make an impartial effort to ascertain facts. I think this profoundly regrettable and I think that progressives throughout the Western World have been led down blind alleys by sycophantic adulation or fanatical hatred of the Soviet Government.

Having said this, I must add that I find your book exceedingly interesting and the facts which it sets forth most worthy to be known. I should like also to add that I greatly respect and admire the stand you have taken against the abominations that have occurred in America, and that I shall be very sorry if you find my questions in any way offensive. But, if I am to write an introduction, I shall have to make it clear that I write as a friend of civil liberties and not as an advocate of oriental police tyranny. In view of all this, it seems to me that you may prefer to get someone else to do the introduction.

Lamont replied at length to Russell's questions on June 11.

I was delighted to have your letter of June 8 and to know that there is a good chance of your writing an introduction to an English edition of *Freedom Is as Freedom Does.* I am not at all offended by your questions and am glad to answer them as fully as possible. Actually, my pro-Soviet reputation has all along clouded the fact that I have always been critical of the lack of civil liberties in the USSR; and I think you will find that we are much closer on this question than you imagine.

To show you from the record exactly where I stand I am enclosing a two page excerpt from my 1952 book, *Soviet Civilization,* and my 1952 pamphlet, *Why I Am Not a Communist,* in which I have checked in red pencil the points which seem especially relevant.

You will note from the quotation on page 27 of *Soviet Civilization* that I agree with you that the offenses against civil liberties in Russia are far worse than those in the United States. Also on page 89 you will see I consider it an "obligation" for Western intellectuals who believe in democracy to criticize Soviet violations of democracy. The quotation from the same page mentions the sad case of Anna Louise Strong.

There is reason to believe that the strong protest that I and other American writers sent to the Soviet ambassador here about Miss Strong was a factor in the Soviet government finally clearing her.

I also agree with you about progressives in the Western World so often adopting either the extreme of uncritical adulation of Soviet Russia or fanatical hatred for it. The passage from page 25 of my book expresses my fundamental position that the USSR is neither a heaven nor a hell—although it has certainly been a hell for the innocent people liquidated by Stalin and his associates.

I believe that the Khrushchev denunciation of Stalin as printed in the *New York Times* of 5 June 1956 is probably on the whole authentic. And I accept Khrushchev's analysis as true in general, although perhaps not in every detail. I think we have to be somewhat guarded on this matter, because the present regime may be exaggerating some aspects of Stalin's character for its own political purposes.

While I was conscious of many mistakes and misdeeds committed by the Stalin regime, I certainly was not aware that he went so far as Khrushchev makes clear. But in my opinion Stalin's behavior as a ruthless and unscrupulous dictator does not negate the work he undoubtedly did in building up the economic and military strength of the Soviet Union, particularly through the Five-Year Plans. At the same time I still believe that Stalin believed and tried to promote on the whole a policy of international peace. I admired Stalin for these positive aspects of his rule and never because it was necessary to *profess* admiration for the benefit of the Communist cause. As a matter of fact, I have never considered myself to be working for the Communist cause, but rather for the much wider end of democratic socialism and according to peaceful methods such as are supported by the British Labor Party.

Finally, in reference to your fourth question, until the Khrushchev revelations I did not realize the terrible extent of civil liberties violations in the Soviet Union. John Dewey and other critics certainly were more realistic than I on this point, although they tended to go on to overall denunciations of the USSR.

Well, this is a long letter and I have perhaps enclosed too much reading material. But I did want to make a thorough answer to the questions you raised. I would be glad to send you my book *Soviet Civilization* by air mail if you desire to glance at it. However, the excerpts I have made will probably serve your purposes.

In *Freedom Is as Freedom Does* the opening sentence on page 5 is meant of course to cover the Soviet Union and every other country. However, in this volume I have steered clear of the un-ending controversy over Soviet affairs, because it is a study of American civil liberties and I did not wish to get mixed up in foreign issues that might distract the reader.

Oh, one more point is that this book plainly demonstrates that I regard civil liberties as applying to everyone from right to left and that I don't support civil liberties merely as a stick to beat anti-Communists with (see also Point 13 in my pamphlet about defending the rights of Trotskyites, Henry Ford and a fascist).

Let me assure you that, having read your letter carefully and having answered it carefully, there is nobody in England whom I would rather have write an introduction to my book than you.

Hook replied to Russell on June 18:

...You ask me whether I have looked into the evidence concerning the Rosenberg and Sobell cases. Until recently I knew only the evidence which appeared in the press at the time of their trials. I have now read the Wexley book on the Rosenbergs. It leaves me utterly unconvinced that they were innocent of the charges made against them. Wexley's book is full of fantastic suppositions for which no valid evidence is given. Its Communist bias is apparent on every page. This does not mean that I am convinced that it was the Mexican government that extradited Sobell. But neither am I convinced as yet that the FBI kidnapped Sobell from Mexico and find implausible Wexley's explanation of the consistent failure of Sobell to state this in court where he could be cross-examined about it. There is an obvious distinction between the truth of the charges that Sobell's asylum was breached by the FBI and the question of his guilt or innocence of the charge made against him. I am no special friend of the FBI. *If* they kidnapped Sobell from Mexico I would be in favor not of a new trial but of his release to Mexico at once since I believe in the right of criminal asylum as well as political asylum...

I expect to do some more reading in the Rosenberg-Sobell case since I am not so certain in this matter as you appear to be, perhaps because having argued with Communists for so many years I am less gullible about them than you are...

My reading shows me that all those who shouted charges about the United States using germ warfare in Korea (before examination, the evidence cooked up by the Communists for these charges was stronger than the evidence that the Rosenbergs and Sobell were framed!) are today shouting charges that the Rosenbergs and Sobell were victims of a conspiracy. I am not saying the converse is true.

The decision to make world propaganda out of the Rosenberg-Sobell case was a political decision in the Kremlin's campaign of political warfare against the United States. I am not saying that you should not make these charges if you believe them true. I am only trying, because of my esteem for you personally, to call your attention to the fact that the Communists build-up of you in their press is motivated neither by genuine regard for you nor by agreement with your ideals.

You are being used—and effectively used—as a weapon in the Communists' political war against the United States. This is apparent from the interview of Belfrage with you as reported in the Communist *National Guardian*...

The interview with Cedric Belfrage to which Hook referred in his letter was published in a May 1956 issue of the *National Guardian*. Belfrage had immigrated to the USA from England in 1936 and in 1953, as editor of the *National Guardian*, he was investigated by McCarthy, arrested, and after fighting the case for two years, spending much of that time in prison, deported to England in August 1955 where he continued to contribute to the columns of his paper, as editor in exile. The interview which touched on many of Russell's central concerns about America also dealt with his most recent view of the USSR:

From his quiet garden villa in the London suburb of Richmond, Bertrand Russell looks back on a life which has never been dull and still, in his 84th year, does not threaten to become so. Among the ruddy-faced snowy haired philosopher's souvenirs are going to jail for his peace activities in World War I, scandalizing the respectable with his free-wheeling co-educational school between wars, and succeeding to an earldom in 1931. He has traveled everywhere in search of truth, interested himself in everything, said just what he thought to everyone, publicly confessed his error whenever he found anything he said or didn't say to have been wrong. The world has come to recognize him as one who has generally been right.

Last March he started another tumult by expressing in the *Manchester Guardian* shame at not having looked into the Rosenberg case "at the time"; "almost certainty" that the Rosenbergs were innocent; and a plea with pungent reference to the background of FBI "atrocities"—for a new trial of the Rosenberg's alleged fellow-conspirator Morton Sobell who is in Alcatraz for 30 years. The indignant ensuing correspondence defending the Department of Injustice and the Federal Bureau of Inquisitions, topped off by a final and even deadlier volley from Russell, has now died down.

Last week I called on him to convey something of what his action has meant to progressive Americans. On the table beside the hospitable tea-tray in his study—which had an electric fire burning and the window wide open to the early summer scents from the garden—were copies of Lowenthal's book on the FBI ("I am just reading it") Reuben's *Atom Spy Hoax* ("I'm just going to read it") and Wexley's *Judgement of Julius and Ethel Rosenberg* which convinced him and inspired his letter. It was in this room last winter that he received Mrs. Rose Sobell, who persuaded him to read the facts and judge from them whether justice had been done to her son.

"I am going into all this," Russell said, lighting his pipe, "because I am an old-fashioned liberal—you might say in the 17th century sense, in that I have always had a great fear of the police and feel that they are the same danger now that kings were then. Lowenthal's book is very instructive. I have been reading about the rounding-up in New York streets in 1918 of men who were supposed to be draft evaders—almost none of them were, but there seems to have been hardly a bleat of protest.

"I recall the time when I was at the University of California at Los Angeles in 1937[7] and they quite suddenly found that one of the lecturers, a man of experience and standing who had defended migratory workers' right to organise, was incompetent. The others did not protest, and I have never seen anything equal the terror in the common room when Sproul, the head of the university marched in to lecture the staff. The university was completely controlled by the banker, Giannini—everyone did what this Italian fascist told them to. Then in 1940 when I was barred from an appointment at New York City College[8]—on the ground that I was "aphrodisiac" among other dreadful lapses, though obviously they didn't know what that meant—not one New Dealer except Mrs. Roosevelt supported me. I can't agree with you that in America there has ever been the same degree of personal liberty that we have here. It doesn't exist for the average man. At all times I have been rather astonished by their lack of protest against injustice.

"Now the way the FBI is behaving is quite extraordinary. Apparently they can find people to testify to absolutely anything. Yet when I meet Americans, if I say anything at all against the FBI it's as if I had talked against the Holy Ghost. How can you? This is holy! I am astounded by the letters I have been getting from Americans, abusing me and exalting the police, most of all the one from the Committee of Cultural Freedom of which I am a member. Is it for cultural freedom or isn't it? What has happened to my old friend Sidney Hook? On the other hand I've had many letters from Americans who say: 'I'm delighted you say these things, I wish I dared.' "

I asked Russell what he thought about the unilateral release of political prisoners and cutting of armed forces by the Russians and their allied countries. He said it was "very embarrassing to the Americans who don't want to do either." I asked: "Do you think the time may be at hand when the world will see America as the country with the only remaining iron curtain?"

"Indeed, it's very likely," he said. "You know, all of Western Europe is very much chilled, in the whole conception of alliance with America, by the fact that there has seemed to be less and less difference between America and Russia. We must stand in with America but we don't like it. I an very anxious for good relations, but all these injustices make it harder."

"How can relations with America be improved?"

"Well, we can't do it until there is greater liberalism in the American administration—that's the only thing that will do it. And so there has to be more frankness about what is going on there. Of course, every government commits misdeeds and feels it must conceal them. We certainly should not be self-righteous in view of our own failures in Cyprus and so on. Governments manage to keep their misdeeds fairly dark at home but abroad they can't. So if they can't keep them dark the only thing is to mend their ways.

"The same is true for us British who commit our sins a long way off, although we're not so bad at home. Of course we shall end by being turned out of Cyprus—what we're doing there is absolutely futile. The whole idea that it's important to have bases is out of date. They are only of use if there's to be a big war, but even then, if we want a big war to destroy practically everybody, we can do it all from Greenland which is not far from Moscow. But people agree there isn't going to be a big war: the chances are at least four to one against it, although the risk is still there."

What did he think about the events in the USSR since Stalin's death?

"I am convinced the Communists really do want to liberalise their regimes. Would I be mistaken in attributing this to the fact that they have really got good hydrogen bombs and so are no longer frightened? But it is quite genuine. They have let out thousands of political prisoners although for years they have been saying there weren't any. What has particularly impressed me is Hungary tearing down the barbed wire along the frontier—because it is an actual physical act. Also I am glad that the genes are now able to behave as they like, not just as Stalin told them.

I have always said that Stalin was the successor to Ivan the Terrible. I think his influence was completely bad. I was in Russia only once, in 1920, and wrote a little book about it.[9] I thought it was horrible—an absolute nightmare—and have had the same view since, although it is getting better now; not what I should like at all, but better. But in any case we've got to co-operate with them whether we like it or not."

I asked him if his views on Western policy toward Russia hadn't changed in recent years. This was his answer:

"The worst thing I ever said—and I am sorry I did—was soon after the last war at the time America produced the Baruch plan for atomic control. I said we must urge the Russians to come in and that, if they wouldn't we should threaten them; and I thought they would yield. I wanted to see atomic power internationalised and thought the Baruch plan a good one.

"I think I said that, and I'm sorry. The moment Russia had atomic power the situation was changed. I thought it was quite possible to persuade Russia to come into the Baruch plan. It wasn't that I wanted a war, or to reform the Russian regime—they have the right to whatever regime they like—but to preserve the peace of the world.

"Within the next five to ten years," said the philosopher with the unclosable mind and the habit of courage, "it is possible that hostility will grow enormously less. It is less already. It rests largely with America." I left him with his books on the American political police and the fruits of their work, promising to lend him my copy of that great contemporary classic, Harvey Matusow's *False Witness*.

Russell replied to Hook on June 26:

...As regards the Sobell kidnapping, you will observe that the Court took care not to deny the statements of Sobell's friends. I cannot think that the Court would have done this if it could have denied them. What the judge said, in effect, was that it did not matter whether Sobell was kidnapped or not. The Russians have been guilty repeatedly of kidnapping and we have all rightly been indignant, but the same offense when committed by the U.S. Government, is considered trivial.

You say "having argued with Communists for so many years I am less gullible about them than you are." I am amazed by your effrontery in making such a statement. You have no doubt forgotten that in 1920 I disagreed violently with almost all my political friends because I thought ill of the Soviet Government. When I first met you in 1924, I was anti-Soviet and you were pro. I have never wavered in my dislike of the Soviet system. You know that Westerners who criticise the Moscow subway system are met with the retort, "How about lynching in America?" Your reply to my criticisms of America is of the same sort.

You say, "your statements about America and the use the Communist world press is making about them are hurting, not helping American liberals fight for a freer America and a freer world." This is the obverse of the argument that you and your friends used against me in 1920 when my criticisms of Russia delighted the reactionaries.

I am glad to see that the Ford Foundation Report has brought out some of the facts about blacklisting, showing that people are sometimes put onto the list through perjury and sometimes taken off again through paying blackmail.

Sidney Hook replied on July 1 but as Russell did not wish to take their argument any further their correspondence terminated. In his final letter Hook had once again contradicted most of Russell's argument and repeated with considerable embellishment his accusations about Lamont's Communist sympathies. Lamont, who had been cited for contempt of Congress in August 1954 and indicted under that charge in October, had fought against this decision and in July 1955 the courts dismissed the indictment. The government went to the Court of Appeals to attempt to reinstate the charges against him but failed. On August 30 Lamont wrote to Russell that the decision of the Federal Appeals Court was "not only a substantial rebuff to Senator McCarthy but also ought to make congressional investigating committees in general operate more carefully."

Footnotes

1. B. Russell, *Autobiography* Vol. 3, (London, 1969) p. 81 (New York, 1969) p. 103.
2. *Ibid.*
3. *Ibid.*
4. *Ibid.*
5. *Ibid.*, p. 81; p. 104.
6. See Russell's review of this book below, pp. 341-5.
7. See *Bertrand Russell's America* Vol. 1.
8. *Ibid.*
9. *The Practice and Theory of Bolshevism* (London, 1920) as *Bolshevism: Practice and Theory* (Harcourt, Brace, New York, 1920).

8 Civil Liberties & the FBI

At the end of October 1956 the British edition of Corliss Lamont's *Freedom is As Freedom Does* was published with a preface by Russell.[1] The London *Daily Express* of October 29 announced:

> Bertrand Russell is called a liar today by the Federal Bureau of Investigation. The 84 year old English philosopher has written a sizzling attack on the FBI in a preface to a book due out tomorrow. This book. a new edition of *Freedom is As Freedom Does* is by 54 year old Corliss Lamont, left wing New York lecturer, who has appeared several times before congressional committees.
>
> Russell accuses the FBI of employing "spies and *agents provocateurs*" and of creating "a terrorist system" in the U.S. Informers are safe, he says, "so long as they continue to do the dirty work. But woe betide them if they repent." The FBI's reply? Said a Washington spokesman: "The History of the FBI will be published in two weeks time. It is accurate and will stand in sharp contrast to what Russell said—a complete falsehood."

The book which had appeared six months earlier in the USA, but without the preface by Russell, now received renewed attention in America because of Russell's contribution. Lamont wrote to Russell on 9 January 1957 enclosing an open letter to Russell from Norman Thomas, the former leader of the American Socialist Party. "Mr. Thomas has hounded me for years," Lamont commented, "because of my sympathy towards the positive achievements of the Soviet Union." Norman Thomas was strongly anti-Communist; he was also a director of the American Committee for Cultural Freedom. The first part of Thomas's open letter published by *The New Leader* on January 7 inveighed against Lamont's Communist

91

sympathies and also against his book which Thomas believed prejudiced "individuals and organizations whose services to freedom have not, like his, been compromised by the application of a double standard." Thomas found it "odd that a philosopher so concerned as you [Russell] with mathematical accuracy and logic should have accepted without more inquiry all Mr. Lamont's statements." Thomas continued:

Yet not only do you lend the weight of your great reputation to endorsing Mr. Lamont's book, you go rather beyond it in statements which his book does not properly support. For example, you write: "Members of the FBI join even mildly liberal organizations as spies and report any unguarded word. Anybody who goes so far as to support equal rights for colored people, or to say a good word for the UN, is liable to be visited by officers of the FBI and threatened, if not with prosecution, at least with blacklisting and consequent inability to earn a living. When a sufficient state of terror has been produced by these means, the victim is informed that there is a way out; if he will denounce a sufficient number of his friends, he may obtain absolution."

Here your exaggeration is so great as to approach falsehood. There have indeed been outrageous offenses in America against individual liberty, notably in the Smith Act and its enforcement— which Communists enthusiastically applauded when Trotskyists and alleged pro-Nazis were the victims. Other grave offenses have been committed in loyalty and security proceedings. Even with the subsiding of McCarthyism, civil liberties still need defense and enlargement. The FBI has been an agent (but not of its own motion the chief sinner) in proceedings which deserve denunciation. However, it is simply untrue to allege that "anybody who goes so far as to support equal rights for colored people, or to say a good word for the UN" is liable to the treatment which you have reported. The FBI does not have spies widely distributed in "even mildly liberal organizations." I speak what I know from wide and long experience. Insofar as vicious economic and social pressure on individuals is concerned, that is less widespread than you imply and is generally the work of unofficial groups (like the Communists themselves in the days of their comparative influence in the labor unions and elsewhere) rather than of the FBI. Your criticism of the official board of the Girl Scouts in letting their *Handbook* be edited by McCarthyists is just, but does not take account of the fact that, even so, the edited *Handbook* contains accurate and favorable information about the UN, respect for which is increasing in America...

I write less in defense of my country than of the truth. I am deeply anti-Communist—as, I think, are you—but that has not prevented me from fighting our Smith Act and spending time and money in defense of certain of its Communist victims. I do not boast when I say that I have better earned my right to correct the record than you to advance your sweeping charges.

Russell's reply to Thomas was published in the February 18 issue of *The New Leader* under the title "The State of U.S. Civil Liberties":

You object to my writing a preface for a book by Mr. Corliss Lamont because of his record as a fellow traveler. Before undertaking to do the preface, I had some correspondence with him, and explained that in the preface I would feel bound to state that I consider the infringements of liberty in Russia very much worse than those in the United States. (This I did.) You may, nevertheless, think that I ought not to have given seeming support to the point of view of a fellow traveler. I was led to do so by the extreme paucity of strong protests by non-Communists against American malpractices. There have been a few such protests, highly honorable to those who have made them. I should mention especially, what has been said by Dr. Harold Urey, the eminent atomic scientist, and Professor Malcolm Sharp, professor of law at the University of Chicago, on the Rosenberg-Sobell case. When I have agreed with Corliss Lamont, it is because what he says is confirmed by independent evidence and would easily be refuted if false....

You say that I go beyond Mr. Lamont's book "in statements which his book does not properly support." You seem particularly surprised at the suggestion that people are exposed to suspicion if they support equal rights for colored people. I should have thought you would have known what is in fact notorious, that, in the South especially, any championship of the rights of colored people, is regarded as evidence of communism, and renders the champion liable to the hardships to which suspected Communists are exposed. I am convinced that what I said on this subject is not exaggerated. Mr. Lamont quotes the chairman of a government loyalty board as saying: "Of course, the fact that a person believes in racial equality doesn't *prove* that he's a Communist, but it certainly makes you look twice doesn't it? You can't get away from the fact that racial equality is part of the Communist line." (See also the Chapter "Mississippi Comes North" in Cedric Belfrage's *The Frightened Giant*.)

I have perhaps said more than Lamont said about the way in which a general state of terror has been produced. I will cite in illustration a case mentioned in the London *Observer* of 18 July 1954. This is the case of a man who was an American University professor, not a Communist or a fellow traveler, but a friend of another professor whose views were more or less those of the British Labor Party but definitely not Communist. This friend was charged with heretical ideas and the hitherto non-political professor came to his support. "The results of my activity" he states "were (1) loss of employment and all that this means; (2) inability to find any work in any other American educational institution; (3) sale of my house and a fine library at a loss, as I could no longer live in a community where I could not find employment and where my children were being abused by their fellow-students because their father was a 'Red.' "

I do not think that you and those who think as you do have the vaguest idea of the general state of fear which exits in American universities among young college professors and instructors and among intelligent students. I have frequent and numerous contacts with men of this kind and it is pathetic to see their joy in breathing the air of free discussion without the dread that an unguarded remark will be reported by supposed friends to some authority with power to inflict ruin...All that I ask of you is that you should study the facts more carefully than you seem to have done, and that, while studying them, you should remember that the sins of others are a poor excuse for our own. Loyalty to the facts should always outweigh loyalty to party, and loyalty to facts entails, in those who make public pronouncements, willingness to ascertain the facts even when they are painful, and especially when care is taken to conceal them.

I also do not think that you have realized a very important matter: If opposition to real evils in the West is undertaken only by Communists, this gives Communists an immense propaganda advantage, and makes American talk about a "free world" appear nothing but hypocrisy.

I do not despair of convincing you that I am in the right where we disagree. You and I, throughout our long lives, have been devoted to not dissimilar causes, and it is much to be regretted if differences about this or that make our divergence seem greater than it is.

The *New Leader* published Thomas's attempted rebuttal of Russell's argument in the same issue of the magazine:

My complaint against the great philosopher's introduction to the Lamont book was that his exaggeration grossly weakened the force of our constructive criticism of our country's failure to live up to its own highest ideals. Now I must repeat that criticism with fresh emphasis, adding to it my fear that unwittingly he plays into the hands of the spiritual neutralists by going as far as he does in denouncing America as well as Russia...

1. Lord Russell damns the FBI by reference to Max Lowenthal's book, *The Federal Bureau of Investigation.* I read that book when it came out and found it in important points unconvincing. In any case, it did not support Lord Russell's fantastic statement (in his introduction) that "anybody who goes so far as to support equal rights for colored people, or to say a good word for the UN, is liable" to visitation and threat by the FBI.

The force of Mr. Lowenthal's book, I must inform Lord Russell, was weakened because he had a personal grievance against the FBI for showing up certain of his associates as men with provable Communist Party records (I am not charging Mr. Lowenthal with communism, but with undue confidence in certain Communists or fellow-travelers)...

2. A second bit of evidence which Lord Russell cites is Cedric Belfrage's book *The Frightened Giant.* I have not read that book, but I know a good deal about Mr. Belfrage and I have before me an excellent review of the book by Dwight MacDonald in the (London) *Sunday Times* of January 27. I agree with Mr. MacDonald that Mr. Belfrage should not have been deported by the United States. I also agree with Mr. MacDonald that aliens in America, as has been established in the Belfrage case and many others, have far better defense against summary deportation than in England where the Home Secretary's power appears to be absolute. There is no question at all about Mr. Belfrage's Communist connections. Sworn and uncontradicted testimony exists that he was a member of the Soviet espionage group headed by Jacob Golos and that he was a secret party member with a party alias. He did not contradict this testimony but pleaded the Fifth Amendment against self-incrimination...

3. Lord Russell's final evidence of the terror under which all decent Americans are supposed to live is a letter published in the London *Observer,* written by an unnamed professor who says that he was outrageously treated for coming to the support of another professor, also unnamed, whose views happened to be "more or less those of the British Labor Party." Over and over, I have admitted the existence of some such cases and denounced them. But I would remind Lord Russell that there are in America 2000 colleges with more than 200,000 professors, the overwhelming majority of whom remain undisturbed in their jobs even though many of them are self-proclaimed supporters of a very absolute type of freedom for Communist professors, regardless of what communism teaches or practices in the field of academic freedom.

It is because we still need the help of men of Bertrand Russell's stature in our struggle for civil liberty and civil rights that I appeal to him once more to refrain from the exaggeration which gives our opponents so much opportunity to scoff...

Finally, may I ask, if we Americans were so sunk in depravity as certain of Lord Russell's statements imply, would our small hope of salvation be worth the ink that he has spent upon it? Fortunately, the facts, bad as some of them are, tell a different story from the one Bertrand Russell has believed.

Russell, who was more concerned to influence Thomas's views than to have the final word in a public debate, replied privately on February 25:

There are a few words which I wish to say to you in reply to your rebuttal in the *New Leader*. In the first place, I am glad you realize that I am not anti-American. In the second place, I must admit that further investigation has led me to the conclusion that I was guilty of exaggeration as regards the FBI in relation to the colour question. I regret this and admit my error. On the other points, I see no reason to modify anything that I have said. You seem to imply that criticisms of the FBI can be ignored if they come from Communists or fellow-travellers. In particular, you point out that Mr. Lowenthal's book had a grievance against the FBI. It is, however, an almost invariable fact that protests against injustices originate with those who suffer from them. I first heard of the Dreyfus case in 1894, but as at that time all the people who complained were Jews, I thought them biased and ignored what they said—wrongly as events proved. With regard to the Sobell-Rosenberg case, my opinion is not based on Professor Sharp's book, though I am glad to find him in agreement with me. My opinion is based upon examination of the evidence. I am sure that in a case not involving political prejudice, the evidence against Sobell would not have been considered conclusive. I think the verdict against Sobell was due partly to bias on the part of the judge and jury and partly to undesirable practices on the part of the FBI. I do not see how any unbiased person can come to any other conclusion.

As to what you say about the "Unnamed professor" whom I quote from the *London Observer*, the fact that he finds it necessary to remain unnamed supports my case. You point out that there are 200,000 professors in America but, as far as my experience goes, those of them whose opinions are at all liberal find concealment necessary, except in a few liberal institutions.

Both in regard to Corliss Lamont and in regard to Lowenthal you make accusations of inaccuracy which are not supported by specific instances and I feel, perhaps mistakenly, that you too readily assume inaccuracy in books by authors whose political opinions you disagree with.

Russell's support for Sobell and his criticism both of the methods of the FBI and the processes of the legal system in the USA were undoubtedly the major factors underlying his sharp controversies with Sidney Hook and Norman Thomas. The fact, however, that both individuals were directors of the American Committee for Cultural Freedom which Russell had repudiated, thereby compromising that body's relationship with its parent organization, made Russell all the more determined to sever all connections with the American Committee. When Nicholas Nabakov, after a delay of almost six months, sent Russell a draft of the Congress of Cultural Freedom's promised statement on their position in relation to the actions of the American Committee[2] Russell was extremely critical. The statement which was intended for publication in the *Manchester Guardian* briefly summarized the essential facts of the original controversy and stated further:

Although we do not wish to enter into the debate on the substantive arguments in the Rosenberg case, the Congress for Cultural Freedom wants to make clear that it did not approve the manner in which the American Committee conducted the polemic, and therefore disassociates itself from its action.

Russell replied to Nabakov on 28 January 1957:

I am afraid you will think me persnickety, but I do not find the draft letter you enclose satisfactory. In the first place, it should be published not only in the *Manchester Guardian,* but in America, as practically every American newspaper published the letter from the American Committee for Cultural Freedom. In the second place, you criticize the American Committee only for its "manner" and not for the substance of its action. In the third place, though I do not contend that it was the duty of your Committee to review the evidence in the Rosenberg-Sobell case, I do think that it was your duty to make it clear that you consider the right to question a verdict an essential part of civil liberties. I note also that your very mild criticism of the American Committee was postponed until the Committee had ceased to exist.

I am reluctantly confirmed in the view that you object to interferences with the liberty of culture much more vehemently when they are committed by Communist nations than when they are committed by those who are anti-Communist.

These various considerations make me feel that I am not sufficiently in sympathy with your organization to remain connected with it and I therefore wish to re-affirm my previous decision to resign.

The Congress for Cultural Freedom made one final attempt to persuade Russell to alter his decision: Nabakov, in two lengthy letters on February 12—one personal, the other official—explained that "it was not our intention to limit the publication of our letter to the *Manchester Guardian*," but that paper was to receive it first as "the issue originated there." Nabakov also argued that "the American Committee has not ceased to exist" but admitted that "its activities have been sharply curtailed." Central to the dispute with Russell however was the question of the "substances of the American Committee's action" which Nabakov protested was not something "we could censor our American affiliate for."

Confirming his decision to resign, Russell's reply of February 25 also revealed the essential contradiction in Nabakov's interpretation of the dispute:

You say that you could not censor your American affiliate for the *substance* of their letter. I do not feel that you are quite justified in saying this. You go on to say that we may all have our individual opinions. But it was just this that the American Committee denied as regards members of its organization. It took a line on a controversial question and found fault with anyone who took a different line. You say "our members have every right to express their own personal views in this matter." But the expression by the American Committee was not merely a *personal* expression and it was certainly implied that a member of the organization ought in the opinion of the organization not have the views that I had expressed.

Because of Russell's concern and his principled role in defending the victims of McCarthyist persecution, his views and support were increasingly sought by those engaged in struggle with the American witch-hunting apparatus. Corliss Lamont, who was by now corresponding regularly with Russell, kept him in touch with developments in America and with his own continuing battle against the investigating committees. Lamont who had for many years been fighting to get a passport informed Russell on June 26 that he had filed a suit against Dulles, the Secretary of State. Lamont explained that "for the past year all application forms have included three questions relating to membership in the Communist Party. I have refused to answer these questions as unconstitutional and am making the first court test of their constitutionality." Lamont in a more general reference to the cause of civil liberties in America expressed hope for the future:

The seven or eight decisions made by the U.S. Supreme Court over the past two weeks have been enormously helpful for civil liberties in America. The decisions concerning Congressional contempt cases have drastically curtailed the powers of legislative investigating committees. I think that we can surely say now that the tide has finally turned toward the re-establishment of freedom in this country.

Russell, too, was convinced that matters had improved in America, but in an article "Three Reasons Why They Dislike Us"[3] published by the *New York Times Magazine* on September 8, he wrote that although there had been improvements "they are not yet such as believers in freedom of liberal opinions can approve." Russell believed that there would be no fundamental improvement "until a more conciliatory spirit prevails on both sides of the Iron Curtain."

Toward the end of 1957, Russell received news from Aaron Katz, who was active in the American campaign to secure justice for Morton Sobell, that sympathy for the campaign was gaining ground in America. He instanced the support of several newspapers as well as the increasing doubts of a number of influential individuals, including Norman Thomas who had been indicating his own misgivings and his readiness to support a hearing. Katz felt that it was Russell who "started Mr. Thomas thinking." In his letter of November 14, Katz paid tribute to Russell's stand on the Sobell case:

I should like you to know that it was your initial letter which appeared in the *Manchester Guardian* which gave a tremendous boost to the campaign for justice for Sobell in this country. It created a major breakthrough in the press and it inspired thousands of previously negative or indifferent people to look into the case.

Katz went on to request a statement from Russell "which might be in the form of an open letter to the U.S. Supreme Court" backing an appeal for a rehearing of Sobell's case. Russell replied to Katz on November 19:

Thank you for your letter. I feel as strongly as ever about Sobell and am entirely convinced that there was no such evidence against him as should have led to his conviction, but I am reluctant to intervene further in a purely American matter. I am very glad that Americans whose opinion counts have taken up Sobell's case and I think it is better to leave the matter in their hands since any intervention by a non-American tends to produce a nationalist reaction.

Footnotes

1. See below, pp. 338-40.
2. January 1957.
3. Russell's title was "Anti-American Feeling in Britain."

9 Russell, Khrushchev & Dulles

In March 1957 the USA, in the face of world wide protest, carried out a series of nuclear weapon tests in the Pacific. The World Health Organization warned of the genetic effects of radiation and when it became known that a further series of tests was planned for May and June by Britain, Russell in an article for *The New Scientist* of 28 March 1957, entitled "The Tests Should be Stopped," argued for the abandonment of all nuclear testing. Russell believed that "an agreement to abandon tests would be a step towards peaceful co-existence" and that such an agreement cut across rival political interests because the hazards resulting from tests affected all of humanity equally. Russell felt that since "the Soviet Government has, on occasion, seemed willing to enter into such an agreement" the Western Powers "ought to show more readiness to test Soviet sincerity." In Russell's view the H-bomb tests diminished rather than increased security:

We know authoritatively from Mr. Dulles that we have been on the brink of war several times in recent years. These are the risks to which we have exposed ourselves by the vain search for security.

Can anybody with any plausibility maintain that there would be greater risks in a policy proclaiming more universal aims and a greater regard for the future of mankind? And if risks must be run, is is not better to run the risks in pursuit of something ennobling and splendid rather than in the perfecting of weapons of man's destruction? For such reasons, I should rejoice if the British Government were to abandon not only the projected tests, but the manufacture of H-bombs.

Despite a demand for the abolition of H-bomb tests from the British Labor Party early in April and despite appeals from the Pope, Schweitzer, Nehru, Russell and others for the universal prohibion of nuclear tests and weapons, the British government exploded its first H-bomb in the Central Pacific on 15 May 1957 and followed this up with further tests culminating on June 19.

After the failure of the disarmament conference in London in September, the breakdown of United Nations disarmament talks and a revelation by *The Times* that U.S. planes loaded with H-Bombs were constantly in the skies above Britain,[1] Russell, who did "not wish to be an accomplice in a vast atrocity which threatened the world with over-whelming disaster,"[2] decided to write an Open Letter to both President Eisenhower and Premier Khrushchev in the hope that he could urge "at least a modicum of common sense to break into the policies of the two Great Powers" and that they would be persuaded that "the things which they held in common were far more numerous and far more important than their differences."[3] Russell's letter appeared in the *New Statesman* of 23 November 1957 and was reproduced in *Look* magazine on 21 January 1958:

I am addressing you as the respective heads of the two most powerful countries in the world. Those who direct the policies of these countries have a power for good or evil exceeding anything ever possessed before by any man or group of men. Public opinion in your respective countries has been focused upon the points in which your national interests are thought to diverge, but I am convinced that you, as far-seeing and intelligent men, must be aware that the matters in which the interests of Russia and America coincide are much more important than the matters in which they are thought to diverge. I believe that if you two eminent men were jointly to proclaim this fact and to bend the policies of your great countries to agreement with such proclamation, there would be throughout the world, and not least in your own countries, a shout of joyful agreement which would raise you both to a pinnacle of fame surpassing anything achieved by other statesmen of the past or present. Although you are, of course, both well aware of the points in which the interests of Russia and America are identical, I will, for the sake of explicitness, enumerate some of them.

1. The supreme concern of men of all ways of thought at the present time must be to ensure the continued existence of the human race. This is already in jeopardy from the hostility between East and West and will, if many minor nations acquire nuclear weapons, be in very much greater jeopardy within a few years from the possibility of irresponsible action by thoughtless fanatics.

Some ignorant militarists, both in the East and in the West, have apparently thought that the danger could be averted by a world war giving victory to their own side. The progress of science and technology has made this an idle dream. A world war would not result in the victory of either side, but in the extermination of both. Neither side can desire such a cataclysm...

2. The international anarchy which will inevitably result from the unrestricted diffusion of nuclear weapons is not to the interest of either Russia or America. There was a time when only America had nuclear weapons. This was followed by a time when only Russia and America had such weapons. And now only Russia, America and Britain possess them. It is obvious that, unless steps are taken, France and Germany will shortly manufacture these weapons. It is not likely that China will lag far behind. We must expect that during the next few years the manufacture of engines of mass destruction will become cheaper and easier. No doubt Egypt and Israel will then be able to follow the example set by the great powers. So will the states of South America. There is no end to this process until every sovereign state is in a position to say to the whole world: "You must yield to my demands or you shall die." If all sovereign states were governed by rulers possessed of even the rudiments of sanity, they would be restrained from such blackmail by the fear that their citizens also would perish. But experience shows that from time to time power in this or that country falls into the hands of rulers who are not sane. Can anyone doubt that Hitler, if he had been able to do so, would have chosen to involve all mankind in his own ruin? For such reasons, it is imperative to put a stop to the diffusion of nuclear weapons. This can easily be done by agreement between Russia and America, since they can jointly refuse military or economic assistance to any country other than themselves which persists in the manufacture of such weapons. But it cannot be achieved without agreement between the two dominant powers, for, without such agreement, each new force of nuclear weapons will be welcomed by one side or the other as an increase to its own strength. This helter-skelter race towards ruin must be stopped if anything that anybody could desire is to be effected.

3. So long as the fear of world war dominates policy and the only deterrent is the threat of universal death, so long there can be no limit to the diversion of expenditure of funds and human energy into channels of destruction. It is clear that both Russia and America could save nine-tenths of their present expenditure if they concluded an alliance and devoted themselves jointly to the preservation of peace throughout the world. If they do not find means of lessening their present hostility, reciprocal fear will drive them further and further,

until, apart from immense armaments, nothing beyond a bare subsistence will be left to the populations of either country. In order to promote efficiency in the preparation of death, education will have to be distorted and stunted. Everything in human achievement that is not inspired by hatred and fear will be squeezed out of the curriculum in schools and universities. Any attempt to preserve the vision of Man as the triumph (so far) of the long ages of evolution, will come to be viewed as treachery, since it will be thought not to minister to the victory of this group or that. Such a prospect is death to the hopes of all who share the aspirations which have inspired human progress since the dawn of history...

I suggest, Sirs, that you should meet in a frank discussion of the conditions of co-existence, endeavouring no longer to secure this or that more or less surreptitious advantage for your own side, but seeking rather for such agreement and such adjustments in the world as will diminish future occasions of strife. I believe that if you were to do this the world would acclaim your action, and the forces of sanity, released from their long bondage, would ensure for the years to come a life of vigour and achievement and joy surpassing anything known in even the happiest eras of the past.[4]

Khrushchev was the first to respond and his reply was published in the *New Statesman* on 21 December 1957.[5] Khrushchev supported Russell's call for the ending of the arms race and the distribution of nuclear weapons. He agreed that this could be achieved and that war would be prevented "if everyone who wants to preserve peace will struggle for it actively and in an organised way." Khrushchev outlined for Russell the various steps taken by the USSR towards preventing the further distribution of nuclear weapons and pointed out that these efforts had met with no response from the Western Powers. He also warned that curbing the deployment of nuclear weapons would not in itself remove the danger of nuclear war:

The Soviet Union considers that the danger of atomic war will only be removed finally and completely when the manufacture and use of atomic and hydrogen weapons will have been completely prohibited and the stockpiles destroyed. For almost twelve years now the Soviet government has been demanding such a solution of this question and has made quite a few concrete proposals in the UN in support of these aims. If the Western Powers would express a sincere desire to end the danger of atomic war, then it would be possible—tomorrow, even—to advance along this path, taking, for a start, such steps as the immediate ending of nuclear weapons tests and renunciation of the use of such weapons. But it must be said straight out that, up to the present, unfortunately, we have not had evidence of any such desire by the American, British or French governments. The fact is that those quarters which formulate the policies of those countries wish to preserve war in their arsenal as a means of securing the aims of their foreign policy.

Supporting Russell's call for a rapprochement between the USA and the USSR and for East and West to "learn to live with the other and substitute argument for force" Khrushchev stated:

You are completely right of course, when you say that one of the chief reasons for the present state of tension in international relations, and for all that is meant by "cold war," is the abnormal character of the relations between the Soviet Union and the United States of America. The normalization of these relations, on the rational basis of peaceful co-existence and respect for one another's rights and interests, would beyond a doubt lead to a general improvement in the international situation. The Soviet Union has always tried for just such a normalization of relations with the United States, and it will continue to do so. We have taken quite a few definite steps in this direction. You will probably remember, for example, that in January 1956 the Soviet government proposed to the government of the USA that a treaty of friendship and co-operation be concluded between our two countries. Our proposal still holds good. We have tried and will continue to try to re-establish Soviet-American trade relations, which were broken off by the government of the U.S. and we want to open up cultural, scientific and technical exchanges with the United States. Negotiations are now, incidentally, taking place in Washington, on Soviet initiative, for the widening of cultural relations between our two countries.

Khrushchev also supported Russell's proposal for a meeting between the leaders of the USSR and USA to discuss questions of co-existence but he felt that there were "forces, both in the United States itself and outside it...which actively oppose any step in that direction" basing their policy on "exploiting the distrust and differences existing at present between the two biggest powers." Khrushchev insisted that Britain too should make a contribution towards reducing the tension by not allowing herself to be used as an American base for nuclear weapons. Concluding his letter, Khrushchev expressed confidence that Russell's call for peace would find sympathetic echoes all over the world:

I fully support this call; my colleagues and I would like to express the hope that your ardent desire for improved relations between states will meet with support also from the leaders of other countries.

Today the struggle for peace, for the ending of the cold war, which sharpens international tension and which could lead mankind to immense disasters; the struggle for the peaceful co-existence of states, is the vital concern of all peoples of the world, of all men of good will. What we advocate is that the superiority of any particular system be proved, not on the field of battle but in peaceful competition for progress, for improved living standards of the people.

Eisenhower himself did not respond to Russell's letter. Some weeks passed before Russell received a reply from John Foster Dulles writing on behalf of the President.[6] Dulles' letter was published in the *New Statesman* on 8 February 1958. Much of his letter was taken up with an attack on communism and in particular the Soviet Communist Party which he believed depended upon "force and violence and could not exercise power anywhere in the world today if they should relinquish that." On the other hand he claimed that the "creed of the United States is based on the tenets of moral law" and it therefore "rejects war except in self-defense." Dulles contrasted examples of the Soviet Union perpetuating its power by force with claims made by Khrushchev in his letter and concluded that "it is indeed quite improbable that the Soviet Communist Party should now abjure the use of force and violence." The United States on the other hand, he maintained, abhorred war:

This abhorrence of war, this determination to substitute peaceful negotiation for force in the settlement of international disputes, is solidly founded in the religious conviction that guided our forefathers in writing the documents that marked the birth of America's independence. Indeed, there are important elements in our religious groups who even decry the use of force for self-defence. I do not think that it is possible to find in the history of the United States any occasion when an effort has been made to spread its creed by force of arms. There is, therefore, no need on our side to "abandon" what Lord Russell condemns. On the contrary, it would be abhorrent and unthinkable that there should be introduced into our creed the concept of its maintenance or extension by methods of violence and compulsion.

Dulles concluded therefore that for the world to "become a happier and safer place in which to live" it was necessary for Russell to "persuade the Communist parties of the world to renounce dependence upon force and violence" while "those who have freedom must be organized to preserve it."

Dulles then outlined for Russell the measures taken by the USA "to assure that the power of the atom should be used for peaceful purposes."

A decade ago, when the United States had a monopoly of atomic weapons and of the knowledge of how to make them, we proposed that we and all others should forego such destructive weapons....We proposed an international agency to control all use of atomic energy everywhere. That proposal was rejected by the Soviet Union with the consequence that nuclear weapons today exist in vast and growing quantities.

In a further effort to stem the increase of nuclear weapons stockpiles and their irresponsible spread throughout the world, the United States joined in proposals that fissionable material should no longer be produced for weapons purposes and that existing nuclear weapons stockpiles should be steadily diminished by agreed contributions to peaceful purposes internationally controlled. This proposal, too, has been rejected by the Soviet Union.

Dulles assured Russell that the USA was determined to "avoid war of any kind, nuclear or non-nuclear, and to renounce all use of force as a means of subjecting human beings to a rule to which they do not freely consent." Dulles quoted to Russell from the Declaration of Independence which he believed best illustrated the creed of America:

It is the creed by which we live in defense of which many Americans have laid down their lives—in France, in the Phillipines, in Korea, and many other foreign lands—in a supreme act of fellowship with those of other lands who believe in the dignity of men and men's right to have governments not imposed on them but chosen by them. Such a creed cannot be imposed by force because to use force to impose a creed would of itself be a violation of our creed.

I revert again to Lord Russell's statement that "it is not necessary that either side should abandon belief in its own creed." Certainly this is true of the United States whose creed comprehends the renunciation of force and violence to spread its creed. The same, unhappily, cannot be said of Soviet Communism, whose creed comprehends the use of force and violence. Therefore, I believe that it is necessary that at least that part of the Soviet Communist creed should be abandoned in order to achieve the peaceful result which is sought by Lord Russell and all other peace-loving people.

It is the steadfast determination of the United States—you may call it a creed if you will—to work in a spirit of conciliation for peaceful solutions based on freedom and justice of the great problems facing the world today.

On 5 March Khrushchev wrote to Kingsley Martin, the editor of the *New Statesman*, asking if he would publish a second letter to Russell "in view of the fact that in Mr. Dulles' letter distortions and inaccuracies are permitted with regard to the foreign policy of the Soviet Union." Khrushchev's rejoinder was published on 15 March. In a 9000 word letter Khrushchev set himself the task of "examining calmly and soberly some of the most important aspects of the present international situation." Basing his argument on a historical appraisal of the "two world systems" and their respective international roles, he rejected Dulles' view that it was the Communist creed which was responsible for the tensions in the world. Khrushchev's contention was that "ideological questions and questions of social organization are the internal affairs of the peoples of each country." He concluded with an appeal to Russell:

Isn't it, therefore, time to think again, to end this duel of words, to eliminate the Cold War, which was not begun by the peace-loving peoples, and turn to concrete negotiations in order, in a business-like atmosphere, paying heed to each other's interest, patiently step by step to advance towards the solution of ripening international problems, including the problem of disarmament? And for this there is no need for either the Soviet Union or the United States of America to renounce its own ideology.

Russell's reply to both leaders was featured in the *New Statesman* of April 5:

...Mr. Khrushchev and Mr. Dulles appear as rival fanatics, each blinded to obvious facts by mental blinkers. If we grant for the moment the hypothesis of each, that the victory of his system would be a boon to the human race, it still does not follow that either side should favour a war in which both sides, as well as non-participants, will be exterminated. This is so simple and so obvious that one cannot but be amazed at the incapacity of intelligent men to grasp its consequences. Mr. Khrushchev himself says: "You know very well, Lord Russell, that modern armaments, atomic and hydrogen bombs, will be exceptionally dangerous during a time of war not only for the two warring states in terms of direct devastation and destruction of human beings; they will also be deadly for states wishing to stay aside from the military operations, since the poisoned soil, air, food, etc., would become the source of terrible torments and the slow annihilation of millions of people. There is in the world today, an enormous quantity of atom and hydrogen bombs. According to the scientists' calculations, if they were all to be exploded simultaneously, the existence of almost every living thing on earth would be threatened."

I have not found any comparable passage in Mr. Dulles' much shorter letter, but I have little doubt that on this point he would agree with Mr. Khrushchev. I think, however, that Mr. Khrushchev comes nearer than Mr. Dulles to advocating the sort of policy which is called for. The most hopeful passage I can find in his letter seems to be the following: "We say: let us act, let us impose a strict prohibition on atomic and hydrogen weapons, immediately cease testing these weapons and establish reasonable controls. Let us come to an agreement on conditions which do not trespass on the interests of the parties concerned, which do not lead to the strengthening of some and the weakening of others, on conditions which would not lead to states losing their independence and sovereignty, whichever system they may belong to, and on conditions which would not offer advantages to some countries to the detriment of others."

It is customary in the West to discount such statements as insincere. I think this is a mistaken policy. They should be accepted at their face value and regarded by the West as a basis for negotiation. If, in fact, they are insincere, negotiations will reveal this. But, if they are sincere, real progress becomes possible. It is, I know, very difficult for a Western reader to avoid feeling irritated by the assumption of Communist rectitude. But Communists are bound to be equally irritated by Mr. Dulles statement that "the creed of the United States is based on tenets of the moral law." If any detente is to be achieved, each side must learn to forget such sayings by the other side and to abstain in the future from remarks which can only irritate.

...This correspondence arose out of my letter inviting President Eisenhower and Mr. Khrushchev to forget the points in which their interests are supposed to differ, and to remember the far more important points in which their interests coincide not only with each other, but with those of mankind. I cannot pretend that the result, so far, is very encouraging. But the point of view that I was presenting is novel and I still have hopes that statesmen on both sides, when they have got over the initial shock, will allow themselves to become aware of what they must do if life on this planet is to continue...

This matter is vital to every man, woman and child in every continent and of every political party. If the politicians who have been trained in outmoded ways of thought have lost the elasticity that the new world demands, the men and women throughout the world who think that a living future is preferable to a dead world of rocks and deserts will have to rise and demand, in tones so loud that they cannot be ignored, that common sense, humanity, and the dictates of that moral law which Mr. Dulles believes he respects, should guide our troubled era into that happiness which only its own folly is preventing.

A little over ten years later Russell recalling this period wrote "I believed then, as I still believe, in the necessity of co-operation between nations as the sole method of avoiding war."[7] This belief, he wrote, had moved him to correspond with Khrushchev and Dulles. "The righteously adamantine surface of Mr. Dulles' mind as shown in his letter." Russell wrote, "filled me with greater foreboding than did the fulminations and, sometimes, contradictions of Mr. Khrushchev."[8] Russell believed that Khrushchev's letter showed "some underlying understanding of alternatives and realities while Dulles' letter showed none."[9] Russell's estimation of the respective attitudes of the two leaders corresponded with his later view of the international role of the USA and USSR by which time "Russia seemed to have recognised the need of co-operation [while]...the United States continued to confound co-operation with domination."[10]

Russell's correspondence with Dulles and the initial reply from Khrushchev received wide coverage in the U.S. press. Corliss Lamont, who was pursuing his suit against Dulles for a passport, described the exchange of letters as a "great blow for peace"[11] and he kept Russell posted with clippings from the New York press. Russell was encouraged by the positive response to his open letter both by the heads of state concerned and the public, and he followed up the theme of his open letter in an article for the *New York Herald Tribune* entitled "The Two Visions" published on 6 January 1958. A summary of Russell's views on the need for East-West negotiations at the highest level was published internationally, including the press in socialist countries. The summary which was originally written as a message to be delivered on January 11 to an annual dinner meeting of U.S. Nobel Prize winners was mainly concerned with what Russell felt would be the most effective principles and procedures to follow in negotiations between the Great Powers:

Negotiations between East and West with a view to finding ways of peaceful co-existence are urgently desirable. Certain principles should govern such negotiations: (1) any agreement arrived at should as a whole be not advantageous to either party; (2) it should be such as to diminish causes of friction; (3) it should be such as to diminish the danger of a more or less inadvertent outbreak of nuclear warfare.

The procedure I should wish to see adopted would be, first, a meeting at the highest level between the Governments of the U.S. and the USSR, not intended to reach binding agreements but to explore the possibility of a compromise which both Powers could accept. The negotiations involved should be secret until the possibility of such compromise had been established. If such a compromise seems feasible, it should be recommended by both parties to the other powers of NATO and the Warsaw Pact.

If an agreement is to be successful in averting the risk of nuclear warfare, it must provide for the destruction of nuclear weapons and the cessation of their manufacture under the guarantee of inspection by an agreed neutral authority. It must also provide for the removal of all alien troops from agreed territory including as minimum East and West Germany, Czechoslovakia, Poland and Hungary. Germany not to remain in NATO or above Satellites in Warsaw Pact. The countries in Eastern and Western Europe must be free to adopt whatever form of Government and whatever economic system they may prefer.[12]

Many Americans were hostile to Russell's views on the desirability of detente with the USSR. His correspondence with Dulles and Khrushchev and his article in the *New York Herald Tribune* were particularly provocative. A torrent of critical and sometimes hysterical letters poured into Russell's North Wales home. Russell replied to Herbert A. Philbrick of New York on 6 February 1958:

I will endeavour to answer the points you make. You say that in my view to secure our own safety we ought to condone the slavery of millions behind the iron curtain. This is not a correct statement of the situation. Only two possibilities are open to us: (a) to seek a detente; (b) to slaughter the "enslaved millions" while they slaughter us. I cannot see the utility of this latter course.

You say "what common interests are held between freedom and slavery?" This is a melodramatic and unreal way of stating the matter. Many people in Russia feel free; many people in the U.S. feel unfree. The Franco regime with which the U.S. co-operates is as unfree as the Soviet regime. In addition to these considerations, those, whether free or not, who prefer to be alive rather than dead have a common interest in avoiding nuclear war. I am not concerned to defend the Communists, but I think your view of them is unduly simplified.

You reject my description of "fanatical groups of men taught by their Governments and their leaders of thought to view rival groups as wicked." The whole of your letter justifies me in this view. You regard the Russians as wicked, and your opposition to them is fanatical, and you have learnt this view from your Government and the leaders of thought in your country. I much regret that the Chinese scholar whom you quote should regard pro-American activities as criminal. I regret equally that you should regard pro-Russian activities. as criminal.

You are allowing yourself to indulge in a fancy picture of the Soviet regime collapsing as a result of Western might. It would be very nice if this happened, but there is no reason to expect it. You say to me "You will remain in chains until the shackles of slavery are broken from everybody in the Soviet slave empire." You do not tell me how these shackles are to be broken, and apparently you are perfectly willing that they should not be broken in Spain.

On February 25 Alfred Kohlberg, the publisher of *Plain Talk*, which had published Russell's "The Prevention of Atomic War" in February1947, wrote to Russell taking him to task for revising his position on the problem of dealing with the USSR. Kohlberg pointed out that Russell's views in his 1947 article were diametrically opposed to those expressed in his correspondence with Dulles and Khrushchev and in an interview with Joseph Alsop published on 18 February 1958 in the *New York Herald Tribune*. Kohlberg questioned "whether it might be possible that the people who denounced you as unfit for publication in 1947 might possibly have been right, even though for the wrong reasons."

Russell replied on March 8:

I have pursued one consistent purpose, namely, to prevent an all-out nuclear war in which both sides possess nuclear weapons. At one time there was one method by which this could be achieved; at another, another. There was no more inconsistency than there is when a man gets out of a train after an accident because the train is not going to reach its intended destination. You quote Joseph Alsop as saying that I am in favour of unilateral nuclear disarmament. This is an undue simplification. I am in favour of Britain disarming unilaterally if negotiations for general disarmament prove futile. If it can be secured that only the U.S. and USSR have nuclear weapons, I favour negotiations between them for abolition of nuclear weapons by both sides. I do hold, however, that if all negotiations prove futile and no alternatives remain except Communist domination or extinction of the human race, the former alternative is the lesser of two evils. You, I gather, do not hold this view.

As for your accusation that the policy I have advocated has changed from time to time: it has changed as circumstances have changed. To achieve a single purpose, sane men adapt their policies to the circumstances. Those who do not are insane.

Ever since the Russell-Einstein declaration in 1955, Russell had been a prominent supporter of the Pugwash movement, founded and sponsored by Cyrus Eaton, a Canadian millionare. Pugwash, which had grown out of the Russell-Einstein Declaration and which was mainly concerned to promote the social responsibility of scientists and the peaceful use of scientific discoveries, was supported by scientists from both East and West. Because of Eaton's efforts to secure the co-operation of scientists from socialist countries he came under the scrutiny of the FBI. In May 1958, he was attacked by the House Un-American Activities Committee and on 21 May Russell wrote to him expressing support and stating that it would be "a sad day for America when activities such as yours are pronounced to be un-American."

Russell also gave his support to Linus Pauling, one of the original signatories to the Russell-Einstein Declaration, and who had also been subject to FBI investigation, when he approached Russell during May requesting a statement for use in promoting his new book *No More War*, "about the nature of nuclear war and of nuclear weapons, and the necessity for abandoning war as the method of solving international problems." Russell contributed his statement on 25 July 1958:

> Dr. Linus Pauling's book *No More War* is a very valuable addition to the works which endeavour to enlighten mankind as to what governments are preparing for them. Dr. Pauling explains, in entirely untechnical language, the various dangers to which human beings are exposed by nuclear weapons and ruthlessly lays bare the misleading character of many official pronouncements. Basing himself upon semi-official data, he estimates the effect of a nuclear war on the United States if it should break out at the present time. He concludes that on the first day of the war forty-two million Americans would die and sixty-six million would be injured; that by the fourteenth day the number of dead would exceed the number of injured; and that after that the slow effects of gradual fall-out would cause a number of deaths which it is impossible to estimate. (Although such figures must be well known to the American Government, Mr. Dulles has recently told the world that America might win a hot war.) Dr. Pauling's book is scientific, careful, factual and balanced. It should be read by all who wish the human race to survive.

Earlier in the year Russell had joined with Pauling and other individuals from the U.S., Britain, Japan, Germany and France as plaintiffs in simultaneous suits against the authorities responsible for nuclear testing in both the USA and USSR. The suits, which became known as "The Fallout Suits," were filed in the respective courts of both countries in June

1958 and sought to secure a permanent bar on the future testing of all nuclear devices.

Norman Thomas, who was one of the American plaintiffs, wrote Russell on August 8 that the suits had been "carried through to an unsuccessful conclusion in the District Court." He informed Russell of the intention to appeal against the decision and thanked him for his part in them and also for what Russell had been saying generally "about war, peace and nuclear weapons."

Russell's writings and activities against the threat of nuclear warfare were beginning, in 1958, to win for him an active following on both sides of the Atlantic. In America the lead he was giving to men of science was recognised with his election on 4 December 1958 to an Honorary Life Membership of the New York Academy of Sciences. In Britain his call for nuclear disarmament was striking a sympathetic chord with increasingly wider sections of public opinion and he was elected President of the newly formed Campaign for Nuclear Disarmament (CND).

On 31 March 1958, just one month after the founding of CND, the USSR unilaterally resolved to suspend nuclear tests and at the same time invited the U.S. and Britain to do the same.

Footnotes

1. "U.S. Atom-Bomber Flights over Britain 'Provocative': Mr. Bulganin Accuses the West." *The Times*, 13 December 1957.
2. B. Russell, *Autobiography* Vol. 3, (London, 1969) p. 102 (New York, 1969) p. 138.
3. *Ibid.*
4. This letter and the ensuing correspondence with Khrushchev and Dulles were later reprinted in *The Vital Letters of Russell, Khrushchev and Dulles* (MacGibben and Kee, London, 1958). This book was the idea of Kingsley Martin, editor of the *New Statesman*.
5. 7 December 1957.
6. January 1958.
7. B. Russell, *Autobiography*, Vol. 3, p. 102; p. 138.
8. *Ibid.*, p. 102; p. 139.
9. *Ibid.*
10. *Ibid.*
11. Lamont to Russell 19 December 1957.
12. Written on 7 January 1958.

10 Nuclear Disarmament

Russell's correspondence with Dulles and Khrushchev and his experience with the Pugwash movement had convinced him that these activities, while helping to alert people to the dangers of nuclear war, could not in themselves lead to nuclear disarmament, and that more effective methods, based on massive public protest, were necessary to persuade governments to renounce nuclear diplomacy. He realized that tremendous pressure would be needed to effect that result and hoped therefore to win the support in the first place, of the British public. As president of the Campaign for Nuclear Disarmament Russell continued to search "to find fresh approaches through which to try and sway public opinion, including governmental opinion."[1] Russell believed that "if Britain gave up her part in the nuclear race and even demanded the departure of United States bases from her soil, other nations might follow suit."[2]

The growing support in Britain for the aims of the Campaign for Nuclear Disarmament made Russell hopeful that the Labor Party might eventually become the Parliamentary spokesman for unilateral disarmament in opposition to government policies. Russell felt that policies "dictated by common sense" were needed and that "if the public could be shown this clearly, I had a faint hope that they might insist upon governmental policies being brought into accord with common sense."[3]

Toward the end of 1958 Russell set himself the task of preparing for publication a book presenting his viewpoint on nuclear warfare. In it he attempted to "show possible means of achieving peace in ways which should be equally acceptable to Communist nations, to NATO nations and to uncommitted nations."[4] Proof copies of *Common Sense and Nuclear Warfare* were sent to various heads of government and on 6 January 1959 Eisenhower acknowledged the book and assured Russell that "no one

115

> "The view that No World is better than a Communist World, or that No World is better than a Capitalist World, is one that is difficult to refute by abstract arguments, but I think that those who hold it should question their right to impose their opinion upon those who do not hold it by the infliction of the death penalty upon all of them. This is an extreme form of religious persecution, going far beyond anything that has been advocated in previous human history."

could possibly pray more devoutly for a just peace than do I." The reaction of the British government was equally discouraging and Russell decided to return "to the piecemeal business of speaking at meetings, CND and other, and broadcasting."[5]

The publication of *Common Sense and Nuclear Warfare* aroused much public interest in Britain and America. Although Russell himself was not entirely satisfied with the book as "it did not tackle the question as to exactly how each individual could make his opinion known and influence policy making,"[6] it did serve to clarify his views on unilateral disarmament about which there had been considerable controversy in the past. In a chapter on "Unilateral Disarmament" Russell insisted that "the view in favour of avoiding nuclear warfare even at great cost is one which applies to both sides equally."[7] Answering his critics Russell stated:

...What I advocate in practice, and not as the outcome of an artificial logical dilemma, is a conclusion of agreements between East and West admitting the inevitability of co-existence and the disastrous futility of war... Many of my critics, though they are in the habit of proclaiming that they value freedom, on this point deceive themselves. They do not think that those who prefer life rather than death, even under Communism or under Capitalism, as the case may be, should be free to choose the alternative that they prefer. Not only the inhabitants of Communist nations—or of Capitalist nations—but the inhabitants of uncommitted nations are denied by them the most elementary freedom, which is freedom to choose survival. The view that No World is better that a Communist World, or that No World is better than a Capitalist World, is one that is difficult to refute by abstract arguments, but I think that those who hold it should question their right to impose their opinion upon those who do not hold it by the infliction of the death penalty upon all of them. This is an extreme form of religious persecution, going far beyond anything that has been advocated in previous human history.[8]

In America Russell was rapidly becoming recognized as the chief spokesman in the West for nuclear disarmament, and co-existence with the USSR. He received daily dozens of letters mostly from Americans, praising or attacking him for his views. Many Americans sought his advice. One anxious correspondent asked Russell if there was any place in the world which might be "comparatively safe" as a refuge in the event of a nuclear War. Russell replied on 19 December 1958:

> I do not think that there is much point in trying to find a safe refuge from radio-active poison. I think it is much more useful, both publicly and personally, to join those who are engaged in trying to prevent a nuclear war....If, however, you wish to find a comparatively safe region, I think one may say that the Southern hemisphere is safer than the Northern and that it grows progressively safer as you approach the South Pole.[9]

The correspondent wrote back expressing incredulity at Russell's advice and Russell confirmed and reinforced his view in this reply of 23 February 1959:

> I was not pulling your leg in recommending the Southern Hemisphere on the assumption that there were a war between Russia and the West. If there were a war between China and Australia, the Southern Hemisphere would of course be very dangerous.[10]

The world tensions resulting from the nuclear arms race eased appreciably at the end of October 1958 with the opening of a conference in Geneva to negotiate the suspension of nuclear tests. A ceasefire on testing was maintained by all three nuclear powers throughout 1959 and on 28 February and 6 March 1960, shortly after the first French atomic tests in the Sahara, Russell discussed the prospects for a continuing ban on tests with Edward Teller, the "father of the H-Bomb," on "Small World" a three-way transoceanic TV program produced by Edward Murrow. Teller argued for a limitation on the ban of nuclear testing allowing for the resumption of underground tests because he believed that the USSR could not be trusted and the "underground explosions of certain kinds, and also, incidentally, some other kinds of explosions in interplanetary space cannot be detected." Teller maintained therefore that "what cannot be detected cannot be policed and what cannot be policed, should not be banned." Russell argued that detection was "much more possible than Dr. Teller is leading us to think." Making his case for a total ban on tests Russell drew an analogy with the question of the need for social laws against murder. "It's perfectly true," Russell stated, "that in some murders, the murderer is never caught." "But, he concluded, "we don't think that's a reason why we shouldn't have a law about murder." On the question of trust Russell reminded Teller of the fact that "in 1955 the Western powers made very admirable suggestions for general disarmament, and to their horror the Russians accepted them, and thereupon, the Western powers withdrew them." Russell felt that the USSR had equal cause for suspicion but that "at the present moment, I don't say always, but now, Russia is much more prepared for disarmament than the West seems to be."

The debate ended on a general note of disagreement and in later years Russell was to describe it as a "most distressing occasion" and said that he was "inhibited" by his " intense dislike" of Teller and by Teller's "disingenuous flattery."[11] The televising of the debate throughout the USA was undoubtedly a reflection of the growth in importance of the nuclear disarmament movement in the U.S., as well as the increasing regard for Russell as its acknowledged leader.

One of the first hostile reactions to Russell's standpoint in his debate with Teller came from Sidney Hook who renewed his attack on Russell in an article "Second Thoughts on Peace and Freedom" published in the *New Leader* on 11 April 1960:

In a television discussion between Bertrand Russell and Edward Teller on Edward Murrow's "Small World" Teller argued forcefully and persuasively that it would be self-defeating for the free world to enter agreements to cease nuclear testing unless they could be properly policed. For if we honorably fulfilled the agreements and the Communists did not, then within a few years they would have such a preponderance of military power that they could easily impose their will on the world. Teller therefore proposed that we now agree to suspend testing nuclear weapons above ground because we can detect violations of the agreement, but for the time being, since no methods exist to distinguish between underground nuclear tests and minor earthquakes, he recommended that we do not agree to suspend such tests until appropriate methods of detection are evolved. Inasmuch as fall-out danger is minimal in such tests, and may lead to diminution of fall-out in *any* kind of nuclear explosion including those employed for peaceful purposes, this proposal seemed reasonable enough.

Surprisingly, Russell demurred on the ground that this evinced a degree of suspicion which was not auspicious for fruitful cooperation. When Teller made an eloquent plea for the survival of a free world, Russell said that although freedom (of which the presence of free speech was taken as the symbol) was, of course, important, peace was more important because it insured survival. The implication was plain. We must be prepared to sacrifice freedom if that is the price of peace.

Hook dealt at great length with the issue of freedom and examined in the light of Russell's arguments both past and present the degree of freedom which obtained in the U.S. and the USSR. Russell, Hook averred, "seems intent upon describing conditions in the Soviet Union as if freedom were increasing there and decreasing in the West." Hook found Russell's views "extraordinary" and commented:

> The truth is that the Kremlin regards Russell today as a valuable, if capricious, ally, in its systematic campaign to disarm the West psychologically and technologically. In their eyes he is playing the same role—though enormously more influential—that Cyrus Eaton does in industry and Niemoller in religion. It is noteworthy that the philosophical hacks in the Soviet Union no longer call Russell "a running dog of imperialism" or employ other choice epithets when they have occasion to mention his philosophical views, although these views have not changed since the days of Zhdanov. Just as they now distinguish between Einstein the physicist, and Einstein the "idealist" philosopher, so they are now distinguishing between Russell, the great "partisan of peace" who has seen the error of his ways and Russell "the subjective idealist."

Making extensive reference to Russell's writings on America in the 1950s and particularly to his strictures on the FBI and McCarthyism, Hook accused Russell of exaggerations which "were of the same order as those of McCarthy himself." "It is not hard to predict," Hook continued, "that Russell will find the West, and particularly the United States, increasingly bereft of its freedom as the years go by in order to make it appear more plausible to himself and others that freedom is not really being sacrificed on the altar of security."

Hook concluded his article with an aphorism which he had composed for the dedication page of one of his books:

> It is better to be a live jackal than a dead lion—for jackals not men. Those who are prepared to live like men, and if necessary, die like men, have the best prospect of surviving as free men, and escaping the fate of both jackals and lions.

Russell replied to Hook in the May 9 issue of *The New Leader*:

> ...Hook states explicitly that, if there is an agreement between East and

West, the West will of course abide by it, but the East is very likely not to. Western Europe, which according to the North Atlantic Treaty Organisation is to be defended by the U.S. if necessary, has lately learned, with understandable dismay, that there is considerable doubt as to whether the U.S. would, in fact, fulfill its treaty obligations. Secretary of State Christian Herter, in response to a question, made the following statement: "I cannot conceive of any President involving us in an all-out nuclear war unless the fact showed clearly we are in danger of all-out devastation ourselves, or that actual moves have been made toward devastating ourselves."

Herman Kahn, in an article in the Stanford Research Institute *Journal* (reprinted in *Survival*, March-April 1960), relates that he asked a number of Americans how many American deaths in a nuclear war they would put up with rather than ignore their NATO obligations if Western Europe and not America were attacked. He reports that all of them, at first, said that of course America would fulfill her obligations, but, after about 15 minutes of discussion and reflection, they decided that there was a maximum to the number of endurable deaths. Some put the maximum at 10 million, some at 60 million, others at various intermediate figures. Kahn concludes, "No American that I have spoken to who was at all serious about the matter believed that U.S retaliation would be justified—no matter what our commitments were—if more than half of our population would be killed." After all the self-righteous assurances that America always abides by treaties, Western Europe has heard these *sotto voce* remarks with bewilderment. It now feels that the "balance of terror" is a trifle terrifying.

Herter's pronouncement, with the comments reported by Kahn, show that the attitude which I hold and which Hook repudiates is, in *fact*, the attitude of the American Government with the support of American public opinion., For it is obvious that, if Western Europe were overrun by the Russians while America looked on passively, the world-wide victory of communism would become very much more probable. The American government and American public opinion evidently prefer this to large-scale American death.

Examples of Western self-righteousness could be multiplied indefinitely. I will give only a few illustrating the freedom which is supposed to prevail in the West. On March 31, a symposium on the continuous culture of micro-organisms was held in London under the auspices of the Society of Chemical Industry. Academician Ivan Malek of the Czechoslovak Academy of Sciences, who, two years ago, acted as host to a similar symposium in Prague attended by many British delegates, had been expected to read a paper, but was refused a visa by the British authorities. On April 10, a conference on nuclear disarmament was held in London at which there were delegates from 20 countries, including East Germany, Poland and Hungary. But the Home Office refused visas to the expected Russian delegates. On April 10, also, five West Germans were sentenced to prison as members of the World Peace Council on the ground that this body is a front for the Communist party...

I hope that Hook will note that I have not said either that the Communists are more trustworthy or have more freedom than the West, or even that they are as trustworthy or have as much freedom as the West. Nor have I said that the West has less freedom than it had. I say only that it has less freedom than it boasts and that it is not as impeccably trustworthy as it sometimes thinks it is. I believe, however, that the Communists have much more freedom than they had a few years ago.

Communists and anti-Communists can live together, or die together, or, just possibly, arrive at the superiority of one of the two groups. For my part, I wish to see them live together, and I wish most earnestly to see them *not* die together. If this worst possibility is to be prevented, it is not enough for each side to bristle with H-bombs ready to be fired off whenever a flight of starlings is mistaken for enemy missiles. It is necessary that each side should learn to treat the other with common courtesy and with the realization that we all live in glass houses. The calm assumption that of course the other side would cheat, but of course our side would not, is made by both sides. But to hear some champions of the West speaking, one would never guess that the other side can be equally sincere in its suspicions...

There is nothing new about fanatical aversions. Hook is much impressed by the fanaticism of Communists, but, for my part, most of the Communists that I have met were less fanatical than Hook. The best answer to fanatical aversions occurs in Act III Scene 1 of *The Merchant of Venice*, which, slightly adapted to modern circumstances, says "Hath not a *Communist* eyes? hath not a *Communist* hands, organs, dimensions, senses, passions? fed with the same fork, hurt with the same weapons, subject to the same diseases, healed by the same means, warmed and cooled by the same winter and summer, as a *Capitalist* is?"

I advise Sidney Hook to look up the original and ponder my adaptations.

Hook replied in the same issue of *The New Leader*[12] under the title "Bertrand Russell's Political Fantasies" that he had been "as severe a critic" as Russell "of evils in the West and of illiberal aspects of its foreign policy." Hook rejected what he termed as "ambiguous lessons from *The Merchant of Venice*, in which Communists are cast as a new oppressed minority, to convince me that they belong to the human race." Hook devoted a major part of his letter to a summary of his protracted controversy with Russell over several years in order to demonstrate what he regarded as inconsistencies and contradictions in Russell's arguments. The first part of his 2500 word reply repeated his previous allegations about the aggressive intentions of the Soviet Union, its "grim system of legal tyranny" and Russell's "lack of balance" in promoting the view "that there is not such a great difference in the degree of freedom betweeen East and West as to justify defending our freedom against attack."

Russell did not trouble to reply to Hook whom he regarded as a "Menshevik who had become apprehensive of Russia ruling the world" and who "thought this so dreadful that it should be better the human race should cease to exist."[13] Russell was gratified with a letter from Corliss Lamont which confirmed much of what Russell felt about Hook. Lamont wrote on June 21:

I have followed your debates with Sidney Hook in *The New Leader* with interest, and have naturally been sympathetic to your position. Since in one of his articles Professor Hook quotes from your special introduction (foreword) to my *Freedom is as Freedom Does*, I feel that some comments by myself might be in order.

In your article of 9 May 1960 you point out some recent violations of civil liberties in the United States. But nowhere in this series has there been any indication of Sidney Hook's own part in the American witch-hunt that has steadily gone on since the close of the Second World War. Since, as you say, Hook has a fanatical aversion to Communists, it is not surprising that on the domestic scene he has campaigned unceasingly in ways that definitely undermine the Bill of Rights.

Hook has taken the position that no member of the Communist Party or so-called fellow traveler should be allowed to teach in schools and colleges. He has attacked many innocent liberals and progressives, not to mention outright Communists, who have tried to protect themselves against prosecution and framed-up perjury charges by relying on the Fifth Amendment's provision against self-incrimination. In his book *Heresy, Yes...Conspiracy, No* Hook lines up with the most reactionary elements in providing an intellectual basis for conspiracy charges and indictments against radicals—always a mainstay for tyrannical governments.

In the famous case of the national Council of Jewish Women v. Betty Levin, an Area Secretary in that organization, Sidney Hook became the chief witness against this young lady accused of being a secret Communist and infiltrating the council by means of "Communist" books such as *Soviet Communism* by Sidney and Beatrice Webb. The case came before the American Arbitration Association; and the Arbitrator, James Lawrence Fly, decided in favor of Miss Levin, referring to Hook as "the eminent philosopher" with an "allergy for red." Mr. Fly stated: "It may well be that in a number of foreign countries the Area Secretary would have been executed. Council has done less. But even it has permanently blighted a career." This was primarily the work of Prof. Hook, who instigated the charges in the first place.

So you see it is no wonder that a good many civil libertarians in the United States regard Sidney Hook as the Joe McCarthy of the intellectuals. Dr. Hook is not only a fanatic towards Communists. In the fall of 1959 when plans were being made in the United States to celebrate John Dewey's Centennial, Hook ruled you out as a member of the International Honorary Committee because, I am told, he claimed that you once stated that Dewey's philosophy led in the direction of Fascism.

Russell replied on July 12:

I am pleased by your information on the subject of Dr. Sidney Hook and delighted by his objections to my attitude towards Dewey. I did not know that Hook had so much influence, but of Such is the Kingdom of Heaven.

In the meantime two events of major international importance had occurred. On 1 May 1960, just two weeks before the opening of the Summit Conference on disarmament in Paris, a U.S. military reconnaissance aircraft was shot down while spying over Soviet territory and on May 7 the U.S. decided unilaterally to resume the underground testing of nuclear weapons. In view of these acts the breakdown of the Summit talks on May 16, the day of opening, was a predictable event.

News of the impact on Americans of the breakdown of the conference reached Russell via Stephanie May, an American friend who had returned home after a visit to England. "It has been very difficult returning to the States at this time," she wrote on May 22, "the U-2 incident, and our stupid blundering following it was simply inexcusable." She was upset by the "distressingly small number of people" in America who felt that their country was "in any way responsible for the breakup of the Summit Conference." May then gave Russell news of a disarmament rally held at Madison Square Garden on May 19:

Every seat in the Garden was sold and there were people standing.
Walter Reuther, Mrs. Roosevelt...Alfred Landon, Norman Thomas,
Governor Williams of Michigan, and many top Broadway celebrities
made speeches or entertained. It was really marvelous...After the Rally
8000 of the audience marched over to the UN Building, arriving for
their services at 1 a.m. It was really quite impressive. We aren't up to
an Aldermaston yet, but at least this was an encouraging beginning.

Russell had earlier sent a message of greeting to the rally[14], in which he
urged the participants not "to expect immediate or rapid success" in their
campaign:

Only by generating an overwhelming public opinion can we secure
victory. But in moments of discouragement we are apt to forget that
public opinion is not a vague, amorphous, external something, but is
the opinion of people like you and me. Each one of us is a unit in the
making of public opinion, and each one of us can hope to win other
units to our side. Human volitions have caused our troubles and
human volitions can cure them. The hope, if we succeed, is glorious.
And if we can make this felt, we shall succeed.

Russell's involvement in the disarmament campaign, and his support
for a negotiated end to nuclear testing caused him to view the breakdown of
the Paris Summit talks with the utmost alarm. Where previously he had
advocated a close alliance with America as the chief means towards British
and European security, he was now increasingly convinced that neutrality
was the only policy which could help to ensure Britain's survival. Russell
believed that Britain's future could best be safeguarded by disassociation
from NATO and by removing American armed forces from British
territory. Russell explained his viewpoint to the American public in an
article entitled "The Case for British Neutralism" published in the *New
York Times Magazine* on July 24. "Recent developments," Russell
wrote, "have necessitated a reconsideration of policy by the West, and more
particularly, by members of NATO other than the United States."

Published together with Russell's article was a reply from Hugh
Gaitskell, the leader of the British Labour party, who believed that any
weakening of NATO would be to the advantage of the USSR and would
allow it to "expand without serious risk or cost to itself." Gaitskell was
unconvinced of the likelihood of nuclear conflagration either by design or
by accident. He was certain however that "the balance of security, though
precarious, does help to prevent war and that it must therefore be
maintained."

> "The United States Secretary of Defense in 1958, summarizing a Pentagon report, maintained that in a nuclear war, there would be 160 million deaths in the United States, 200 million in the USSR, and, in the United Kingdom, everybody."

Russell wrote in rebuttal of Gaitskell's views, and his letter was published by the *New York Times Magazine* on August 14:

Mr. Gaitskell's reply to my arguments in favor of British neutralism calls for a rejoinder on certain points. First, as to the likelihood of a nuclear war by accident: Oskar Morgenstern, a politically orthodox American defense expert, in an article reprinted in *Survival* says, "The probability of thermo-nuclear war occurring appears to be significantly larger than the probability of its not occurring."

Ohio State University inaugurated a study of the possible causes of unintended war, which are numerous and have already on several occasions very nearly resulted in disaster. Adlai Stevenson has said: "There can be no deterrent to war by accident." I suppose it is proneness to such remarks which caused him to be thought unfit to be President.

The next question is what would occur in a nuclear war. Mr. Gaitskell brushes this aside with an acknowledgement that it would be horrible—which is oddly combined with a refusal to adopt policies making it less probable. The United States Secretary of Defense in 1958, summarizing a Pentagon report, maintained that in a nuclear war, there would be 160 million deaths in the United States, 200 million in the USSR, and, in the United Kingdom, everybody.

Some authorities are more optimistic. A.G. Field, our civil defense expert, has stated: "It cannot be said categorically that in these countries (NATO allies of the U.S.) there would be no survivors after a nuclear attack."

I should certainly agree that this cannot be categorically asserted. Until the experiment is made, doubt is permissible, but it seems somewhat remarkable that the British Government, with the connivance of a majority of the Labour Front Bench, should support a policy of which the best that can be said is that it may leave a few Britons alive.

We were impressed by the seriousness of Hitler's threat to Britain in 1940, but it was not nearly as serious as the U.S. threat to Britain at the present moment. This threat arises, not only from a possibility of a general war, but also from an entirely different source—namely, the risk that we might be dragged by the U.S. into acquiescence in measures regarded by the USSR as provocative, and that we might, in consequence, be subjected to a completely destructive attack directed against Britain alone, and not, also, against the U.S.

Mr Gaitskell is suprised that I should consider this not unlikely. I cannot understand his surprise. At the time of the U-2 crisis, Khrushchev and Malinovsky loudly proclaimed that this would be their policy if incidents such as the U-2 flight continued. Malinovsky said of any NATO nations other than the U.S. which tolerated such incidents: "We shall deal them such a blow that nothing will be left of them."

He uttered on this occasion no similar threat against the United States. All the British newspapers, especially on May 10 and 11, were full of these threats, which were headlined. But apparently Mr. Gaitskell failed to see them.

Mr. Gaitskell asks, as if it were an argument against me: "Need brinkmanship continue?" Of course, we need not; but it will continue if the governments of the West persist in present policies which Mr. Gaitskell, in the main, supports.

A third point for which Mr. Gaitskell finds fault with me is as to the expense of the arms race. At present (to quote Sir R. Adams' "Assault at Arms") we in Britain spend only 30 pounds per head per annum for every man, woman and child, but already we are being told that the estimates will have to be increased, and in America the Democrats have adopted a program rejecting any attempt at a ceiling for expenditure on armaments. I think Mr. Gaitskell seriously underrates the ingenuity of armament experts of both East and West in inventing new weapons.

The manned bomber is obsolescent; the guided missile is to have its little day: but clearly the future lies with unmanned satellites containing H-bombs. My arithmetic does not run to computing what they would cost.

Mr. Gaitskell rejects my view that ideological differences play a very small part in the hostility between East and West. I do not believe that, even if Russia became as liberal as our ally Franco of Spain, we should become friendly to the Soviet regime. We have been sometimes friendly with Russia, sometimes hostile, without any change in the Soviet governmental system. Mr. Gaitskell says (1) that a nuclear war will almost certainly not happen, (2) that "the present peace is highly precarious." Which does he mean?

I do not wish to think that the whole world will become Communist, but I wish even less to see mankind obliterated. Neither disaster need occur. Mr. Gaitskell speaks favourably of disarmament, but fails to note that the most serious approaches to disarmament have been made by the USSR and have been foiled by niggling opposition from the West.

Western policy, through blindness. has done everthing to pose the alternative "Red or Dead." Those who advocate a policy which would evade this alternative are regarded as fellow travelers. As to this, however, public opinion in Britain is changing and there seems now some hope that in spite of our "patriots," there may be Britons alive at the end of the present century.

The ensuing letters selected from the columns of the *New York Times Magazine* were on the whole unsympathetic to Russell's position.[15] A professor of Russian from New York University was "convinced that the policies Lord Russell has urged in your newspaper and elsewhere can only help bring about the catastrophe of nuclear destruction" and a Vermont correspondent questioned whether Russell "with such a confusion of ideas and values" was "so important an interpreter of the present crisis... as to deserve being consulted as an oracle." Other letters, addressed to Russell in Wales, were less restrained in their criticism. A "patriot" wrote that he had read a quotation attributed to Russell "stating that you would gladly crawl on your belly tomorrow to surrender, rather than have your beloved England subjected to a Hydrogen bomb attack. I am not surprised," he wrote, "to hear this coming from you after all your years of making like an intellectual idiot."[16] Russell replied on September 6:

> Your letter consists of vulgar abuse. The remark about crawling upon my belly to Moscow is an invention of my opponents, if it has ever been made at all. Nonetheless, if I thought that such a feat were within my powers at the age of eighty-eight and would have any effect towards preserving my compatriots, or any human beings, from the imminent destruction by means of nuclear warfare, I should endeavour to do it, though I fear that I should also have to crawl to Washington. That the extinction of the human race is all too likely to come about in the near future seems to me to be owing largely to the angrily closed minds of rigid dogmatists.[17]

Representative of the many complimentary letters Russell received was that of Barrows Dunham written on 2 August 1960:

> Allow me to express my whole-hearted admiration for your article in the *New York Times Magazine* of July 24th. You there state the case unanswerably and with the utmost refinement of exposition. It is, as you say, true that the enmity between the two greatest powers is more dangerous to them both and to the rest of the world than socialism is to the capitalist nations or capitalism to the socialist. People may hold what political theories they hold, but the survival of mankind must

first be ensured before any theory can be other than pointless.

So far as I know, there never has been another social problem in which the values are so clear, together with their application. Ordinarily these things are rather muddy. Acccordingly, one waits with growing anxiety to see whether pure reason (for if ever there was a case of pure reason, this is it) will triumph over the old vicious habits of power politics. For myself, I cannot conceive that there is anything in Marx or Jefferson (if we let these names represent what is best in the two sides) which would entail the extinction of our race.

How to make governments show by their policies that they are aware of the risks they run is another matter. In this, your labors have been more effective than those of anyone else. Every living person owes you a debt of gratitude for their own continuing lives and for the lives of their grandchildren. I am sure you know by this time, that they are aware of the debt and are happy to pay it.

Footnotes

1. B. Russell, *Autobiography* Vol. 3, (London, 1969) p. 105 (New York, 1969) pp. 142-3.

2. *Ibid.*, p. 104; p. 142.

3. *Ibid.*, p. 105; p. 143.

4. Preface to B. Russell *Common Sense and Nuclear Warfare* (London, 1959), (New York, 1959).

5. B. Russell, *Autobiography* Vol. 3, p. 105; p. 143.

6. *Ibid.*

7. B. Russell *Common Sense and Nuclear Warfare* p. 87.

8. *Ibid.*, pp. 88-9.

9. B. Feinberg and R.Kasrils (eds.) *Dear Bertrand Russell* (London, 1969), p. 70 (Houghton Mifflin, Boston, 1969), p. 35.

10. *Ibid.*

11. B. Russell, *Autobiography* Vol. 3, p. 107; p. 146.

12. *The New Leader* prepared the book *The Strategy of Deception: A Study in Worldwide Communist Tactics* and was secretly paid $12,000 by the U.S. government. When the U.S. Information Agency asked a House Appropriations Sub-Committee to increase its allowance for "book development" from $90,000 to $195,000, the Agency assured the legislators that the funds would go for books "written to our own specifications" and having "strong anti-communist content." (*The New York Times*, 3 May 1964).

13. B. Russell, *Autobiography* Vol. 3, p. 108; p. 146.

14 Based on a speech made to the Campaign for Nuclear Disarmament at the Central Hall, Westminster on 15 February 1960.

15. 14 August 1960.

16. B. Feinberg and R. Kasrils, *op. cit.* p. 65; p. 29.

17. *Ibid.*

11 Civil Disobedience

There is little doubt that the growing movement against nuclear arms was proving an embarassment to the American government. The work of leading scientists, particularly through the Pugwash movement, in revealing the true nature and hazards of the nuclear arms race, was giving great impetus to those struggling for the abolition of tests and for peaceful coexistence with the USSR. Linus Pauling, who had been particularly active in exposing the perils of nuclear testing, was under constant harassment from powerful forces in the government who wished to silence all opposition to the resumption of the nuclear arms race. In January 1958 Pauling had presented to the United Nations a petition signed by 9,235 scientists from all over the world "urging that an international agreement to stop the testing of nuclear bombs be made now."[1] The petition, which included 37 Nobel Laureates and the names of 2,875 American scientists as well as 3,769 scientists from socialist countries, had been initiated and organized by Pauling without the assistance of any organization. Russell had been a signatory to the petition, and when Pauling was ordered to appear before the Senate Internal Security Subcommittee on 15 September 1960 to consider contempt proceedings against him, after he had refused to reveal the names of those individuals who had helped him to organize his petition, Russell wrote on August 16:

I am horrified by the action of the Internal Security Subcommittee of the Senate. It seems to me that they demanded of you what almost any honourable man would feel to be a dishonourable action. I earnestly hope that they will repent before going to extremes.

Russell also wrote on August 25 to individuals organizing a campaign of support for Pauling, that he hoped that "this obscurantist attempt to suppress the spread of information will be abandoned owing to an overwhelming volume of protest." Pauling's case was by no means an isolated one. Corliss Lamont informed Russell on October 7 that "we are having a recrudescence of McCarthyism here with the Senate Internal Security Committee grilling in Washington some 36 people who have been working with the National Committee for a Sane Nuclear Policy." Lamont also sent Russell a donation of $1000 towards the work of the Committee of One Hundred which had recently been formed in Britain under the Presidency of Russell. Russell had helped to create the Committee of One Hundred when he became convinced that "Pugwash and CND and other methods that we had tried of informing the public had reached the limit of their effectiveness."[2] The Committee of One Hundred, he felt, would be more effective if it was to base its campaigning on acts of civil disobedience which "might grow into a mass movement...so strong as to force its opinions upon the Government directly."[3] The establishment in November 1960 of the first American Polaris nuclear missile firing submarine base in Britain at Holy Loch in Scotland, was a catalyst to the Committee's plan of campaign. Their first activity, a "sit-down," was announced by Russell at a press conference on December 14, to take place outside the Ministry of Defense in London on 18 February 1961.

Russell was also concerned through his writing to disabuse the British and American public of the notion fostered by their governments that "civil defence" measures including an "early warning system" could effectively protect populations from the devastation of a nuclear attack.

In a letter of 10 November 1960, to Dr. Alan M. Clarke of California, Russell argued "that the civil defence plans put forward both in the United States and in Britain seem to me to have no purpose except to deceive the population and to allow our murderous military experts to carry out their devilish plans without hindrance from their victims." The letter was written in reply to Dr. Clarke's request[4] for Russell to both contribute an article to The Los Gatos Times-Saratoga Observer, and to answer a letter from Dr. Edward Teller minimizing the effects of a nuclear war, which appeared in the columns of that paper. Russell fulfilled both requests. His letter to the editor of The Los Gatos Times was dated November 10:

In your issue of October 11 there is a letter from Dr. Edward Teller written in his usual pontifical style and making dogmatic assertions which do not accord with the opinions of such experts as have no reason for bias. He says that it is "nonsense" to maintain that an all-out nuclear war might put an end to the human race. He also says that it is "incorrect" to suppose such a war would "wipe out our technical civilization." He thinks it unnecessary to support these statements by anything except his personal authorization as the inventor of the H-bomb—a weapon which he apparently considers much less formidable than it is generally thought to be. In fact, no one knows what percentage of the human race, if any, would survive such a war as Dr. Teller has made possible. I hope nobody ever will know. Whatever the percentage may be, it will certainly be much smaller that Dr. Teller pretends. I do not think there is a single disinterested expert who will deny this."[5]

In his article published as "Hostility not only Wicked but Silly" in the *Los Gatos Times* on November 17,[6] Russell examined the feasibility of civilian populations surviving a nuclear attack through the employment of an early warning system:

I find it quite impossible to believe that those who have devised this fantastic palliative can think that it can serve any useful purpose. Let us consider, stage by stage, what would be likely to happen. Imagine the whole population of (say) New York faced with the prospect of almost certain death if they remain on the surface for another twenty-five minutes, and officially advised to get into the shelters during this very short time. Everybody knows the sort of thing that happens when a fire in a theatre causes a stampede. If you compare the number of people in a theatre with the number of people in New York, you may get some idea of the twenty-five-minute stampede which the Authorities recommend. It must be obvious that a very large proportion of those seeking the shelters would be trampled to death, and that the only people who would reach the shelters alive would be males muscularly vigorous and morally ruthless. At an optimistic estimate, one might hope that one percent of the population of New York would reach the shelters undamaged.

On the eve of the Committee of One Hundred's "sit-down" outside the Ministry of Defence, Russell received a letter from his American friend Stephanie May who wrote on 17 February 1961, "I wish I could be with you to join your protest and to move ahead to a sane and disarmed world. Your courage is an inspiration to us all." May enclosed a clipping giving news of the arrest of two American pacifists who had attempted to hitch a raft to a submarine tender which was accompanying a nuclear submarine, the "George Washington," on its voyage to the Polaris Base at Holy Loch in Scotland.[7] The newspaper reported that "the raft, about 12 by 12 feet in size and equipped with a stove and tent, was named Bertrand Russell, after the British philosopher and advocate of nuclear disarmament."

The "sit-down" outside the Ministry of Defence which was planned to coincide with the arrival of the U.S. submarines at Holy Loch, prompted *Newsweek* to discuss the British nuclear disarmament movement in its issue of February 27:

The U.S. has its nuclear submarine boarders and its Committee for a Sane Nuclear Policy...But it is in Britain that the idea of unilateral disarmament has put down its deepest roots. Britain's Campaign for Nuclear Disarmament, the parent body from which Russell's group is a militant offshoot, claims 10 million sympathizers...They have made deep inroads into the powerful trade unions and fired the imagination of British youth...And they have seen their principles adopted by...the British Labour Party last October, despite the all-out opposition of party leader Hugh Gaitskell ...Russell broke away from the parent body last year to form a "Committee of One Hundred" dedicated to awakening the public by illegal action, if necessary; the London demonstration was the first real test of his new policy of civil disobedience. "Make no mistake about it" Russell told *Newsweek*'s Peter Webb last week"...the risk of war by accident is very great. These people at Thule (U.S. early warning station) can't tell the difference between the moon and Russian missiles. The only hope for world disarmament is for Britain to disengage from the Western Alliance and head a group of neutral powers which could draw up a disarmament plan that both East and West could accept without having to lose face."

In an article for the *New Republic* published on April 3 Russell cited references to support his conviction that the Soviet Government was seeking detente with the West. Under the title "Thermonuclear War: Battle of the Experts"[8] Russell reviewed two "statements of policy," *On Thermonuclear War* by Herman Kahn and *The Character of Modern War* by Major General Talenski. In examining the respective arguments of the two authors Russell imagined himself to be "a member of one of the newly emancipated nations" and as a result "was considerably disquieted by the thoughts which the two pronouncements were likely to generate in such a reader." With regard to Herman Kahn Russell argued:

If...those who agree with Mr. Kahn remain in control, thermonuclear wars will succeed each other until there is nobody left to fight them. This is a bleak and cheerless outlook, but it is the best that Mr. Kahn can offer us even by stretching optimism to the very limits of credibility. Nowhere in this long book does he consider the possibility which would prevent a thermonuclear war by the ending of the cold war.

As for Major General Talenski who "expresses Soviet official policy" Russell felt that he was "quite astonishingly different from Mr. Kahn in his outlook and hopes." Contrasting the approach of the two authors, Russell favored Talenski who Russell believed:

> ...does not seek ways of making such lawful destruction "acceptable," but, rather, looks to disarmament agreements to remove from the world the threat of nuclear war...We must, he concludes, "struggle even more stubbornly and consistently for the destruction of all armaments, for the exclusion of war from the life of human society, for peace in the whole world."

Russell gave much of the credit for current Soviet policy to Khrushchev and as a result he felt that continued American opposition to "Khrushchev's hopes for peaceful co-existence" might persuade the Soviet Government to remove their leader and revise their policies. "The danger to mankind" Russell concluded "comes primarily, not from communist countries, but from the military authorities of the U.S."

On June 3, just a few months after his inauguration as 35th President of the U.S., John Kennedy met with Khrushchev in Vienna for talks on the international situation. From Vienna Kennedy went directly to London for talks with the British Government. Russell, in anticipation of Kennedy's visit to Great Britain, wrote an open letter to the president which was left in the care of the American embassy in London. The letter asking Kennedy to "take cognizance, not only of governmental opinion, but also of that very large and rapidly growing section which is opposed to the establishment of a Polaris base," was dated June 2 and signed by Russell on behalf of the Committee of One Hundred. He received no reply although excerpts appeared in the *New York Times* of June 6. Russell, however, continued to be inundated with letters from ordinary Americans; peace organizations, student bodies, professional and trade associations, plied him continuously with requests for his sponsorship, his signature to petitions, his greetings to meetings and conferences and for his presence as a lecturer and debater in America. Russell dealt conscientiously with this illimitable flow of letters despite a full program of nuclear disarmament activities which included regular speaking engagements, recording statements and interviews, and the writing of many articles and letters for the press.

A bad attack of shingles confined him to bed for several weeks but he used this opportunity to complete a new book *Has Man a Future?* in which he developed the arguments begun with *Common Sense and Nuclear Warfare.*[9] The publication of *Has Man a Future?* coincided with the Committee of One Hundred's "Hiroshima Day" demonstrations in London on August 6, which were organized "to remind people of the circumstances of the nuclear bomb at Hiroshima."[10] Russell, who attended the demonstration at the Cenotaph, was later prevented by the police from addressing a mass meeting. Corliss Lamont, who was in Tokyo at the time, commented later in his letter to Russell of August 8 "your great exploits ring round the world" and he enclosed a clipping from the *Mainichi Daily News* of the same date which carried a report datelined August 6, under the headline "Police prevent Earl Russell from speaking":

> London police today prevented Earl (philosopher) Russell from addressing a mass meeting at Hyde Park organized as a sequel to this morning's Whitehall demonstration in observance of Hiroshima Day. Earl Russell was prevented from speaking because he was using a loudspeaker for which special permission is essential. A crowd of several thousand "anti-atom bomb movement" supporters chanted "Shame," and "Leave him alone," as a policeman snatched the loudspeaker (held aloft by a supporter) through which Russell was speaking.

Exactly one month later, the Russells were summoned to appear at the Bow Street court in London to be charged with "inciting the public to civil disobedience."[13] In the meantime the disarmament talks at Geneva ended in disagreement on August 30 and within a few days both the USSR and the USA announced their intention to resume their respective nuclear tests. On September 6, a week before the Russells were due to appear in court, Russell wrote to the U.S. Ambassador in London warning that the resumption of underground tests could "only increase tension and make nuclear war more likely." The U.S. Government had also threatened to resume atmospheric tests if the USSR persisted in its own. On September 12, the Russells appeared at Bow Street Court, refused to be bound over to keep the peace for 12 months, and were sentenced to 2 months imprisonment, commuted to one week each on the grounds of health.

The jailing of the Russells (Bertrand now 89) caused a storm of protest, and letters of support poured in from all over the world and especially from individuals and organizations in America. Twelve philosophy professors from the University of California expressed their "deepest esteem" for the Russells' "moral courage and integrity" and described Russell's life as "an inspiring symbol of the philosophical calling in our time."[12]

Women for Legislative Action, an organization of 600 women in Southern California "deplored" the imprisonment while stating that Russell's ideas and leadership could "never be restrained within prison walls."[13] Otto Nathan, the trustee of the Estate of Albert Einstein, wrote from New York:

I am one of the many millions throughout the world whose respect and admiration for you, if such was possible, further increased in the last few weeks...How Einstein would have admired and appreciated the forthrightness and integrity of your position.[14]

Congressman James Fulton wrote from Pittsburgh, Pennsylvania:

I am writing to compliment you on your firmness in the principles in which you believe. It is refreshing in this world today to find people willing to stand up to public opposition and adhere to peaceful proposals and solutions regardless of the public clamor at the time. In my own small way, at the time of many patriotic speeches given on the floor of the House of Representatives at the time of the Berlin Crisis, I gave a speech calling for moderation, patience and understanding, which was not received with great acclaim.

I was shocked that Britain, of all places, would justify a sentence for refusing to keep the peace upon citizens who are publicly advocating peaceful means and peaceful settlements. The comment in the London Dispatch to our U.S. papers was humorous when the prosecutor, John Matthew, told Judge Bertram Reece that the action was brought "to *prevent* deliberate breaking of the laws." I congratulate you on refusing to state that you should be content to be bound to enter into the recognizance to keep the peace and be of good behavior for 12 months. Under the circumstances, this was a ridiculous request.[15]

From prison, Russell issued a statement which was read to a massive nuclear disarmament demonstration at Trafalgar Square in London on September 17:

At any moment of any day the slightest miscalculation can bring nuclear war. Rockets are poised at a few minutes' notice. H-bombers are continually in the air, radar is totally unreliable. Radioactivity kills and maims our children. War is always imminent.

To use the vast scheme of mass murder which is being prepared, nominally for our protection, but in fact for universal extermination, is a horror and an abomination. We call upon people everywhere to rise against this monstrous tyranny.

We call upon scientists to refuse work on nuclear weapons. We call upon workers to "black" (boycott) all work connected with them and to use their industrial strength in the struggle for life. We will not tolerate the incineration of human beings because governments are occupied with idiotic matters of prestige.[16]

Once released from prison Russell immediately plunged back into his activities. He also replied to his many supporters and well wishers. He wrote to James Fulton on 30 December 1961:

I am very grateful to you for your letter, and I wish to apologise sincerely for the long delay in replying to it, but I have been overwhelmed with correspondence since my release from prison. At this moment the planet is covered with rocket bases on a hair trigger. H-bombers patrol continuously and the radar on which they rely cannot distinguish a goose from a missile. In the light of this, nuclear war is a matter of statistical certainty. I feel there is almost nothing I can do which can compare with the enormity of the evil facing men today.

In Britain we are organising a resistance movement which we hope will be international and co-ordinated as such. The Committee of One Hundred encourages people to resist through systematically obstructing the entire technology of extermination. I have been very much encouraged by your letter and your interest and I am enclosing some recent literature which I hope you will find pertinent.

Russell was profoundly alarmed by the breakdown of the moratorium on nuclear testing and by what he felt to be a growing bellicosity in America. He intensified his efforts to help organize and publicize civil disobedience. On 29 October 1961 fresh from his ordeal in Brixton prison he addressed a Committee of One Hundred demonstration in Trafalgar Square. Quoting from a policy statement of the U.S. Air Force Association which he described to his audience as "the most terrifying document that I have ever read"[17] Russell argued his view that there was a "rapidly growing feeling in America in favour of a nuclear war in the very near future."[18] Russell believed that the American Government was coming under increasing pressure and influence from the armament lobby whose aims, he declared, were embodied in the document from which he quoted:

It begins by stating that preservation of the *status quo* is not adequate as a national goal. I quote: "Freedom must bury Communism or be buried by Communism. Complete eradication of the Soviet System must be our national goal, our obligation to all free people, our promise of hope to all who are not free." It is a curious hope that is being promised, since it can only be realised in heaven, for the only "promise" that the West can hope to fulfill is the promise to turn Eastern populations into corpses. The noble patriots who make this pronouncement omit to mention that Western populations also will be exterminated. "We are determined" they say, "to back our words with action even at the risk of war. We seek not merely to preserve our freedoms, but to extend them." The word "freedom" which is a favorite word of Western warmongers, has to be understood in a somewhat peculiar sense. It means freedom for warmongers and prison for those who oppose them....This ferocious document, which amounts to a sentence of death on the human race, does not consist of the idle vapourings of acknowledged cranks. On the contrary, it represents the enormous economic power of the armament industry, which is re-enforced in the public mind by the cleverly instilled fear that disarmament would bring a new depression....the armament firms exploit patriotism and anti-communism as means of transferring the taxpayers' money into their own pockets. Ruthlessly, and probably consciously, they are leading the world towards disaster."[19]

Russell then repeated his belief that "Britain would be safer as a neutral" outside NATO, without American bases and without the "illusory protection of the American bomb."[20] He drew attention to the gathering support for Committees of 100 which were being set up in other countries and called upon the meeting to help build up a "great worldwide mass movement of people demanding the abandonment of nuclear weapons, the abandonment of war as a means of settling disputes."[21]

Evidence of the international support for the aims of the Committee of 100 Movement was contained daily in Russell's mailbox. The activities of the Committee of 100: their sit-downs at American air bases, the prosecution of 5 of their leaders under the Official Secrets Act, and Russell himself braving a snowstorm to address a mass meeting in Trafalgar Square on 26 February 1962, caused world-wide press attention and inspired the growing movement for nuclear disarmament, particularly in America.

Norman R. Lee, Chairman of the Central New York Committee of 100 wrote to Russell on 27 February 1962, "You are the individual who has most influenced my thinking." Explaining the problems encountered in propagandizing nuclear disarmament in New York, Lee appealed for a message from Russell to boost membership of his organization which he assured Russell was "anxious to follow your leadership; to take actions as you direct."

Russell replied on March 18 enclosing a message of support and "conscious of the difficulties under which you must work" suggested ways and means by which the New York Central Committee of 100 could carry their protest to a wider public.

The Reed Students for Peace from Reed College in Oregon were anxious to secure Russell's advice and support for the plan to send a boat "preferably with an international crew into the new testing ground for American bombs on the British owned Christmas Island.'" In their letter of March 7 the Reed students anticipated that Russell "as one of the leaders of the peace movement in the Western World" might be able to help them "in finding some boats that we might be able to use for this purpose." Frustrated by the lack of governmental response to all orthodox and legal efforts for peace and disarmament they assured Russell that "if we must break laws and go to jail in order to save our lives and the lives of most of the world's population we are willing." Although unable to give material assistance Russell replied with his fullest support on March 17.

A young group of nuclear disarmers in Milwaukee informed Russell of President Kennedy's impending visit to their city and asked Russell for his advice on the most effective way of informing President Kennedy of their views.[22] "The members of our group, who are from fifteen to eighteen years of age, anxiously await your advice on holding such a demonstration. In view of your activities and concern with youth, we felt it proper to beseech you for guidance in this matter." Russell replied on 19 April 1962.

I should at once say that I cannot suggest any form of demonstration which one can guarantee will not lead to arrest. However, I would suggest that you consider picketing the entrance to the party headquarters, or the route along which Kennedy will travel, with posters and placards explaining your views. You could also have a leaflet printed at a fairly small cost, and distribute it among the crowd, or throw it into the president's path. It would seem to me that there are three considerations to bear in mind in order that your protest may be as effective as possible. In the first place, the incident that a number of young people are utterly opposed to American atmospheric testing should be firmly imprinted in Kennedy's mind. Secondly, you should ensure by previously contacting the press that as much publicity for your action in obtained as possible. Thirdly, as many people as are there should clearly see your physical presence, as distortion in the press will enable many readers to ignore the real nature of your action, whereas it is difficult (or at least *more* difficult) for people to distort what they themselves see.[23]

The U.S. government's intention to resume atmospheric testing had been announced by President Kennedy during the first week of March 1962 when it became apparent that the then current round of disarmament talks at the Geneva Conference were proving unproductive. Cyrus Eaton, the sponsor of the Pugwash movement, immediately cabled Russell on March 4:

...The United States has merely been maneuvering at Geneva with no intention of agreeing to a Test Ban. Kennedy's speech Friday evening confirms that additional nuclear tests in the atmosphere has always been a policy of the American Government! Deceit and dis-simulation have been the chief characteristics of our negotiations with the Soviets. Arthur Dean, the Wall Street lawyer who now heads American nuclear negotiations is a leading expert in hypocrisy and double talk.

Quoting extracts from Kennedy's speech to illustrate his contention, Eaton appealed to Russell:

Only your brilliant pen and eloquent voice can call the world's atten-tion to the shallow insincerity of the Kennedy speech and American policy.

Russell replied to Eaton on March 17 assuring him that he had been "spending every spare moment on the preparation of massive demonstra-tions in protest against the resumption of atmospheric tests by the United States."

Russell had in fact already delivered a personal protest to the Ameri-can Embassy and on March 24 led a Committee of 100 "occupation" of Parliament Square which disrupted traffic in the area for two hours. Just three days before the U.S. commenced its series of tests in the Pacific Russell cabled various leaders of neutral nations asking them to help prevent the tests by sending ships into the test area.[24] Although none of those contacted were prepared or able to send vessels, Nkrumah, Tito, Nehru and Sukarno responded warmly to Russell's request and expressed support for his idea. Following the resumption of American atmospheric tests on April 25 and in the weeks leading up to his 90th birthday on May 18, Russell received many tributes from America.

Corliss Lamont sent a further donation of $1000 towards the work of the Committee of 100 and commented in his letter of May 1:

Since the renewal of nuclear atmospheric testing by the Kennedy administration, there have been good stories in the New York City press about the demonstrations you and the Committee of 100 have been leading in Great Britain. It is splendid that your Committee has continued this invaluable work...

Linus Pauling wrote on May 10:

We suffer year after year, from the onslaughts of a partially hostile environment—cosmic rays, radiation from radio-active substances, the disrupting effect on molecules of thermal agitation, harmful sub-stances that are added to our foods—and our tissues suffer a corresponding deterioration. You have shown that the brain—at any rate, *one* brain, one of the most extraordinary in the world—has an astounding resistance to these onslaughts.

I congratulate you on the great contributions that you have made to the world over a period of more than three score years. The greatest of all contributions to world sanity and world peace. It may well be that if any one man deserves the credit for having saved the world from nuclear destruction, you are that man.

The philosopher Rudolf Carnap wrote from the University of California on May 12:

I am in complete agreement with the aims for which you are fighting at present...By nature I am inclined to turn away from the insane quarrels of parties and governments...But at present, when the survival of civilization is at stake, I realise that it is necessary to at least take a stand...[25]

Russell replied to Carnap on June 21:

...in this country we are having a much greater success than seems evident in the United States, although it is obvious that protest in the United States requires far greater courage and dedication than its equivalent here. Nonetheless, I am hopeful that the effect of our minority resistance may grow and find a co-ordinated international expression.[26]

Russell then informed Carnap of the Committee of 100's intention to demonstrate on September 9 at the Air Ministry in Whitehall and that the demonstration would involve civil disobedience. "I shall be taking part in the physical demonstration itself," Russell continued and commented "I believe that men are starved for an answer to the terror and that they will respond if this sense of helplessness can be overcome."

Russell and the Committee of 100 hoped to secure massive support for their September demonstration. To stress the importance of the demonstration and the need for a substantial turnout the Committee undertook to secure pledges of participation from at least 7000 people as a condition for going ahead. Because he was anxious to establish the co-ordinated and international character of the Committee of 100's work Russell set about inviting various international figures to take part in the demonstration. Russell wrote to Linus Pauling on June 26 that it was his hope that "people such as Dolci, Schweitzer and Sartre may participate and that "if it is possible for you to join me and to be at my side at this demonstration, I should be very happy." Although Pauling agreed to come to England to attend the demonstration, some of the 7000 pledges hoped for by the Committee of 100 failed to materialize and the demonstration was consequently called off.

Despite Russell's "great sympathy with the early aims and actions of the Committee"[27] and despite his conviction that mass civil disobedience was "one of the most effective ways of attacking present international policies,"[28] he was becoming increasingly skeptical of the effectiveness of the Committee of 100 in the campaign against nuclear armaments. The need to abandon the September demonstration and the mounting disputes within the ranks of the Committee itself reinforced his belief that the "Committee was disintegrating and had outlived its usefulness."[29]

Russell's activities with the Committee of 100 continued to create widespread interest in America. The transmission throughout the U.S. of a TV interview of Russell by David Susskind in which Russell argued the case for civil disobedience as a way to achieve nuclear disarmament brought a large response from American viewers.[30] Letters of support for Russell's views poured in from all over the U.S. There were also many appeals for Russell's intervention on behalf of Americans who were in prison or facing trial because of their disarmament and other peace activities. One such appeal came on behalf of Don Martin who, in the course of a civil disobedience demonstration, had entered a restricted government area. Martin had already served one year of a six year sentence. Russell wrote on June 26 to the *New York Times* which published the letter on August 30 under the title "Russell Pleads for Pacifist":

I am often told that Americans have a high opinion of my attempts to arouse people to an awareness of the imminent danger of nuclear annihilation. If this is in fact the case then perhaps Americans will join me in condemning the sentence of six year's imprisonment imposed on a 21 year old student because of his participation in a demonstration of civil disobedience in your country. I should like to remind you that if I were an American, I should only do exactly as he has done and I should do it often.

If freedom, as you understand it, means freedom for those who agree with you and six years for those who do not, then perhaps you will begin to understand why we who are not possessed of fantical interest in a conflict which could only lead to nuclear annihilation, find your behaviour on a par with the Russians.

I hope that Don Martin will be released, having served one year, and that you will find another way of saving conscience if not face.

Russell also wrote to President Kennedy on July 1 describing Don Martin as "a man of conscience who believes, with me, that hydrogen missiles are weapons of genocide and cannot be acquiesced in." Russell appealed to Kennedy to "consider the meaning of six years' imprisonment for a person aged twenty and to consider the nature of civil liberty if such a sentence is possible for such an offence."

Russell once again raised the issue of civil liberty when in July 1962 he cabled Attorney General Robert Kennedy on behalf of William Worthy, a young black journalist. Worthy, who was a well-known contributor to the Baltimore *Afro-American* had been indicted under the McCarran-Walter Immigration Act for re-entering the U.S. after visiting Cuba without a passport. Passport requirements had been in effect since January 1961 when the U.S. had severed diplomatic relations with Cuba owing to its new revolutionary government. Russell protested that "Restrictions on William Worthy and his indictment under the McCarran Act evidence the disappearance of your civil liberties and disgrace America in the eyes of reasonable men. I urge you to quash the indictment."

When the campaign on behalf of Worthy revealed that more than 200 white U.S. citizens had visited Cuba since the imposition of the travel ban, and returned to the U.S. without interference by the U.S. government, there was widespread domestic and international protest. It became clear that the prosecution of Worthy resulted more from his favorable reports about the situation in Cuba, and in particular his praise of the steps taken against racial discrimination by the Castro government, than from any considerations of the law. In the face of this protest Worthy was sentenced to three months imprisonment, although it had been expected that he would receive the maximum possible sentence of five years.

The Worthy affair was soon overtaken by the events of the Cuban crisis in October 1962. It was against the background of this crisis that Russell issued a statement published in the *New York Herald Tribune* of 29 September 1963, supporting Worthy in his appeal against his sentence:

...The United States Government has systematically bullied a smaller nation, namely Cuba, and has stuck at nothing to undermine, intimidate and destroy its Government. One of the consequences of so unjustifiably aggressive a policy is the hiding of the truth about the Government of Cuba, its policies, its philosophy and its popularity.

William Worthy is a spokesman for the right to question authority and the right to unbiased knowledge about political events. Despite every intimidation he has risked his freedom by travelling to Cuba and by reporting fairly on Cuba and world opinion.

I am appalled that for exercising his elementary democratic rights and for fulfilling his moral duty as a citizen and journalist, he now faces a sentence of three months. On the right to inform Americans accurately and to use liberty to challenge orthodoxy will rest the prospect for survival in this dark age.

Footnotes

1. Linus Pauling, *No More War* (Victor Gollancz, London, 1958) p. 160.
2. B. Russell *Autobiography* Vol. 3, (London, 1969) p. 109 (New York, 1969), p. 148.
3. *Ibid.*, p. 110; p. 149.
4. Clarke to Russell, 12 October 1960, and 2 November 1960.
5. Published 16 November 1960.
6. Written 9 March 1960 for WDET broadcasting station of Wayne State University, Detroit.
7. Unidentified and undated.
8. See below, pp. 346-9.
9. B. Russell, *Has Man A Future?* (London, 1961) (New York, 1962).
10. B. Russell, *Autobiography* Vol. 3, p. 114; p. 156.
11. *Ibid.*, p. 115; p. 157.
12. Cable dated 14 September 1961. The signatories were: Rudolf Carnap, Montgomery Furth, Donald Calaish, Abraham Kaplan, Douglas Long, Hans Mayerhoff, Richard Montague, Herbert Morris, Donald Piatt, J. Wesley Robson, Patrick J. Wilson, Robert Yost.
13. Letter of 8 October 1961.
14. Nathan to Russell, 13 October 1961.
15. Fulton to Russell, 17 October 1961.
16. *Daily Telegraph* 18 September 1961, reprinted in *I.F. Stone's Weekly* 25 September 1961.
17. B. Russell, *Autobiography* Vol. 3, p. 147; p. 209.
18. *Ibid.*
19. *Ibid.*, pp. 147-8; pp. 209-10.
20. *Ibid.*, p. 148; pp. 210-11.
21. *Ibid.*, p. 149; p. 212.
22. B. Feinberg and R. Kasrils (eds.) *Dear Bertrand Russell* (London, 1969) pp. 95-6 (Houghton Mifflin, Boston, 1969) p. 62.
23. *Ibid.*, p. 96; pp. 62-3.
24. Text of cable published *The Observer*, 22 April 1962.
25. B. Russell, *Autobiography* Vol. 3, p. 132; p. 182.
26. *Ibid.*, pp. 132-3; p. 184.

27. *Ibid.*

28. *Ibid.*, p. 125; p. 171.

29. *Ibid.*, p. 122; p. 167.

30. A two hour interview first broadcast on "Open End" in New York on 10 June 1962; reported in *New York Times*, 11 June 1962 and *Newsweek*, 18 June 1962.

12 Cuban Crisis

The persecution of William Worthy was a clear reflection of the official U.S. attitude to the newly established revolutionary government in Cuba. American hostility had been mounting ever since the Castro-led rebellion had overturned the Batista dictatorship in 1959 and succeeded in removing Cuba from the orbit of American big business interests. Commenting on President Kennedy's promise to the American people that he would restore freedom to Cuba, Russell argued:

It must be understood that he means freedom for the children (of Cuba) to die from hookworm and for the rest of the population to be subject to a ruthless and brutal government of corrupt dictators who will provide riches for inhabitants of the U.S. and a very few of Cuba.[1]

After the abortive Bay of Pigs invasion by U.S.-supported Cuban emigres in April 1961, the situation continued to deteriorate with the growing likelihood of direct American intervention.

Defending Cuba's sovereignty, and fearful that U.S. provocation lead to a nuclear confrontation, Russell appealed to the American government and people in February 1962:

The hysteria that has been created in the United States about the Cuban Revolution is a grave danger to the peace of the world. Those responsible for creating this psychosis should carefully consider if they will always be able to control it. The United States has already sponsored an invasion of Cuba, which was defeated because the vast majority of Cuban people quite clearly supported the government of Dr. Fidel Castro. It seems possible that the United States is contemplating a further attempt to force upon the Cuban people a regime which is against its own wishes.

146

No state has the right to dictate to Cuba, or to any other nation, how she is to run her own affairs. At long last Cuba, after half a century of American domination, is able to build houses and schools, to stimulate education and culture, to abolish poverty and disease and human misery. The Cuban revolution deserves hope and encouragement, not blind hostility.

Vast corporations such as United Fruit are afraid of losing a profitable empire in Latin America. The military-industrial complex needs continual armament and preparation for war if it is to retain its position and power and profits. These forces in the United States, with their paid liars—be they scientists or industrialists or Congressmen—have created a pathological hatred of the Cuban Revolution which is a grave threat to the independence of Cuba, and a grave threat to the peace of the world.

I appeal to the Government of the United States to allow Cuba to solve her own problems without interference. I appeal to the people of the United States to ignore the hysterical speeches of their leaders. I appeal to the Governments and Peoples of Latin America to uncompromisingly reject any measures against the Cuban revolution. Cuba is a sovereign and independent nation, with the inalienable right to solve her own problems as she pleases.

United States action against Cuba could lead to a nuclear war. Such a war would destroy civilisation, and probably the whole human race. Let us remember our humanity, and forget the rest.[2]

In the face of America's strenuous efforts to overthrow their government, the Cubans turned to the Soviet Union for aid and assistance. When the U.S. placed an embargo on Cuban sugar the Soviet Union agreed to purchase the crop. When Cuba sought arms with which to defend itself against threatened invasion the Soviet Union agreed to provide the arms. The U.S. was enraged by what was termed "Soviet interference" while Russell commented that Castro's "overtures to communism are the effect and not the cause of American hostility."[3]

Russell was in contact with the Cuban Ambassador in Britain who hastened to inform him towards the end of August of his government's expectation of an imminent invasion and global crisis since war-fever in the U.S. was at an unparalleled height. Russell promised to assist in whatever way he could and issued a statement to *The Guardian* expressing his fears and seeking to caution both the United States and the Soviet Union.

The situation of Cuba involves a serious threat to the peace of the world. The Cubans have every right to the government they wish and if it is a Communist government it in no way justifies American intervention. If the United States invades Cuba it may provoke dangerous warlike action from the Soviet Union. If Russia supplies arms and troops to Cuba the danger of unwise and warlike action by the Americans will be increased with the imminent risk of world war. The situation demands a definite undertaking by the government of the United States not to invade Cuba and by the Soviet Union not to give armed support to Cuba. Precipitate action by either may provoke world wide disaster.[4]

Russell's statement was not published by *The Guardian*, yet its warnings could not have been more crucial nor more timely. In the ensuing weeks the crisis mounted with alarming rapidity and fears of the "imminent risk of world war" materialized.

In his subsequent account of the events of the crisis, *Unarmed Victory*, Russell wrote:

During the days of October 24 and 25, those who had knowledge and imagination went through an anxious time. It seemed probable that, at any minute, war between America and Russia would break out and would involve, in all likelihood, the extinction of the human race.[5]

The crisis had erupted on October 22 when President Kennedy imposed a blockade on Cuba and threatened the Soviet Union with nuclear annihilation if certain conditions were not met, or if the Soviet Union resorted to reprisal actions anywhere else in the world. Kennedy declared that any ship trading with Cuba would have to submit to being boarded and searched or be sunk. Specified arms supplies would not be allowed through the blockade. Kennedy made the dramatic revelation that Soviet nuclear missiles had been "discovered" on the Island and that unless these were dismantled forthwith the U.S. would wage war in order to remove the threat to its security.

On the eve of Kennedy's expected announcement Russell had urged his fellow countrymen to "come out in the streets of your country and demonstrate our demand to live and let live" should there be any suggestion of war "or of an action calculated to provoke war."[6]

Russell found that Kennedy's speech brought "humanity to the edge of nuclear death."[7] According to him the U.S. president had "arrogated to himself the right to threaten the Soviet Union publicly with nuclear destruction unless the Soviet Union bowed to American will."[8] Russell felt that the question of Soviet missiles in Cuba "was infinitely less important than the action taken by the President, for there were missiles round the world, all of them reprehensible, but it was the combination of military blockade and the threat of nuclear war which brought mankind to utmost peril."[9]

The whole world tensed for the expected confrontation as Soviet ships—already on the high seas—sailed towards the Caribbean where the U.S. blockade awaited them. Russell found that "never before in the course of a long life have I experienced anything comparable to the tense anxiety of those crucial hours....Hour by hour headlines appeared in the Press such as those in the *Daily Sketch* of October 25: "Khrushchev orders 'Sail on—or sink' "....Hour by hour...came news of war preparations in America...hour by hour nothing happened to stem the impending destruction of mankind."[10] The crisis had proceeded so swiftly that the "usual forces making for conciliation"—the United Nations, neutral countries, peace organizations—"had no time to act,"[11] and Russell "with little hope of success" decided to appeal directly to the heads of states involved.

On October 25 he cabled Kennedy immediately after the U.S. President's speech:

> Your actions desperate. Threat to human survival. No conceivable justification. Civilized man condemns it. We will not have mass murder. Ultimatums mean war. I do not speak for power but plead for civilised man. End this madness.[12]

At the same time he appealed to Khrushchev:

> I appeal to you not to be provoked by the unjustifiable action of the United States in Cuba. The world will support caution. Urge condemnation to be sought through United Nations. Precipitous action could mean annihilation for mankind.[13]

Russell also urged the British Prime Minister "to prevent American madness from bringing on nuclear war,"[14] and exhorted UN Secretary General U Thant to condemn the U.S. action.

The Committee of 100 were geared to demonstrate against any sign of brinkmanship, and Russell in support of their actions issued a statement to the press at the same time as he was busy cabling the heads of state:

> Kennedy's speech brings humanity to the edge of nuclear death. Tonight people are in the streets. All who wish to survive must protest now. Tomorrow, the Committee of 100 will prepare mass action at the American Embassy in Grosvenor Square at 8 p.m. I appeal to every sane man and woman to join it.[15]

Recognizing that the Press had an important role to play at this crucial hour, when acceleration of events would in all likelihood outrun public knowledge, Russell made a special plea to the news media:

> I appeal to the press of this country to allow the people to know of the grave danger facing mankind and to urge people to demonstrate and to act against death, and on behalf of human survival.[16]

On the 24th, with huge crowds protesting outside the American Embassy in London, Russell issued an urgent leaflet to the British public:

YOU ARE TO DIE
Not in the course of nature, but within a few weeks. And not you alone, but your family, your friends, and all the inhabitants of Britain, together with many hundreds of millions of innocent people elsewhere.

WHY?
Because rich Americans dislike the government that Cubans prefer, and have used part of their wealth to spread lies about it.

WHAT CAN YOU DO?
You can go out into the street and into the market place proclaiming: Do not yield to ferocious and insane murderers. Do not imagine that it is your duty to die when your Prime Minister and the President of the United States tell you to do so. Remember rather your duty to your family, your friends, your country, the world you live in, and that future world which, if you so choose, may be glorious, happy and free.

AND REMEMBER
CONFORMITY MEANS DEATH—ONLY PROTEST GIVES A HOPE OF LIFE.[17]

The press had been either ignoring or greatly abridging Russell's numerous messages and appeals but during the afternoon of the 24th he was suddenly besieged by the media as news came through of a positive response to his efforts at mediation on the part of Premier Khrushchev. As Russell laconically observed: "The Press...suddenly discovered that I had been rather concerned about the crisis in Cuba."[18]

Khrushchev had publicized through the Soviet news agency, Tass, a long letter in reply to Russell's cable.[19] In it he expressed "sincere gratitude" for the concern Russell had displayed "in connection with the aggressive actions of the United States." Russell found that the letter brought a "ray of hope" in Khrushchev's assurances that "the Soviet Government will not take any reckless decisions...will do everything to prevent war from breaking out."[20] Khrushchev called on the U.S. government to "display reserve and stay the execution of its piratical threats" and proposed "a top level meeting...to remove the danger of unleashing a thermonuclear war."[21]

The New York Herald Tribune of October 25 in common with most important dailies gave the initiative major prominence, reporting under the front-page banner headline: "Khrushchev calls for Summit Meeting with Kennedy—He Replies to Lord Russell." In its account of Khrushchev's response to Russell the newspaper carried the comment: "Tass was in such a rush to get Mr. Khrushchev's words on the record that it published them long before Lord Russell could have received the letter. It was clear therefore that Mr. Khrushchev was anxious that his words have immediate impact on world opinion."

Khrushchev had made it clear that the Soviet Union would not give way "if the American government should carry out the program of piratic actions outlined by it,"[22] and Russell therefore promptly cabled him:

Thank you for your heartening reply. I congratulate you on your courageous stand for sanity. I hope you will hold back ships in Cuban waters long enough to secure American agreement to your proposal. Whole world will bless you if you succeed in averting war. If there is anything I can possibly do please let me know.[23]

As a result of these developments Russell again cabled Kennedy:

I urge you most strongly to make a conciliatory reply to Khrushchev's vital overture and avoid clash with Russian ships long enough to make meeting and negotiations possible. After shots have been exchanged it will probably be too late. I appeal to you to meet Khrushchev. If there is anything I can do please let me know.[24]

The first Soviet ships to enter the blockade area permitted the Americans to board and search them. These did not carry any arms shipments and were allowed to sail on, but it was known that other ships which were carrying arms were within an hour's distance of the blockade

This was the crucial hour and in Russell's words:

The world waited breathlessly in expectation of the fatal news that Russian and American ships had met and shots had been exchanged. No such news came. And at last it was learnt that Khrushchev had ordered some ships to turn away and others to submit to American inspection. It was this decision of Khrushchev's which made the preservation of peace possible. It was a unilateral act and a very brave

"The American action in Cuba is unqualifiably mad...It might be interesting to speculate on American reaction to spy-planes sent by Cuba over Washington. But what of the actual complaint that America makes? Does she think that nuclear submarines are acceptable but stationary bases are not? Does she think that Polaris submarines in the Holy Loch are 'defensive' and not 'aggressive?' And Turkey? And Siam?"

act, since it exposed him to the charge of yielding to threats...For this magnanimous act he deserves the gratitude of the world.

With the news that Soviet ships had been ordered to alter course it was realized that immediate disaster had been avoided, although this only meant that temporary respite had been gained since America's ultimatum with regard to the missile sites kept the crisis at danger point.

Russell hastened to issue the following press statement:

Premier Khrushchev is personally responsible for the avoidance of a war of nuclear devastation. He has acted with the greatest restraint in a crisis of the first magnitude.

He has carried out every letter of the promise contained in his message to me. He promised to do nothing rash and nothing which would risk conflict and twelve Russian ships turned back from their destination at Cuba. He has stopped all further shipments. This leaves Cuba blockaded. Mr. Khrushchev's desperately important moderation makes it incumbent upon President Kennedy to accept his offer to meet and discuss outstanding issues at the highest level. The blockade violates international law. It is illegal. It is immoral. If the blockade is defensible when applied to Cuba then it is just as applicable to Great Britain. America should consider the war of 1812. If nuclear bases are intolerable in Cuba they are intolerable everywhere. This is the heart of what I have been saying to the British people for the length of our campaign for nuclear disarmament. Nuclear bases threaten the peace of all. Now is the moment for us to realise that we have been on the very edge of the end of human life on our planet. Mr. Khrushchev's offer to meet and discuss the source of conflict must be supported by every sane man and woman.[26]

Russell's statement was reported out of context and in such a way as to suggest he supported the presence of missiles in Cuba. In a message to the Committee of 100 which had been organizing demonstrations outside the American Embassy, he declared:

152

"As for the voice of Britain as part of NATO we have again seen that if America were to declare the planet flat and the Tories a host of baboons, the Prime Minister would spend fortunes to persuade us all that gaping primates were a grand species, especially fitted for the new and adventurous conditions provided by the flat earth we all have desired since the Americans told us to do so."

During the past week we have been brought to the very edge of extinction. The American action in Cuba is unqualifiably mad. If missile bases are intolerable in Cuba, they are intolerable in Great Britain, and if a blockade which amounts to war can be justified for Cuba, then Khrushchev, by the same argument, should blockade Great Britain. Let us consider American justification. They say offensive missiles are in Cuba. This may or may not be true. Certainly their spy-photographs are indicative of nothing in themselves. It might be interesting to speculate on American reaction to spy-planes sent by Cuba over Washington. But what of the actual complaint America makes? Does she think that nuclear submarines are acceptable but stationary bases are not? Does she think that Polaris submarines in the Holy Loch are "defensive" and not "aggressive"? And Turkey? and Siam?[27]

The British Government had given the U.S. unqualified support. Denouncing the Soviet Union as "untrustworthy," Lord Home, Britain's Foreign Minister, characterized the placing of missiles in Cuban hands as "calculated double-dealing"[28] and condemned the Soviet Union for upsetting the balance of miltary power. Russell attacked the position of the British Government in trenchant style:

The double-dealing of which Lord Home speaks is a fitting description of American double-thinking and the double standard of Macmillan's so-called sovereign government...As for the voice of Britain as part of NATO we have again seen that if America were to declare the planet flat and the Tories a host of baboons, the Prime Minister would spend fortunes to persuade us all that gaping primates were a grand species, especially fitted for the new and adventurous conditions provided by the flat earth we all have desired since the Americans told us to do so.[29]

On October 25, Russell finally received a reply to his earlier communique to Kennedy, who cabled back:[30]

I am in receipt of your telegrams. We are currently discussing the matter in the United Nations. While your messages are critical of the United States, they make no mention of your concern for the introduction of secret Soviet missiles into Cuba. I think your attention might well be directed to the burglars rather than those who have caught the burglars.[30]

Russell, who "could understand the hysteria that swept over the U.S."[31] upon hearing of Soviet missiles in Cuba because the U.S. had not previously known "powerful enemies upon its borders,"[32] replied to Kennedy at once:

Thank you for your reply to my cables. I understand your anxiety about nuclear missiles. My point is that a blockade which threatens the sinking of Soviet ships brings mankind to the edge of annihilation. I beg you not to invade Cuba or to risk nuclear war. Could you accept United Nations inspection of bases and offer bases in Turkey in exchange?

The removal of any bases from the Russian perimeter would immensely strengthen America's stand on behalf of peace and would bring a comparable Soviet response.

I am appealing to Dr. Castro to accept United Nations inspection in exchange for your solemn pledge that Cuba will not be invaded by the United States. It is in your hands to transform a situation of grave crisis into one of immense hope. Peaceful initiative from you now would bring the world's gratitude.[33]

Russell felt that the whole point of the Cuban affair was to avoid war whatever the provocation. As to President Kennedy's remark about "burglars" which was widely publicized in the press ("Behold the Burglars Kennedy Tells Russell" reported the *Washington Evening Star*) Russell has written:

Nobody could accuse the Cubans of being burglars, since they had not left their own island. As for the Russians, they came at the invitation of the Cubans and were no more burglars than are the American forces in Britain and Western Europe. But in view of the repeated American threats of invasion of Cuba, the Americans were at least contemplating "burglary."[34]

In view of the American government's threat to wage war unless Soviet missiles were immediately withdrawn from Cuba, Russell cabled Khrushchev, who in his opinion "seemed to have a firmer grip of the terrible issues at stake than was held in the U.S."

"Stripped of diplomatic verbiage, the position of the U.S. government is this: 'unless everybody everywhere does exactly what we wish, we'll exterminate the human race'...I think, though with great reluctance, that sane people ought to yield as far as is necessary to avoid catastrophe. The end of the human race would be definitive, whereas American insanity may be temporary."

May I humbly appeal for your further help in lowering the temperature despite the worsening situation. Your continued forbearance is our great hope. With my high regard and sincere thanks.

On the same day, October 26, Russell sent the following cable to Dr. Castro:

I feel great compassion for yourself and for the beleaguered people of Cuba. I appeal to you with all my heart to allow the United Nations inspection of Cuba, and to seek United Nations protection. Such a gesture from you is not required by international law. It would give mankind a reprieve from certain conflicts and make survival possible.

To defend Cuba against American invasion can now mean only the annihilation of the whole human race. I ask you humbly to accept the unwarranted American demands regarding supposed missiles. This would remove the pretext for invasion. The world would rise to support you in thankfulness.

I beg you for the sake of humanity to accept dismantling of any missiles, even if only defensive, in exchange for a solemn pledge that Cuba will not be invaded.[36]

Castro was quite prepared to accept UN mediation, and agreed to UN inspections of Cuba as long as the U.S. agreed to UN inspection of American invasion centers in Florida and Georgia. This did not appeal to Kennedy and neither did the Soviet suggestion of trading a disbandment of U.S. bases in Turkey as a *quid pro quo* for their dismantling of the missiles in Cuba. An impasse was again reached with Russell observing that "the only hope for mankind was for one of the nations involved in the dispute to give way."[37] He wrote in *Unarmed Victory*:

...I believe it is quite possible for people with various religions and people with various economic and political systems to live together in this world. At this juncture of history it appeared to me that not my

155

own "Free World" but only the Communists involved in the dispute understood the significance and probable consequences of their actions.[38]

The U.S. refused to respond to the Soviet and Cuban offers and it seemed that a clash between the two great powers was now inevitable unless someone backed down. In desperation Russell cabled Castro and Khrushchev on October 28. He appealed to Dr. Castro as follows:

In the light of America's total and dangerous unwillingness to respond to moderation, could you make a great gesture for humanity and agree to dismantle the bases? The fate of mankind rests with your decision...[39]

Russell sent a lengthy cable to Premier Khrushchev:

The U.S. rejection of your proposals to trade Soviet installations in Cuba against NATO installations in Turkey is totally unjustifiable and is a sign of insane paranoia. Stripped of diplomatic verbiage, the position of the U.S. government is this: "unless everybody everywhere does exactly what we wish, we'll exterminate the human race." They have the power to do this and it seems they also have the will. What are sane people to do in view of this armed madness?

I think, though with great reluctance, that sane people ought to yield as far as is necessary to avoid catastrophe. The end of the human race would be definitive, whereas American insanity may be temporary. It seems to me, therefore, that you ought to dismantle Soviet installations in Cuba under the guarantee of inspection by UNO demanding only, in return, that when UNO gives the necessary guarantee, the American blockade of Cuba should be lifted. I think it should be made evident to world public opinion that this action is only taken in response to a kind of blackmail which is neither sane nor morally justifiable...[40]

Later that day came the dramatic news that the Soviet Union had offered to dismantle the missiles in Cuba and comply with American demands, on the understanding that the USA would respect the sovereignty of Cuba. According to Russell: "Khrushchev had offered salvation to mankind. The relief was overwhelming."[41] As a result he issued the following press statement:

...I cannot praise sufficiently the sanity and magnanimity, the willingness to do all required to solve this overwhelmingly grave crisis. It is absolutely essential to examine what Mr. Khrushchev has done. He has stopped his ships from entering the blockade area. He has promised to take no rash action or to run the risk of nuclear war. He has offered to dismantle the bases and has asked for the exchange of some of those which ring his country. He has now unilaterally removed all Cuban bases and has yielded to demands made under the threat of force. I pay tribute to him. It is important to see that he has also offered to prevent other conflicts from occurring which could lead to world war. President Kennedy is under a moral obligation imposed on him by humanity, and has an absolute duty to meet with Mr. Khrushchev and to earnestly pursue the removal of NATO and the Warsaw Pact, to achieve disarmament, and, as Mr. Khrushchev has said, to consider all issues of peace and war.

If ever words have been matched by deeds, they have been so by the Soviet Union. The concrete deed is the ending of this crisis. If the United States has ever been sincere in its claims to be willing to agree to end the Cold War, on the condition that Russian deeds matched her words, then now is the time for the United States and for Mr. Kennedy to prove it.[42]

As an expression of his own "profound gratitude" to the Soviet Premier, Russell cabled Khrushchev:

I should like you to know of my personal feelings about your solving the Cuban crisis. I have never known any statesman act with the magnanimity and greatness that you have shown over Cuba and I wish you to be clear that every sincere and honest human being pays you homage for your courage.[45]

In his assessment of the settlement of the crisis Russell wrote:

Until this moment, there had not been very much to choose between American and Russian policies. But when Khrushchev gave this indubitable proof of his determination to avoid general nuclear war the USSR became the more rational of the two contestants.[44]

In regard to the charge that he was biased in favor of communism, Russell found it repeatedly necessary to clarify his position, which he did as follows:

I must repeat...that my opinions as to the Cuban crisis are not due to any love of communism...but I think that the prevention of nuclear war is an issue which transcends in importance all other issues in international affairs, and, whenever this issue is relevant, I feel that support is due to the more pacific party. It is only for this reason that since, though not before, Khrushchev decided not to challenge the blockade, I have thought him more praiseworthy than his opponents ...Regardless of the relative merits of capitalism and communism, the world must, in this matter, regard Khrushchev as preferable to the politicians of the West. He has been engaged in trying to create an atmosphere in which successful negotiations between East and West may become possible and the Cold War may be brought to a peaceful solution.[45]

While many prominent individuals and peace organizations spoke out forcefully in favor of a negotiated settlement it is clear that Russell's unique status enabled him to play an important role in the crisis. "Many people sent letters to the Heads of State involved," Russell later stated, "I had good luck in being answered and at considerable length."[46]

The fact that Russell's voice was heeded was due to his tireless efforts ever since 1945 to arouse humanity to the dangers of nuclear warfare. The number of people who came to rely on his judgement and activities during this crucial period was considerable. That he regarded his involvement in the Cuban crisis as a climax in his life's work is indicated by this letter, typical of his response to messages of goodwill from his many supporters:

Thank you for your kind wishes. I was pleased to receive them. As you might appreciate, the crisis was such that it was not clear that we should survive the week, but I can assure you that the solution to the crisis made the week one of the most worthwhile of my entire life.[47]

Footnotes

1. B. Russell, *Unarmed Victory* (London, New York, 1963), p. 27.
2. Published in *Revolution* Havana, 4 February 1962.
3. Unidentified newsclipping
4. September 1962
5. B. Russell, *Unarmed Victory*, p 9.
6. *Ibid.*, p. 36.
7. *Ibid.*, p. 37
8. *Ibid.*, p. 29
9. *Ibid.*, p. 30
10. *Ibid.*, p. 35

11. *Ibid.*, p. 10.

12. *Ibid.*, p, 39.

13. *Ibid.*

14. *Ibid.*

15. 23 October 1962. Unpublished.

16. 23 October 1962. Unpublished.

17. B. Russell, *Unarmed Victory*, p. 40.

18. *Ibid.*, p. 42.

19. *Ibid.*, p. 44.

20. *Ibid.*

21. *Ibid.*, p. 46.

22. *Ibid.*

23. 24 October 1962, *Ibid.*, p. 47.

24. 24 October 1962, *Ibid.*,p. 47-48

25. *Ibid.*, p. 50.

26. *Ibid.*, pp. 51-52.

27. *Ibid.*, p. 52.

28. *Ibid.*, p. 49.

29. *Ibid.*, pp. 52-53n

30. *Ibid.*, p. 55.

31. *Ibid.*, p. 56.

32. *Ibid.*

33. 26 October 1962, *Ibid.*, pp. 56-7.

34. *Ibid.*

35. 26 October 1962. *Ibid.*, p. 57.

36. *Ibid.*, p. 58.

37. *Ibid.*, p. 62.

38. *Ibid.*, pp. 62-63.

39. *Ibid.*, p. 63.

40. 28 October 1962. *Ibid.*, pp. 63-64.

41. *Ibid.*, p. 64.

42. *Ibid.*, pp. 64-65.

43. 28 October 1962. *Ibid.*, pp. 66-67.

44. *Ibid.*

45. *Ibid.*, pp. 74-75.

46. *Ibid.*, p. 12.

47. B. Feinberg and R. Kasrils (eds.) *Dear Bertrand Russell*, (London, 1969), p. 77; (Houghton Mifflin, Boston, 1969) p. 42.

13 Rationality of the Arms Race

Russell's role in the Cuban crisis, his praise of Khrushchev and his criticism of American policies and Kennedy's actions, brought him, perhaps more than ever before, to the critical attention of the American public. The news media with the exception of the very small left-wing press were unanimous in their bitter condemnation of Russell's views. In the months following the crisis hardly a day went by without the American press carrying some attack against him. His advanced age and his philosophical reputation were more than once used to cast aspersions on his political judgement. Fairly typical of this criticism was an editorial in the *Idaho State Journal* of 6 November 1962, which, under the heading "The Philosophy that Failed," accused Russell of not serving "the cause of liberty" and declared that "nothing is easier in this world than to stand on a box and shout: Disarm!" and that what is needed "are men who will not waste their energies proclaiming the goal but address themselves instead to the complex, agonizing, endless task of building a basic, enduring sense of trust in a now divided world...It is not too late even for the aged, misguided Lord Russell to begin this hard quest."

Russell received daily many letters from individual Americans whose confusion and indignation at his stand over Cuba had been reinforced by the press assault. On the other hand Russell continued to receive many indications of support. "Last week you seemed to be the one remaining hope that the world would be saved," wrote Clark Foreman on behalf of the Emergency Civil Liberties Committee on October 30. "All of us in the future must look to you as one who used most effectively his right to speak out." Foreman went on to inform Russell that his Committee had decided to present Russell with the Tom Paine Award for 1962 "for the person who has made the greatest contribution in the spirit of Tom Paine." The award was normally confined to Americans but Foreman explained "we now feel that you belong to all who wish for freedom, peace and sanity in this world," and "it is offered with the greatest degree of gratitude and appreciation for your role in saving humanity."

Russell, who greatly admired Paine, was deeply moved by the award.[1] In accepting the honor he sent a statement to the Emergency Civil Liberties Committee on November 8. The statement was published in *I.F. Stone's Weekly* on December 17:

> You honour me in a way I deeply appreciate. Tom Paine symbolized for Americans the articulation of a radical consciousness that human welfare and intellectual integrity depend upon courageous insistence upon freedom for men and women. Freedom cannot effectively exist where it is understood to mean no more than the toleration of occasional differences about matters which are of small importance.
>
> Disputes, for example, about the comparative merit of consumer produce or the total of farm expenditure may be cited as examples of freedom, but only by those who are dead to its life and deaf to its death. The vision of Tom Paine was that of a serious public involvement in the direction of those affairs which affected people's lives. He struggled for the right to partake in radical change and in the constant debate as to how the good life might be provided for the American people.
>
> Values and great beliefs live on after their institutional expressions have ceased to live. So it is with the nominal civil liberties enjoyed today either by Americans or by citizens of other countries.
>
> Thousands of years of human effort, of great suffering, of unique achievement are in daily jeopardy because the absence of freedom strived after by Paine prevents men from forestalling consummate folly.
>
> Today, the exercise of power is so remote from the daily lives of men and women and the control of the very springs of thought so concentrated in the hands of those sycophantic to power, that freedom is increasingly an abstraction with which we are deluded.
>
> Delusion takes the form of public incantation over values and beliefs which are dishonored even as they are invoked. President Kennedy speaks of human freedom as he takes actions which may condemn hundreds of millions of human beings to agonizing death.

Future generations are forfeited to the paranoia of those who compulsively act for garrison states. So it is that I believe that we delude ourselves if we fail to realize that the genocidal power possessed by the few condemns us all to futile death and empties our formal rights of meaning or of viable life. Only to the extent that we are able to remove those who would perpetrate this crime against humanity can "freedom" be seriously our possession or our right.

I feel honoured in a way I do not find easy to acknowledge. I am an Englishman and so was Tom Paine by birth. I believe that human freedom and the civilised ends to which that freedom was to have been directed are not spoken for by the Governments of either of our two countries. I find it difficult to express the feelings I have upon receiving this award because I know how Tom Paine would feel about the country he left and the nation he helped to found. The pity of it. The disgrace to all that is best in man's long odyssey. The intolerable affront to the dignity of us all contained in the readiness to annihilate whole continents in pursuit of the insane dictates of power.

If there is one message, one sentiment, I should wish to give you it is that I cannot bring myself to believe that mankind is so base that none of its representatives will struggle for a more excellent way of life, no matter the chances of success. Thank you for your honour to me. We share the conviction that the struggle must go on.

In the January 1963 issue of *Harper's Magazine*, the editor, John Fischer, took Russell and other scientists to task for pronouncing on matters which he felt were the exclusive concern of political and military experts. In the process Fischer misrepresented Russell's views on issues of war and peace. Russell wrote to *Harper's Magazine* on 4 March 1963:

You published an article in your January issue by a Mr. J. Fischer. This article is not sufficiently serious to warrant the time necessary to examine it, but it may be worthwhile to mention that the views attributed to me by Mr. J. Fischer bear no relation to what I have advocated and it seems clear from the context of his article that he has attributed these false views to me with foreknowledge. I shall charitably assume that this was due to oversight and I shall, therefore, seek to explain briefly what it is I am saying in sufficiently simple language such as to enable J. Fischer to understand more clearly.

I am contending that human beings live, at the moment, in immediate danger of total annihilation. I do not say this rhetorically, but base the statement upon the fact that rocket bases and nuclear missiles cover our planet and rest upon warning systems of a few minutes. This entire apparatus of global butchery depends upon radar, radar which is incapable of distinguishing natural phenomena from missiles. Many of *Harper's* readers will be familiar with the kinds of statements made by insurance companies concerning the possibility and likelihood of accidents with regard to aeroplane flights and automobile transport. We know there will be a mean number of accidents each year, although we cannot say which cars will crash or planes fall. So it is, as a simple problem of mathematical statistics, that with each day the possibility of total annihilation through accident increases to a point of near certainty.

In the cold war, the two giants competing for power ruthlessly extirpate every semblance of human decency wherever they are able to do so in pursuit of their mad struggle. The United States, for example, imposes intolerable regimes upon Asian, Latin American and Middle Eastern countries, and economically exploits the great majority of mankind who live at below subsistence level to support American profit. Similar things can be said of the Soviet Union, but Americans need reminding of the nature of the society they inhabit. Devil theory, fanaticism such as was practiced in the Thirty Years War and evident in the conflicts between Catholics and Protestants, Christians and Moslems, will eliminate life from our planet. The Russians are not devils. Their record is comparable to that of any other nation state, not better, little worse. The American Government pursues a policy of genocide. This is a plain statement of fact. You, like Eichmann, acquiesce in this policy and you, like he, have the imperative moral responsibility to demand an end to such a policy. It can be done, if cowardice is put aside for clarity.[2]

John Fischer replied to Russell on March 10:

Thank you for your letter of March 4. It is the best possible illustration of my main point in that article to which you refer: that when scientists stray outside of their own field, they are likely to come up with some rather curious notions.

For example, it is a simple, easily verifiable matter of fact that the American nuclear-missile system does *not* "rest upon warning systems of a few minutes" nor does its apparatus "depend upon radar, which is incapable of distinguishing natural phenomena from missiles." The primary purpose of the Polaris and Minuteman systems is to eliminate dependence upon any sort of warning system, and to make possible a deliberate, slow reaction. If a Russian missile were to land on American territory, therefore, there need be no immediate retaliation. The President could take whatever time might be necessary to find out whether the missile was fired by accident, or whether it was fired as part of a deliberate attack. Moreover, this country has established an elaborate system of safeguards which makes it virtually inconceivable that a missile could ever be fired by accident; and it seems quite probable that the Russians have developed similar systems of their own.

I doubt you will convince many Americans that their government is pursuing "a policy of genocide," that it "imposes intolerable regimes" upon other countries, or that we are exploiting other peoples "to support American profit." On the contrary, other peoples are exploiting us at the rate of a good many billions of dollars a year given them as foreign aid.

Finally, I was puzzled by your suggestion that the article misrepresented your views. Do you mean that you are *not* advocating unilateral disarmament?[3]

Russell answered Fischer at length on March 15:[4]

You suffer from what theologians call *"invincible* ignorance." You also lack acquaintance with elementary logic. *Ad hominem* comment is no help to argument. Even if the absurd contention were made that men of particular intelligence are less well equipped to comment on public affairs than men of practiced ignorance, it would still be necessary to examine the remarks of the former on their merits in order to refute their claims. It will not help you to call scientists names. To complain of their training as a means of coping with their contentions is not an argument but a prejudice.

I shall examine the facts since you show so unbelievable an ignorance of them. You assert unabashedly: "It is a simple, easily verifiable matter of fact that the American nuclear missile system does *not* 'rest upon warning systems of a few minutes,' nor does its apparatus 'depend upon radar, which is incapable of distinguishing natural phenomena from missiles.'"

And I thought that the Americans were telling the truth when they justified blockade of sovereign Cuba by invoking the danger provided by wicked Russian missiles. These missiles were dangerous because they reduced the warning time, said Mr. Kennedy. But perhaps he was following the procedure announced by Mr. Sylvester and 'lied in the national interest.'"[5]

The DEW-Line system and NORAD are a fantasy, I suppose. This radar network is designed to detect oncoming missiles, and the firing of American missiles is said to depend upon the information provided by DEW-Line and NORAD. The warning system upon which SAC works is fifteen minutes. The warning system in Britain is four minutes. All of the rocket bases are primed according to signals expected on radar registering missile attack. Would you claim that SAC and rocket bases abroad are *not* part of the American nuclear missile and bomber system?

So much for that contention. With regard to the reliability of radar, Sir Robert Watson-Watt, who is the inventor of radar, has declared unequivocally that radar cannot distinguish natural phenomena from missiles. The Director of Jodrell Bank, Sir Bernard Lovell, has stated that it would not be possible to distinguish on radar between meteorites and missiles. There have been a large number of accidents due to the faultiness of radar. NORAD interpreted the rising of the moon as an invading Russian armada and on the basis of this error the signal to attack was given; only the freak occurrence of an iceberg cutting an underwater cable delayed it sufficiently to cause doubt in the mind of a Canadian commander.[6]

The Mershon National Security report, published by Ohio State University Press, on 28 June 1960 itemizes fifty incidents involving nuclear weapons including twelve major accidents. It predicted accidental nuclear war during the 1960s as a matter of statistical probability. It lists the accidents caused by radar and confirms the statements concerning its faulty character made by Watson-Watt and Lovell. So much for the infallibility of radar.

You say categorically that the safeguards taken make it inconceivable that a missile could be fired by accident. In 1958 twelve Nike missiles were fired because of an electrical short circuit. Twenty-four warheads were scattered less than a day before the missiles were to be fitted with hydrogen warheads. The Mershon report lists comparable examples.

As regards the Minuteman missile, Professor Ralph Lapp states: "It might go by accident, it might be tampered with by saboteurs, or fired by fanatics."

After discussing safety precautions concerning ICBMs, President Kennedy stated: "All the safety factors leave a serious loop-hole in the control of ICBMs."

Lloyd V. Berkner, organizer of the International Geophysical Year, stated: "As large numbers of fast flying missiles come into the possession of both sides, ready for use, critical command will tend to devolve to lower and lower echelons. To some extent this is already occurring. If we are going to be able to retaliate effectively, it will become less practical to assemble Congress or to call together the Cabinet or even for the President to be consulted when missiles with the ultimate destructive power are seen flying toward us."

As Professor Lapp put it, "in the era of missile warfare, the control of nuclear weapons steadily becomes more diffuse and the danger of war through accident, miscalculation, or madness must rise accordingly."

The President of the American Psychological Association, Dr. Charles E. Osgood, stated: "The maintenance of peace depends upon rational behavior by those in control; yet in the present era of great danger we are more than ever at the mercy of 'the unpredictability of human behavior under stress.' " On the same subject, Professor Lapp stated: "This unpredictability applies equally to chiefs of state and to lower echelons. But with the diffusion of control of nuclear weapons to more and more hands, the chances of someone breaking under the stress are multiplied."

Stockpiles of nuclear warheads are available at bases of the West German Air Force and may, according to President Kennedy, be turned over to the Germans in emergency! When a B-52 bomber had to jettison a 24-megaton bomb over North Carolina, five of the six "safety" mechanisms had been triggered. One switch separated us from the obliteration of a vast area.

So it is that the following men have stated the danger:

"Accidental nuclear warfare is extremely likely."

Lord Hailsham

"Future generations will look back with amazement if war is averted."

John Foster Dulles

"These modern weapons are simply too hot to handle and as time goes on, the curve of probability that they will go off will steadily rise."

Thomas K. Finletter

"If developments continue as they have during the last fifteen years, I believe all-out nuclear war is, in the long run, inevitable."

Harrison Brown

"Every year, every month lost is not just marking time...but a lightening-fast slide to the line separating peace from the blast of rocket nuclear war."

Andrei Gromyko

As for genocide, this is a simple matter of definition. The utilization of the nuclear rockets will entail the murder of hundreds of millions. This is genocide.

I shall list the intolerable regimes supported solely by American capital and American guns: Vietnam, South Korea, Paraguay, Peru, Chile, Ecuador, Bolivia, Guatemala, Haiti, Formosa and Spain.

There are others. There are even more who are tolerated for just as long as they do not challenge American economic exploitation. Greece, Portugal and France are tyrannies and all three maintain camps for political prisoners.

I enclose a copy of my article in the *Bulletin of Atomic Scientists* in which I once again repeat my position as stated in *Common Sense and Nuclear Warfare* and in *Has Man a Future?* It can be found in countless articles and interviews. It is perfectly clear you have never read my writing on the subject and I challenge you to provide the source for the view you attribute to me in your article.

It amuses me to have you suggest that I am unfamiliar with the issues about which I write, and that questions of war and peace are not my province. I have written on social issues since 1896 and on matters of peace and war and international politics for over fifty years.

I cannot say whether your ignorance on these matters is real or whether you suppress the facts which alarm you. I can say that it is abominable for a man who edits a journal to be both so ill-informed and so prepared to write on subjects of which he has no knowledge. This practice spreads ignorance and untruth.

The above article, when eventually published in the June issue of *Harper's Magazine* was footnoted with two editorial observations. The first, in reference to Russell's quote about "Mr. Sylvester" and the possibility that President Kennedy "lied in the national interest," commented: "Presumably Arthur Sylvester, Assistant Secretary of Defense for Public Affairs; if so, the words in quotation marks are a misquotation." Russell's quote was not precise but Sylvester had spoken of "the inherent right of the government to lie" and claimed that "the generation of news by action taken by the government becomes one weapon in a strained situation." The second footnote referred to Russell's account of a Canadian Commander's role in not acting upon a NORAD signal to attack Russia and commented "Where Lord Russell heard these alarming tales is unclear." The alarming "tales" involving Canadian Air Marshal Roy Slemon were in fact reported in the *Manchester Guardian* of 28 November 1960; *The Washington Evening Star* of 7 December 1960; *The New York Times* of December 8 and 23, and in many other newspapers.
Fischer's reply to Russell was dated March 21:

Your main trouble, it would appear from your letter of March 15, is a confusion between warning time and reaction time. This is not surprising, since there was a period some years ago when the two concepts were closely related. During that period the American deterrent was made up entirely of bombers, based on highly vulnerable air-fields. Consequently it was necessary for them to get off the ground within about fifteen minutes after a radar warning might be received of an enemy attack. (This did not mean, of course, that they had to launch a retaliatory attack of their own on such short notice, but the reaction time was still relatively short; that is, a decision would have to be made within a few hours that a plane could stay in flight.)

Within the last two years, we have been in the process of replacing manned bombers and the early, vulnerable type of missiles such as the Thor, Jupiter, and Titan, with new varieties of missiles which are largely invulnerable to enemy attack. These are the Minutemen, located in "hardened" underground sites scattered over a very wide area, and the Polaris, which can be fired from submarines under water. It is most unlikely that even a massive enemy attack could knock out more than a very small percentage of either the Minuteman or Polaris systems. Consequently, they have become entirely independent of the radar warning network. This network is still maintained for whatever minor service it might be to unhardened installations and to the civilian population, but the firing of American missiles is *not* dependent upon the information provided by DEW-Line and NORAD as you suggested in your letter of March 15. These new missiles would not need to be fired until after enemy missiles had actually landed on American territory, and if it seemed advisable, any retaliatory action could be delayed for days or weeks until it could be fully determined whether the enemy attack was accidental or intentional.

As the Minuteman and Polaris systems are being completed, the obsolescent bomber bases and early-generation missiles are being taken out of service both here and abroad. The manufacture of strategic bombers has already been stopped, and—as you may know— American bombers and early-generation missiles have been removed from a number of overseas sites, including Turkey, England, Italy and Morocco. Within a year or so it is anticipated that all of these vulnerable systems, which necessarily work on a short reaction time, will be replaced with Minuteman and Polaris systems which operate on long reaction times quite unrelated to the missile warning system.

(In the version published in *Harper's Magazine* this last sentence was deleted.) Fischer continued:

Two other misconceptions mentioned in your letter deserve comment:

(1) The Nike missile is a short-range anti-aircraft weapon; it is not fitted with a hydrogen warhead. There has never been an accidental explosion of a nuclear weapon.

(2) The statement of Dr. Ralph Lapp's which you quoted about the Minuteman missile was apparently made while this weapon was in the early stage of development. I can't be sure, since you did not mention the date of the quotation. I have discussed these problems with Professor Lapp repeatedly in recent years however and I'm confident that the quoted statement does not represent his current position. If you are interested in the precautions taken to prevent accidental firing of a Minuteman missile, you might like to glance through the attached reprint.

Since you seem to speak frequently on these matters, and since you state rather emphatically, that you are opposed to the spreading of misinformation, I thought you might want to acquaint yourself with some of the current facts.[8]

(Fischer's reference to his discussion with Professor Lapp was deleted from the version published in *Harper's Magazine*.) Russell replied to Fischer on March 24:

Our controversy has centered on the issue of accidental war and the nature of American policy. You are unable to refute the overwhelming evidence of specific and statistical kind. You are unable to "unwrite" the Mershon Report, the work of the Pugwash scientists whose competence in their fields is real, the statements of Kennedy, Dulles, Gromyko, Hailsham and scores of others. And you are unwilling to grasp what you would never deny with regard to the data of insurance companies on accidents in many spheres. Insofar as hundreds of millions of lives are involved, I have no compunction in saying to you that you enhance the prospect of annihilation by your journalism.

The electrical failure which detonated Nike missiles in 1958, the instance of total mental breakdown such as has recently been recorded for American missile officers, the occurrence of a mad first-strike act by a rebellious commander are all part of the data concerning accidental nuclear war. Kennedy's remarks were directed to "hardened" ICBMs.

The "invulnerability" to hydrogen attack from 100-megaton weapons may delude you but its absurdity deludes few other than military propagandists. The errors on radar which give false evidence of massive attack will provoke reply. The Institute for Strategic Studies assessed the strategic strength for early 1963 on the part of the United States to include over 1,600 medium-range bombers, 600 long-range bombers, 250 medium-range missiles, and 500 long-range missiles. If you think that this arsenal will not come into use should radar show a massive attack, I leave you to your delusion. If the missiles which detonated in 1958 are now said to have been anti-aircraft weapons, the claims of the time were lies. The danger is in no way lessened.

Finally, Polaris submarines are increasingly detectable and sinkable. So much so that there is serious consideration of going over to surface vessels. As the day approaches that radar is not felt to give "warning" or "reaction time," the likelihood that either side will feel compelled to strike first will increase. There are many crises brewing in this world, many of them because of the American exploitative policy I have specified, and in each the probability of an error of judgement is high.

Any claim that "accidental war is impossible," any statement that rational acts are guaranteed and American judgment is infallible, are lunatic. I note in this discussion your insensitivity to the issues couched in such grand and pseudo-technical jargon. The issues concern vast suffering and agony, mass murder and devastation. How extraordinary that men so diminished as those who can discuss this without awareness of what they do should escape universal opprobrium. In a long life during which I have often observed the vanity and cruelty of men I cannot cite a more cold-blooded parallel.

I should be grateful for your permission to publish this correspondence.

In his reply of April 4 Fischer agreed to the publication of their correspondence "provided it is published in full including this letter":

Our recent correspondence leaves me with a certain feeling of frustration, because we seem to be talking about different things—and because I apparently have failed completely to make my position clear. May I try once more?

(1) I have never suggested that "accidental war is impossible," that rational acts are guaranteed, or that American judgment is infallible. Obviously nothing is impossible and no one is infallible. I do regard accidental war as more unlikely, and I have tried to set forth some of the facts on which this view is based. Your own view—that accidental nuclear war is inevitable, or at least highly probable, seems to me to be based on some facts which are now obsolete, other "facts" which never existed, and on an almost total misconception of American policy.

(2) So far as I know, we do not disagree on two points: that a nuclear war would be an unparalleled catastrophe, and that every conceivable effort should be made to reach a satisfactory agreement on nuclear disarmament. What reasonable man could believe otherwise?

(3) Where we do differ, apparently, is on what would constitute a "satisfactory" disarmament agreement and how it might be reached. If

I correctly understand your position—as set forth in your letters, your article in the March 1962 issue of the *Bulletin of the Atomic Scientists*, and your other recent writings and speeches—you would like to see Britain abandon nuclear weapons and adopt a position of neutrality, and break up the NATO alliance. This in itself would constitute a considerable degree of unilateral disarmament by the West, and (in my view) would bring war dangerously close by tempting the Soviet Union to further aggression.

In addition, if your statements have been correctly reported in the British press, you advocate American acceptance of a disarmament agreement that contains no adequate provisions for verification or inspection. This simply would be the equivalent of complete unilateral disarmament by the West, since there is no reason to believe, on the basis of the historical record, that the Soviet Union would keep such an agreement for a moment.

(4) It is also part of this historical record that the United States made the first and most sweeping proposals for nuclear disarmament— offering, *at a time when we had a monoply of nuclear weapons* to abolish them and to turn all nuclear technology over to an international agency (the so-called Baruch-Acheson-Lilienthal proposals in 1946). Since that time, American negotiators have persisted, with infinite patience, in trying to reach an agreement that will effectively control or eliminate nuclear arms. So far, apparently, they have been unable to evoke any serious interest from either the Russians or General de Gaulle. Under these circumstances, I am at a loss to know what further steps this country might take.

(5) There is no point in arguing with you about the nature of American society or American policy. Anyone who really believes that "the power of decision" in this country rests "in the hands of semi-literate paranoids, compulsively acting out their sick hates and their blind malice"—as you put it in the *Bulletin* article—obviously is beyond persuasion.

On a few subordinate matters, however, I do hope that you might be willing to re-examine the facts. For example, no nuclear weapon, so far as I can discover, was ever detonated by accident; the Nike is and always was a short-range anti-aircraft weapon, and I can find no published suggestion to the contrary; I know of no evidence of "total mental breakdown...recently recorded for American missile officers," or of a "mad first strike act by a rebellious commander." (If you have any such evidence I shall be glad to hear of it). President Kennedy has never proposed that nuclear warheads "be turned over to the Germans in an emergency"; that would be contrary to treaty obligations and to

American law. There is no "serious consideration of going over to surface vessels" as a replacement for the Polaris submarines because they are "increasingly detectable and sinkable." (The suggestion that a European multi-national nuclear force might use surface vessels was advanced because they are cheaper than submarines, not because they are less vulnerable; they are not. And such a force would be intended to supplement, not replace, the Polaris.) All I am suggesting is that you should examine such documents as the so-called "Mershon Report" with the same intellectual vigor that you once applied to the arguments of G.E. Moore and Wittgenstein.

(6) Finally, rising population pressures throughout the world seem to me a greater danger, in the long run, than the existence of nuclear weapons, since if they are not checked they will make war virtually inevitable. Is it too much to hope that you might enlist your considerable energies as a propagandist in this kind of peace movement?[10]

The correspondence was published by *Harper's* in their June issue under the title "Bertrand Russell on the Sinful Americans." Despite Fischer's wish to have the correspondence published in full he omitted from his magazine version of the exchange, Russell's final letter of April 11:

I should not be frank with you if I did not say that I believe there is something basically unhealthy in the approach that you and those who think as you do take to the problem of nuclear war. I am reminded of the most recent bit of inane thinking to issue from Washington— namely the view that a "no cities" strategy is something which is tenable. This view, which one is given to believe is now popular in Washington, holds that nuclear war has become so devastating and over-whelming in its destructive character that the only way in which it will be possible to have such a war would be if there were a prior agreement on the part of both Heads of State to exclude cities as targets. So we are treated to the suggestion of a calm discussion, while the missiles are flying, held between Kennedy and Khrushchev, in which each will bargain over cities and stop short of their destruction. Then there will be a truce, the Cold War will begin again and, presumably, further nuclear war will be ruled out through agreement.

I mention this because I consider it to be of great importance insofar as it teaches us something of the mentality of those who now offer themselves as apologists of American policy. It does not occur to them that the agreement and the calm discussion of which they speak could precede a nuclear war. It does not occur to these people that they have a real psychological need for this nuclear holocaust and they will contrive any argument, however insane, such as will allow them to have their holy conflict. I am appalled by your recent letter. I am appalled because it so shamelessly shifts the ground and evades the real issue. Your history of American innocence is fantasy. The United States and the Soviet Union have committed numbers of crimes against each other and greater numbers against mankind during the course of their conflict.

I have sought to show you that the United States maintains the most ruthless dictatorships and resists any suggestion of social change where such change may challenge economic interests in your country. This you reject in terms of such unctious self-righteousness as to make one despair of any hope at all of America facing the reality she is inflicting upon mankind. Nothing prevents the United States from agreeing to disarmament with inspection, if she were prepared to agree to substantial disarmament as well as to inspection. The American record of duplicity in Indo-China is as outrageous as any I have encountered. I refer you to the Geneva reports and an excellent summary of the situation in Indo-China by Anna Louise Strong, whose political opinions you may dislike but whose factual evidence is overwhelming and irrefutable.

This detailed discussion of the comparative inequities of the two systems, is, for me, a minor issue in comparison with the grave danger. I shall continue to insist that men recognise that for the most obscure and unjustified differences and on behalf of the most extraordinary struggle for power between two authoritarian giants, they are placing all of human civilization at the mercy of an error in judgment or an electrical failure. In your first letter to me you made the following bold statement: "This country has established an elaborate system of safeguards which make it virtually inconceivable that a missile could ever be fired by accident." You now claim that all you intended to say is that accidental war is not likely. You rest your case on the belief that the improvement of technique has reduced the likelihood of technological accident. The truth of the matter is that the very refinement of technique has reduced the time margin during which any decision can be made, and as a result, has immensely enhanced the risk of error and the likelihood that such an error would go undetected or could not be corrected in time. If it is true that you are concerned to see agreement on nuclear disarmament, then it is your responsibility to recognise that the United States has a very great share in the danger to which mankind is exposed and in the failure to eliminate it.

If you wish to publish this correspondence and to refute my suggestion that men of power in the United States who make decisions are compulsive and behave as semi-literate paranoids, I demand that you publish the evidence I advanced in the *Bulletin of Atomic Scientists* for this statement. That evidence begins with page 9 where I discuss the Air Force Association document and quote statements by General Nathan Twining, Admiral Arthur Radford, the Air Force Association and General Powers, and General Orval Anderson. The statements which I have quoted from these men indicate what I consider to be insane paranoia and they are indicative of the indoctrination which has informed all military people and which infects civilian figures such as yourself. I am not using language by way of epithet, I am choosing these terms with care and I believe them to be exact and accurate.

If you wish to publish this correspondence in full, then I request you to include the following information as part of this, my last letter. "The Cordiner Report of 1958 placed the value of property owned outright by the American Department of Defense at 160 billion dollars. This does not include property leased to the Department or dependent upon buildings of the Department for its value. Outright ownership of this kind has reached thirty-two million acres within the United States.

"Kennedy's budget for 1962 called for seventy-seven cents out of every one hundred to be spent on past wars, the Cold War and preparations for future war. Military assets are three times as great as the combined assets of the U.S. Steel, American Telephone & Telegraph (the largest U.S. corporation), Metropolitan Life Insurance, General Motors and Standard Oil. The personnel of the Department of Defense is triple the number of *all* the above mentioned corporations and their subsidiaries.

"Military power and the power of big industry are joined through the interchangeability of their personnel and the billions of dollars provided by the one and fulfilled by the other in military and quasi-military contracts. In 1960 21 billion dollars were spent on military goods alone and this was only a part of the military budget for that year. Three other corporations—General Dynamics, Lockheed and Boeing—receive over one billion dollars on such contracts in one year. General Electric and North American Aviation secure over 900 million dollars.

"These awards are conferred at the discretion of public men recently executives in the very industries receiving such contracts. Military officers who champion a weapon produced by one corporation, retire to its board of directors. There are over 1400 such retired officers *above the rank of major* in the one hundred vast corporations which divided between them sixteen billion dollars. This list includes 263 generals and flag-rank officers, 27 admirals and the former Secretary of the Army. The sixteen billion were secured in one year.

"Subcontracts from major war contracts spread to every part of the American economy and society. The Defense Department alone hires over 3½ million people and four million people work directly in defense industries.

"In many cities, missile production produces over fifty percent of all manufacturing jobs. In San Diego, California, it is over eighty-two percent. In eight states, one out of three jobs are *directly* in defense industry. In Los Angeles more that fifty percent of *all jobs* depend on defense expenditure. Finally in the United States of America as a whole between *one quarter and one third* of all economic activity hinges upon military expenditure and it is predicted that this will soon reach fifty percent of all such economic activity.

"The psychological, political and economic involvement in preparations for mass murder affect every food store and petrol station proprietor, every industrial worker, every politician—in fact the entire nation. This is the Warfare State."

Some weeks ago an American Air Force Officer was retired on the grounds of instability. He had in his charge missiles. This is only an example of the possibility of total mental breakdown of those in charge of such weapons to which I referred in my earlier letter. The possibility of a mad *first strike* act by a rebellious commander is also, as I have said, part of the data concerning the possibility of accidental nuclear war.

You have maintained that I advocate surrender on the part of the West. This is a lie. I have advocated that Britain become neutral and use its influence to promote settlement. Whether or not you consider this to bring war closer is your own business, but it is not justified for you to say that I have advocated surrender. I repeat, this is a lie, I have not advocated acceptance of any disarmament agreement containing "no adequate provision for inspection." I have requested that the United States show a genuine willingness to take unilateral initiatives to make possible a disarmament agreement. By distorting my views you do not succeed in removing the danger or the necessity for what I advocate. You are wrong with regard to the detectability of Polaris submarines. I have been informed by Pugwash Scientists on advances made in such detective processes. You suggest that I apply intellectual rigour to the consideration of the Mershon report. I suggest that you read it and that you consider the facts contained in it.

I am not clear what Moore and Wittgenstein have to do with our controversy, but I believe that you are not either. I am pleased to learn of your philosophical interests.[11]

On 12 February 1963 the 17 nation disarmament conference resumed in

> "Vietnam has a starving, illiterate and diseased population under a barbarous military dictatorship which is financed, officered and directed by the United States. Opposition to it in the form of a desire for social reform is repressed with napalm jelly-gasoline and pronounced Communist to justify the barbarism; as if Communists are quite alright burned alive."

Geneva and almost at once became bogged down by disputes between the major powers. Russell, who remained firm in his conviction that Cold War rivalries were irrelevant when faced with the overriding considerations of preventing a nuclear war, expressed his anxieties at the "delays and difficulties now taking place in Geneva with regard to the banning of nuclear tests" in a letter sent to the *Washington Post, Pravda* and *The Times* on March 8. Describing the hazards involved for mankind in the continuation of tests Russell asked "What would Governments say if Pakistanis and Indians in their dispute over Kashmir...poisoned the atmosphere of the planet in the course of it?" Russell questioned the right of Governments "to make the people of the world hostage to every petty squabble they might entertain," and appealed for a cessation of testing "irrespective of what the other side is prepared to do." Russell elaborated his views on the Cold War in a reply to Victor Lieberman, an American student who had argued to Russell his belief that "Russia's inflexible determination to establish world hegemony is the basic reason for the Cold War."[12] Russell's letter was dated March 7:

> ...Each side, East and West, has accepted the prospect of hundreds of millions of deaths and has brought us to the verge of this with their Bismarkian power politics. Rockets and missiles depend on faulty radar and the likelihood of disaster increasingly looms before us. This is a madness in which the United States and Russia share and all of their citizens have the same responsibility as Eichmann to oppose the murderous policies of their Governments.
>
> As for the behavior of America, she promotes ruthless dictatorships and cruelly subdues all opposition to them in the name of "anti-communism." This is the nub of her foreign policy in all Latin America, Asia and the Middle East. In Africa she is content with economic domination and imperialism of an indirect sort.
>
> The countries you itemise are as follows: Vietnam, Korea, Iran, Greece and Turkey. You might well have added France, Spain and Portugal. Nonetheless, I shall content myself with those you list. Vietnam has a starving, illiterate and diseased population under a barbarous military dictatorship which is financed, officered and

directed by the United States. Opposition to it in the form of a desire for social reform is repressed with napalm jelly-gasoline and pronounced Communist to justify the barbarism; as if Communists are quite alright burned alive. Korea has a military dictatorship. Persia terrorises all peasant opposition. Greece maintains concentration camps for political opponents, over one thousand of whom rot after seventeen years, many of them kept interned when found in Nazi built prisons after the war. Turkey is not what one might call a haven of happiness.

...The old saws about "world hegemony" cut two ways. The true need is for the courage to attack one's own Government where it is wicked and to worry less about the perniciousness of others. The latter is, more often than not, a reflection of one's own actions.

Lieberman replied on March 15 accepting Russell's view that "assigning guilt for the conflict is a rather absurd occupation" in view of the threat of annihilation to both sides. Lieberman continued:

Despite biased newspaper reports of your activities, your arguments on the Cold War enjoy a considerable following in my country. Among young people, weary of the dogma that has ruled their parent's lives, you are especially popular. Nearly every U.S. college has Student Peace Union members, and friends in my personal social group read many of your books.

In the midst of his continuing struggle with the American Press and in the certain knowledge that he was fighting an uneven battle for the support of the American public Russell was grateful for Lieberman's letter, and wrote to him again on March 27:

It is extremely encouraging to me to find that someone who enquires about my views respects what I say and actually changes his mind in the light of it. This is gratifying to me and I feel I should thank you, not for agreeing with me, but for being willing to treat these issues on their merits. In the climate of our times, this is no small thing.

Footnotes

1. See "The fate of Thomas Paine" in B. Russell, *Why I am not a Christian,* London, 1957); (New York, 1957).
2. Published in the June 1963 issue of the magazine.
3. *Ibid.*
4. *Ibid.*
5. See below p. 167.
6. See below p. 167.
7. "The Case for British Nuclear Disarmament," March 1962.
8. *Harper's Magazine*, June 1963.
9. *Ibid.*
10. *Ibid.*
11. Published in the July 1963 issue of *The Minority of One*, together with the preceding correspondence, under the title "On the Rationality of the Arms Race."
12. Lieberman to Russell, 2 March 1963.

14 *The New York Times* & Vietnam

As a result of his treatment by the press during and following the Cuban crisis Russell was determined to combat all those tendencies in the U.S. which he felt served to strengthen government control of the press so as to use it as a weapon in the Cold War. After reading "The Management of News," an article by Lester Markel, associate editor of *The New York Times*, published in the February 9 issue of *Saturday Review*, Russell wrote to the *Saturday Review* and his letter appeared on 16 March 1963 under the heading "The Press as a Weapon":

> Should the American Government decide to sterilize "subversives," "liberals" would be concerned to see that there was a proper right of appeal.
>
> Lester Markel's article "The Management of News" is most astonishing for its lack of self-consciousness. The "news" is now acknowledged as that information which suits governmental convenience. Orwell would have admired Mr. Markel's subtlety of mind. Most American apologists for nuclear genocide are less frank than Mr. Markel. It would be well to examine what it is he assumes and asserts.
>
> He assumes that the function of the press is to criticize the efficiency of governmental operations in the Cold War, which, he declares, is as crucial as any hot war and in which the press is a vital weapon.
>
> The American government systematically lies about the consequences of nuclear fallout. It pursues policies the consequence of which can only be nuclear annihilation. The Cuban crisis is a primary example. Mr. Markel, however, would have us accept the totalitarian function of the press for simple reasons. He assumes that the Cold War

is desirable, that the government should lie and suppress truth in the pursuit of it, and that criticism should never begin with the criminal assumptions of American policy.

I submit that the eager readiness to eliminate several hundred million human beings, the sublime conviction that American rockets are permissable but other rockets are wicked, the refusal to allow that sane men (including journalists) have a duty to tell the truth about the danger to mankind, establishes once again the shameful betrayal of America by "liberals" who embrace the conception of the world prepared for the American public in the Pentagon and the exploitative centers of corporate capitalism.

Lester Markel was accorded right of reply in the same issue of *Saturday Review*. He indignantly rejected Russell's criticisms and denied that he had suggested that the government was entitled to lie in pursuit of the Cold War. He claimed that he was arguing that "if we are to engage in secret operations (which I believe to be necessary in this kind of war) you cannot expect the government to put out all the facts while these operations are in process."

The U.S. Government applauded "the thoughtful and valuable article by Lester Markel" in the form of a comment by Robert Manning, the assistant secretary of state, whose letter the *Saturday Review* deemed fit to feature together with Markel's "rebuttal" of Russell.

The controversy between Russell and Lester Markel presaged a much more serious and bitter confrontation in the columns of the *New York Times*, beginning less than three weeks later. Russell, for many years a regular reader of the *New York Times*, had followed closely the newspapers reportage of the Vietnam War. Through piecing together information gleaned from scattered news items "buried in inside pages" of the *New York Times* and other newspapers, he was able "to assess the character of the war from evidence and documentation which could not be easily dismissed."[1] It was Russell's view that "when the *New York Times* stood to gain nothing from the publication of an article, it was likely to have no other motive than a desire to print a truthful account."[2] Because Russell believed that it was rare for anyone to "fabricate reports and evidence which are inimical to his interest" he accepted the authenticity of the "isolated pieces of horrifying information about the war in Vietnam.[3] Commenting several years later, Russell argued that the press had at that time:

no intention of forming a coherent picture of the war from these reports and every intention of preventing others from doing so. The informed press knew that there was something seriously wrong about the war, but restricted themselves to pedestrian comments and perpetual criticisms. This course preserved their "responsible" stance but prepared the ground for a later *volte face* when their earlier attitude was widely discredited.... As the war in Vietnam escalated, slowly and steadily, the *New York Times* came under increasing pressure not to print articles which exposed the lies and distortions of the American Government.[4]

When Russell was informed by Corliss Lamont, in a letter of 11 March 1963, that some remarks from Russell on the Vietnam War "would help greatly to educate the American public," he immediately wrote to the *Washington Post* on March 22. The *Washington Post* which had the previous week printed, as an advertisement, a copy of an open letter to President Kennedy protesting against U.S. military intervention in South Vietnam, signed by 62 prominent Americans including Lamont, declined to publish Russell's letter.

Russell then sent the identical letter to the *New York Times* and it was published on April 8:

The United States Government is conducting a war of annihilation in Vietnam. The *sole* purpose of this war is to retain a brutal and feudal regime in the South and to exterminate all those who resist the dictatorship of the South. A further purpose is an invasion of the North, which is in Communist hands.

The real concern which brings the United States to pursue the brutal policy abandoned by France in Indochina is the protection of economic interests and the prevention of far reaching social reforms in that part of the world.

I raise my voice, however, not only because I am in profound disagreement with American objections to a social change in Indochina, but because the war which is being conducted is an atrocity. Napalm jelly gasoline is being used against whole villages, without warning. Chemical warfare is employed for the purpose of destroying crops and livestock and to starve the population.

The American government has suppressed the truth about the conduct of this war, the fact that it violates the Geneva agreements concerning Indochina, that it involves large numbers of American troops, and that it is being conducted in a manner reminiscent of warfare as practiced by the Germans in Eastern Europe and the Japanese in Southeast Asia. How long will Americans lend themselves to this sort of barbarism?[5]

The lead-off item in the editorial columns of the paper commented:

Bertrand Russell's letter on this page reflects an unfortunate and—despite his eminence as a philosopher—an unthinking receptivity to the most transparent Communist propaganda. It stems from the delusion than communism is no longer a menace and the real threat to world peace comes from the West's efforts to check Communist aggression.

This newspaper has repeatedly made it clear that it does not mirror the Kennedy Administration's viewpoint about American policies in Vietnam. We have criticized its too rigid support of the autocratic Diem regime, which has insufficient popular backing, and we have urged greater freedom for the individual and more rapid social and economic reforms. We have been deeply concerned, as most thinking Americans have, about the increasing military commitment in South Vietnam, and we have not shared Washington's excessive optimism about American successes.

But Lord Russell's letter represents something far beyond reasoned criticism. It represents distortions or half-truths from the first to the last sentence.

The United States Government is not supporting a "war of annihilation" in Vietnam. There are some 12,000 uniformed Americans there as advisers and trainers, whose bearing, moderation and judgment have done a great deal of good. Their purpose is not to "retain a brutal and feudal regime in the South and to exterminate all those who resist," but to prevent an armed takeover of the country by Communist guerrillas, encouraged and in part supplied, trained, led and organized from North Vietnam or Communist China or both. In the never-never land in which Mr. Russell lives, he twists the Communist infiltration of South Vietnam into an imagined U.S. program to invade the North.

Napalm has been used by the South Vietnamese air force against real or imagined havens of Vietcong guerrillas. Its use has certainly killed innocent people as other weapons have done in all other wars. American advisers have opposed its employment, on both moral and practical grounds, against all except clearly identified military targets. Defoliation chemicals (common weedkillers) have been employed largely in attempts, so far with limited success, to strip leaves from heavy jungle growth near lines of communication and base areas.

Lord Russell's statement that "the real concern" of the United States is "prevention of far-reaching social reforms" is arrant nonsense, as even he in his heart must know. There are many questions to be raised about the extent and the wisdom of the American commitment in South Vietnam, and about the need for reform of the government that the United States is supporting there; but to call the United

States the aggressor and to say nothing about the Communist push for domination against the will of the inhabitants in Vietnam is to make a travesty of justice and a mockery of history.[6]

Russell's reply to the *New York Times,* written on April 12 was not published until May 4:

Your editorial of April 8 calls for a reply from me on various counts. You accuse me of an "unthinking receptivity to the most transparent Communist propaganda." In fact, I base my remarks about the war in South Vietnam upon careful scrutiny of reports in Western newspapers and in publications of the British and American Vietnam Committees. My belief derived from this study is that the U.S. support of Diem is driving more and more of the inhabitants of South Vietnam into the arms of the Communists—a result to be deplored.

You accuse me of distorting the truth or of speaking only half truths, but this is a charge which may be turned against you. I agree with the point of view that you express in your second paragraph. But, in my letter, I give reasons for my point of view: it is, I suppose these reasons to which you take exception. They are: 1) that the purpose of the war is to retain "a brutal and feudal regime in South Vietnam and 2) to exterminate all who resist Diem's dictatorship"; 3) that the U.S. is pursuing a "brutal policy (abandoned by France in Indochina) in order to protect economic interests and to prevent far-reaching social reforms in South Vietnam; and 4) that the war is an atrocity. It is an atrocity because such things as napalm bombs are being used—bombs which do not simply kill, but which burn and torture—and that chemical warfare is employed to destroy crops and livestock and so to starve the people of South Vietnam. I did not mention innumerable appalling atrocities carried out by Diem's Government because for these America has only the indirect responsibility involved in the continued support of Diem.

You say in your fifth paragraph that napalm bombs have been used, but only against "real or imagined havens of Vietcong guerrillas" and have "certainly killed innocent people." You say, however, that American advisers "have opposed the use of these bombs." This may be true, but it is less than a half truth. You have said in your fourth paragraph that Americans are in Vietnam only as advisers and trainers. This is not true, and invalidates your explanation concerning napalm bombs. I suggest you read the report of Richard Hughes on conditions in Vietnam in the (London) *Sunday Times,* 13 January 1963—a journal by no means pro-Communist, anti-American or even very liberal—in the course of which he speaks of "the Washington fiction that no United States troops are involved in combat and that United States officers and 'trainers' are on the scene merely to 'advise, observe, support and assist.' " He says also: "The Americans are now operating more than 200 helicopters and scores of reconnaissance and troop transport planes in the combat areas. Probably half of all bombing and strafing missions by the South Vietnam air force are undertaken by Americans serving as pilots and co-pilots."

In your fifth paragraph you also endeavour to minimise the effect of "defoliation chemicals" by calling them "common weedkillers." If sprayed, as they must be to achieve the end for which you say they are intended, certain common weed killers would destroy many crops and animals. But, in fact, chemicals other than common weed killers have been used (some of these were once used as "common weed killers" but were found to be too dangerous). The U.S. Government has been charged by the South Vietnam Liberation Red Cross, after a year's study by them of the chemicals sprayed in South Vietnam and their effect upon the health of human beings, animals and crops, with using weed killers which in the large dose used, are harmful; with using white arsenic, various kinds of arsenite sodium and arsenite calcium, lead manganese arsenates, DNP and DNC (which inflame and eat into human flesh), and calcic cyanamide (which has "caused leaves, flowers and fruit to fall, killed big cattle like buffaloes and cows and seriously affected thousands" of the inhabitants of South Vietnam); with having spread these poisonous chemicals on large and densely populated areas of South Vietnam. Admittedly, the South Vietnam Liberation Red Cross, is, as its name suggests, allied with those opposing the U.S. supported Diem regime, but its published findings cannot be ignored since it has urged international investigation of the situation. The use of these weapons, napalm bombs and chemicals, constitutes and results in atrocities and points to the fact that this is a "war of annihilation."[7]

I criticise "atrocities" where I find them. I was considered too anti-Communist by the liberals of the U.S. in Stalin's day for objecting to the atrocities that occurred in Russia at that time. I have recently been carrying on a correspondence concerning the hardships suffered by Jews in Communist countries. I see no reason to suppose that atrocities are to be condoned when committed by Western governments. It is not I, but you, who, in attempting to whitewash U.S. action in South Vietnam, is speaking half-truths and is thereby doing the very thing of which you accuse me: ignoring the Communist push for domination. Moreover, the emulation of what the West says it considers most dastardly in Communist behavior is unlikely to win support for what the West says it stands for anywhere in the world. It makes a mockery of the phrase so beloved by the West—"The Free World."

Two other accusations you make against me: you say that "to call the U.S. the aggressor and to say nothing about the Communist push for domination against the will of the inhabitants in Vietnam is to make a travesty of justice and a mockery of history." The latter is a fine peroration. But I would call to your attention the fact that you yourself had already said (paragraph 2) that you have criticized the U.S. Government's "support of the autocratic Diem regime which has insufficient popular backing." I would also call your attention to the following bit of history: The Geneva Conference of 1954 proposed compromise concerning Vietnam which was admirable and which would have solved the problems of that country if it had been observed. The signatories were Molotov and Selwyn Lloyd who signed as co-chairmen representing East and West respectively. The agreement reached by this Conference was, with the backing of the U.S., not observed by South Vietnam. A new regime was established in South Vietnam under a dictator named Diem of whom *Time* says (21 November 1960): "Diem has ruled with rigged elections, a muzzled press, and political re-education camps that now hold thirty thousand."

I can only deduce that, in your failure to face the facts, and to publicize them, concerning the war in South Vietnam you are, to use your own phraseology, indulging in "arrant nonsense as even you in your heart must know."[8]

Russell was appalled to find that the crucial section of his letter providing evidence of the use of chemicals and insecticides in the war, supporting his defense against the *New York Times* editorial, had been omitted from the published version of his letter. He wrote at once in protest:

I am profoundly shocked by the journalistic standards of the *New York Times*. I have been engaged in a public controversy with the *New York Times* concerning a matter of international importance, namely, the atrocities presently being carried out by the Government of the United States in Vietnam. You attacked me in an editorial, accusing me of arrant nonsense and of stating things without evidence to substantiate them. In my reply to that attack, I presented the evidence in the course of a long letter. You published my letter, omitting my evidence and without even an indication by means of dots to suggest that the letter had been cut or shortened. I have had correspondence and controversy in the pages of *Izvestia* and *Pravda* and I wish to point out to you that never have I been so shabbily treated, never have

Izvestia and *Pravda* behaved in a manner comparably dishonest. I am writing to request you publish the evidence which you omitted from my last letter.[9]

Russell enclosed a copy of the omitted text but neither this nor any of the ensuing correspondence was ever published by the *New York Times*. John B. Oakes, the editor of the editorial page replied to Russell on May 17:

The *New York Times* journalistic standards, which you denounce, need no defense from me. The fact is that *The Times* has given you more than ample space in which to air your views.

Your second letter (published May 4) was longer than the maximum we allow. We will not permit even you to monopolize our letters columns. In accordance with long standing procedure, we reserve the right to cut without notice—and in this instance we did find it necessary to cut an overly long letter of yours to bring it down to the required length. The excision was made solely on account of excess length of the original and for no other reason, nor did it in any way alter the sense of your letter.

We exercise our own judgment in selecting the paragraph to cut. The one selected contained detailed allegations relating to the general charge of chemical warfare. I have not the slightest doubt that you would have objected equally as vociferously no matter which paragraph, sentence or phrase had been cut. In respect to the dots you mention, we never use them in our letters column.

Permit me to remind you that in our editorial of April 8, replying to your first letter (which was also published that day), we fully acknowledged that chemicals—specifically napalm—had been used in South Vietnam by the Government forces. This is not and never was the point at issue. The phrase "arrant nonsense" was specifically applied to your (and the Communist) allegations that the United States' "real concern" is to prevent social reforms in South Vietnam. That charge still stands as the arrant nonsense we said it was.[10]

Russell replied to Oakes on June 5:

I note that you now maintain that what you denied emphatically in an editorial in your newspaper was entirely known to you. I suggest therefore, that it is not the journalistic standards of the *New York Times* which need denouncing but the integrity of its Editor.

You say that you have not the slightest doubt that I should have objected equally no matter which paragraph or sentence or phrases had been cut. That is not so. The reason it is not so is that you took such care to omit precisely those sentences which specify the chemicals used and the absence of which provoked an attack upon me by the *New York Times* previously. The further point that these chemicals were not merely weedkillers, but destroyed livestock, crops, and killed human beings was never admitted by the *New York Times*.

I further point out that the *New York Times* of 19 January 1962, states that of 2,600 villages in Vietnam, nearly 1,400 have been destroyed because of military action by the United States and the Diem Government, in which both chemicals and napalm were used. You take exception to my designation of this conduct as "a war of atrocity." You attack me publicly for making such charges without substantiation. You omit the evidence in my reply to your attack when publishing it, and you write me a letter in which you say that you allow me ample space in which to air my views. You say further, that you need make no defence of the journalistic standards of the *New York Times*. I am impressed by your confidence, and, therefore, request permission to publish this correspondence forthwith.[11]

Oakes replied to Russell on July 3:

Your letter of June 5 is again full of the kind of "distortions or half-truths" which we correctly ascribed to you in our editorial of April 8. For example, we did not deny in our editorial that napalm was used; we specifically admitted it. We did not deny that defoliation chemicals were used; we specifically admitted it. We did not challenge you to specify the other chemicals, if any, that were used; yet you insist that this is the question that "provoked" our editorial attack on you.

What "provoked" our editorial was your own letter of March 28, sent to the *Times* for publication, and published on April 8, in which you accused the United States of "conducting a war of annihilation" in Vietnam, the "sole purpose" of which was "to retain a brutal and futile [sic] regime in the south," to protect economic interests and to prevent "far-reaching social reforms in that part of the world." As I have already informed you in my letter of May 17, this is the kind of language that we described in our editorial of April 8 as "arrant nonsense"; and arrant nonsense, I repeat, it is.

Appropos of your comment about *Pravda* and *Izvestia*, do you honestly believe that they would have published a letter attacking the USSR, written in terms comparable to those you used about the United States in your letter of March 28?

If you publish this correspondence, I trust you will also publish it with your letter to us of March 28 and our editorial reply of April 8, as well as this letter.[12]

The correspondence closed with Russell's letter to Oakes of July 27:

Let us consider where the "half-truths" lie. You did not deny that napalm was used, but you did deny that Americans were involved in its use. In your editorial of April 10, you state: "American advisers have opposed its employment, on both moral and practical grounds, against all except clearly identified military targets." This is not true. Your own reports of 19 January 1962 refer to the destruction of nearly 1,400 villages. "Napalm and chemicals were used in the course of this devastation."

You stated that chemicals employed were common weedkillers and were intended solely to strip leaves from jungle growth. This is untrue. The evidence in my letter which you suppressed establishes its untruth which is, of course, why you disallow it.

Considering that my charge of atrocity is based upon the ruthless use of chemicals and jelly-gasoline, the wholesale devastation of civilian populations in their villages and the use of concentration camps, it would appear that these are the facts to which you object when you refer to my statement as "arrant nonsense, distortion and half-truth from the first to the last sentence." Clearly "the first to the last sentence" is at least inclusive of my remarks on chemicals and napalm. You chose to cut my paragraphs on the specific chemicals used because the paragraphs served to show that the chemicals affected human beings and animals and were not merely weedkillers. You are not honest when you contend that this information was already acknowledged by the *New York Times*. It is precisely the distinction between chemicals which are weedkillers and chemicals which rot human flesh and kill those who come in contact with them that I have sought to make in the course of making clear to the American public the nature of the barbarous war conducted by their Government in South Vietnam.

That Diem's regime is "futile" and serves American economic interests, I should be willing to stand by before any impartial mind.

I agree that *Pravda* and *Izvestia* might well suppress a letter attacking the USSR as forthrightly as my letter on Vietnam attacks the United States. This, however, was not the point I was making, as you well know. Never have *Izvestia* or *Pravda* purported to publish a letter of mine while omitting surreptitiously the very evidence in dispute in the course of an exchange. This form of dishonesty is, to my mind, more perfidious than the absence of publication of a letter. It is conscious fraud.[13]

In the course of his correspondence with the *New York Times*, Russell received scores of communications indicating support for his stand. Many of these came from South Vietnam itself. Nguyen Xien, President of the Committee of Protest Struggle Against U.S.-Diem Persecution of Intellectuals in South Vietnam, and Secretary General of the Vietnam Socialist Party, wrote on April 16:

> Your letter as well as the open letter on March 1 of 62 American intellectuals and personalities...constitute a great stimulus for the struggle of our entire people....We earnestly hope that you will use your high prestige to continue condemning the U.S.-Diem crimes, especially their use of toxic substances as a war means to massacre South Vietnamese people.

Me Nguyen-huu-Tho, President of the South Vietnamese Liberation National Front Central Committee wrote:

> We have seen that there are no questions having a bearing on the fate of mankind to which you remain indifferent...Our people have closely followed your unswerving struggle for the elimination of the nuclear threat, and admire your unshakeable courage in standing out, despite your age, against repressive measures and vile slanders. That was why we hoped that you would voice your opinion on the biggest bloodshed now going on in the world. This hope has now been met.[14]

Russell received copies of many letters which had been sent to the *New York Times* supporting his view. One such letter from Rockwell Kent, the artist, dated April 15 but found unacceptable for publication, drew attention to the *New York Times'* accusation that Russell's statements were derived from Communist sources:

> Whatever the sources of his information may have been, his charges are fully sustained by articles that have appeared in the American press, notably *Life* magazine (January 25), *The Nation* (January 19, March 2) and the *St. Louis-Post Dispatch*. They are likewise endorsed by 60 prominent Americans in an *Open Letter to the President* recently published (as an advertisement) in the *Washington Post* and the *New York Times*.
>
> Or, in the spirit of the late Senator McCarthy, are these American publications to be considered as Communist fronts and the Open Letter's signatories as mere dupes? Your readers will doubtless decide for themselves.

"Don't let the fatherly strictures of the *New York Times* affect you in the slightest" wrote W.H. Ferry from the Center for the Study of Democratic Institutions in California.[15] "You are doing just fine. Since we lack a Russell ourselves, we have to make do with the wonderful reverberations from Wales." Richard Morrock wrote from Bard College, Annandale-on-Hudson, New York, "several years from now you will be able to say to the United States, 'I told you so.' "[16] Morrock also congratulated Russell for his article in the *New York Times* magazine section "about the need for East-West peace."

That article entitled "Is Communism a Menace?" had been written in response to the *New York Times* magazine asking Russell to clarify his position. Published on April 7 there is little doubt that the article helped to provoke the *New York Times'* editorial attack on Russell of April 8. "My own belief," states Russell in his opening paragraph, "is that, although communism was something of a menace in the days of Stalin, it is so no longer. It has been replaced by another menace, namely the fear of Communism." Russell argued his view that while communism up until the Khrushchev era had based its policies on the inevitability of a great war with capitalism, it had now changed its approach, for two reasons:

The first was his (Khrushchev's) realization that a nuclear war could not produce such a world as Communists desire. The second was that Russia, after a long period of hardship and scarcity, was at last in a position to produce consumer goods in abundance, provided peace was preserved.

Russell continued:

I am firmly persuaded that friendly gestures from the West would now produce an enthusiastic response and that communism, now, is only a menace because it is thought to be so.

Russell then restated his position on the Cuban crisis as well as on the Sino-Indian border dispute in which the actions of the USSR on the one hand and China on the other hand led him to believe that both those countries had realized that the "avoidance of nuclear war is a vital interest of every country in the world."

Russell's article, followed as it was by his attack on American Vietnam policy in the *New York Times* of the next day, raised a hornet's nest. The *New York Times* magazine was inundated with angry letters.[17] "I am more than ever convinced that outside the field of mathematics Lord Russell is a presumptuous and reckless thinker," wrote one irate reader. "How many readers will swallow this sophistry" demanded another. Yet another counselled "it seems to me that sadness and compassion are more appropriate: 'Old age is a dirty trick' my physician once said. The once pre-eminent thinker is a victim of that inevitable trick."

While the columns of the *New York Times* reflected an overwhelmingly hostile reaction to Russell, the response to him personally was much more evenly balanced, with many letters of support. Abe Pivowitz of New York wrote on April 13:

...I reach across the Atlantic to shake your hand. Your truthful actions on behalf of mankind are an inspiration to all of us who are working for peace, freedom and human justice.

Allen Kimbell, a Student Peace Union activist wrote to Russell on April 17 describing the disputes within the American peace movement over attitudes to the Vietnam War. His organization had participated in a "New York Easter Peace Walk and Demonstration" at which they displayed "No War in Vietnam" signs which included quotations from Russell's letter to the *New York Times:*

When we held these signs up at the UN rally, we were attacked from the microphone and by people around us...There were many reasons for this, among them the compromising and non-provocative attitude of the organizers who managed to make the march as non-effective as possible.

Kimbell asked Russell for advice on "improving our demonstrations and raising the morale of the people in them." Russell replied on May 27:

Thank you for your recent letter, which I was most interested to read. I am well aware of the difficulties which face the peace movement in the United States and of the fact that several peace organisations there are not offering serious and effective resistance to American foreign and military policy.

I hope that it will be possible for you in the New York area to contact other people, as you have done in your chapter of the Student Peace Union, and discuss with them the creation of effective resistance to war. Our experience in Britain has been that out of such meetings of determined people can come the enthusiasm and imagination to create genuine resistance. I doubt whether the problem is to improve existing organisations if they are attacking you for radicalism. This suggests to me a shameful timidity on their part. Whilst they doubtless deserve a public rebuke and constructive criticism, they may well still be of some service in bringing people into the peace movement in the first instance.

Our main concern, however, must be for a radical growing edge to the movement. Here I can offer you no blueprint, but I am enclosing some literature from the earlier days of the Committee of 100, which I hope you will find of interest and value.

I am greatly encouraged by your opposition to war in Vietnam and should wish you to know, as I explained recently to the Student Peace Union, that my second letter to the *New York Times* on this subject was mutilated by that newspaper, which had attacked me editorially for not producing evidence and sources for my statements and then deleted from my second letter all the documented evidence for which it asked.

On May 11 the New York City Student Peace Union had held a forum against war in Vietnam at which they read a statement they had requested from Russell, which he had sent them in a cable on May 9:

Greatly heartened by your opposition to atrocious war in South Vietnam by United States Government. Extend my hand in common cause and hope our efforts will induce government to desist. Urge you publish widely data on chemical warfare which I am sending as *New York Times* has censored my evidence.

Russell's revelations about the nature of American involvement in Vietnam were helping to stimulate a powerful reaction to the war on the part of militant sections of the American peace movement. Students in particular were turning increasingly to Russell both for inspiration and as a source of information on the war. On 5 June 1963 Irving Kirsh, an office holder of the Student Peace Union, informed Russell of the success of their forum and of the production of a pamphlet on Vietnam consisting of Russell's exchange with the *New York Times* and including his evidence on chemical warfare.[18] Kirsch also informed Russell of his organization's plan to hold a demonstration in front of the United States mission to the United Nations on June 29:

The demonstration will be centered around the information you have supplied concerning the U.S. war in Vietnam. We are inviting all organizations that are opposed to this atrocity to join with us. There may also be simultaneous demonstrations in other cities.

Repeating the Student Peace Union's support for Russell and for Russell's hope for united efforts to end the war, Kirsch asked if similar protests were being planned in England. Russell had been as concerned to influence British public opinion against the war, especially in view of Britain's role as co-signatory to the 1954 Geneva Conference on Vietnam. At the time of his controversy with the *New York Times* he was writing similar letters to the British press explaining his opposition to U.S. involvement as well as calling upon the British government to honor its commitment to the decisions of the Geneva Conference. The response from the British press closely paralleled that of its American counterpart, condemning Russell for making charges, especially concerning chemical warfare, without evidence. In a letter to *The Guardian* of May 5, Russell provided the evidence necessary to substantiate his claim of American atrocities and demanded:

> Are you so blinded by the dictates of the Cold War that you have lost the capacity to condemn such barbarism when the facts cry out to you?

The Guardian declined to publish his letter.

On 29 September 1963 Russell announced to the international press the launching of the Bertrand Russell Peace Foundation and the Atlantic Peace Foundation which, acting together, were to place on an institutional basis Russell's efforts to develop a movement of international resistance to the threat of nuclear war. The developmment of the Foundation became Russell's principal interest. It was not only the vehicle for his activity in the remaining years of his life, but was planned to continue the work after his lifetime. Russell explained that although the various peace movements had achieved a certain amount of publicity about the danger of nuclear war, and the need for disarmament, that publicity had been "distorted, inadequate and sporadic." It was among the Peace Foundation's intentions, Russell declared, "to develop our own media of communication" which would "not depend upon establishment controlled or governmental intimidated press."[19]

Owing to Russell's critique of the press he was approached, early in October, by the *New York Times* to do an article for them on his idea of what constitutes a good newspaper. Russell's reference to "the establishment controlled or governmental intimidated press" was the "newspeg" upon which the *New York Times* wished him to comment in his introduction to the article.[20] Russell prepared an article which he entitled "My idea of a Good Newspaper" and submitted it to the *New York Times*. The first part of the article was devoted to supporting his contention that newspapers were subject to pressure from powerful sources such as the government, advertisers and big business interests. In addition to these "specific sources of misinformation," Russell maintained that there was a "diffused desire for what one may call respectability." Explaining this view he wrote:

> Respectability, as I am using the term, means conformity with the opinions and interests of the powerful. For anyone who has contact with those who wield power, whether secret or overt, life is very much

pleasanter if they side with men of influence than if they oppose them. For all these various reasons, influential newspapers seldom give truthful accounts in controversial matters. There is a reciprocal causal relation between public opinion and the press. The press creates a certain kind of public opinion, and public opinion, in return, makes the press still more misleading in supporting the bias that it has created.

He then proceeded to give specific instances of "suppressions and distortions."

A good example of the former kind of distortion is the question of shelters. It has become exceedingly probable that in a nuclear war the Soviet Government would employ very large bombs, the chief danger from which would be firestorms, not fallout. Governments, however, have continued to advocate shelters against fallout and have tried to conceal the uselessness of shelters against firestorm in which the occupants of even very deep shelters would be either roasted or asphyxiated for lack of oxygen. Very few newspapers, except unpopular journals appealing to minority opinion, are willing to mention these facts about shelters, and most are quite willing to abet Governments in deceitfully luring their citizens to a vast horror of agonising death....

There are other dangers, at least as great as those from nuclear bombs, about which most people have been kept ignorant, by the popular press. Take, for example, non-nuclear gas bombs, of which it is estimated that the U.S. government has a stockpile of 130,000, each of which is said to be capable of destroying all life in an area of 3,500 square miles. If these estimates are correct, and they are the most accurate obtainable, the American stockpile of non-nuclear nerve gas bombs is capable of destroying all organic life on the land surface of the earth eight times over, and of destroying all organic life in both land and sea two and a half times (*Window on the World*, M.H. Weik, July-August 1963).

Another matter in which misleading statements by Governments have been reiterated by the press is the Soviet attitude to the inspection that must accompany a disarmament treaty. It is stated untruly that the Soviets reject any inspection until the whole process of disarmament is complete. The position of the Russians has been and is as follows: if the West agrees to the *principle* of general disarmament the Russians call for internationally recruited inspection teams to be placed in every country *before any measures* of disarmament are begun. If general disarmament were agreed to, the Soviets have stated that they would permit: 1) thousands of United Nations inspectors on

Soviet soil before any reduction of armaments is started; 2) these inspectors could control on the spot disbanding of 60 percent of Russian manpower and 100% of the means of delivery of missiles and all other carriers (*A Summary of Disarmament Documents, 1945-1962*, National Lawyer's Guild, San Francisco, California).

Russell explained why in his opinion the popular press was willing to "follow its Governments in suppressing and distorting the dangers of present nuclear policies":

...the Cold War, so long as it can be kept cold, is a source of profit to very powerful interests, notably the armaments industry. So long as the Cold War continues, the risk of a Hot War will remain....practical politicians, successful newspapers, and very large sections of the public are content to go on running this risk and to support their reckless policy by suppressions and even downright lies.

Advancing his guidelines for an ideal newspaper, Russell concluded:

The first thing that is to be desired is a separation of news from opinion. Ideally, the presentation of news should not be affected by the editorial opinion of a newspaper, which should be expressed in articles quite separate from reports of what has occurred. A closely related matter in which impartiality is to be desired is the selection of news and the amount of space given to this or that item. In both these respects a newspaper should be guided by the importance to the world of the news item and not by the question of whether it favours this side or that in any controversial issue....

The misleading use of words implying censure is a very frequent method of giving false impressions to readers. In various countries, notably Laos and South Vietnam, there is opposition to the government which is generally labelled in the Western press "Communist" or "Communist inclined" even when, in fact the resistance to the Government has nothing to do with communism—only, possibly, a natural dislike of being slowly tortured by burning napalm oil. There are many such question-begging epithets which a journalist can use according to taste—for instance, "red dictators," "red infiltration," "terrorists." There are also methods of ridicule which can be employed with considerable success. When there is an anti-nuclear demonstration in London, many newspapers will state that the men taking part in the demonstration were all bearded and long haired. I have seen this statement accompanied by a photograph of the demonstrators in which there was not a single beard. One must deem it fortunate that newspapers are sometimes careless. A good newspaper, as I imagine it, would not employ such terms or such devices indiscriminately, but would content itself with calling a spade a spade and not a beastly shovel.

Cliches such as "free world" have a powerfully misleading effect upon very large parts of the population of Western countries. When the term "free world" is used, it seems in practice, that part of the world which is opposed to Moscow or Peking. Whether there is or is not freedom in a country which is labelled part of the "free world" is not considered. Many such countries are dictatorships—Spain, Portugal, South Vietnam—and others, such as South Africa, Angola and the Southern States of America, allow freedom only to a section of the population. I am not pretending that the Communist world is free. I am only contending that the anti-Communist world is not nearly as free as the received cliches suggest. Again, the ideal newspaper would employ them only with the greatest discretion.

Newspapers which publish something definitely false should be under an obligation to publish a denial (with equal prominence) as soon as the falsehood of what has been stated is brought to their notice.

On October 28, the London representative of the *New York Times* informed Russell that her editors had requested a revision "since they do not feel you have provided us with the article we ordered." The editors felt that Russell had given his opinions "on a variety of other subjects, but there is very little on what an ideal newspaper would be like."

Russell replied on October 29:

Since receiving your letter of October 28, I have looked over the article to which your editors object. I have failed to see how I could deal with the theme of which your editors wished me to treat in any other way than as I have done. You asked me, in your letter of October 7, to begin by justifying my phrase about the "establishment-controlled or government-intimidated press." I did so. You asked me to continue by describing the ideal newspaper as I conceived it. I did so. I could not give instances of such a newspaper since there are none. Consequently, my only way of describing the ideal newspaper, and of illustrating and making clear my points, was to mention ways in which it would differ from the actual present-day practices. In order to spare the sensibilities of American readers, I drew almost all my instances from the British press. Though the article doubtless "tells" my "opinions" on a variety of other subjects, the accurate precis of the article, which I send herewith, seems to show that your editors are wrong in saying that "there is very little" in it "on what an ideal newspaper would be like." I am left wondering if the reason they have given for turning down the article is their real reason. I cannot help feeling that they will continue to object to the article so long as it supplies justification for my phrase "establishment-controlled or government-intimidated press," and precise detail about what the ideal newspaper should and should not do. In view of this doubt I do not feel that I can spend further time and effort to provide, as you suggest, some substantial inserts.

Footnotes

1. B. Russell, *War Crimes in Vietnam* (London, 1967);(Monthly Review Press, New York, 1967) p. 29.
2. *Ibid.*, p. 30.
3. *Ibid.*
4. *Ibid.*, pp. 30-31.
5. *Ibid.*, pp. 31-32.
6. *Ibid.*, pp. 32-33.
7. This paragraph was omitted by *The New York Times.*
8. B. Russell, *War Crimes in Vietnam*, p.. 33-36.
9. *Ibid.*, p. 37.
10. *Ibid.*, pp. 37-38.
11. *Ibid.*, pp. 38-39.
12. *Ibid.*, pp. 39-40.
13. *Ibid.*, pp. 40-41.
14. 1 April 1963.
15. Undated April 1963.
16. 8 April 1963.
17. 21 April 1963.
18. Student Peace Union (New York City), *Bertrand Russell on the War in Vietnam.*
19. Published in full in *The Minority of One*, November 1963.
20. Heather Bradley, London Editor, to Russell, 7 October 1963.

15 The Myth of American Freedom

Russell was disturbed by the fact that due to the antagonism of the press on both sides of the Atlantic he was not able to make known to the public at large his views on American policies and he had to rely increasingly on the limited resources of the radical press to publicize his information. *Liberation, IF Stone's Weekly, The Nation, Frontier* and *The Minority of One* were among those American journals most sympathetic to Russell's position. Russell had joined, at the end of 1962, the Board of Sponsors of *The Minority of One*, an "independent monthly for an American alternative, dedicated to the eradication of all restrictions on thought," edited by M.S. Arnoni.

The magazine, which also included among its sponsors Albert Schweitzer and Linus Pauling, contained in its May 1963 number, Russell's article "The Myth of American Freedom" which had first appeared during April in *Frontier*.[1] "The active presence of freedom in American life is vanishing small." With this opening statement Russell proceeded to argue that there were three interrelated developments in America "which have made talk of freedom and individual liberty empty talk." These developments were: "Overt and unabashed police state techniques; the evolution of institutional life incompatible with freedom and liberty; and the power struggle between...America and Russia."

Analyzing developments in America since the end of World War II Russell asserted that in this period the road to political power had been "characterised by the crudest persecution of dissident opinion," the object of which had been to impose "an acceptance of capitalism and the power of large industry." Russell explained how radical opinion in the U.S. had been discredited by equating it with communism:

> "The result of this pervasive and systematic terror [McCarthy-ism] has been that Americans first respond to political discussion by seeking to attach labels to ideas, the better to dismiss them without having to consider them."

The elimination of dissent was achieved by identifying dissent in the popular mind with support of the...inconceivably wicked Russians... Russia was the means of ending American radicalism.

Commenting on "the atmosphere of hysteria" which had been "sedulously cultivated by the press and the government of the United States" in the post-war years, Russell judged that:

The result of this pervasive and systematic terror has been that Americans first respond to political discussion by seeking to attach labels to ideas, the better to dismiss them without having to consider them. It is not possible to have such an environment for fifteen years without profound effect. Americans prefer to say that the witch hunt was a passing phase of hysteria created by nasty men such as McCarthy. On the contrary, the persecution which America has witnessed and largely embraced was created by men of power to destroy political opposition. McCarthy was an excrescence upon this fact.

Because of these years of "persecution, systematic conditioning and the eradication of political opposition," Russell felt that "the political democracy of which Americans speak is, for me, largely without serious meaning."

Citing Morton Sobell as a victim of persecution Russell described his case as "one of the more obvious examples of 'freedom' in the United States." Russell had remained closely involved with the campaign to secure freedom for Sobell, issuing statements, writing to the parole board and meeting with Sobell's wife on her campaign visit to England. The Campaign Committee had been conducting a prolonged fight through the courts, and after Russell learned that the U.S. Court of Appeals had refused to grant Sobell a new trial, despite condemning the conduct of the prosecution in the Rosenberg-Sobell case as "wholly reprehensible," he issued the following statement:

The persecution of Morton Sobell is a case as infamous as that of Dreyfus or Sacco and Vanzetti. No contemporary example of political injustice is as clear and shocking as the case of Morton Sobell. He was illegally kidnapped. He was convicted on the basis of a perjuror's evidence, a man whose perjury was admitted by himself in the very Court which passed sentence on Morton Sobell. There was no evidence whatsoever other than the accusation of this confessed perjuror. We now learn that even the United States Court of Appeals acknowledges in a unanimous decision that the law under which Sobell was tried and the tactics employed by the Prosecution required, at the very least, a re-trial. How is it possible that a man can be sentenced to thirty years on no evidence and that the trial can be conducted in so reprehensible a manner as to be condemned by a Court of Appeals, and yet the man so unjustly convicted is refused a new trial?

Morton Sobell was given a wartime sentence of thirty years. It was not wartime. The jury was not asked to find what it was Sobell was supposed to have done, either in war or in peace. He was accused of no specific thing. Despite all this, the conclusion to which the Court of Appeals comes with regard to Morton Sobell is that although it is true he may be innocent, and although it is true, whether innocent or not, the trial through which he was convicted was so suspect as to be set aside fo a new trial—despite, all this Sobell must remain in prison without a new trial because he has already served thirteen years and it is too long a time for the case to be re-opened. It is too long ago to allow the case to be re-opened again. Could anything be more monstrously unjust than this?

To my mind, Morton Sobell is a symbol of the evil of fanaticism. He is a victim to this evil, and his case is a blot on the American conscience. I plead for a new trial or a parole for him.[2]

Russell prepared this statement for a filmed interview in London as part of a documentary which included similar pleas for clemency by many eminent Americans. The film was shown at New York's Carnegie Hall on 19 June 1963, the 10th Anniversary of the execution of Julius and Ethel Rosenberg.

In the June 1963 edition of the *Minority of One* Russell contributed the first of his series of "Notes and Comments" which he was to use as a means of communicating monthly information he felt to be important, which had been ignored or rejected by the national press. One such item of information concerned Maurice Paul, a foreign-born trade unionist, against whom the Immigration and Naturalization service of the Justice Department has issued a deportation order. Paul was one of the many hundreds of non-citizens who as a result of the Walter-McCarran Act of 1952 had been made subject to deportation proceedings because of civil rights and trade union activities.

Russell's message of 26 March 1963 to the Trade Union Committee for Defense of Maurice Paul was published in the July issue of *The Minority of*

One together with the news that the Government's case against Maurice Paul had been dropped:

> That a man should spend the greater part of his life in a country—forty years—partaking in its public life and in all respects an admirable citizen, and yet be subject to deportation is an appalling reflection upon the standards of justice in the United States. What is Maurice Paul's crime? His crime is that he is a trade union organiser who has made the cause of those who live in the slums and who are subject to appalling economic conditions his own. He has been subject to the crudest political persecution and the usual treatment of a paid perjuror. It is an outrage that he should be deported and I appeal to all decent Americans to oppose this act of tyranny.

As a result of Russell's protest on behalf of Maurice Paul he was approached by the Methodist Federation for Social Action in Oregon, whose representative Mark A. Chamberlin informed Russell of the predicament of Hamish MacKay and William Mackie, "two long-time resident aliens of Portland, Oregon" who had been deported in 1960 under the Walter-McCarran Act after being charged with membership of the Communist Party. MacKay, a carpenter, had been a resident of the United States for thirty-six years and Mackie, a painter, for fifty-three years. Both had dependents in the United States and both had been denied citizenship on political grounds. Russell wrote to Chamberlin on August 8:

> ...I most strongly urge all those concerned to grant this travesty of justice their immediate and favourable attention. The future of civil liberty in the United States depends largely on the outcome of this case and others like it. The use of exile and of the threat of exile as a political weapon have no place in a free society.

Several months earlier Russell had described the Walter-McCarran Act as "a symbol of neanderthalism in our time." In a tribute to Professor Louise Pettibone Smith, a national co-chair of the American Committee for the Protection of Foreign Born, and to the late Dr. Royal France, Russell wrote under the title "What does America offer Humanity?":

> Human liberty is an abstraction which men of power have profaned. They have profaned this idea, not alone because they have violated it, but because they have invoked it. Men of power today invoke the noblest concepts of our species in the name of their cruel and insensate brutality. It is in the name of human liberty that policies of mass

destruction, of genocide, of extermination, are being perpetrated. It is in the name of human liberty that the American government is prepared to incinerate human beings in the hundreds of millions. It is, therefore, clear that to preserve a policy of this kind, again in the name of human liberty, the most primitive and savage legislation of repression must be enacted.

When such men of power have at their disposal the means of conditioning an entire population, it is a source of extraordinary pain and desperation for those individuals who see the perversity both of the practice and the language in which the practice is couched. When we consider the McCarran Act and the entire legislation of repression which has been enacted in the United States, we must consider it in the context of a whole range of activity. Paid informers, investigating committees operating in conjunction with a slanderous press, subversive lists, a secret political police, loyalty oaths—all of these—have been part of an attempt to reduce the American people to a condition of servility and of hysterical fanaticism with respect to independence of thought.

Professor H.H. Wilson has referred to this climate and this pattern of behaviour and has called it the development of "a concentration camp for the mind." I wish to consider the way in which this concentration camp for the mind has been used by men of power. It has been used by them to keep themselves in control of a society and to remove from the people the right to question that control without the very loyalty of these people to their country being called in question. This power has been utilized to sustain a struggle for international power which is likely to lead to the extermination of human life on our planet. The Cold War, the struggle for power betwen the Soviet Union and the United States, is a reflection of the mentality of those who have prepared the McCarran Act and who would utilize it to create conditions of tyranny in the United States. I believe that it is very important that this relationship be understood...[3]

During August Russell received information from Jeffrey S. Gordon of Berkeley, California, a member of the Committee Upholding the Right to Travel, that 59 students who had defied a government ban and visited Cuba, were returning to the U.S. where it was believed they would be subject to "possible prosecution and definite persecution of one type or another." Gordon asked if Russell would "serve as a sponsor of CURT."[4] Russell agreed to sponsor the Committee. A further letter from Gordon[5] informed Russell that because his "position on peace and the need for constant interrelations between all peoples is well known in the United States" a message from him to a meeting to welcome home the students "would be a great boost to us." Russell sent a message on September 16.

Shortly afterwards it bccme known that the students were all indicted and Russell wrote on October 1 to the *New York Times*:

> I am concerned to point out to Americans the totalitarian nature of the current persecution of the students who travelled to Cuba. They were exercising what ought to be considered their elementary rights in a democratic society. For travelling to another country they are charged under acts which make them liable to five years imprisonment or a fine of $20,000. They are accused of such things as acting as "foreign agents" and of conspiring to make an illegal trip.
>
> Apart from the fundamental violation of their freedom, I should have thought that the guarantee of the Bill of Rights against excessive bail would have prevented their being held under a bond of $5,000.
>
> This tyrannical victimisation of courageous citizens is as reprehensible as the silence of the American public and press. It is apparent both how fearful the American Government is of independent information regarding Cuba and how indifferent Americans are to attacks upon individual liberty.[6]

Russell's article "The Myth of American Freedom" was written at a time when the persecution of dissident opinion in America was intensifying in response to the challenge posed by the example of Cuba and the incipient black revolt. The case of the three "Bloomington Students" was illustrative of Russell's contention that the anti-Communist "witch-hunt" was not a "passing phase" but had been created "to destroy political opposition."[7] The students concerned were office holders of a Young Socialist group at the University of Indiana and had been indicted under a 1951 state law "to exterminate communism and Communists and any and all teachings of the same," after organizing a student meeting on the "Black Revolt in America." Russell became the honorary chairman of the Committee to Aid the Bloomington Students who faced prison terms of up to six years if convicted. Russell wrote to the Committee on September 23:

> Thank you for your information concerning the intolerable persecution of the Indiana University students. I have been a socialist for over half a century. I am disgusted that three courageous people can be sentenced to up to six years imprisonment for no other offence than membership in a Young Socialist Society. How ludicrous the propaganda about the "Free World." Not only does this "free world" consist mainly in tyrannies all over the globe, but those who dare to point this out are imprisoned for doing so in the "free" United States. I offer them my every support and assure you that I shall raise the matter in Great Britain.[8]

Footnotes

1. See below pp. 356-60.
2. Published in *The Minority of One*, August 1963.
3. Published in Journal of the *Louise Pettibone Smith Committee*, 12 October 1962; reprinted in *The Minority of One*, November 1962.
4. Gordon to Russell, 12 August 1963.
5. Gordon to Russell, 9 September 1963.
6. Not published.
7. "The Myth of American Freedom; see below p. 358.
8. A letter from Russell protesting the case appeared in the London *Sunday Times* of 6 October 1963.

16 The Kennedy Assassination & Aftermath

On 5 August 1963 America, Britain and the USSR signed a partial test ban treaty in Moscow. Although the treaty meant an end to all nuclear tests in the atmosphere, in space and underwater, and was undoubtedly a victory for all those who had campaigned against nuclear tests as well as, in Russell's view, "a first step towards the ending of the Cold War,"[1] Russell remained apprehensive about the future, especially in view of the Chinese Government's opposition to the treaty. China regarded the treaty as evidence of rapprochement between the U.S. and the USSR directed against China. Russell believed that the retention of this attitude by the Chinese, coupled with the prospect that she was certain to soon have her own nuclear weapons, would be "an increasingly dangerous obstacle to world peace."[2]

On September 22 Russell wrote to President Kennedy to congratulate him upon the signing of the treaty and raised the problem both of China's attitude to the treaty as well as the absence of U.S. recognition of the Chinese Government:

Clearly, no lasting peace is possible without understanding with China and no disarmament agreements are tenable unless China is a signatory to them. Is it not time to approach China with regard to establishing relations with her and with regard to the recent proposals of Premier Chou? I have reason to believe that such a move on the part of the United States would be well received by China and serious disarmament agreement could well be the result.

The alternative, I fear, will be Chinese nuclear tests and weapons combined with deeply felt resentment at her isolation and ostracism.

The largest country on earth in terms of population can only be softened through mutual respect and discussions and I am anxious about the rapidity with which this opportunity is disappearing...

I remember with gratitude your speech as a Senator urging a reconsideration of American policy towards China and I hope very much this may now be possible.

Russell's chief concern, however, remained the ending of the Cold War and peaceful co-existence between the U.S. and the USSR and he took up this question with Kennedy:

It has been said widely by American officials that the major barrier to disarmament...with the Soviet Union is her refusal to countenance inspection on her soil or controls over disarmament.

In the Soviet proposals for disarmament advanced in 1961 it was stated that were the government of the United States to agree to the principle of general disarmament, the Soviet Union would:

a) Call for internationally recruited inspection teams to be placed in every country *before any measures of disarmament are begun.*

b) Allow thousands of United Nations inspectors on Soviet soil before any reduction of armaments is started.

c) Allow these inspectors to control on the spot: the disbanding of sixty percent of Soviet manpower, and one hundred percent of the means of delivery of missiles and all other carriers in agreed stages.

I am most anxious that, in view of this, some accommodation should be reached enabling disarmament to occur and the dangerous Cold War to be liquidated. This opportunity will clearly depend on the inclusion of China in consultations and agreements. I await with hope and interest your views on these urgent matters.

William E. Foster, the Director of the U.S. Arms Control and Disarmament Agency, replied on October 29 on behalf of Kennedy:

...I have noted your comments on the need for the participation of Communist China in any disarmament agreements and on the attitude of the Soviet Union toward inspection and controls over disarmament.

The overwhelming vote of ratification in the United States Senate of the test ban treaty accurately reflects the strong support by the Government and people of the United States for measures which can serve to halt the arms race and facilitate progress toward general and complete disarmament. The United States will persist in its efforts to halt and turn down the arms race, which brings security to no nation...

Russell had also informed Kennedy on October 2 of his plans concerning the formation of the Bertrand Russell Peace Foundation and the Atlantic Peace Foundation. On 5 November 1963 Thomas M. Judd, on behalf of President Kennedy, acknowledged Russell's letter and indicated that the U.S. Government supported the aims of the Bertrand Russell Peace Foundation. Russell replied that he was sure that "Mr. Kennedy will understand that we should welcome his support in these aims."[3] Just two weeks later Russell "in common with the rest of the world"[4] was stunned by the assassination of the U.S. president in Dallas, Texas on November 22. His surprise however, was modified by his awareness of "the growing acceptance of unbridled violence in the world and particularly in the United States."[5]

Russell shared with many people strong doubts as to the true facts behind the assassination; the allegation that this was the work of a lone assassin, Lee Harvey Oswald; the linking of Oswald with the shooting of Patrolman Tippit; Oswald's subsequent murder by Jack Ruby; and the role of the Dallas police, and the press in general in accounting for the killings.

Expressing these doubts Russell has stated:

When President Kennedy was assassinated, confusion and hysteria were widespread in the United States. The suspicion in the world of political motivation alarmed the military-industrial groupings ruling the United States. It was essential to come up with an assassin. Within fifteen minutes of President Kennedy's death, official U.S. agencies proclaimed not merely the apprehension of his assailant, but the apprehension of the sole individual responsible. Lee Harvey Oswald was convicted from that moment, in one of the most unrelieved and intimidating propaganda campaigns. This was the work of the mass media and official bodies. Even this campaign was insufficient to erradicate the suspicion surrounding the confused version advanced by officialdom, and when Lee Harvey Oswald was murdered in the midst of Dallas police, the widespread doubt became contemptuous disbelief.[6]

It seemed to Russell "that there had been an appalling miscarriage of justice and that probably something very nasty was being covered up."[7] Russell's suspicions were confirmed when in June 1964 he met Mark Lane, a New York lawyer who had been acting on behalf of Oswald's mother and who had compiled very compelling evidence challenging the official version of the assassination.

Mark Lane, who had encountered extreme hostility in America towards his investigation, came to Europe to seek a platform and support for his Committee of Enquiry into the circumstances of Kennedy's murder. Russell felt that "it was quite clear from the hushing-up methods employed" by the American authorities "that very important issues were at stake."[8] Russell was impressed by "the energy and astuteness with which Mark Lane pursued the relevant facts" as well as by "the scrupulous objectivity with which he presented them.[9] He agreed to do everything possible to assist Lane, and together with his colleagues on the Bertrand Russell Peace Foundation, established the British "Who Killed Kennedy? Committee," with himself as Chairman.

On the basis of Lane's findings, Russell compiled a document entitled "Sixteen Questions on the Assassination" which vigorously criticized the official handling of the case:

> The official version of the assassination of President Kennedy has been so riddled with contradictions that it has been abandoned and rewritten no less than three times. Blatant fabrications have received very widespread coverage by the mass media, but denials of these same lies have gone unpublished. Photographs, evidence and affadavits have been doctored out of recognition. Some of the most important aspects of the case against Lee Harvey Oswald have been completely blacked out. Meanwhile the FBI, the police and the Secret Service have tried to silence key witnesses or instruct them what evidence to give. Others involved have disappeared or died in extraordinary circumstances.[10]

Russell found that in common with Lane's his challenge of the official view was "well and truly vilified"[11] and that strenuous attempts were made by the British and U.S. press and government agencies to "frustrate our efforts."[12] In calling for support for Mark Lane from all those who wished for "the peace of the world...and who valued the truth,[13] Russell declared:

> There is no precedent for Mark Lane's remarkable attempt to investigate the truth regarding the assassination of President Kennedy. When Zola sought to uncover the truth concerning Dreyfus, he had the advantage that Dreyfus was alive. Oswald has been murdered, and this *cause célèbre* concerns the assassination of a President in the nuclear age.
>
> Mark Lane's evidence comprises one of the most remarkable documents I have seen and is an unanswerable indictment of the Government's attempt to suppress the truth and conceal the circumstances surrounding the death of the President. There has never been a more subversive, conspiratorial, unpatriotic or endangering course for the security of the United States and the world than the attempt by

the United States Government to hide the murderers of its recent President....[14]

When the Warren Commission, which had been appointed to investigate and pronounce on the assassination, issued its voluminous report in September 1964, Russell immediately disputed its findings. The news media generally acclaimed the Report without critical examination "aggressively stating that no one could doubt its conclusions,"[15] but Russell refused to regard it as "holy writ."[16] His statement on the Report concluding that "the Warren Commission's lack of integrity is fully exposed," was issued on September 27:

The murder of an American President affects the peace of the world: a plot to kill him would have the gravest implications. For these reasons alone, the Warren Commission had to explain the disturbing anomalies which have attended the murder and its aftermath. With all the resources of the White House, the FBI, the Secret Service, the Dallas police, the CIA and other governmental agencies available to the Commission, their report conspicuously fails to dispose of the doubts as to the latest official view of the assassination.

We have seen medical evidence altered, three contradictory official versions of the assassination, the circulation of Oswald's description as Tippit's murderer more than twenty minutes before Tippit was shot, a fabricated report from the Dallas authorities, eye-witnesses ignored, lies about the number of bullets—a parade of distortion and doctored evidence. These facts have been established by the investigations of Mr. Mark Lane.

The Warren Commission itself consists of men so close to the investigatory agencies of the United States that they would be ineligible to serve as jurors. They have persistently leaked information about the report they now present. The report evades the facts presented by Mr. Lane, and suppresses the evidence supporting them. It is a sorrily incompetent document and covers its authors in shame....[17]

As a result of Russell's forthright condemnation of the Warren Report, editorial attacks were mounted against him in leading American and British newspapers. "Word went about," commented Russell, "that I was talking through my hat and had not even read the report."[18] Answering this accusation Russell wrote to the newspapers concerned, including the *Washington Post* on 9 October 1964. In his letter Russell added two further contradictions about the assassination which had come to light:

Your editorial attack upon me is based upon misinformation and I should be glad of an opportunity to place the facts before your readers.

Owing to suppression by the press, people have been unaware of the fact that I am the author of an article entitled "16 Questions on the Assassination." This article, which was published in September, considers with considerable care the contradictions in the official versions of the assassination and the anomalies in the evidence advanced. Mr. Mark Lane, whose findings our Committee in Britain disseminates, obtained an early copy of the Warren Commisssion Report and prepared a six thousand word reply which was in my hands before the Report was released. I was also apprised of the Summary and Conclusions of the Warren Commission Report, which consists of its final findings and is part of the Report itself. My press statement referred to the failure of the Report to deal with the very question I had posed in my previous article. I also referred to Mr. Lane's damning indictment of the Warren Commission Report—an indictment which I, for one, consider unanswerable, except by plain abuse.

It is unfortunate that the American and British press have shown themselves unwilling to examine critically the omissions and distortions which were documented from the Warren Report itself.

1) The rifle claimed to be the murder weapon and also the weapon ordered by Oswald from the Chicago mail order firm, is two and a half pounds lighter and 4.2 inches shorter than the weapon ordered from the Chicago mail order firm, as claimed.

2) The Report falsely states that Jack Ruby denied attending a meeting at the Carousel Club with Tippit, Weissman and another man.

The Report is not holy writ. I feel confident that every word of Mr. Lane's statement and my own will stand up to scrutiny. Will the *Washington Post* test its confidence in the Report by allowing me space to acquaint its readers with all of the failings of the Warren Commission investigation and findings? Perhaps after permitting me an article, the *Washington Post* will deal with our case and abandon personal abuse.

Neither the *Washington Post* nor any of the other newspapers concerned were willing to publish Russell's views, nor were they prepared to publish his letter. With regard to the British press Russell wrote in the *Daily Worker* of October 10:

With the exception of the *Daily Worker* the press has treated the Warren Commission Report as holy writ....I cannot recall treatment more shameful than that which has been accorded the British "Who killed Kennedy? Committee" by the British press.

The only American journal to feature Russell's "16 Questions on the Assassination" was the *Minority of One* which, in January 1965, also published an article of Russell's entitled "Post-Kennedy World Outlook." Russell's main hope was that President Kennedy's increasing willingness to negotiate with the USSR on nuclear issues, exemplified by the partial test-ban treaty, would continue to develop under President Johnson. With a presidential election due later in the year Russell considered whether Johnson would display the initiative necessary to bring about further agreement with the Soviet Union:

> The assassination of President Kennedy was undoubtedly a disaster not only for America but for the world. But how great was the disaster, it is not yet possible to know. President Johnson has stated that he will continue Kennedy's policies and has already proved that in the matter of civil rights he intends to show as much energy as his predecessor had been showing. In international affairs, it is not so easy to form a judgment. He has stated that, before renewing negotiations with the Soviet Government, he will need time to study President Kennedy's not yet matured suggestions. As the time is short before a new presidential election, this makes it very doubtful whether anything of importance as regards East-West relations will be accomplished during the months before that event.

Outside the central problem of Soviet-American relations was the question of China and her nuclear potential. Russell had written to Johnson in this connection on 21 December 1963:

> I write to express my appreciation of your policy towards the important issue of peace and future relations with the Soviet Union. I am particularly hopeful that your Administration will find a way of involving China in the essential discussions related to disarmament and an end to the Cold War.
>
> I hope you will agree that Chinese intransigence is both unfortunate and remediable. The exclusion from world affairs and the grievances the Chinese profess to feel could, if redressed, result in considerable advance as may be shown by the extensive proposals for nuclear disarmament advanced by the Chinese Government in *Peking Review*. It has further come to my notice that Premier Castro would welcome lessening of tension with the United States and I very much hope this will be possible despite political differences.
>
> The feeling is growing that the grave and imminent danger of mass extermination can be finally ended and I wish to assure you of the widest possible support in that pursuit among all those who have

worked against nuclear war over many years. I enclose for your interest some literature concerning the recently formed Peace Foundations. I should value your opinion of these efforts and, still more, your support of them.

Russell continued to emphasize that a real detente was impossible as long as the United States pursued hostile policies towards Cuba as well as China. Russell, accordingly, wrote to Johnson on 3 May 1964:

I have followed with great approval your efforts towards the establishing of better relations with the Soviet Union and for the relaxation of tension in the Cold War. I hope, therefore, you will understand the motives which prompt me to write to you about the situation in Cuba.

I cannot see that a tolerant policy towards Yugoslavia and improved relations with the USSR are compatible with so hostile a policy towards Cuba. The only hope for peace must lie, surely, in the diminution of hostilities in troubled areas of the world and it is hard to see why the island of Cuba should represent any threat to peace or American security. The declaration that the United States may fly craft over Cuban territory is entirely in violation of Cuban sovereignty and unacceptable by any State in the world today. The United States possesses missiles on her territory but would not permit Soviet or Cuban craft to violate her air space because this is so.

I fear the consequences of the continuation of this practice and the maintenance by force of an unwanted military base at Guantanamo Bay. Surely it is this sort of action on the part of a large neighbour towards a smaller one which the United States has professed to deplore.

I appeal to you to establish normal relations with Cuba and to forego flights over her territory so that the hopes for peace built so arduously in recent months may not be dashed. I feel certain this course is in the vital interests of the United States, will promote immeasurably the cause of peace and will win worldwide approval for American magnanimity.

At the same time he addressed a similar letter to the major U.S. newspapers which for once received widespread publication. "The blind spot America displays over Cuba threatens to dash the hopes of peace so arduously built," declared Russell.[19] Also written in May 1964 was "Detente or New Entanglements?" in which he stated:

The decision on the part of great sections of powerful opinion who were previously architects and promoters of the Cold War to become reluctant advocates of detente is of very great importance. It seems that President Kennedy reflected this change and, to some extent, President Johnson does so as well. His statement that he will meet the Soviet Union more than half way in the matter of Germany is very welcome. President Johnson's description of Soviet fears regarding a rearmed Germany indicates the extent to which the Cold War is changing. He described Russian fears as understandable and described himself as one aware of the dangers of German rearmament. Such developments suggest that the calamitous character of a nuclear conflict is at last becoming understood by politicians. It does not mean, necessarily, that they will find the wisdom to extricate themselves from the pointless conflict which they have imposed on the world. It does mean that they may be more susceptible to such schemes as may be advanced towards that end.[20]

Russell, however, warned against those powerful forces in the United States working against detente. He felt that "hesitant supporters of detente" like Johnson could succumb to the pressures of those who insisted upon "the increase of the arms race and the extension of the conflict wherever possible":

Those who are struggling to end the Cold War and to bring rational planning to the affairs of mankind must begin by opposing and exposing dangerous policies now prevalent in the United States toward Cuba, China and Southeast Asia. If the good sense President Johnson has shown about the question of Germany could be extended to Cuba and Southeast Asia, his words of peace would acquire substance and American leadership would have some claim upon the respect of the world. This will require forthright, open opposition to the extraordinary power exercised by the secret American Government which resides in the Pentagon and the Central Intelligence Agency, and which draws upon the vast financial resources of American industry. It is to be hoped that the civilian Government and American industry can be won to the program of sane development, rather than one of Armageddon and the suicidal pursuit of policies which, although portrayed as national policies, are, in fact, conspiratorial ones, totally at variance with true national interest and the peace of the world.

The nomination in June 1964 of Senator Barry Goldwater as the Republican candidate for the presidential elections confirmed Russell's fears that "those who essentially desire both Cold and hot War threatened the new moves towards peaceful co-existence.[21] As a result of fresh Cuban initiatives towards normalizing relations with the USA, and fearful that Johnson under pressure from the Goldwaterites would reject the overture, Russell released a statement to the British press on July 20:

We are often advised that unless governments show willingness to come to terms with those who have been their opponents, there is little hope that peace may be achieved on our planet. In the light of American belligerence towards Cuba—an attitude which has encompassed an attempt at invasion, an economic blockade, and persistent efforts to overthrow through subversion the legitimate Government of that country—it is remarkable that Fidel Castro has given the assurances which he has in his recent interview with the *New York Times.*

Dr. Castro made a very conciliatory and generous appeal to the United States to improve relations between them and to remove the sources of misunderstanding. It is a disappointment that the American State Department has rejected this magnanimous offer on the part of Dr. Castro out of hand. It is to be hoped that the press of the world will take the part of Cuba in this recent exchange with the United States. It cannot have been easy for the Cuban Government to approach the United States in these terms, particularly with the prospect of a dangerous summer ahead. The advent of Goldwater into the presidential arena in the United States confronts us with a most grave and urgent dilemma. One of the candidates for the Presidency is a man who would take steps which would lead to nuclear devastation. It will require the utmost courage on the part of Mr. Johnson to improve relations with Cuba. I have no doubt that were this step taken, his courage would be rewarded. It is the duty of all who can see the issue clearly to urge Mr. Johnson to stand for peaceful coexistence and for settling of outstanding disputes through negotiation.

There can be no better place to begin than with Cuba. Cuba represents an unnecessary and unjustified point of conflict in the world. American-Cuban understanding would make peace greatly more secure.

If President Johnson seeks to compete with the lunatics who oppose him in the United States in the name of anti-communism, he will play into their hands and will fail to state clearly the issue which is at stake—man's survival on this planet. I urge the press of this country to recognise their responsibility. It is not an American question, it is a world question, and we are all obliged to raise our voices to prevent disaster from overtaking us.[22]

Goldwater's nomination aroused world-wide alarm since his policies were clearly a threat to peace. With the presidential elections due in November Russell initiated an international campaign to make known to American people the extent of opposition to Goldwater's policies.

During August Russell circulated a manifesto called "An Appeal on the Danger to the World of Goldwater's Policies," to trade unions, international organizations and eminent persons in Britain, Western Europe, Africa, Asia and Latin America. It met with an enthusiastic response. In his covering letter soliciting support for the manifesto Russell argued:

> Many people will attempt to say that the American election is no concern of ours and we have not the right to interfere. This notion fits the world of the nineteenth century, but not one in which an action by an American president could result in mass annihilation...

The manifesto declared:

> The world hovers on the edge of destruction. The decision rests with a few powerful men and is the most important concern of every human being. Nuclear war and world peace are no longer national matters. The advent of Goldwater is an imminent threat to the survival of man. His candidacy increases the danger and halts all signs of hope. His election will mean unmitigated disaster. Goldwater has stated:
>
> 1. We are, in no uncertain terms, against disarmament.
>
> 2. We should liberate all Communist states, including Eastern Europe, the Ukraine, Armenia, Latvia, Lithuania and Estonia.
>
> 3. We should give the decision to use nuclear weapons to Field Commanders and the head of NATO.
>
> 4. We should abrogate the Test Ban Treaty and resume testing.
>
> 5. We should have nuclear weapons in space and abrogate the agreement prohibiting this.
>
> 6. We should give only military aid and only to anti-Communist states.
>
> 7. We should leave the United Nations.
>
> 8. We should withdraw diplomatic recognition from the Soviet Government.
>
> 9. We should invade Cuba.
>
> 10. We should use nuclear weapons in Vietnam and attack the North.

These policies will inevitably cause a nuclear war. The world's peoples are the victims. It is an imperative duty for the people of the world to make known their view so that the American people will realise the depth and strength of world feeling. Goldwater has uttered a sentence of death on all of us. Goldwater and his policies must be defeated.

Inevitably there was criticism that Russell's campaign constituted foreign interference in the American elections. In a letter to *The Times* of September 14 Russell defended himself:

You publish a letter from Professor W. Winks (*The Times*, 14 September 1964) objecting to British criticisms of Goldwater's policy. As this policy, if carried out, will lead to the death of all inhabitants of Britain, I do not see how our objection to this policy can be blamed.

Americans who take Mr. Winks' line apparently think that Britons should go to their death unresistingly. If this is America's attitude, I do not see how that country can be considered friendly to Britain. I do not believe that a majority of Americans can expect the rest of the world to remain dumb while their death is being arranged.

It is said that foreign criticism will help Goldwater. If, however, all those who feel strongly speak out, it may be confidently hoped that a large majority of Americans will decide to avoid becoming objects of the world's hatred.

As the election of Johnson would bar the way to Goldwater, Russell was concerned to influence Johnson towards adopting an alternative policy for peace. Russell addressed an open letter to Johnson on 19 October 1964:

...China and Russia call for an international congress of which the purpose should be to abolish all nuclear weapons. We are told by many in the West that such a proposal is premature. This means only that those who advance this argument have not yet thought out plausible ways to bring about the failure of such a conference.

It is open to you, if you so choose, to add your immense power to the influence of those who advocate such a congress, in the sincere hope that it may remove the imminent peril of universal destruction.

If you do this you will lift the burden of fear from all the millions of human beings who watch with paralysed terror the march of mankind toward the abyss.

You will be hailed in every country and in every continent as a saviour, as one who in a mad world has shown the road to sanity; and you will have the satisfaction of knowing that you have performed a service to humanity more noteworthy and more immense than has been performed by even the greatest of your predecessors.

In the name of mercy, and in the name of humanity, I implore you not to let this opportunity pass unused.[23]

Under the title "Who Spawned Goldwater?" the *American Dialog* of October-November published a statement by Russell in which he explained the advent of the Senator's candidacy as "part of a pattern of violence in the United States enhanced by a fanatical hatred of Communism which bears little relation to reality."

Citing instances of American policies of "economic exploitation coup d'etats, assassinations and wars of oppression" where the CIA has been used as "an international agency of subversive intrigue" Russell described the ideology of the Cold War as "a myth intended to mask the presence of rapacious power."

It was these conditions, Russell maintained, that had produced the radical right:

the vigilante bands of fascist Minutemen, the atmosphere of political persecution and brutality, the death of thousands of Negroes and the plot to kill the President of the United States in Dallas.

These were also the conditions, Russell concluded, that had made Goldwater "a major contender for the presidency." Russell declared: "On the principle of no annihilation without representation the world protests in horror against Goldwater and the appalling conditions which have spawned him."

Russell developed this theme in a major article entitled "The Increase of American Violence."[24] Describing America as "a country in ferment," Russell demonstrated how violence and lawlessness had led to "the creation of a trigger-happy population in which violence is admired and mildness is regarded as a proof of cowardice and in which hate is constantly inculcated." Russell felt, therefore, that, "it is scarcely surprising that a country in this mood should produce men willing to murder its president." Russell commented on Goldwater's acceptance speech which he regarded as the best indicaton of what the Senator's policy was likely to be if elected:

In this speech he rejected all attempts at accommodation with the Communists. He stated that hostility to communism should be the basic policy of the United States, and should be pursued by the methods of brinksmanship....

It is impossible to judge in advance whether Goldwater will be elected in the coming election or not. American opinion has been educated to accept a totally false opinion both of communism and of America. It is very largely believed in America that America stands for freedom, whereas communism stands for the hated tyranny of a minority. Both these beliefs are false, and until they are abandoned, it is difficult for America to play a rational part in world politics. Goldwater heads the irrational part of America. If he wins, the prospect is dark, and so it is if he personally loses but his policy is adopted by his opponents. So far, appearances suggest that the most likely outcome is the rejection of Goldwater and the adoption of his policy.

The first part of Russell's expectations were fulfilled when Johnson won a sweeping victory over Goldwater in the November election. His fears about the adoption of Goldwater's policies were to preoccupy him in the coming years.

Footnotes

1. B. Russell, letter in *The Times*, 15 August 1963.
2. *Ibid.*
3. B. Russell to William C. Foster (for Kennedy), 7 November 1963.
4. B. Russell, *Autobiography*, Vol. 3, (London, 1969) p. 165; (New York, 1969) p. 236.
5. *Ibid.*
6. From a Preface written for, but not published in, *Rush to Judgement* by Mark Lane.
7. B. Russell, *Autobiography*, Vol. 3, p. 165; p. 237.
8. *Ibid.*
9. *Ibid.*
10. *The Minority of One*, September 1964.
11. B. Russell, *Autobiography*, Vol. 3, p. 165; 237.
12. *Ibid.*, p. 166; p. 238.
13. Statement from *The Minority of One*, September 1964.
14. *Ibid.*
15. B. Russell, "Warren Report is not Holy Writ," *Daily Worker*, 10 October 1964.
16. *Ibid.*
17. Not published.
18. B. Russell, *Autobiography*, Vol. 3, p. 166; p. 238.
19. *New York Herald Tribune*, 7 May 1964.
20. Published by *The Minority of One*, August 1964.
21. "Detente or New Entanglements." *Ibid.*
22. Not published.
23. Published by *St. Louis Post-Dispatch*, 25 October 1964.
24. See below pp. 382-91.

17 The Black Revolt

In many ways Russell's article on "The Increase of American Violence" was a crystalization of his overall view on the United States at this time. Russell believed that America's internal crisis together with its aggressive international policies was the main threat to world peace. In regard to the ferment within America Russell felt that "the present alignment of Negroes and white men is the most dangerous and explosive particular problem now existing in the United States, and the most difficult to solve."[1] In his message to the Civil Rights Freedom March in Washington, which took place on 28 August 1963, Russell stated:

> The treatment of the American Negro is an atrocity which has a history of three hundred years in what is now the United States of America. The number of Negroes who have died through torture, lonely murder and systematic maltreatment in this period without doubt is in excess of those killed by the Nazis in the course of their unparalleled barbarism in Europe.[2]

Russell released the full text of his message to the press in London on 27 August. The statement continued:

> More than this has been done to the American Negro. He has suffered an experience of systematic terror in which he could, and indeed can today in many parts of the United States, be shot down at will. In the South he is subjected to what amounts to slave labour and a peonage system, in which he is told he "almost got out of debt" when it comes time to receive his pay. A casual glance can send him to the gas chamber. The Negro has had to experience depravity shown him not on one occasion, but over many generations. I have heard Negro

"The treatment of the American Negro is an atrocity which has a history of three hundred years in what is now the United States of America. The number of Negroes who have died through torture, lonely murder and systematic maltreatment in this period without doubt is in excess of those killed by the Nazis in the course of their unparalleled barbarism in Europe."

music, and if there need be an indictment of the experiences of the Negro in the United States, it is contained in its lyric and its mood.

A nation which can commit this crime is unhealthy. The crime against the Negro is the price paid not only for brutality. It is the cost of America's indifference. This indifference is the most serious indictment of all. I am convinced that the march on Washington is a turning point in the history of the United States. The Negro in the United States is on the move and he will not stop. The meaning of this is that the values and the practices which have formed the United States over three hundred years are being fundamentally challenged. This march is the real emancipation proclamation, and if it is to be implemented and if the United States is to be saved from the brutality which has both subjected the Negro and now threatens mankind with obliteration, the march on Washington must lead to an end to indifference, to suffering and mass murder, in short, a revolution in the thinking and acting of Americans.

I, for one, am with you heart and soul. "Let my people go" was no parochial cry on behalf of a small nation. It was a cry for an end to barbarism and cruelty and the voice was for all of mankind. So it is with you today."

The first part only of Russell's statement was taken up by the *New York Times* on August 28, the day of the march, under the dramatic heading "Russell hails rally: Likens U.S. negroes to Hitler's victims." *The Times* commented:

The comparable Nazi death toll, not including military deaths, has been estimated at more than 6,000,000 persons. A total of 333,500 negro slaves were imported into the United States up to 1808, according to figures in *An American Dilemma* by Gunnar Myrdal. The 20th anniversary edition of the book, published in 1962 by Harper and Row, estimates that at least a half a million more Negroes were smuggled into the country between 1808—when the Slave trade became illegal under the Constitution—and 1860. Thus more than 800,000 Negroes were brought to the United States in the slave trade.

As to mortality in the trade Mr. Myrdal writes: "Available evidence is contradictory as to the extent of mortality during the period from the seizure of slaves in Africa to their ultimate sale in America. The old standard evidence pointed to a death rate as high as five-sixths of all Negroes captured. Some recent sources of information, however, mention a mortality as low as 13 percent."

The *New York Times* version of Russell's statement was quickly picked up by other national newspapers and Russell was subjected to intensive criticism and abuse from news columnists and readers alike. The Canadian press also joined the chorus of condemnation. Andrew Feldman, a Canadian student, informed Russell that "on August 29, in the two major Toronto papers (*Star* and *Telegram*) comments appear on your message...under headings, respectively, 'Knowing when you are old' and 'Impudence.' Both articles are derogatory, in fact shameful."[3] From San Antonio, Texas the Rev. D.W. Edmunds, a self-styled "miracle healer," challenged Russell to produce evidence to support his statements.[4] Russell replied on September 7:

I wish to correct you on several points. The first concerns the number of Negroes who had died over 300 years as a result of their treatment. This estimate referred to the course of the slave trade, the killing and maltreatment over the generations and effects of extreme terror on any population. The *New York Times* published a fraction of my total statement on the crime against the American Negro. That part published referred to my comparison of the crime with that of Hitler. This statement, of course, is shocking in American opinion. I am surprised, however, that living in the South you can be unfamiliar with the treatment of the Negro. You disclaim that Negroes can be shot down at will in many parts of the USA. Any glance at the Negro press will disconfirm this. It is a common occurrence in the rural south, although, it is true, that American papers rarely consider it worth mentioning in print. The outstanding recent examples are (1) Rev. Lee of Mississippi (2) Gus Courts (3) Emmet Till. These are outstanding because they were committed in public or because the victim was northern. The number of unknown rural Negroes so murdered and the number who never emerge from police stations when picked up on spurious charges is legion. The Negro press bears this out as does the proud boasting of rural southern sheriffs who sound in their statements like the S.S. There is nothing fanciful about the experience of the rural Negro nor is there in my account of it. As for the "casual glance" I should remind you that Emmet Till was shot down at the age of 14 for "looking" at a white salesgirl while purchasing chewing gum. "Rape by leer" is a southern statute and it carries the death penalty. I did not, in my statement, refer to the crimes of mutilation committed against Negroes; perhaps you are familiar with the occurrence of these. They are often reported in the Negro press. The gas chamber is one of the modes of execution in several American states. This was very well published at the time of the killing of Caryl Chessman and I should have thought you would have recalled it.

I am interested to show that the Negroes in rural America have suffered reckless murder through the decades and that they have had virtually no recourse. The role of the "county farm" and the penitentiary camps is infamous. The mode of intimidating labour is a significant part of the development of American institutional life. I am concerned that Americans understand the nature of the damage done to this people. The deaths through malnutrition, inadequate health facilities, hard labour and life shortening are a terrible indictment. I refer you to the songs of the Negro, the scholarship of Basil Davidson, Gunnar Myrdal and Alan Lomax and the essays of James Baldwin and the record of violence reported in the Negro press over the years. We have witnessed sustained violence, legal terror and lifetimes of despair. You say that you are familiar with the prejudice and misinformation about the USA. I am familiar with and worried about the blindness and prejudice of those who inhabit it.

I should wish you to examine the circumstances of American Negroes in Southern rural areas and Northern slums more closely. I should wish you to oppose them publicly.

With respect to the miracle healing of which you say you are capable, may I suggest you read my book *Why I am Not a Christian* in which my views are set out?

Russell's continuing concern for civil liberties and the plight of minority groups in the USA had led him to read extensively on the history of the Afro-American. His investigations had revealed that only one sixth of the Black people shipped to America in the course of the slave trade survived their transplantation. It was clear to Russell that from these statistics the slave traffic alone had accounted for four million deaths.

Russell was also concerned to study more contemporary sources so as to arm himself with information on the immediate issues facing the Blacks in America. His growing interest and activity in this field caused many journals and writers to send him the newest writings; some to seek his views, others to simply keep him informed. James Baldwin sent Russell his *The Fire Next Time* and Russell communicated to Baldwin his admiration of "the book's precision and intensity of feeling." "It is difficult," Russell commented, "to write honestly of suffering, and the mastery of despair."[5]

To Leo Huberman and Paul Sweezy, editors of *Monthly Review*, Russell indicated his admiration for *American Revolution: Pages from a Negro Worker's Notebook* by James Boggs which they had sent him. Russell in his letter of August 20 also commented on *Monthly Review*:

Your journal has been of the greatest interest to me over a period of time. I am not a Marxist by any means...but I recognise the power of much of your own analysis and where I disagree I find your journal valuable and of stimulating importance.

Russell also wrote on 20 August 1963 to James Boggs congratulating him on his book which he found "remarkable" and which he hoped would have "the widest possible circulation in the United States." Russell was much impressed with the book's "power and insight" and was interested to know the author's views on two questions:

The first concerns the degree of conditioning which has taken place in the United States since 1945. Do you think that American workers and middle-class people will become involved in conscious revolt as the process of automation advances? Will they not embrace a more harsh authoritarianism and delve for new victims, particularly as the witch-hunt has found great support in the population? The second question concerns the extent to which American whites, whose living standards have depended upon the exploitation of American Negroes and non-European peoples, will understand the American Negro revolt. If they fail to make common cause with it, will not the result be a further impetus towards the neo-Fascist government?

James Boggs replied at length to Russell on 5 September:

...I believe that it will probably be in the north rather than in the south that the bitterness of the whites will overflow in spontaneous actions of a Fascist character. As you probably know, for over a hundred years it has been alright for a Negro to be a carpenter, a brickmason or a plumber in the south. In fact that is why the Tuskegee Institute was accepted by southern whites, because in the south they let the Negro do any kind of work as long as they, the white man, could be boss. But in the north, stemming from the infamous deal that was made in 1877 and the lie that the north had fought the civil war to free the slaves, there are more hypocrites than there are in the south. So that in the south you know your enemy, while in the north, whatever the white man says you never know whether he really means it or not. But nowadays, the question of what he really means is going to be tested in the economic sector. That is, the Negroes are going to demand what I maintain America cannot now give—jobs. I do not believe that America can give the Negroes jobs except at the expense of whites who are waiting for these jobs...

I would not say, at the moment, that these northern workers in particular are Fascist-inclined. The southerners are really more organically like the South Africans and the Nazis. But if the southerners are to remain in the U.S. there is a threat hanging over their heads which they know very well. That is, the Negroes in many areas in the south are a majority or nearly a majority. For example in Tuskegee, Alabama there are 22,000 Negroes to 5,000 whites. Which means that the Negroes could easily win political power if they had the use of the ballot or if it came to a test of physical strength, head on, the Negroes could slaughter the whites. But in the north the whites still have their illusions of quantitative strength and in many areas they are the actual majority...

As to the immigrant whites. The Polish in the United States, in Detroit and Chicago in particular, aren't too different from what they were in Marx's time, full of prejudices, and could easily be led to join with the fascists. However, in New York City this situation does not prevail because of the large concentration of Russian Jews, Italians, etc. But if the economic philosophy of individual self-interest, which is projected particularly by the labor unions and the government as well as by so-called progressive groups in the U.S. continue to prevail, then one can only expect the worst from all of the immigrants, workers or not.

I do not feel able to predict exactly what will occur. However a certain feeling remains with me that there is going to be blood running in the streets between the so-called progressive class-conscious workers and revolutionary Negroes. In fact, I think that conditions in some areas are already those of a pre-civil war character. The question is who will make the sparks explode into a full-scale conflagration and who can keep them from exploding. As of now, you will note that the U.S. has kept its armies as a go-between. The armies act as a peace-maker, rushed in wherever there is a possibility of a full-scale civil clash. And so far the army itself has not taken sides seriously...

The issues here, as far as one can foresee, are going to be issues between the white population and the black population because so far, with the exception of the students there has been no *social force* in the white population which the Negroes can respect, and a handful of liberals joining in a demonstration doesn't change this one bit. In fact, the average white worker has not been out in a demonstration in the last ten years and with the decline of the union he has no cause but the defense of what he personally has accumulated.

Russell wrote to Boggs once again on September 18:

> I cannot see how the Negro revolt can stop short of a challenge to capitalism in the United States. The rural peonage in the south and the meaning of serious political consciousness among northern Negroes seems to me to lead to direct identification with those exploited in Africa and Asia. Moreover, without the arms race, how can the United States answer the stark needs of slum dwellers. The arms race entails cold war. I do think that the Negro revolt could be the means of opposing effectively and for the first time the assumptions of the United States and the race towards nuclear annihilation...

It was to be many weeks before Russell was to hear from James Boggs again but towards the end of October he received a letter from an American friend Alice Mary Hilton who was also an acquaintance of James Boggs. Hilton, an expert on the social consequences of automation had, like Russell, been impressed with Boggs's book and recently visited him at his home in Detroit where Boggs had shown her his correspondence with Russell. "After many hours of very frank conversation with the Boggs's," Hilton wrote in her letter to Russell of October 24, "I believe that it is necessary for me to make some additions to Jim Boggs' letter of September 5." Hilton put to Russell her view of recent trends in American society affecting Black Americans as well as her hopes and expectations for the future:

> I want to make it clear why I am so concerned about the struggle of the Negro. I believe that this dichotomy of Negro and white, the degradation of one human being by another, is disastrous to both, and unbearably degrading to both. It is a problem, which like the South African problem, reaches far beyond the borders of the United States. It could, ultimately, be the cause for thermonuclear war...I believe that the effects of automation is the major problem mankind must solve, and the American Negro problem is one aspect of it...The march on Washington was a tremendous experience for the uncommitted white American...The dignity and decency of the demonstration accomplished in minutes more than anything else that had happened in a century of the Negro struggle...I believe that this impact could be felt throughout the country. Subsequent press stories, but more significantly, the stories I heard from personal and trusted friends, bear this out...

I would like to tell you my fears and the primary reason for this long letter. Jim Boggs is part of a Negro movement whose numerosity and power are difficult to estimate. A short time ago, it was thought the the so-called Black Muslim movement had about 100,000 members. Jim Boggs is not exactly a Black Muslim, because he is not religiously involved, but he believes in segregation, and in violent separation and revenge...

Jim writes to you that there are conditions of pre-civil war character. This is not yet true. So far, acts of violence have been quite isolated and there has not been much enthusiasm. He further writes that he does not know who will make the sparks explode into a full-scale conflagration and who can keep them from exploding. Fortunately, I believe this to be largely "wishful" thinking (on his part)...

The worst error the Boggs's make, it seems to me, is their assumption that things must get a lot worse before they can get better, and that the sooner they get worse, the sooner they'll get better. Upon those assumptions they base their arguments that Canadian autoworkers in Detroit should immediately be replaced with American Negroes—thereby adding international to racial conflict, that all whites should be thrown out of their jobs, automation introduced as quickly as possible, and the remaining jobs given to Negroes. This is, of course, impossible, not because I want to "protect" the whites more than the Negroes, but because the further automation progresses, the more highly skilled the work that must still remain to be done by human beings, the more preposterous to put an unskilled person, regardless of their color, on the job. In order to help things get worse sooner, the Boggs's recommend and hope for the election of Goldwater. I believe that this would be unmitigated disaster for the world. Under Goldwater the worst elements of the military-industrial complex—those who frightened Eisenhower—would certainly take over the country. They would risk war by invading Cuba, use this opportunity or any Negro riot to declare martial law. If they get away with the invasion of Cuba—which seems doubtful to me—they will demand more...

Although I find myself in disagreement with the Kennedy administration more often than in complete agreement, I believe that Kennedy is essential simply because he learned his lesson perfectly clearly—that war must not be committed. I believe much of his action is due to political uncertainties. He has lost a great many votes because of his stand on civil rights for Negroes, and he has not made too many friends among the Negroes. I believe he has compromised too much— and yet, there is the unalterable and ghastly fact that he has not been able to get the civil rights bill through Congress.

If Goldwater is elected in 1964, it would be sheer disaster. I believe that your influence with Jim Boggs would be tremendous. If you would just remind him—and all of us, really—continually that nothing can be done without peace, and that the Negro movement, or movements, must support first of all peace. If there is a riot and bloodshed, I am afraid the white people who are now on the way to reason, to identification with the Negro—no, the human—cause, this precarious fledgling enlightenment will be killed. The reaction will be worse than anything could ever have been before.

The Negro people have been patient for so very long. They have shown great restraint, good sense, and desire for peace. I do not want them to wait any longer. I simply want them to keep on the road they themselves have built. I think the vast majority of them still are. I think a few are hopelessly fanatical and bitter. But I think Jim Boggs can be saved for better things than the bloodshed he envisions or the holocaust he wants to help unleash. I know that you would wield great influence, and I beg you, in the name of all you have so magnificently fought for all your life, to exert this influence on him...

P.S. Jim Boggs is invited to speak at Town Hall, N.Y. on Nov. 21. If you could possibly reach him before then he might speak a little more reasonably.

Russell replied to Hilton on November 16 stating his complete agreement with her views on the "disastrous consequences of Negro violence should it occur on a large scale." He enclosed a memorandum entitled "Should the Negro movement in the U.S. remain non-violent?"[6] which he asked her to pass on to Boggs "or to make any use of it that seems to you suitable." In the memorandum Russell stated:

The movement towards equality between the Negro and the white populations of the United States is one which has my whole-hearted and complete sympathy. I consider the white prejudice against Negroes to be both stupid and brutal, and I should wish to see it disappear entirely, but I do not believe that this end will be achieved if the Negro movement adopts methods of violence.

There is, at present, a rapidly increasing sympathy with the Negro cause among large sections of the white population. I fear that this sympathy will very largely cease if the movement abandons persuasion and attempts, instead, to use force. There is some reason to think that the spread of automation will cause such general widespread unemployment as will bring about a combined movement of white and black unemployed. This is much to be desired if the problems raised by automation are to be solved in a rational manner. But there is another possibility—namely, that the spread of unemployment in the white population will lead to a demand for a preference of white labour at the expense of Negroes. Such an unfortunate result is much more likely to occur if the Negro movement becomes violent and renders co-operation between white and black unemployed difficult, if not impossible. I think we must also face the reaction of the white population to any violence on the part of the Negroes. The effect would be of two kinds: many previous sympathisers would become hostile, and those who are already hostile would become more ready to meet violence with violence. In such a clash the white population would indubitably be victorious, and the victors would be more vicious and intolerant than they have been for many decades. It is easy to imagine a conflict so bitter as to cause something like ruin in many parts of the United States, but it is not easy to imagine an outcome to violent conflict which would be in any degree beneficial to the Negroes.

The spread of automation will require a great deal of fresh thinking and fresh feeling about the position of labour in an industrial community. It is hardly to be supposed that such thinking will be sane or beneficial if it has to take place in an atmosphere of civil war with its inevitable accompaniment of cruelty and atrocity and bitterness.

Alice Hilton received the memorandum in time to have it read at the New York Town Hall meeting of November 21 sponsored by *Monthly Review*. Commenting on the meeting Hilton wrote Russell on November 22 that "your reasonable words were not heeded. Jim Boggs expressed his appreciation, but—he said—'unfortunately, Bertrand Russell does not understand revolution. Nothing can be accomplished without violence. The Negro cannot hope for freedom and equality until the blood flows in the streets of America.'"

In the same letter Hilton expressed her great shock and sorrow at the assassination of President Kennedy which had occurred on the morning of her writing to Russell:

None of us can even find so small a consolation as to believe this to have been the act of a madman. A madman he may have been, but his act was carefully planned and organized. The next few days may not show who was guilty, but they will show who is going to be blamed...

Kennedy's assassination was taken up by James Boggs in his reply to Russell of December 29.

...A President of the United States has been assassinated and in turn his alleged assassin has been assassinated. We have a new President, and

228

still nothing has changed, except that there are a lot of people, who for some silly reasons believe that some things have changed and that they are going to be better...

Boggs went on to deal with the New York Town Hall meeting which he had attended and to which Russell's memorandum had been read:

I who was speaking next had to say that whereas I too would like to hope that the issues of our revolt might be resolved by peaceful means, I believed that the issues and the grievances were so deeply imbedded in the American system and the American people that the very things you warned against might just have to take place if the Negroes in the USA are ever to walk the streets as free men...

It is because in this country the counter-revolution is forcing those who want to struggle to take more drastic steps because the consensus in the country is that the Negroes have already gotten enough and that they must earn their right to more and wait for legislative channels to grant it to them. And we know that they are not going to grant us anything and we also know that the civil rights bill about which you have undoubtedly heard a great deal, is not going to give us anything, but that to get anything from it we will have to do just what we had to do in regard to the Supreme Court decision, get out in the streets and fight.

And I do not believe that the temper of the Negroes is such that they will take eight more years of the kind of beatings and jailings that they have taken since 1954, just to prove that they are entitled to the things that everybody else has. In fact, I believe that period is over; that the black masses will either retaliate—or they won't act at all. But the one thing that they will not take any more is beatings. The one thing that always goes unnoticed in all the eulogizing of the non-violent behavior of the Negroes is the open, direct violence of the American whites against the Negroes. So that the eulogizing of the non-violence of the Negro has also been implicitly in readiness to accept the violence of the white. And if a nation has not felt aroused by the bestialities of whites, it has no right to expect anything different from the Negroes who have been on the receiving end of these bestialities for over 300 years. This is what we have to face as we enter the new year...

It would be very interesting for me to see how you yourself would describe what America has been all these years when you take into consideration that historically it has been considered a democracy even though all the while there has been fascism for so many millions.

If the majority chooses to be racist, which is what the majority of the Americans have chosen to be, then democracy is also fascism. The main point is that the American system is much older than any other non-democratic system now in existence. So it must be judged on its record. And on its record, it is a system which any responsible historian will have to judge as having operated by race exploitation. These are the truths which the Negro struggle is bringing to light, and I believe that it is your responsibility as I believe that it is my responsibility to recognize and record this, so that in the future words do not confuse the struggle but help to clarify it. This is what I think philosophers should make clear. Because even though Negroes in the United States still think they are struggling for democracy, in fact, democracy is what they are struggling against.

Russell replied to Boggs on 4 January 1964 recommending to him the December 9 issue of *I.F. Stone's Weekly* which contained an article on the assassination of President Kennedy. "As to my own views on the struggle of the American Negro" he referred Boggs to the October issue of *The Minority of One* which had reproduced Russell's message to the Washington Freedom March under the title "Let My People Go." Russell then took up the various points that Boggs raised in his letter:

...I consider your view of the Negro struggle in the United States ill-conceived in certain respects. I have the feeling that you sometimes confuse what you wish to see take place with what the circumstances are likely to create. I hope you will not mind my saying this.

In the first place, I see no evidence whatever to justify the conclusion that the unemployment induced by automation will inspire in white victims a desire to make common cause with their fellow Negro victims. On the contrary, I should expect them to embrace racialism and to blame the Negro for their unemployment.

I appreciate that democracy in the United States does not mean very much and I tried to set out my own reasons for thinking this in my essay "The Myth of American Freedom." I cannot, however, agree that this is a justification for violence on the part of persecuted, oppressed and deprived Negro workers in America.

It is important to distinguish between a desire for violent reprisal and a clear notion of what results will ensue. Without the latter, the former assumes the character of an indulgence which is irresponsible because it is not a result of true concern for those advised to use violence.

I warn against organised Negro violence because Negroes are outnumbered in the United States, because violence is not controllable, rational or humane...

I do not wish Negroes to become "like other Americans" either. Nor do I wish to mute resistance or shrink from the prospect of Black

Americans taking positions of power in their own interest as opposed to seeking to lobby whites in supplication.

What I urge is an intelligent appreciation of the true situation, a sense of historical perspective, a courageous evaluation of the meaning of a real "explosion" on the part of those now oppressed beyond continued endurance.

The political party you are now promoting and the uncompromised groups now forming which insist on political and economic rights now give a far more rational response and one more likely in organizational terms to have effect, than a vague call to violence with no more said as to how this makes political and human sense.

I consider it sophistry to suggest that "even though Negroes in the United States are struggling for democracy, in fact democracy is what they are struggling against."

Democracy should mean rather more that majority rule. Majority support for atrocities does not, in my view, bring democracy unless Hitler is to be hailed as a leading democrat of our time.

Respect for minority rights, individual liberty, complete freedom of dissent, independent judicial proceedings are important components of democratic life. That they are absent in the United States and in most other countries today I accept. I cannot accept that it follows from this that these values are to be put aside because they are absent. I should regret it if the oppressed embraced the values of their oppressors although this too is common enough in history and in our own time.

I hold violence to be the result of the failure to find a political solution and to create more problems than it solves. For a beleaguered *minority* it is a counsel of complete despair...

The full text of Russell's memorandum on "Should the Negro Movement in the U.S. remain non-violent?" had been published by the *New York Times* on December 8 under the heading "Negroes warned by Lord Russell." Kenneth B. Clark of the the Northside Center for Child Development in New York, who had persuaded James Baldwin to send Russell a copy of *The Fire Next Time*, wrote to Russell on December 30 in reference to the publication of the memorandum.

Your remarks seemed to have been taken out of context. For example, it was not clear from the story whether you thought that there was any danger of American Negroes resorting to organized violence in seeking their rights. As I see the problem the danger of violence does not stem from the Negro groups, but is a constant risk which the Negro must take as he seeks his rights. Those who would deny him his right—the extreme segregationists—are the ones who have resorted to violence, and probably will continue to do so. The Negro groups cannot control this reality, particularly since these perpetrators of violence have generally gone unpunished. The only thing that Negroes can do to avoid this type of violence is to accept the existing injustices and chronic cruelties without effective protest.

Clark enclosed with his letter a copy of his book *The Negro Protest* which contained transcripts of interviews he had held with James Baldwin, Malcolm X and Martin Luther King. Clark expressed the hope that Russell's reading of the interviews would contribute to his understanding of "some of the more complex aspects of the Negro's struggle for democracy in America."

Russell had been until then unaware of the *New York Times* use of his memorandum. He replied at once to Clark, drawing attention to his earlier statement in *The Minority of One* which concerned "the history of the maltreatment of the American Negro."[7] He further assured Clark that he appreciated "the initiative in violence is in the hands of the whites" and that "in parts of the south and north organised and official white violence occurs and Negroes have no effective recourse."

Russell then explained to Clark the circumstances which gave rise to his memorandum:

I have been having an intermittent correspondence with James Boggs since writing to him upon reading his remarkably interesting book *The American Revolution: Pages from a Negro Worker's Notebook.*

Mr. Boggs believes that the onset of automation will enlarge the "submerged class" in the United States. He believes the unskilled and non-unionised workers will find common cause which will have class as well as racial content. He writes convincingly of the degree of force which this discontent already possesses...

In the course of my correspondence with Mr. Boggs I found that he feels the situation in the United States to make Negro violence inevitable and possibly desirable. I disagree.

I appreciate the intolerable difficulty but consider the use of violence disastrous. I do not take this view because I approve of white violence or because I am unaware of the pressures on Negroes who are victimised.

At a meeting organised by *Monthly Review* Mr. Boggs advocated violent defense and spoke of the inevitably violent course of Negro resistance. The publication *Liberator* often advances impressive arguments along similar lines and it seems apparent from the speeches of Malcolm X that non-violence is equated with acquiescence, weakness and/or collaboration. I appreciate the appeal of violence to people who are immeasurably oppressed but I do not believe in its political efficacy under the conditions which are in existence in the United States today. It is possible that my knowledge is inadequate but, such as it is, these are my views...

It was clear to Russell that his memorandum, published as it was outside the context of his views indicating his understanding of the conditions which promoted black militancy, was open to much misinterpretation. He attempted to rectify the situation by clarifying his attitude in a letter to the *New York Times* of 7 January 1964:

In your issue of 8 December 1963 you published an article which set out my views on the question of violence in the Negro revolt. As these views were part of a theoretical memorandum and did not refer to present or past violence on the part of Negroes a wrong impression as to my views has been gained which I should appreciate the opportunity to put right.

The initiative in violence in the United States is entirely white in origin and the most brutal things are occurring. I know of the terrible circumstances under which protest for human rights for Negroes in America must be conducted.

I am fully aware that Negroes are very often without any recourse in the face of white violence in the rural South and the urban North. I neither wish to mute Negro resistance nor to suggest that Negro resistance is responsible for violence. On the contrary, I urge militant resistance and support the attempts to secure positions of political power for Negroes so that they may act for their own safety and well being and need not be dependent upon supplications of white authority.

I caution against the adoption of violence in the future as oppression and despair mount in the Negro community because violence is dangerous, inhuman and politically unwise in the very interests of the Negro struggle. It is important that militant resistance to evil should not be equated with violence and it was in looking to the future of the struggle for Negro rights in America that my memorandum was written.

Russell asked the Letters Editor of the *New York Times* to send him a clipping "should, as I very much hope it will, this article be published," but on February 3 he was informed that the *New York Times* was "unable to make use of your letter."

Russell's commitment to the cause of civil rights was not confined to theorizing about social history or debating on questions of strategy and tactics. His understanding of and compassion for the plight of Black Americans grew with his increasing knowledge of and involvement in their daily struggle against bigotry and injustice. During the last months of 1963 Russell, as a result of an appeal from the Emergency Civil Liberties Committee, issued a number of statements and letters to the U.S. and British Press calling attention to the case of Reverend Ashton Jones, a white Californian who had been "beaten and imprisoned several times in the course of his struggle for Negro rights."[8] On January 8 Russell wrote once again to the press giving further details of the case: his letter appeared in the British *Sunday Times*:

With reference to my earlier letter about the Reverend Ashton Jones, who was imprisoned because he brought a Negro and white child to the First Baptist Church of Atlanta, I should wish to bring the following facts to the attention of your readers:

The Reverend Ashton Jones of California last June, with another white and two Negro friends, sought to worship in the main auditorium, called "sanctuary," and brought two children with him for that purpose, instead of in the basement of the wealthy First Baptist Church of Atlanta, to which Negroes have been consigned by the church's deacons. For protesting direction to the basement, the Hospitality Committee of ushers called the police and the group was arrested for disturbing divine worship under a law of 1792. Mr. Jones, whose age is 67, was dragged down the steps by the police, who dragged him by his heels, his head hitting the concrete. Bail was set at $500.

At the trial on August 28, the others were dismissed, but Judge Durwood Pye sentenced Reverend Jones to a fine of $1000 and 18 months in prison, six months at hard labour, and, on appeal, bail at $20,000. The bail for whites who bombed the Negro churches in Birmingham in which several children were killed was $300. The Constitution of the United States prohibits excessive bail.

In gaol, a white prison officer beat Mr. Jones badly and he went on a hunger fast for over a month to secure better treatment from the guards. Appeals to the Judge, the Governor, the Solicitor—General and Congressman, and the picketing of the church have been in vain, and it is learnt that forceful intravenous feeding was initiated out of fear that Mr. Jones would die.

Leaders of the pickets are a Negro couple, both professors, who are not allowed to visit Mr. Jones in the segregated gaol. Mr. Jones will allow no payment to bail bond brokers.

An announcement has been made that the First Baptist Church has voted to open its sanctuary to everyone, but Negroes are still denied eligibility for membership...

It should be pointed out that those who are so treating the Reverend Ashton Jones have recently been guilty of electric torture and so treated men and women who were on a peaceful march. The Police Chief, Laurie Pritchard, of Albany, Georgia, was congratulated by Attorney-General Robert Kennedy two years ago for keeping law and order.

I should hope that British protest would be brought to bear in this appalling situation.

Towards the end of March Russell learned that the protest on behalf of Rev. Ashton Jones had been successful and he had been released from prison. A *New York Times* news item datelined Atlanta 15 March 1964, and headed "Cleric Returns to Church," stated briefly:

A Los Angeles non-sectarian minister and two Negro girls attended a service today at the First Baptist Church, where he was arrested last summer for trying to have it integrated. The Rev. Ashton B. Jones, 67 years old, said he and Misses Myrna Holt and Barbara Smith were received "just like anyone else."

In the first half of 1964 Russell received scores of letters from individuals and organizations involved in the cause of civil rights for Afro-Americans. This flow of letters paralleled the rise of Black protest in America. The harsh realities of ghetto life and social discrimination in the northern cities were the cause of increasing agitation from the Blacks and increasing concern from the whites.

Marvin Adler, an editorial board member of the Education Journal of the United Federation of Teachers wrote on January 26 asking Russell to contribute a "philosophical" article on the struggle for integration in education. Adler informed Russell of some of the problems facing "the more than forty thousand teachers of New York City's Public Schools:"

As you might know, New York City is faced with the threat of a school boycott by the Negro community. Although New Yorkers think they're relatively free of prejudice, comparing themselves with southern-style discrimination, the fact is that New York City heads the list of the percentage of schools with between 60 and 90% non-white enrollment. There must be something wrong with their thinking and actions when the facts show the *de facto* segregation to be so very extensive.

Russell replied on February 7:

I do not see that the problem of the treatment of Negroes in the United States is a matter for philosophy. It is a question of political behaviour and personal responsibility. The matter is simple. The Negro has been a suppressed group in the United States which has been subject to cruel treatment in order to perpetuate its subjection. Whites have, by and large, acquiesced in this state of affairs, and are not willing to face consequences of truly seeking to alter them. This, no doubt, is because it would affect their own comfort and would require far-reaching change in the institutional life of the United States. It is a matter for political struggle, and I hope this political struggle will be increasingly supported by white Americans.

Shortly after the enactment of the Civil Rights Bill by the Johnson administration on 2 July 1964. Black discontent erupted into violence in the ghetto areas of New York.

Russell, concerned that the British people should understand what he regarded as the underlying causes of this event wrote to the press on July 28. His letter appeared in the *Daily Telegraph* of August 2:

The unrest in Harlem, Bedford Stuyvesant and Rochester in New York among Negroes, while set off by the killing of a fifteen year old boy by an armed police lieutenant, results from longstanding and genuine grievances. The nation-wide effort in America for equal rights for Negro citizens is not restricted to securing a cup of coffee at all-white luncheon counters or the right to attend all-white schools. For the entire American Negro population it is often a matter of life or death. Thirty-five years ago, the infant mortality rate was twice as high for Negroes as for whites. Today it remains twice as high. Thirty-five years ago, twice as many American Negroes died from pneumonia as did whites. Today twice as many still die. The rate of tuberculosis in Harlem today is ten times that of the rate outside. In the south the Negro can be shot virtually at will. In the north police brutality is notorious and constant.

The Negro in America must observe that while thousands of Africans are securing freedom, his own modest efforts for some fair share of that which he has helped to produce in America are denied. To these efforts, live ammunition, night sticks, steel helmeted white police officers, many of them bigots of the worst order, are no answer. The request for an impartial civilian Review Board to investigate police brutality is sound and one wonders why New York City has resisted this. The insistence by the City administration that the

"Harlem is a city occupied by an oppressive army serving what amounts to an outside power. In Harlem there are more rats than people and more cockroaches than rats. Its inhabitants are brutalised every moment of their lives by police, poverty, and indignity. If in any country in the world city after city rose up for days on end, taking to the streets, battling the police, barricading boulevards and smashing shops, it would rightly be called a rebellion or a revolution. In the United States it is called a Black riot."

Review Board should be composed only of police officers indicates a refusal to understand the purpose of such an agency. It is a sad comment upon justice in New York that there is need for such a Review Board. If the courts were fair and impartial in evaluating the testimony of police officers and those charging them with brutality, there would be no need for this agency. But, it is generally recognised, even by the City administration, that the courts are notoriously prejudiced in favour of the police and that those seeking redress are often denied justice.

The violence in the Negro communities of New York, in response to police violence, is a demand by Negroes for an end to subservience, brutality, economic misery—in short the status of a colonial people. American wealth should be directed to the tearing down of all America's Harlems and to the provision of decent living conditions. Only when the Negro rebellion is met by justice and by the prospect of effective political expression can the race problem end and America regain world respect.

The summer of 1964 had witnessed mass demonstrations by Black people in numerous American cities and in the wake of this upheaval many Black leaders were brought to trial. One of the most important of these trials was the indictment of Bill Epton for "trying to overthrow the government of the State of New York."[9] Russell became a sponsor of The Committee to Defend Resistance to Ghetto Life, to whom he addressed, on 31 March 1965, a statement of support:

Harlem is a city occupied by an oppressive army serving what amounts to an outside power. In Harlem there are more rats than people and more cockroaches than rats. Its inhabitants are brutalised at every moment of their lives by police, poverty and indignity. If in any country in the world city after city rose up for days on end, taking to the streets, battling with the police, barricading boulevards and smashing shops, it would be rightly called a rebellion or revolution. In the United States it is called a Black riot.

Nothing more clearly indicates the hand of oppression in America than the indictment of American radicals for having instigated these riots. Mr. Epton has been indicted for trying to overthrow the government of the State of New York. Five others face long gaol terms. The Grand Jury which has returned these indictments holds those radicals who have championed the Negro cause responsible for the Black revolution. How pathetic. The very people responsible for the decades of misery in Harlem indict the passionate opponents of their practice.

This is a struggle which will not end until the system of society which allows these conditions to obtain and such Grand Juries to wield power is overthrown. Were I in New York, I should certainly be guilty of trying to overthrow the Government of the State of New York. Anything less is an evasion of responsibility in the face of brutality and injustice.[10]

Although Russell had been critical of the earlier writings of Malcolm X, he had become aware of the Black leader's subsequent views and had shown an interest in meeting him. "I should be glad of an opportunity to see you when you are next in this country" he had written to Malcolm X, on 16 February 1965, while expressing his distress at "the outrageous bomb attack upon your house." Very soon afterwards Malcolm X was assassinated and Russell issued a press statement on February 23:

The murder of Malcolm X is a terrifying indication of the disintegration affecting American society. The violence and chaos which increasingly greet us from America must give pause to all who are conscious of the fact that American decisions determine the fate of mankind. A society in which people are shot down at will is a society which will plunge the world into disaster.

Malcolm X was reviled in the United States and Britain by the established press not because of his advocacy of armed defense for the Negro against attacks, but because he showed that the same standards which promoted cruel and unrelenting wars of atrocity in Vietnam, the Congo and other parts of the world were responsible for the suffering of the Negro in the United States. Now these American standards have claimed his life. American opinion has not been troubled by the atocities imposed by the U.S. Government on Vietnam and the Congo. Liberal opinion in America apparently contends that by offering Negroes equal opportunity to oppress others as they have been oppressed, the problem of Negro-white relations would be removed. Malcolm X exposed this hypocrisy and was feared because he asked for something more than equality in corruption.

The violence of Harlem is America's violence and it is to be feared that America's violence will become the violence of the world. There is no evading the fact that his death is a symbol of the American condition today.[11]

On the invitation of William Worthy and Grace Lee Boggs, Russell became chairman of the International Commission to investigate the murder of Malcolm X. Russell's growing commitment to the cause of Black Americans was becoming widely recognized. Martin Luther King cabled him on 29 March 1965 to enlist his support "for a national and international boycott" of Alabama until "the admission to the voter registration books of at least 50 percent of the Negro citizens of voting age". Russell cabled his reply on April 1:

Wholeheartedly support boycott of Alabama until all Afro-Americans registered voters. Urge militant demonstration in Washington. Only such bold steps by leadership can deter continued murder and bloodshed.

When Dick Gregory, the Black comedian and campaigner for civil rights informed Russell that he had been hospitalized after his arrest following a demonstration in Chicago, Russell released a statement on June 14:

The beating of Dick Gregory is a further shocking example of the brutality which is becoming characteristic of American life. It is inevitable that the conscienceless violence imposed by the United States on helpless people in Asia and Africa will return to plague the United States itself. That the most brave and conscientious of Americans should be the first victims is a warning to all who can see it. I hope the indignation felt at the treatment of Dick Gregory will cause people to follow his brave example in resisting immoral and cruel policies in the United States.[12]

"The oppressed Negro nation is rising against its three hundred year subjection," Russell wrote in August 1965 following the upheaval in Watts, Los Angeles, widely regarded as the most explosive of the ghetto rebellions that shook America that year. In his article "The Negro Rising"[13] Russell, who characterized the Watts events as a "revolutionary uprising," went on to explain:

Suppression of deprived people historically has inspired revolution, but when these people suffer humiliation and contempt on racial grounds, the cruelty of the oppression is magnified and the uprising assumes a national character.

Russell pointed out that Black Americans were becoming increasingly aware of the connection between their own conditions and those people subject to U.S. domination abroad:

American Negroes are discovering the unreformability of the system which oppresses them. It is not possible for the American military-industrial system to depend upon exploitation and domination in Vietnam and, also, to effect a revolutionary transformation of the conditions of the Negro within the United States. I suspect that only the American Negro is able to understand fully the nature of U.S. oppression in Vietnam, the Congo, the Dominican Republic or other areas of Latin America, Asia and Africa.

Indicative of the growing identification of Black Americans with other subject peoples was Martin Luther King's emergence as an opponent of America's war in Vietnam. Like Russell, King believed that no program for advancing the cause of Black Americans was possible without a fundamental change in the U.S. and while the U.S. continued its war of oppression in Southeast Asia. In keeping with the antagonisms heaped on both King and Russell for their opposition to U.S. policies, a columnist of the *Los Angeles Times* on 20 August 1965 warned that "Martin Luther King could share Bertrand Russell's pitiable Fate."[14] Describing Russell as a "philosopher of distinction babbling erratic nonsense as a senile and garrulous old man," the columnist argued that Martin Luther King "by his decision to use the prestige won in his campaign for civil rights for the purposes of conciliation in Vietnam," was "in danger of becoming the Bertrand Russell of the United States."

Footnotes

1. "The Increase of American Violence," see below pp. 384.

2. Published in full in *The Minority of One*, October 1963.

3. Feldman to Russell, 3 September 1963.

4. Edmunds to Russell, 31 August 1963.

5. Russell to Baldwin, 18 September 1963.

6. Published in *The New York Times*, 8 December 1963.

7. Russell to Clark, 1 January 1964.

8. From Russell's letter in *The Times* of 1 November 1963.

9. From Russell's statement of 31 March 1965, below.

10. Extracts in *New York Times*, 7 April 1965; published in full in B. Feinberg and R. Kasrils (eds.) *Dear Bertrand Russell* (London, 1969), pp. 83-84; (Houghton Mifflin, Boston, 1969), pp. 48-49.

11. Not published.

12. Not published.

13. Originally published as "Los Angeles Negro Rising" in *The Week*, 16 September 1965; as "Bertrand Russell on the revolt in Los Angeles" *World Outlook*, 17 September 1965; reprinted as "The Negro Rising" *The Minority of One*, October 1965. See below pp. 392-3.

14. See Illustrations pp. 304.

18 Escalation of the Vietnam War

Russell's anxieties about the future course of U.S. policies and the prospects for peace, following the death of Kennedy, were exacerbated by America's increasing involvement in Vietnam. Early in 1964 it became clear that the war in Vietnam was not only to be continued by the Johnson Administration but stepped up. Russell redoubled his efforts to arouse the American people to the cruel nature of the war and of their government's role in extending it. He wrote to a number of leading American papers and his letter appeared in the *New York Herald Tribune* of January 17:

Do Americans understand the nature of their war in Vietnam— chemical warfare, the wholesale destruction of villages (1400 out of 2600) and the herding of the peasant population into barbed-wire encampments because of the sympathy they have for the insurgents?

Napalm with its torturous effects is widely employed. The jellied gasoline can neither be rubbed off nor washed off. The victim must slowly burn to death. Its purpose is to terrify all who observe its effect. Therefore this warfare is as atrocity-ridden as any ever conducted.

The United States undertook this war instead of permitting the elections for a unified Vietnam agreed on in the international conference. The regime in the South is tyrannical. Recent suicides indicate the population is more unhappy than ever. The overthrow of Diem resulted from his attempt to negotiate with the North for a neutral and united Vietnam.

The war can be ended now and the suffering stopped by a neutral government neither pro-West nor pro-East.

Russell also wrote to the London *Observer* demanding an impartial investigation of the most recent evidence of "the use of chemical poisons by

242

American and South Vietnamese Governmental forces." He expressed his determination to bring to the notice of the British people "the strong indication that the U.S. is indulging in chemical and gas warfare of an atrocious kind." The *Observer* published Russell's letter on February 9 together with comments form Dennis Bloodworth, their Far Eastern correspondent,who attempted to refute Russell's charge that the defoliants harmed humans or animals and accused Russell of obtaining his information from North Vietnam propaganda sources.

A reply from Russell, published on February 16, was given similar treatment, with Bloodworth casting further doubt on Russell's assertions. Russell pursued the controversy with a third letter, quoting extensively from the British press to corroborate his views, but this the *Observer* declined to publish:

I am pleased that Mr. Bloodworth finds my proposal for an impartial international inquiry into the use of chemicals in Vietnam "unexceptionable." I accept his suggestion that I should initiate one.

It is noteworthy that defoliants and pesticides used in the United States and Great Britain were found to be so harmful that Dr. Weisner, the chief science advisor to President Kennedy, declared them "more dangerous than radioactive fallout." (*Guardian*: 17 May 1963). *The Times* (16 May 1963) disclosed the death by pesticide of birds of fifty-eight species and described fifty pesticides in widespread use as responsible for "acute poisoning" of animals and human beings. President Kennedy found it necessary to halt their use and began a formal investigation. I hope it is now clear that chemicals kill human beings and even "weedkillers" have consequences.

This atrocious war, which has been conducted in Vietnam since the ceasefire in 1954, is in brazen violation of international agreements. These agreements call for elections in South Vietnam which were never held.

Mr. Bloodworth fails to mention that the population which was not permitted to vote freely was uprooted, deprived and ruthlessly regimented in "strategic hamlets" by force. Sixty-five percent of the total population of 7,800,000 were moved to these camps, surrounded by barbed wire and moats (*Observer* 3 November 1963).

Napalm, which destroyed 1400 villages, is a chemical which burns unremittingly and cannot be extinguished. The victims suppurate before terrified observers. The United States has spent over one million dollars daily on this war, four thousand have been killed or wounded each month (*Observer* 8 September 1963). Private armies have been financed by the CIA at a cost of 250,000 pounds monthly (*The Times* September 1963).

All this has taken place against an "enemy" which now controls nearly 70 percent of South Vietnam. The majority of the Vietcong was described as *non-Communist* in the *Observer* by former Premier Tran Van Huu. The Vietcong official policy demands a neutral and disengaged South Vietnam. A popular front which has fought an appalling tyranny in South Vietnam has been opposed by the United States at an incalculable cost to the population. Even the Communist North has declared through Ho Chi Minh that it wished to be unified with the South on terms of neutrality in the cold war and "indepen-dence of Russia, China and the West (*The Times*, 5 November 1963).

The truth is that America has waged a war of conquest against a popular uprising which claims the support of the vast majority. The war is in violation of international agreements, uses techniques employed by the Japanese in the Second World War, and has the sole aim of frustrating neutral and stable government independent of Western dominance. Will the *Observer* demand its immediate cessa-tion?[1]

American opposition to the Vietnam War was growing in proportion to the intensification and expansion of the conflict. Students were in the forefront of this developing protest movement and Russell was concerned to encourage their activities.

The Peace Caucus at Stanford University in California wrote to Russell on 21 February 1964 informing him of their plans for a campaign based on "rejecting increased American involvement in the conflict and calling for negotiations toward the neutralization, and possibly, the reunification of Vietnam." They enclosed with their letter a tape on which they hoped Russell would record a statement of his views on the war and on American policies. Congratulating the students on their efforts Russell sent them a 1500 word recorded statement based on facts which had "passed unscathed through the crucible of American denial" and which Russell believed to be "incontrovertible."[2]

The Stanford students replied on March 13 giving a detailed account of their many activities and of the use to which they had put Russell's recording which they described as a "most valuable contribution to our common endeavor." They also informed Russell of their plans for a demonstration in San Francisco on Easter Sunday which would "involve a great number of groups from throughout the Bay Area in protest to American action in Vietnam."

Russell was very impressed with the industry of the Stanford students and on March 21 he wrote sending them a message for their Easter Sunday demonstration: "I am immensely encouraged by the opposition of American students to this oppressive war," Russell stated, "for until a real and sane alternative foreign policy is formulated and adopted in the United States the immoral willingness to engage in wars of annihilation will threaten mankind with extinction." He advised the students that he would soon send them an article which was an expanded version of the tape recording he had sent them. Entitled "War and Atrocity in Vietnam,"[3] the article outlined the history of first French then American involvement in Vietnam from 1946. Again, making his customary use of quotations from the Western Press, Russell demonstrated how "atrocity has characterized the conduct of the war throughout its history," and concluded:

The tragedy in Vietnam indicates the extent to which it is possible to hide or disguise terrible crimes and it is time that people in the West raised their voices for an end to the bloodshed.

Among many other letters received from American student organizations engaged in protest against the Vietnam War was one from R.D. Stetler, Jr., on behalf of his group at Haverford College in Pennsylvania who had been raising money for medical supplies for the South Vietnam National Liberation Front.[4] Stetler informed Russell of the forty men at his college who had signed a petition "listing those who refuse to fight in the war against the Vietnamese people." He also provided Russell with details of the May 2nd Committee which represented "a number of colleges and universities from the northeastern part of the U.S. and a number of political groups from the much fragmented American left" who had combined to take concerted action on Vietnam and who were organizing simultaneous nationwide demonstrations on May 2.

Russell was heartened by Stetler's news and in his reply of March 20 he asked Stetler to make contact with the Peace Caucus at Stanford University "as they have begun a very intensive campaign against the war." The Haverford students soon came under attack from the Philadelphia School Board for their activities and Russell wrote to the *Philadelphia Daily News* on April 24 expressing his "whole-hearted support for the action of the Haverford students who are raising money for medical supplies for the National Liberation Front in South Vietnam." Repeating his condemnation of American aggression and the threat to world peace arising out of the war Russell then concluded:

Those Americans who have the courage to speak out against this war and its extension, and to appeal for individual responsibility for the policies conducted in the name of the American people deserve world wide support. The dispatch of medical supplies to the victims of American crimes is the minimum duty incumbent upon the Americans whose government has behaved so atrociously.

Like so many other of his pronouncements this letter was not published.

July 1964 marked the 10th anniversary of the agreements reached by the Geneva conference on Indo-China which provided for the establishment in Vietnam, Laos and Cambodia of three independent and neutral states. The occasion was marked by world wide demands that the war in Vietnam should end and that the 14 Nation Geneva Conference should be reconvened. Russell, who was in the forefront of this campaign wrote on July 15 to inform U Thant, secretary general of the United Nations, with whom he had had much friendly contact: "I met with Linus Pauling and J.D. Bernal recently and we are preparing wider support for a campaign to reconvene the fourteen nation Geneva Powers." As part of this campaign Russell led a British delegation that met on 20 July 1964 with David Bruce, the American ambassador in London.

A critical point in the Vietnam War was reached on 2 August 1964 when American warships off the North Vietnam coast were involved in a conflict with North Vietnamese torpedo boats in the Gulf of Tonkin. As a result of the incident the U.S. launched serious bombing raids into North Vietnam on August 5. Russell immediately issued a press statement:

> The grave situation in Vietnam is the outcome of American refusal to begin a negotiated settlement of the war in accordance with the Geneva agreements. American bombings of villages in North Vietnam have resulted in reprisal against her ships off the North Vietnamese coast. The attacks are unwarranted and the North Vietnamese reprisals unwise.
>
> The Secretary General of the United Nations has urged the convening of the 14 Nation Geneva Conference. I appeal to President Johnson to agree. World opinion desires settlement and not a war which will engulf mankind.
>
> President Johnson must have the courage to make peace if he does not wish to destroy humanity to appease Senator Goldwater.[5]

On the same day Russell cabled President Johnson:

> I appeal to you to halt any further attacks on North Vietnam. No result beneficial to peace can occur without negotiations now for a neutral settlement of the entire question of Indo-China. World opinion backs U Thant in asking the convening of the Geneva 14 Nations Conference. For the sake of peace and America's name I beg you to take this step while time permits.

He also cabled Premier Ho Chi-Minh:

American attacks threaten world peace and American refusal to negotiate an end to the war is indefensible.

Nonetheless, I appeal to you not to respond so as not to provide pretexts for U.S. extension of the war, bringing disaster.

Russell received a cabled reply from Ho Chi-Minh on 10 August 1964 which explained his government's action against the American forces:

I welcome your condemning U.S. [who] provoke war and endanger peace in our country and Southeast Asia. Our people and government have always respected and strictly implemented 1954 Geneva Agreements. But in view of U.S. imperialists act of war, we have been compelled to take necessary action in self defense to safeguard our sovereignty and security. We are always attached to peace and stand for peaceful settlement of Vietnam problem. Thank you for concern over serious situation created by American imperialists in our country. Respectful greetings.

Russell replied to Ho Chi-Minh on August 15:

I am very grateful to you for your cable. I entirely sympathise with your position and your people. The United States is behaving with appalling arrogance and is a danger to world peace. I very much approve your prudence and conciliatory practice in the light of this provocation. I assure you that I shall raise my voice for an end to the war and settlement along the lines of the agreements entered into in 1954. Your request for the reconvening of the 14 Nation Geneva Conference is entirely just.

In the meantime Russell had had talks with U Thant who had been in London during July and in a letter to the secretary general of August 7 wrote:

...Recent events cause grave alarm. It is my view that the American attacks on North Vietnam were planned over a considerable period and were launched after the creation of a suitable pretext. If the United States behaves in this way there is small hope for the peace of the world and I cannot believe that the attempt to appease Goldwater can cause anything other than disaster. I view with hope your talks with President Johnson and wish you every possible success.

By August 7 more information had emerged regarding the Gulf of Tonkin incident and Russell had elucidated this in a statement of that date which was delivered to the U.S. Embassy in London:

"The war in South Vietnam has seen 7 million people placed in barbed wire camps patrolled by machine gun bearing guards and police dogs. 160,000 have died, 700,000 have been maimed, 350,000 imprisoned and 16,000 internment camps constructed by the end of 1963."

The American attacks on North Vietnam are a grave threat to world peace. They have no justification. The Seventh Fleet had ships off the North Vietnamese coast and North Vietnamese villages had been bombed by American planes flying from Laos. Todays *Daily Mail* reports that Pentagon sources reveal that American ships took part in the inspection of North Vietnamese ships on the North Vietnamese coast. The United States attacks reflect the disastrous consequences of United States policy in Southeast Asia.

The war in South Vietnam is a popular national revolution which has a non-Communist leadership and massive national popular backing. The war is conducted despite the offer of all parties but the Americans to accept a neutral solution in accordance with the Geneva Conferences of 1954 and 1962. The war in South Vietnam has seen 7 million people placed in barbed wire camps patrolled by machine gun bearing guards and police dogs. 160,000 have died, 700,000 have been maimed, 350,000 imprisoned and 16,000 internment camps constructed by the end of 1963.

In one year, 50,000 air attacks were made by United States planes. In one year 14,000 villages were destroyed.

This brutal policy has done irreparable damage to the United States apart from the horrible suffering it has caused the people of Vietnam.

The United States must be made to stop this war and to agree to the request of U Thant and of world opinion to negotiate now. The Geneva 14 Nation Conference should be immediately convened after a cease-fire.

I hope the United Nations will demand American agreement to a Conference such as that held in 1954 or condemn the United States as an aggressor. The alternative will be acquiescence in American extension of this war to the North, the involvement of China, and quite inexorably, a world war. This must not be permitted. What worse can Goldwater do if the men who oppose him do so by outbidding him in madness and suicidal belligerence?[6]

With the exception of Wayne Morse the U.S. Senate supported the extension of bombing to North Vietnam and Russell who had followed

Morse's public statements "with the greatest approval and admiration for your courage" wrote to him on August 7: "Yours is the lone voice on the madness of U.S. policy in Southeast Asia and I wish to congratulate you on all that you are doing." Russell was most concerned to counter the U.S. government's use of the Tonkin incident to escalate the war and he wrote to the *New York Herald Tribune,* who did not publish his letter of August 14:

Your readers may not be aware that in Europe and in other places outside America the explanation offered by the American Government for the recent attacks on North Vietnam are not accepted. Even the American State Department has now acknowledged that the North Vietnamese islands, Hon He and Hon Ngu, were attacked by vessels from South Vietnam with the American Seventh Fleet stationed nearby. It was after these attacks that replies came from North Vietnamese torpedo boats. It is hard to understand why full-scale air attacks should then be launched by the United Staes, when the initial attack came from South Vietnam, with American cover.

We are left with the following conclusion. The United States is prepared irresponsibly to risk the widening of a war which could be ended any time the United States showed willingness to enter into negotiations which accord with the Geneva Agreements of ten years ago. It is the United States which has persistently violated these Agreements and which, by these attacks, shows itself a threat to the peace of the world. Senator Morse's solitary vote in the Senate was a vote for world opinion.

Russell, who did not view America's aggression in Vietnam as an isolated event, but rather as a consequence of a global strategy, linked U.S. policy in Southeast Asia with developing U.S. activity in the Congo. In a letter to *The Guardian* published on August 22 he commented on this theme:

Your editorial on the Congo does well to show the relation between American intervention in Vietnam and present American activity in the Congo. The United States is assuming the arrogant right to intrude militarily wherever her economic interests are endangered. These interests reflect the power of private industry and what Fred Cook has rightly called "The Warfare State." The "Warfare State" is controlled by industry in alliance with the military, from which so much of its profit derives.

American intervention in the Congo, as in Vietnam, comes to brazen economic and political imperialism, masqueraded as opposition to communism. The United States must be made to cease its perpetual intervention in countries which are so wicked as to use their resources for their own advance, as opposed to American and Western aggrandisement. Rebels do not worry the United States, as we know from their efforts with regard to Cuba. The real concern is neither absence of freedom, instability in a given country, nor the peace of the world. It is time a spade was called a spade where American policy is concerned.

Vietnam was now consuming most of Russell's time and energy and his tireless activities were making an impact on increasingly wider sections of the American people. James G. Patton, President of the National Farmers Union, wrote to Russell on September 25 with an invitation to address his organization's convention to be held the following year. "If you can come we would like to make a special award to you as a world citizen for your efforts on behalf of the people of the world," Patton notified Russell, and continued, "since 80 percent of the people of the world are rural and farm people, we think this is in keeping with your great life work and the deep respect which the people of the world have for you."

On November 7 the George Washington Carver Memorial Institute informed Russell that they had voted him their "Supreme Award of Merit and Honorary Fellowship for outstanding contribution to better race relations, human welfare, art and literature, and the cause of universal peace."

The May 2nd Movement asked Russell to become an international sponsor of their campaign against the Vietnam War and Russell in accepting sent the students a message on December 3:

The war of atrocity in Vietnam confronts Americans with a duty not unlike that faced by Germans during the Nazi era. It is not necessary to compare the gas chambers of Nazi Germany with the internment camps employed in South Vietnam to make clear that the record of torture and atrocity for which the United States is responsible challenges Americans with the same moral duty to protest. Forced labour, chemical warfare and appalling mutilation has characterised the war directed by America in Vietnam during the past decade. I consider the May 2nd Movement to speak for the conscience of Americans and I urge all who value the good name of their country to join in its work.

With the Vietnam conflict continuing to escalate and the prospect of confrontation with China mounting, Russell, on November 27, cabled President Johnson who had recently been re-elected to office:

The Vietnam crisis is one which concerns not only the citizens of the United States and of Vietnam but all human beings, since the lives of all are at stake. The American Government is hesitating (so it appears) as to whether the war should be extended to North Vietnam and to China. The war against China, if it is not nuclear, is likely to drag on inconclusively for years. It is likely that the Russians will patch up their differences with China and come to its assistance. Indeed, they have already said that they will come to the assistance of North Vietnam. It will soon become evident, in that case, that neither side can defeat the other except by employing nuclear weapons. In the heat of battle, each side will consider such employment essential. The result will be the extermination of the human race.

Is it worthwhile to risk such a result merely because the majority of the inhabitants of South Vietnam wish to be neutral in the cold war?...

Excerpts from Russell's cable appeared in the *New York Times* of November 28 but he received no reply from President Johnson.

While, in general, Russell met with official silence from the U.S. government, his contact with the Vietnamese was developing particularly through a regular correspondence with Ho Chi-minh. Both the government of the Democratic Republic of Vietnam and the Liberation forces in the south had come to recognize Russell as the most outstanding figure in the West calling for a just and peaceful settlement of the Vietnam conflict. Towards the end of 1964, Christopher Farley, Russell's secretary and an office holder of the Bertrand Russell Peace Foundation, visited North Vietnam on Russell's behalf to gain first hand information on the situation. Russell wrote to Ho Chi-minh on December 30 with new year greetings, thanking him for "your kindness to my associate Mr. Farley" and stating:

As I write there are reports of a wider recognition, both in the United States Senate and among the public, that the United States will have to withdraw entirely from Vietnam, and I hope that this offers you some small encouragement.

In his article "Free World Barbarism" published in the December edition of *Minority of One* Russell drew attention to "Plan Six" which had been advanced by W. W. Rostow, the director of the State Department's Policy Planning Board, which provided for "a naval blockade and air raids against North Vietnam."[7] Quoting from Western news sources Russell revealed:

Melvin Laird stated in a committee of the U.S. House of Representatives that "the U.S. administration is preparing plans for a strike into

North Vietnam." The Associated Press reported a combat force of fifty jet bombers training in the Philippines in preparation for bombing of targets in North Vietnam.

Supporting his contention that "the United States has been deliberately provoking North Vietnam" Russell catalogued a series of statements in the U.S. press which had commenced in April 1964 with a *New York Times* report that "Secretary of State Dean Rusk told SEATO nations the U.S. [was] absolutely committed to remain in South Vietnam and reiterated that the war may be brought to North Vietnam soon."[8]

Russell was convinced that the August attack on North Vietnam, resulting from the Bay of Tonkin incident, was the prelude to a premeditated move by the U.S. to extend the war into the North. "The time for protest is overdue," Russell warned, "we may hope it is not too late."[9]

On 7 February 1965, the U.S. launched a full-scale bombing raid deep into North Vietnam and Russell immediately issued a statement. copies of which he addressed to President Johnson, Prime Minister Harold Wilson and Premier Ho Chi-minh on February 9:

The American attack on North Vietnam is disastrous on two grounds: one, that it is unjust, and two, that it exposes mankind to an appalling danger. Americans have been trying for years to subdue the desire of South Vietnam for independence and to compel it against its will to serve American purposes. South Vietnam wishes to be independent and neutral. America will not permit this. This is imperialism of an old-fashioned kind.

But the graver objection to the American action is that it involves the danger of war with Russia and China. In such a war, civilisation will be extinguished for a century or two and it is not impossible that the human race will be exterminated. Is it worthwhile to pay this price in order to prevent South Vietnam from its legitimate desire for independence? It is intolerable that the British Labour Government should support a policy involving such dangers through a cowardly desire to support the United States whatever that power may decide to do.

I hope that the American action in North Vietnam will be condemned as aggression at the United Nations and that it will be abandoned as a result of protests in every part of the world.[10]

Harold Wilson replied to Russell on February 16 that in his government's view "the dangers of the situation in Vietnam were not created by the action taken by the United States"[11] and Chester L. Cooper writing on behalf of President Johnson informed Russell on February 24 that his "views on the situation in Vietnam" had been "added to the many other opinions received at the White House."

In the meantime Russell had attacked the British Labour Government's foreign policies, including it's "craven and odious support for American madness" in a speech delivered at the London School of Economics on February 15.[12] Describing American attacks on North Vietnam as "desperate acts of piratical madness," Russell urged "world protest at every U.S. Embassy" and "meetings, marches, demonstrations and all other forms of protest" directed at the British Government's support for American actions in Vietnam. In an emergency statement prefacing his speech Russell declared:

Once more America summons mankind to the brink of war. Once more America is willing to run the risk of destroying the human race... Either America is stopped now or there will be crisis after crisis...[13]

To the American Youth Against War and Fascism, who had embarked on a course of protest action, Russell cabled on February 18, "urgently appeal for nationwide demonstrations in America in defense of peace and people of Vietnam...all good wishes to you for your action today."

Russell kept up a barrage of letters and articles to the British and American press few of which would ever have been published but for the *Minority of One* which Russell described as "the leading American journal in the fight for peace" and "the most incisive publication of which I know."[14] In Britain the *Daily Worker* published his "Danger in Southeast Asia" under the title "U.S. has shocked Mankind" on March 27. "The Americans have at last succeeded—too late, alas—in shocking the conscience of mankind." Russell wrote and continued:

They have been engaged for years in various kinds of atrocity in endeavouring to subdue "inferior" races at home and abroad, but these acts have been excused as occasional excursions of a too energetic population. The British Labour Government has applauded them and has made itself an accomplice in unspeakable cruelties...We have been told on high American authority that the next step America will take will be the destruction of China. When China has been destroyed, Americans will turn to giving assistance to their henchmen in the British Labour Party in their struggles in Malaysia. She will then "liberate" various other...countries in Asia and Africa. When these tasks have been accomplished America will rule the world....There is only one hope for the world, which is that the better elements in the American population will refuse to follow collective mass murderers on their fatal course....These are, I am convinced, the great majority of

Americans...It should still be possible, though it is getting daily more difficult, to induce more Americans to choose a Government not composed of savage exterminators....The British people, despite the attitude of the leaders of the two great parties, can help bring this about. The action of the ninety four Labour MP's and of important trade unions in protesting against the American aggression, is a step in the right direction.

The first official change in the character of U.S. military intervention in South Vietnam ocurred on 24 March 1965 when American pilots who along with other military personnel had previously been employed only as "advisors" were involved in bombing raids on National Liberation Front positions. This was followed just two weeks later by the landing of 3500 Marines at Da Nang, the first American troops to be sent into South Vietnam in an admittedly combat capacity. The extent of American firepower was indicated by Ho Chi-minh who informed Russell in a cable of March 18:

Situation very dangerous. USA brought more troops into South Vietnam to intensify war. Since January 1965 U.S. warships and aircraft attacked 18 and 9 times respectively various places in DRV killing women and children, destroying houses and villages.

"American military men are all persuaded that the only way to win a small war is to turn it into a big one" Russell wrote at the time in "Prospects of Escalation in Southeast Asia" for the May issue of *The Minority of One*. "With every day that passes, the escalation to World War becomes more probable."

Many Americans reacted with horror to these new developments. Congratulating Lewis Mumford, the author, who had written an open letter of protest to President Johnson, Russell wrote on April 8:

American policy, which the British Government supports, seems to me completely mad and in danger of ending in utter disaster. I wish more people would speak out against it as you have done.

Mumford replied on April 16:

Thank you for saying what you did about my open letter to President Johnson: in taking a stand on such issues you have set a standard for all of us. The letter has met with an encouraging public response. Though it was not printed in any of the Eastern newspapers where it was sent, it has now achieved countrywide circulation, and possibly has had an effect in stimulating student-teacher demonstrations in Columbia, New York University, University of Michigan, and Berkeley; likewise, perhaps on the advertisement signed by 2500 clergymen, under the headline: "For God's sake stop it!" The rejection of the U.S. government's Vietnam policy is far more widespread than the newspapers and networks indicate: and it has a note of militancy that's been happily carried over from Martin Luther King's campaign for Civil Rights. But this has mainly been confined to the young—the people of weight and position have been shamefully silent for the most part....

Russell also received encouraging news from City College of New York, where, he was informed, a Committee to Aid the South Vietnamese National Liberation Front had been set up. "All funds raised will be used to provide the people of the National Liberation Front with necessary materials, exclusive of armaments" wrote John R. Osborne on April 19, "the materials supplied will, in the main, consist of medicines and hospital equipment. Russell sent a message of support on April 28.

Reflecting the growing public concern about the war were the student inspired "teach-ins" which served to scrutinize U.S. government policy. Among the first of these was that held at the University of California, Berkeley on May 21 and 22. Russell was invited to send a recorded message to this event.[15] "The world is confronted with a great danger, the danger of subjection to the United States. This danger has been growing for some years, but it is now coming out into the open," Russell began his statement. Going on to examine what he termed "the latest and most flagrant of United States misdeeds" Russell dealt with the landing, at the end of April, of 20,000 U.S. marines at Santo Domingo in order to reinstall the recently overthrown dictatorship of the Dominican Republic:

In Santo Domingo, the United States, assuming its moral right to control the Western Hemisphere, has acted to preserve its sphere of influence. In Vietnam, the U.S. is waging a massive war on the boundaries of China. China, because it is a communist country, is not permitted to have a sphere of influence—that would be aggression. There is one law for the United States and another for the rest of the world. Both laws are made in Washington.

Returning to the main theme of Vietnam, Russell explained that "when it became apparent to the United States that not even two million dollars a day could buy enough friends, and the war in the South was being lost, the bombing of the North was started." Welcoming the student's action at Berkeley Russell concluded that it was of "supreme importance that ways should be found of stopping America before it is too late."

With President Johnson's policy becoming committed to stepping up the bombing of North Vietnam and the involvement of American combat forces in the South, Russell issued a statement on June 6:

President Johnson's decision to bring full scale war to Vietnam shows his contempt for world opinion. He will be noted as the most brutal and incompetent of all American Presidents to date. I appeal to Americans to hold a new March on Washington in protest against the madness apparent to all but the isolated and purblind members of a few benighted governments.[16]

While Russell was anathema to American officialdom and was subjected to continuous press censorship, his world stature ensured that he would be approached from time to time by certain sections of the media to state his views. Merv Griffin, a well-known U.S. television personality, invited Russell to do a recorded interview for his nationally syndicated program. The interview was filmed at Russell's home in Wales and broadcast on 28 June 1965 with wide national viewing and publicity. Griffin was interested to question Russell on America's role in Vietnam and the world, and in the half hour discussion Russell dealt with numerous questions in both a humorous and serious vein.

Griffin, describing himself as "speaking as an American" and adding that Americans "love to avoid any kind of war," questioned Russell on the steps necessary to attaining world peace. Russell replied that everybody wanted peace but that there were various ways of achieving it. "The first thing would be," Russell explained, "for America to give up aggressive war, give up the habit of invading peaceful countries and torturing them."

In a long discussion on Vietnam and America's deepening involvement Russell asserted that while most "ordinary Americans" believed their government was conducting a "protective war...against wicked Communists," they were in fact waging war "against people who were, until they were attacked, entirely in favour of neutrality." Those people, Russell added, had now "learned what American troops are."

Dealing with the escalated American presence in Vietnam, Russell stated that the U.S. had first sent advisors and then "troops to advise the advisors." When Griffin asked Russell why he thought young Americans were "fighting in lands thousands of miles from us" Russell retorted: "They're fighting there in order that your rich men may be richer. That's quite simple."

In answer to Griffin's question about a solution for the "great problem in Vietnam" Russell stated:

What ought to be done...is exactly what the Geneva Conference recommended. North and South Vietnam ought not to be divided.

They ought to have a general election...I think there's no occasion for anybody to interfere with Vietnam. At the same time I think that it'll be very difficult for Vietnam to get normal again because the whole population has been uprooted. And I think they'll need a lot of help. But there's no difficulty whatever in seeing what the solution ought to be. It ought to be, simply, that all foreign troops are withdrawn from Vietnam, and North and South Vietnam, together if they like, or separately, if they like, should vote.

Griffin then asked Russell for his views on America's relations with "Red China" to which Russell replied:

Well, the Americans have found it convenient to make the Chinese into a bogey. The Russians are no longer an adequate bogey. And so they have had to find another...They want to have a war with China. When I say America I mean the governing forces in America, who are not the nice people who are kind and so forth....Yes, they want a war with China. And they think that Vietnam is a convenient jumping-off place.

Russell rejected Griffin's suggestion that continued American nuclear superiority might be the overall solution in dealing with the world's problems:

No, that's no solution! The Americans are so abominable. To have an American autocracy throughout the world would be one of the most dreadful things that could happen. The only thing worse is a nuclear war.

In South Vietnam the instability of the Saigon government was marked by frequent changes in the leadership. When Air-Marshal Ky emerged as the new Prime Minister, Russell wrote to the press on July 8:

The Prime Minister of South Vietnam, Air-Marshal Nguyen Cao Ky, stated: "My only hero is Hitler. We need four or five Hitlers in South Vietnam."

Eighty percent of the territory of South Vietnam is controlled by the National Liberation Front, and it enjoys the support of virtually the entire population. The United States, however, in support of Prime Minister Cao Ky, who is an avowed admirer of Hitler and Nazism, continues to bomb with napalm and phosphorous and razor dart weapons the people of Vietnam, without discrimination or respite. The day is not far off when those who perpetrate this policy will have to answer for it.[17]

> "The United States has over 3,300 military bases in the world. These bases guard the spoils of United States capitalism, e.g. nearly 60 percent of the natural resources of the world."

The deteriorating situation of the Saigon regime with its army suffering heavy defeats at the hands of the Liberation forces, on the one hand, and increasing world-wide pressure for the withdrawal of U.S. troops as a step towards implementation of the Geneva Peace Agreements, on the other, led President Johnson to propose "unconditional discussions" while announcing the phased dispatch of a further 300,000 troops to Vietnam. Commenting on these developments, Russell, in a message to the Seattle Chapter of the American Fellowship of Reconciliation, stated:

> The U.S. has employed the language of peace talks at the very moment that it blueprints the dispatch of 300,000 troops to Vietnam. It bombs within 40 miles of the borders of China at the same time that peace missions are proposed.
>
> In short, words of peace camouflage U.S. acts of war. What must be remembered is that negotiations were already held in 1954. These led to international agreements prohibiting the presence of foreign troops in Vietnam. It is in violation of these very international agreements that U.S. troops are in Vietnam. This is aggression. The only solution is the withdrawal of U.S. troops in conformity with the already negotiated Geneva Agreements. Until the aggression ceases and the U.S. troops are withdrawn there can be no peace in Vietnam.

The Fellowship had requested from Russell a message to a broadly based "Rally to End the War in Vietnam Now" to be held on Hiroshima Day, August 7, in conjunction with Canadian peace groups at Blaine on the U.S./Canadian border. "Your determined witness for peace over the years is a great inspiration to thousands of us on this continent," the organizing committee informed Russell in their letter of July 29, adding that "some word from you will be greatly appreciated and heartening as we carry on the fight against this miserable war in Vietnam.

Much of the content of Russell's message was incorporated in an article "On Vietnam" for the September issue of *Frontier*. In his article Russell asserted that Americans had allowed "corporate capitalism to identify its selfish and rapacious aims with the national interests of the American nation." In wishing Americans to understand the meaning of their government's policy, Russell pointed out:

> The United States has over 3,300 military bases in the world. These bases guard the spoils of United States capitalism, e.g. nearly 60 percent of the natural resources of the world. As the United States

contains only 6 percent of the world's population, it is clear that this vast international system of military control is required to suppress a world revolution against conditions of poverty, disease and unrelieved misery for the peoples of Africa, Asia and Latin America.

Discussing the atrocious nature of the Vietnam War, Russell claimed that it qualified "the directors of American policy for trial and execution as war ciminals in the same manner as those Nazis convicted at Nuremburg." Referring to President Johnson's recent proposals for unconditional negotiation, Russell stated:

Words of peace which are contrived to cover acts of war are reminiscent of Hitler and should not deceive people. Americans should try to understand that there is no Vietnamese fleet in Long Island Sound containing nuclear weapons. St Louis, New Orleans, Denver, Los Angeles and Chicago have not been made into furnaces with jelly gasoline. The American people have not suffered bombing, gas burning, poisoning and torture for ten years. Fifty-nine percent of the American population has not experienced forced labour in concentration camps at the hands of a Vietnamese or Chinese occupying army, even in the capacity of advisors. What American would accept negotiations under such conditions unless the troops and the authority which had perpetrated such crimes were removed from his country?

Commenting that the U.S. was intervening militarily in countries throughout the world "wherever poor people with rich land are in rebellion" Russell asked of his readers "what then is our responsibility in the face of such behaviour?" and declaimed:

In my view we must acknowledge and state openly that the Cold War and the danger of world war are the responsiblity of the United Sates, or more accurately, of American imperialism. As long as the American government is controlled by corporate capitalism and its military arm, America will be represented by a policy of counter-revolution and brutality and the world must stagger from one crisis to another...

We must oppose and expose this. The people of Vietnam deserve our full support and solidarity in the same manner as the heroes of the French resistance to Hitler. For my part I salute the National Liberation Front and its struggle for the emancipation of Vietnam from the brutal domination of the United States.

President Johnson's decision to greatly increase American ground forces in Vietnam took effect during September 1965 with the arrival of

20,000 troops. Troops continued to pour in. Far from suppressing the guerilla struggle, resistance increased. Russell wrote to the *New York Herald Tribune* on October 11 after it had reported cases of torture by Saigon troops on their prisoners:

> During the French war of oppression in Algeria, nearly a million French troops were unable to defeat the Algerian revolution. The same number of French and Vietnamese troops were unable to defeat the Vietminh. Japan, France, and the United States have, in turn, tortured and bombed indiscriminately in their efforts to suppress the struggle for national liberation in Vietnam. The *New York Herald Tribune* reported:
>
> "One of the most infamous methods of torture used by the Government is partial electrocution or 'frying' as one U.S. advisor called it. Wires were attached to male genital organs, or to the breasts of a Vietcong woman prisoner. Other techniques designed to force onlooking prisoners to talk, involve cutting off the fingers, ears, fingernails or sexual organs of another prisoner. A string of ears decorates the wall of a government installation."
>
> When will the people of the United States realise that what their government is doing compares to Germany's occupation of Eastern Europe? The next generation of Americans will be asking the present generation why they kept silent while war crimes were committed in their name. It is not too late for Americans to resist the barbarous actions of their Government.[18]

Russell, in common with the broad peace movement in Britain, believed that the most effective way the British people could contribute towards ending the war in Vietnam was by exerting pressure on their government to oppose U.S. policy. When the U.S. began bombing dams in North Vietnam, Russell led a delegation of prominent Britons to see Prime Minister Wilson in protest at the British Government's failure to react. In a statement issued on August 23, prior to the meeting with Wilson, Russell described the bombing of dams as "a horrible and vindictive act against a civilian population."[19] His statement continued:

> We know that serious consideration has already been given in the United States to the bombing of the Red River dykes for which the destruction of the dam is apparent preparation. If this happens, between two and three million people will drown. The rice crop will be destroyed, causing mass starvation. Is there no ounce of humanity left in this Government that it should fail to condemn and publicly reject this barbarism? A delegation to Prime Minister Wilson is being

assembled urgently to demand that Britain should forcibly inform President Johnson of its detestation of this wickedness.

Russell's strong condemnation of the "perfidy of the Labour Government under the premiership of Harold Wilson,"[20] especially in regard to Vietnam, which he saw as a betrayal of socialist principles, led to his public resignation from the Labour Party on the eve of big demonstrations in London to end the war in Vietnam.[21]

The Bertrand Russell Peace Foundation issued a press statement following Russell's action:

In a speech delivered on October 14 at Mahatma Gandhi Hall[22] Bertrand Russell spoke of the Labour Government's policies during its first year as "the carrying out of Britain's old imperialist policy involving concurrence with the deliberate bombing of schools, hospitals and orphanages in Vietnam." Lord Russell described the war in Vietnam as one of savagery and unbridled cruelty and accused the U.S. Government of trying to gild "a very rotten and stinking lily." Lord Russell tore up his Labour Party card after fifty-one years of membership, stating: "I find myself confronted with the most shameful betrayal of modern times in this country. Hitler, at least, never professed humanity, but these men who now pollute the chairs of office professed, before election, the most noble and lofty ideals on human brotherhood. It has done everything in its power to prevent a knowledge of the atrocities which are taking place, let alone a knowledge of the reasons for the Government's complacence in face of them.

Lord Russell declared: "For my part I feel that I can no longer remain a member of this so-called 'Labour' Party and I am resigning after fifty-one years. It is time that a new movement, leading to a new party more nearly like the movement for which Keir Hardie struggled, be formed to carry out the aspirations of those who have, hitherto, upheld the present Party." Lord Russell said that the British Government, through its subservience to America, was helping to bring the world to complete disaster.[23]

Because of repeated insistence by the U.S. Government that it was confining its bombings in North Vietnam to military installations, Russell had been requesting and receiving information from the Vietnamese concerning the results of American bombing. Consequently, he was in a position to release an important letter to the British press on 13 October 1965:

During the past ten years I have received information from the Government in North Vietnam about the war which has been waged by France and the United States. I have subjected all such information to the most careful scrutiny and double checked it against western sources. I have never found data provided me by the North Vietnamese to be without substantiation and wish to call to the attention of your readers the following facts which are fully documented.

American air attacks have deliberately included as targets medical establishments such as hospitals, infirmaries, maternity and medical stations and clinics. By 11 July 1965, 30 medical establishments were destroyed among which were Tuberculosis and Leper Sanatoria. Hospitals in the following places were destroyed by bombing: Vinh Linh, Quang Binh, the provincial capitals of Son La and Yen Bai, Quang Trach, Nghia Dan and Huong Khe.

Sanatoria and Maternity Stations were bombed at Cho Moi, Cua Lo and Ba Don. These establishments were bombed and strafed between 7 and 14 times, killing physicians treating previous bombing victims. Patients limping away on crutches were strafed.

The Leper Sanatorium of Quynh Lap, between the 12 and 22 of June, the T.B. Hospital at Than Hoa (July 8) and the Hospital at Than Hoa (July 9) were destroyed. Quynh Lap Sanatorium was the largest of its kind, carrying out research and treatment for leprosy. It consisted of 160 buildings, treated 4,000 lepers and accommodated 2,600 patients. The T.B. Hospital had 600 beds and all scientific facilities. These institutions were destroyed by bombs, rockets and napalm reducing all buildings to ash. In the neighboring province, hospitals and the Epidemiology Station were bombed for three consecutive days. Physicians, pregnant women and children were killed apart from the destruction of houses and all x-ray laboratories and research facilities.

My documentation pertains to all North Vietnam. It shows a sustained military policy. Our Government's support for American action in Vietnam places the people of Britain in the position of Germans who were silent during Hitler's reign. These crimes are on our conscience, and, for my part, I will not rest until those responsible for them are removed from public life.[24]

Russell projected this information at every opportunity to the American public. In a message to a "teach-in" at the University of California at Los Angeles, on November 12, he informed the assembly that "in one year alone 50,000 air attacks with napalm were conducted by the United States and its puppet government" in Vietnam. Appealing to the students, Russell declared:

What is one to think of a war in which the most powerful industrial nation on earth uses all the ingenuity and resources at its disposal to annihilate the people of a backward, agricultural country thousands of miles away?... It is our duty to condemn and oppose the United States war of aggression in Vietnam. We must work, in whatever ways are available to us, to create a society in which the conditions which have created the Vietnam War are overthrown, never to re-occur. There must be an end to the distortions which condemn the majority of the peoples of the world to a life of misery, while others enjoy unprecedented wealth and privilege. Only in this way can peace be finally assured.

From whatever quarter the war was viewed Russell was a central figure. At the end of 1965, he received information and an urgent request from the South Vietnam Peace Committee, based in Hanoi, to intervene on behalf of two American soldiers, George E. Smith and Claude McClure, who had been released from captivity by the National Liberation Front of South Vietnam as a gesture of good-will. On their release the men had been placed in detention by the U.S. army in Japan, and the South Vietnam Peace Committee cabled Russell to "use your authority and influence to set up suitable means aiming at guaranteeing liberty to those two American army men."[25] Russell promptly issued a press statement on 30 December 1965:

The two American soldiers who were released after capture by the National Liberation Front of South Vietnam are receiving unwarranted treatment at the hands of U.S. Army authorities in Okinawa. What is their crime? They have stated their detestation of the brutal war waged by their Government against the people of Vietnam. They have given voice to the stirring conscience of the American people themselves, and so they are held, without trial, and denied their elementary rights as U.S. citizens.

All who abominate the terrible atrocities committed by the U.S. government in its unjust and aggressive war will protest in the strongest terms this persecution accorded two American soldiers, who bring honour to the United States by their courage and commitment to the truth. I hope people in all countries will demand their release.[26]

Footnotes

1. Russell to the editor of the *Observer*, 16 February 1964; published in *Tribune*, 28 February 1964.

2. The statement, composed 27 February 1964, formed the basis of "War and atrocity in Vietnam." See below pp. 361-70.

3. Published in the Spring edition of *Views;* reprinted B. Russell, *War Crimes in Vietnam* (London, 1967); (Monthly Review Press, New York, 1967).

4. Stetler to Russell, 17 March 1964.

5. Not published.

6. Excerpts in *The New York Times*, 8 August 1964.

7. See below pp. 371-8. Reprinted B. Russell, *War Crimes in Vietnam.*

8. *Ibid.*

9. *Ibid.*

10. *Mr. Wilson speaks "frankly and fearlessly" on Vietnam to Bertrand Russell,* (Bertrand Russell Peace Foundation, 1968) p. 8.

11. *Ibid.*, pp. 8-9.

12. *Ibid.*, pp. 28-38.

13. B. Russell, *Autobiography*, vol. III (London, 1969), p. 205; (New York, 1969), p. 302.

14. Russell to *The Minority of One*, 22 February 1965.

15. Published as "American ambition can kill us," *The Week*, 20 May 1965.

16. Not published.

17. Not published.

18. Not published.

19. Published in *Le Monde*, 25 August 1965.

20. B. Russell, *Autobiography*, Vol. III, p. 165, p. 234.

21. 14 October 1965.

22. Published as "America's Rulers Justify Cruelties Equalling Those of Hitler" in *World Outlook*, 29 October 1965; reprinted in B. Russell *War Crimes in Vietnam* as "The Labour Party's Foreign Policy."

23. Not published.

24. Not published.

25. Cable dated 30 December 1965.

26. Not published.

19 War Crimes Tribunal

Towards the end of 1965 Russell prepared a major statement to be read on his behalf in Havana to the First Solidarity Conference of the Peoples of Africa, Asia and Latin America. "Peace Through Resistance to American Imperialism"[1] was the theme of the statement and it was published in January 1966 in America by the *Minority of One* under the title "Does the U.S. Make Peaceful Coexistence Possible?" Characterizing American imperialism as "a world system of oppression" Russell examined the economic and political policies of the U.S. which he felt represented "the true threat to peace and the true source of the danger of world nuclear war":

> In every part of the world the source of war and of suffering lies at the door of U.S. Imperialism. Wherever there is hunger, wherever there is exploitative tyranny, wherever people are tortured and the masses left to rot under the weight of disease and starvation, the force which holds down the people stems from Washington.

Russell believed therefore that peace could not be realized by depending on the "goodwill of those whose power depends on the continuation of such exploitation and on the ever-increasing scale of military production." Russell called for "a united and coordinated resistance" on the part of all oppressed people to "remove the resources from the control of U.S. imperialism."

In a statement issued to the press on January 14 Russell described those in the West who cooperated in deceiving their people about the nature of the Vietnam War as having "the same guilt in relation to those events as Germans who acquiesced in Hitler's acts." He demanded that people everywhere should call for "the indictment of President Johnson, Dean Rusk and Robert McNamara as war criminals."

"In every part of the world the source of war and suffering lies at the door of U.S. imperialism. Wherever there is hunger, wherever there is exploitative tyranny, wherever people are tortured and the masses left to rot under the weight of disease and starvation, the force which holds down the people stems from Washington."

In Vietnam a ceasefire had been in operation since Christmas 1965 but on 31 January 1966 the U.S. renewed its military actions including the bombing of North Vietnam. In a statement to the press on the same day Russell demanded an end to "this senseless ravaging of an essentially agricultural country":

> The resumption of bombing in North Vietnam is the clearest commentary on the so-called "peace offensive." The Pentagon has no desire for peace. What they want is control of Southeast Asia and they are prepared to go to any length to achieve their aims despite ever more persistent warnings by their own advisors that such a policy might soon lead to total war. This policy must be halted at all costs before it becomes too late.[2]

On February 5 President Johnson met his top advisors in Honolulu and announced his intention to move ahead "on the military front" in defeating the Communists while at the same time, "on the social and political front," helping the Vietnamese people to realize their "deepest aspirations."[3]

As American casualties were growing and it was becoming increasingly clear that there could be no hope of a military solution to the war without further massive increases in U.S. combat commitment, many Americans were outraged by Johnson's pronouncement. Corliss Lamont in his letter of February 18, enclosing a contribution of $2000 to the Bertrand Russell Peace Foundation, remarked:

> I have doubled my gift this year to offset in some slight degree the fact that most Americans are profiting financially from the economic boom which is being so greatly stimulated by President Johnson's horrible war of aggression in Vietnam.
>
> Since Johnson's statements at the Honolulu Conference, I have been calling him Liar-in-Chief of the United States.
>
> We are considering here a petition to the United States Senate, to be printed as an advertisement and calling on the Senate to impeach Johnson for his various crimes.

Russell was most interested in Lamont's plans for a petition calling for Johnson's impeachment as he had himself been "searching for some effective means to help make known to the world the unbelievable cruelty of the U.S. in its unjust attempt to subjugate South Vietnam."[4] By January 1966 he had begun to prepare for the convening of a War Crimes Tribunal which could examine evidence of atrocities committed by the U.S. and its allies in Vietnam and assess the responsibility of President Johnson and other American leaders.

In order to gather evidence for such a Tribunal Russell sent Ralph Schoenman, an office holder of the Bertrand Russell Peace Foundation, and an American, to North Vietnam towards the end of February. Schoenman was also to assess the possibilities of sending into Vietnam investigatory teams who would systematically collect specialized evidence.

Informing Russell of the arrival and subsequent activities of Ralph Schoenman, Pham Van Dong, the prime minister of the Democratic Republic of Vietnam, wrote on March 3:

> ...We believe that your future activities and those of your "Peace Foundation" will be of an important contribution to the mobilisation of the world and American people to strongly condemn the U.S. aggressors and vigorously support the just and surely successful struggle of the Vietnamese people.
>
> President Ho Chi Minh and I beg extend to you our best greetings and wish you good health, longevity and noble contributions to humanity. Your image, that of a champion of the just cause of the Vietnamese people will forever remain in our hearts.

Aside from his correspondence with leaders in Vietnam, Russell was also in regular communication with the London and Paris representatives of the North Vietnamese Government. During May it was arranged that he should prepare a taped statement in support of his plans for a War Crimes Tribunal which would be sent for broadcast on Radio Hanoi. The statement was recorded on May 24.[5] Directing his speech to American soldiers serving in Vietnam Russell appealed to them "to accept personal responsibility for the criminal acts which are occurring every day against the Vietnamese. Your Government has abused your rights," Russell declared, and argued that it was "not sufficient to say that you have been ordered to do these things." Russell then explained why he was calling for a War Crimes Tribunal and asked for American soldiers not only "to come forward with evidence and to make public the torture and the special war crimes with which you are familiar every day," but also to refuse to participate further in the war. He assured his listeners that they would not be alone in this decision:

Hundreds of thousands of people are demonstrating in the United States. The public opinion polls show a majority of the people in the United States have ceased supporting the war...The rising tide of disgust and determined resistance is occurring everywhere.

At the same time in "An Appeal to the American Conscience,"[6] Russell informed the American people of his War Crimes Tribunal and its purpose of trying "President Johnson, Dean Rusk, Robert McNamara, Henry Cabot Lodge, Gen. Westmoreland and their fellow criminals." In his article Russell explained how the Tribunal would function:

I am approaching eminent jurists, literary figures and men of public affairs in Africa, Asia, Latin America and the U.S. itself. Vietnamese victims of the war will give evidence. Full scientific data concerning the chemicals used, their properties and their effects will be documented. Eyewitnesses will describe what they have seen and scientists will be invited to examine the exhibits in the possession of the tribunal. The proceedings will be tape recorded and the full evidence will be published. There will be documentary film material concerning the witnesses and their evidence. We aim to provide the most exhaustive portrayal of what has happened to the people of Vietnam. We intend that the peoples of the world shall be aroused as never before, the better to prevent the repetition of this tragedy elsewhere. Just as in the case of Spain, Vietnam is a barbarous rehearsal. It is our intention that neither the bona fides nor the authenticity of this tribunal will be susceptible to challenge from those who have so much to hide.

To unify British public protest against the war on the basis of active support for the North Vietnamese and the South Vietnam National Liberation Front, Russell, together with his Peace Foundation, set up the Vietnam Solidarity Campaign in June 1966. This organization was also seen as a means to secure a nucleus of British support for the projected War Crimes Tribunal. Addressing the founding conference of the Solidarity Campaign on June 4, Russell declared:

When I think back to 1940, during the Blitz, and recall the mood of Englishmen at that time, I know clearly and without hesitation what our responsibility is to the Vietnamese. Do you remember our feelings when the Nazis were bombing our cities? Do you recall the determination which swept Britain, never to surrender and never to accept a Nazi occupation of our country? Did we suffer gas and chemicals at that time? Was our country cut in half? Were our people in concentration camps? Was our countryside razed with gas, chemicals, jelly-gasoline and fragmentation bombs? No, none of this occurred. And yet Churchill spoke for all of us when he declared that we would fight on the beaches, but we would never surrender.

The purpose of this conference is to declare our fervent hope for the victory of the people of Vietnam, total, unequivocal and swift. The purpose of this conference is to build a movement in Britain worthy of the heroism of the people of Vietnam themselves; a movement which will not equivocate or pander to the economic power of the United States. We wish to build a movement capable of exposing the sordid squalor of our Prime Minister's subservience and greed.

We wish to create a movement which will evolve concrete forms of action, such as a War Crimes Tribunal, which will call before it victims and witnesses of the great panoply of horror which is the war of aggression waged by America in Vietnam.

Our movement will be broadly based. It will seek its support amongst the working people of this country, from the trade unions, from the teachers, from the students, and from all those who see in the struggle of the people of Vietnam that decency and dedication which calls forth the best responses in human beings. For let us have no doubt that we do the Vietnamese no favour by declaring our solidarity. Their struggle against economic domination is a guide to the road we ourselves must travel.[7]

The first mass demonstrations organized by the Vietnam Solidarity Campaign were held in London early in July. The Campaign's unequivocal declaration of support for the National Liberation Front brought immediate condemnation from the national press. Russell as president of the Campaign wrote to the *New Statesman* and his letter was published on July 8:

There is a basic moral and political difference between the Vietnamese resistance and the American aggression. A tiny, physically weak country has been barbarously assaulted by a colossus. Is there no spark of human decency in those who fail to understand the monstrous injustice involved in the use by the United States of its massive power to obliterate a non-industrial and hungry Asian people struggling for the most elementary rights of self-determination and social advance?

A peace movement which is blind to the David and Goliath character of this conflict is unworthy of the name. That the U.S. with all its air power and destructive force, with poison, gas, chemicals and razor bombs, can bombard and torment a small people without evoking an immediate response of solidarity for the beleagured victim against the savage bully, speaks for itself.

Expulsion of the U.S. from Vietnam can only be effected through the struggle of the Vietnamese and the courage of people in the West to undertake resistance against their governments not unlike that undertaken by those few Germans who did what they could to stop Hitler.

What is called support for the "Military victory of one side" is support for the rights of victimised human beings everywhere who ought to be regarded as our brothers and not as the occasion for the unpleasant display of undisguised callousness.

The Solidarity Campaign stands with the people of Vietnam. We do them no favour. The barbarism against which they struggle virtually alone is our own and we may yet learn what napalm and torture mean if we do not stop it.

The *Manchester Guardian* published a letter from Russell under the title " 'Vietcong' wrong?" on July 13:

"Miscellany" (July 6) refers erroneously to the "Victory for the Vietcong" banners of the Vietnam Solidarity Campaign. "Vietcong" is a slang expression meaning "commie" and it was invented by the United States Information Service. Our support is for the National Liberation Front which leads the people of South Vietnam in their 12 year struggle against American aggression. The NLF is a broad alliance ranging from Catholics to Communists and it is important to note that our banners avoid the term "Vietcong."

Through Russell's campaigns and in particular his broadcast over Hanoi Radio he was becoming well-known to the Vietnamese people. Dr. Le Dinh Tham of the Vietnam Committee for the Defense of World Peace based in Hanoi, indicated this in his letter to Russell on July 9:

I wish to particularly welcome your initiative to form an international court for the judgement of the criminal clique of Johnson, McNamara and Rusk, those who have perpetrated and are perpetrating numerous crimes against the people in both zones of our country....

It is clear that regarding the U.S. imperialists, there is no other way than to have them tried before an international court like the Nuremburg Process which dealt with the Hitlerite fascists.

We feel that your initiative is in complete conformity with the desire of all progressive mankind including the American people who are vigorously condemning the criminal war of the U.S. Government in Vietnam. The Vietnamese people are greatly thankful to your initiative and deem it our duty to supply witnesses, data and necessary material for such a tribunal. We believe that the tribunal will be of great use in denouncing largely and comprehensively the war crimes perpetrated by the U.S. imperialists, thus contributing to the mobilisation of the world people to push forward their struggle for staying the bloody hand of the U.S. aggressors...

In a reply to Le Dinh Tham of July 20, Russell assured him that "we will spare no effort to bring the Tribunal to fruition with the most extensive impact possible on world public opinion." Russell remarked that "the full support and encouragement of the Vietnamese people is moving and of the greatest importance."

In a letter of the same date to President Ho Chi Minh Russell reported:

...At the time of writing we are working relentlessly for the preparation of the tribunal. Among those who have joined are Jean-Paul Sartre, Simone de Beauvoir, Josue de Castro, President Cardenas, Danilo Dolci, Lelio Basso, Peter Weiss and Isaac Deutscher. Most importantly, Stokely Carmichael, president of the Student Non-Violent Coordinating Committee (SNCC) has expressed the desire to join and is holding a meeting of his national council to arrange their full support...

Shortly after Russell wrote this letter American aircraft began bombing Hanoi and Haiphong claiming that their targets were the oil depots on the outskirts of both cities. Russell, who was dismayed at the prospect of North Vietnam being left to the mercy of American bombers, cabled Kosygin, the Soviet prime minister, appealing that the Soviet Air Force should be employed in the defense of Vietnam. Kosygin replied on August 2 fully sharing Russell's "anxiety about the gravity of the situation in Vietnam." Summarizing the "material and technical assistance" his government was providing to the Democratic Republic of Vietnam, Kosygin expressed the Soviet Union's "readiness to send volunteers" to Vietnam if invited to do so. "We regard highly, that your voice is raised in support of the Vietnamese people," Kosygin informed Russell, and added:

The Soviet public share your feelings and support the demands for the condemnation of American aggressors in Vietnam for the War Crimes they commit.

The Times reported this exchange under the heading "Soviet forces ready to aid Hanoi" on August 18 and gave an account of a meeting between Russell and the Soviet Charge d'Affaires in London:

In a three hour meeting with Lord Russell, Mr. Vassev...emphasized that Mr. Kosygin's letter was a declaration of intent that the Soviet

Union not only stands ready with its military manpower, but also with its Air Force, the moment the request comes..."Mr. Kosygin offers full support for the War Crimes Tribunal which Bertrand Russell has initiated."

Parallel with this appeal for military assistance from the USSR Russell continued to encourage Americans to do all they could to support the Vietnamese people, including, as a practical measure the provision of medical aid for the National Liberation Front and the Democratic Republic of Vietnam. When the House Un-American Activities Committee subpoenaed a group of Americans involved in organizing this aid Russell protested to the *New York Times* in a letter of August 16:

I am writing to express my indignation at the latest outrage of the House Un-American Activities; namely the inquisition regarding the stand of Dr. Allen M. Krebs, Mr. Jerry Rubin, Mr. Walter Teague and others on the war in Vietnam. Throughout the Cold War the House Committee on Un-American Activities has had an unenviable record as the most overt instrument of reaction in the United States Government. In a majority of cases its members have been elected by a handful of whites who continue, by their use of terror, to prevent black Americans from voting. It has been aptly described as a "bulwark of segregation." I am not surprised that these racists have now turned their attention to the war in Vietnam. What could seem more "Un-American" to them than humanitarian aid for the victims of racist aggression? Their decision to conduct an investigation of medical aid to the National Liberation Front and Democratic Republic of Vietnam reflects how threatened they feel when confronted with men of courage who have articulated their solidarity with the struggle of the people of Vietnam...

Those subpoenaed speak for the conscience of the American people. To label them "un-American" is mirthless irony. Hitler used the calumny "un-German" against those who resisted the incineration of the Jews. We must do all in our power to expose the nature of the war in Vietnam, and we must defend those who are under attack for doing so. The guerillas in Vietnam are the world's soldiers for justice. Those in the West who stand in solidarity with them must command full respect and our most vigorous support.[8]

On August 25 Russell wrote to President Johnson:

I write in connection with the International War Crimes Tribunal which has been under preparation for a period of time. This Tribunal concerns the conduct of the war in Vietnam by the United States Government. Within living memory only the Nazis could be said to have exceeded in brutality the war waged by your administration against the people of Vietnam and it is because this war is loathed and condemned by the vast majority of mankind that demands are heard throughout the world for a formal international tribunal to hear the full evidence.

Your Secretary of Defense, Mr. McNamara, has stated that the tonnages used in Vietnam exceed any used in Korea or World War II. These approach 1,500 tons daily high explosive dropped on hospitals, schools and sanatoria systematically. Poison gas, chemicals, napalm, phospherous and fragmentation bombs of a particularly horrible order are freely used by your Government on your instruction against densely populated civilian areas. But no attacks have occurred on the United States. Vietnamese have not bombed one school or village or violated U.S. territory. Their troops occupy no part of the United States. The vast bombardment of their agricultural land, their villages and towns by the United States cannot be resisted by a Vietnamese air force. This war is like that waged by fascist Japan and Nazi Germany in Southeast Asia and Eastern Europe, respectively...

I ask you to appear before this tribunal in your own defence to answer charges contained in the evidence and eyewitness testimony concerning the acts carried out on your instruction. If you are unwilling to appear personally I request you to appoint officially persons who will seek to defend the actions of your Government...

Here, then, is the challenge before you: will you appear before a wider justice than you recognise and risk a more profound condemnation than you may be able to understand?[9]

When President Johnson failed to respond to the letter Russell observed that "unfortunately" the President "was too busy planning the bombardment of the Vietnamese."[10]

The first full sessions of the War Crimes Tribunal were planned to take place in Paris during April 1967. In order to announce the structure, statement of aims and time-table of the Tribunal a special preparatory meeting of the members was arranged in London on 13 November 1966. Early in September Russell learnt that Stokely Carmichael, the black American leader, who as a Tribunal member was due to attend the London preparatory meetings, had been arrested and imprisoned in America. Russell issued a statement to the press on September 12:

The imprisonment of Stokely Carmichael is a terrorist act by a vicious Government. There are two main reasons for Mr. Carmichael's arrest.

The first is his militant and uncompromising leadership of America's persecuted Negro people. The second is his clear denunciation of the war in Vietnam and the decision taken by him and his national organisation SNCC, to play a major role in the forthcoming War Crimes Tribunal.

Thirty percent of American soldiers in Vietnam are American Negroes. The American Negro soldier knows that his real struggle is at home against misery, persecution and death. In Vietnam, he is used by those who do all these things to his people for the purpose of repeating that persecution against the people of Vietnam. The arrest of Carmichael will not stop the struggle of the Negroes in the United States or the appeal of their leadership to their brothers in Vietnam to join them in opposing the war.[11]

Elucidating his view on the racist character of the American war in Vietnam and its relation to the persecution of blacks in America, Russell prepared, on September 19, a message "To American Negro Soldiers in Vietnam" for broadcast on Hanoi radio:

I address myself to you, American Negro soldiers, because you are engaged in a war so unjust and cruel, against an Asian people who wish only to live better and be left alone. Today, in the United States, the brutality which the Vietnamese experience at the hands of the American army is experienced by American Negroes, whether in the North or South of the United States.

You may know that I have established an International War Crimes Tribunal which has been set up to examine and condemn the terrible crimes committed against the people of Vietnam. Gas, chemicals, jelly-gasoline, acids, lazy dogs, torture and mutilation of prisoners—all these horrors are being committed by American soldiers in Vietnam, on orders from Washington. At the same time in Harlem, Watts, Chicago, Detroit, Atlanta and in Mississippi, American Negroes are tortured and killed. Humiliation and brutality are imposed on Negro children and families across the United States...

I appeal to you, American Negro soldiers, to think where your real struggle lies, is it in Vietnam, or is it in defence of your own people against oppression inside the United States? Refuse to fight this dirty war any longer! Come forward with evidence of the crimes of Johnson and the U.S. Government in Vietnam. I have already appealed to American soldiers in general to do this, but I am addressing this particular appeal to you personally, as Negroes, because the American Negro is made to suffer more than any other group, both in the United States and in Vietnam.

You know that 30 percent of the U.S. army in Vietnam consists of American Negroes. You are used to fight the dirty wars of the Johnson Government, not only because the U.S. Government assigns to its Negro population the dirtiest and the most dangerous jobs, but because the Johnson Government fears courageous and alert Negro men in the United States, who will defend their people against racism, poverty, police brutality and death. Militant Negro organisations are supporting our War Crimes Tribunal in the United States and condemning the war in Vietnam. This is because the struggle against the war in Vietnam and the struggle for the rights of American Negroes is the same struggle against the same enemy.

I extend to you my greetings and my warm feelings, and I earnestly hope that you will respond to the appeal of your people in the United States and your brothers who are the Vietnamese people themselves.[12]

Russell's statements on American racism were serving to strengthen his contact with many prominent Afro-Americans. Under Russell's sponsorship Dick Gregory travelled via London to North Vietnam on a factfinding tour. On his arrival in Britain the *Evening News* of 5 December 1966 reported:

Comedian Dick Gregory arrives in London tonight to place himself in the hands of fate and Bertrand Russell and travel on to Hanoi....it was Dick Gregory the pacifist who approached Lord Russell when he was in London 2 weeks ago and asked him to arrange a visa for Hanoi.

Russell was also consulted by the Vietnamese about less sympathetic individuals who wished to visit North Vietnam. "They asked my advice as to the desirability of permitting Mr. Harrison Salisbury, assistant managing editor of the *New York Times*, to visit Hanoi as a journalist," Russell recalled.[13]

Suspecting that Salisbury would not be able to ignore the evidence of the bombing of civilians, Russell "recommended that his visit was a risk worth taking, and was pleased to read...his reports from Hanoi, which caused consternation in Washington and probably lost him a Pulitzer Prize."[14]

When Muhammed Ali suffered persecution because of his refusal to serve with the U.S. army in Vietnam, Russell issued a press statment on 23 May 1967 in his defense which hailed Ali as a "heroic figure...resisting a racist war."[15] Anticipating further official action against Ali, Russell sent him a letter of encouragement on May 31:

I have read your recent statements with the greatest admiration and personal respect. In coming months there is no doubt that the men who rule Washington will try to damage you in every way open to them, but I am sure you know that you speak for your people and for the oppressed everywhere in your courageous defiance of American power. They will try to break you because you are a symbol of a force they are unable to destroy, namely the aroused consciousness of a whole people determined no longer to be butchered and debased with fear and oppression. You have my whole-hearted support.

Ali replied to Russell on September 11:

Please accept my sincere apologies for the belated answer to your very wonderful and warm statement in support of my position against being drafted into the army for the purpose of fighting in Vietnam. Your support was indeed inspiring and the wonderful way in which you worded your letter has caused me to treasure it and to keep it with me wherever I go.

Perhaps when this is all over and I am able to travel again, I will be able to visit you and thank you personally for all the wonderful things you have done—not only for me but for the betterment of the oppressed people of the world.

Please accept the enclosed copy of my favorite boxing picture as a token of my regard.

Russell wrote again on October 17:

...You are providing an important example to the men of your generation by your refusal to be conscripted for service in a criminally racist war. Though you suffer abuse, your honorable position will earn you the respect of decent men everywhere. I can only pity the twelve thousand American men who have already died in Vietnam, as I pity the American taxpayer who must finance a war which costs seventy million dollars per day. Such conformists are indifferent even to self-interest. I earnestly hope that acts of conscience like your own will erode this conformity and indifference.

Please keep me informed of the progress of your legal actions and let us know whether any of the evidence of the International War Crimes Tribunal would be useful to your Defence Counsels.

Ali replied to Russell on November 15:

I found myself reinspired by your recent thoughtful and sensitive response to my humble letter. I am not sure whether there will be any possibility of using the evidence of the International War Crimes Tribunal in my defense, however, I appreciate your suggestion and I shall forward your letter to my lawyer.

Your letter sounded so youthful and healthy that I can only say I would like to be around when you live a hundred more years and receive a letter when you are indeed much older.

My great regret is that my right to travel has been taken away and I cannot come to England to thank you in person. It would be something to tell my grandchildren of your magnificent efforts to make a world safe for them to survive. In fact, so kind and receptive have the English people been to my plight that I almost regret the drubbing I had to give Mr. Henry Cooper and Mr. Brian London upon my last visit there. However, if these gentlemen are still around, I again shall give them a crack at the title after I am released from jail.

An indication of Russell's deepening involvement with the struggle of Black Americans was his introduction to a pamphlet containing a report from the Student Non-Violent Coordinating Committee and a speech by Stokeley Carmichael.[16] Russell restressed the relationship between the "oppressed in Vietnam and the Black oppressed in the United States":

The struggle against American oppression in Vietnam and the struggle against brutality on the part of black militants in the United States are part of the same international resistance to exploitation and aggression—a long arduous and heroic battle to which all of us must commit ourselves.

In his speech to the preparatory meeting of the War Crimes Tribunal in London on 13 November 1966, Russell had remarked on the "historic role" of the Tribunal's investigations:

We must record the truth in Vietnam. We must pass judgment on what we find to be the truth. We must warn of the consequences of this truth. We must, moreover, reject the view that only indifferent men are impartial men. We must repudiate the degenerate conception of individual intelligence, which confuses open minds with empty ones.[17]

Presenting to the meeting his document entitled "Western Press and U.S. War Crimes" composed entirely from reports culled from British and American sources, Russell circulated copies to the Tribunal members.[18] "These reports" he commented, "should make it clear that we enter our enquiry with considerable *prima facie* evidence of crimes reported not by victims but by media favourable to the policies responsible."

While defining its function and aims, the Tribunal, which was due to convene its opening session in Paris during April 1967, set itself the task of answering, among others, the following questions:

1. Has the United States Government (and the Governments of Australia, New Zealand and South Korea) committed acts of aggression according to international law?
2. Has the American army made use of or experimented with new weapons or weapons forbidden by the laws of war (gas, special chemical products, napalm, etc.)?
3. Has there been bombardment of targets of a purely civilian character, for example: hospitals, schools, sanatoria, dams, etc., and on what scale has this occurred?
4. Have Vietnamese prisoners been subjected to inhuman treatment forbidden by the laws of war and, in particular, to torture or to mutilation? Have there been unjustified reprisals against the civilian population, in particular, the execution of hostages?
5. Have forced labour camps been created, has there been deportation of the population or other acts tending to the extermination of the population and which can be characterised judicially as acts of genocide?[19]

The Tribunal concluded its preparatory session with a renewed invitation to the U.S. government to "instruct their officials or representatives to appear and state their case" to the Tribunal hearings.[20]

To facilitate the work of the Tribunal it was decided to hold certain of its sessions in London. In order to obtain visas for Vietnamese witnesses invited to give evidence at those sessions, Russell, as Honorary President of the Tribunal, wrote to Roy Jenkins the Home Secretary on November 25. In his reply of 5 January 1967, Jenkins informed Russell that "it would not be in the national interest to grant the facilities you seek."[21] Russell then wrote to Harold Wilson, the prime minister, on February 9, appealing to him to "reverse this decision."[22]

In his reply to Russell on March 14, Wilson drew attention to his Government's efforts to "bring the fighting to an end" in Vietnam and in explaining why he could not reverse the decision of his Home Secretary stated:

The one-sided character of the International War Crimes Tribunal you are proposing to hold would make the Government's peace making efforts substantially more difficult. The basis of our approach has been to refuse to single out the suffering caused by acts of war on one side alone, but to use our influence to end the war itself. Many other

Governments share the view of Her Majesty's Government about the damage your Tribunal could do to the cause of peace.[25]

Russell replied to Wilson on March 27:

...You say that I must be aware of your efforts to bring the fighting to an end. I must tell you plainly that your repeated public apologies for the United States have ensured the failure of any such effort. In these apologies you have at times gone further than anything emanating from even Saigon or Washington. A recent example of this was your claim in the House of Commons that during the four day Tet truce "the massive southward movement of troops and supplies in the North...threatened to create a severe military imbalance." No other Western spokesman, however enthusiastic about the pursuit of the war, claimed that troops as well as supplies had been moved south, let alone that what did not happen could produce a severe military imbalance. You must know that what happened during the truce was exactly the reverse of what you claimed. The Chicago Daily News service reported from Saigon on February 10 that U.S. officials knew of no troop movement from the North into the demilitarised zone. But on the first full day of the truce "a new one-day record of 2,762 tons was set for cargo delivered by air to units in the field" by U.S. forces. The same service reported that, according to U.S. figures, "U.S. planes—not counting truck and ship movements, at all—carried 7,042 tons of supplies and more than 17,000 men during the first three days of the cease-fire." Similar reports appeared in the *Washington Post* of February 12. *Le Monde* of February 12-13 reported massive U.S. reinforcements being taken during the truce to the boundaries of War Zone C. The *New York Times* of February 12 reported that during the truce "extraordinary amounts" of supplies and ammunition were taken by U.S. forces to "forward positions." *Le Monde* of February 25 described the use of the Tet truce by U.S. forces to prepare the "Junction City" military operation. Many of these reports were summarized in a front-page dispatch from Washington in *The Guardian*.

I do not mention these reports in many Western newspapers in order to encourage you to ban their entry into Britain, but to show that what you are telling the nation about the war is quite untrue. In addition you have refused steadfastly to condemn American atrocities, in spite of the numerous appeals of your own supporters and of liberals in the United States itself. You continue to ignore the resolution of the Labour Party Conference which called for "the cessation of the bombing by the United States of North Vietnam." You have not ever intervened to prevent the issue of British medals to belligerents on the side of the aggressor. You maintain a series of military and diplomatic links with the aggressor which positively abets his aggression. You are financially indebted to the present American Administration on a large and inhibiting scale. In spite of the fact that less than three years ago you told the Trades Union Congress that if you "got into pawn" you could not afford an independent foreign policy, you nonetheless claim continually that your attitude, which seems to nearly everybody in the world to be grotesquely subservient, is not influenced by that circumstance.

It seems to me that when you call for an end to the murderous aerial attacks on a defenceless population; when you publicly condemn the systematic use of anti-personnel weapons such as the "lazy-dog" and the "guava" against peasants and their children; when you inform President Johnson that his policies in Vietnam call forth the utmost revulsion and horror among all civilized men, then it will be possible to accept that you might begin to make a welcome, if disgracefully belated, contribution to the search for a just peace in that country.

In the context of your present almost total commitment to the American War effort, it requires no little gall on your part to claim that the International War Crimes Tribunal with which I am associated is "one-sided." The Tribunal is composed of persons whose reputation for commitment to humane values and to the pursuit of truth is unchallenged throughout the world. It might have been hoped that you would have approached such persons, all of whom have made an authentic contribution to civilisation, with a certain modesty.

After all, you did not always condemn as "one-sided" support for oppressed peoples in the world. In rightly opposing United States's policy in Vietnam in May 1954, you quite properly said: "Asia, like other parts of the world, is in revolution, and what we have to learn today in this country is to march on the side of the peoples in their revolution and not on the side of the oppressors."

The principal difference between yourself and the members of the War Crimes Tribunal appears to be that they are not prepared to abandon their fundamental convictions in order to secure temporary preferment. If you take stock carefully of your position I hope that you will agree with me that you have no moral right to impede the work of the International War Crimes Tribunal, and you will quickly see that any attempt to do so can only bring down upon your head the justified contempt of civilisation.[24]

In a tersely worded reply of April 17, Wilson confirmed his original decision and informed Russell that he saw "no value in commenting on the assertions" in Russell's letter.[25]

In the meantime the War Crimes Tribunal which was endeavoring to convene its opening session in Paris was being obstructed by the French Government who, despite its criticism of the American intervention in Vietnam had decided that the presence of the War Crimes Tribunal would compromise French relations with the U.S. Explaining his Government's decision to ban the Tribunal, President de Gaulle wrote to Jean Paul Sartre, the Executive President of the War Crimes Tribunal on April 19:

The organisers of the "Russell Tribunal" are undertaking to criticise the United States policy in Vietnam. There is nothing in that which might lead the government to restrict their usual liberty of assembly and expression. After all, you are aware of what the Government thinks of the war in Vietnam and of what I myself have stated, publicly and unequivocally. Aside from the fact that the pen and speech are free in our country, there can thus be no question of inhibiting private individuals whose opinions are moreover, in line with the official position of the French Republic on this subject.

Neither is it a question of the right of assembly nor of free expression, but of duty, the more so for France, which has taken a widely known decision in the matter, and which must be on guard lest a State with which it is linked and which, despite all difference of opinion, remains its traditional friend, should on French territory become the subject of a proceedings exceeding the limits of international law and custom.[26]

As a result of the French ban on its proceedings the Tribunal transferred to Sweden and opened its first session in Stockholm on May 2. In an opening address read on his behalf to the Tribunal Russell referred to the "frantic" attempts by the "United States Government to stop us":

Lies are hurled like napalm bombs. The fragments of these planned untruths find their way into the media of communication so responsible for the deception of ignorant men. The Government of France exposes itself before the world as a pathetic citadel of hypocrisy and spinelessness.

This is no token of our weakness. It is the very opposite. The feverish effort to conceal American crimes is matched by the frantic campaign against those who stand against them. Let us take this as a tribute.[27]

"It is clear to all who have the will to see that the United States Government is committing genocide in Vietnam. The Secretary of Defense informed the Senate that approximately 4,000,000 pounds of bombs fall daily on Vietnam. The tonnage exceeds all the bombing in the Pacific theater during the entirety of World War Two. It exceeds the bombing in Western Europe, during that same period."

In the months leading up to the opening of the Tribunal an abusive press campaign was mounted against Russell, especially in America. *Look* magazine ran a major feature entitled "The Tragedy of Bertrand Russell"[28] in which Russell was described as "the intellectual captive of a mysterious young American [Ralph Schoenman] who wants to put LBJ on trial for murder." Sidney Hook, Russell's old adversary, accused him of becoming "almost pathologically anti-American." Writing in the pages of the *New Leader* Hook characterized Russell's role on Vietnam as "more appropriate to Lord Haw Haw than to Lord Russell."[29] *The New York Times Magazine* commissioned Bernard Levin, a London journalist who had recently publicly affirmed his support of American actions in Vietnam, to describe Russell as having "fallen into a state of such gullibility, lack of discrimination, twisted logic and rancorous hatred of the United States that he has turned into a full-time purveyor of political garbage indistinguishable from the routine products of the Soviet machine."[30]

The British publication in January 1967 of *War Crimes in Vietnam*, a compilation of Russell's key statements, speeches and articles on the Vietnam situation, added fuel to the anti-Russell campaign.[31] Russell was particularly concerned that the book should have appeared in America at the same time but, unlike all his previous books, it was accepted by no major American publisher. It was several months before it eventually appeared under the imprint of the left wing *Monthly Review Press* in New York. Despite a uniformly hostile reception from the press in Britain, and later in America, Russell found it "a pleasure to learn that the paperback edition was sold out within a fortnight of its publication" in Britain.[32]

Russell was upset by the concerted campaign of personal vilification as it was clearly an attempt to destroy the credibility of the Tribunal. "This method of diminishing my effectiveness," he later remarked, "alarms and angers my friends and affronts me, but," he pointed out, "from the point of those who differ with me, I dare say it is their only retort."[33] And referring to the repeated accusations that he was senile, Russell quipped: "If the charge is true, I fail to see why anyone troubles to remark on my babblings."[34] Russell was also amused by the fact that many of the critics questioning the impartiality of the Tribunal had been "among the staunchest supporters of the Warren Commission."[35]

Appealing directly to the American people Russell recorded a message for a "spring mobilisation" of Americans against the war in Vietnam, on 7 April 1967:

It is clear to all who have the will to see that the United States Government is committing genocide in Vietnam. The Secretary of Defence informed the Senate that approximately 4,000,000 pounds of bombs fall daily on Vietnam. The tonnage exceeds all the bombing in the Pacific theater during the entirety of World War Two. It exceeds the bombing in Western Europe, during the same period.

This concentration of explosives is taking place in a relatively tiny area—in a country the size of New York and Pennsylvania The *Washington Post* of March 17 reported that in the month previous, the United States Air Force dropped 68,000 tons thus raising the daily total of bombardment to 4 and a half million pounds daily. This is 4 times the Korean total.

Four and a half million pounds daily of bombardment in a small peasant country is terror bombing aimed at the population. Reports from North Vietnam brought by our investigators make clear that roads, bridges and railways are rarely hit. Villages, towns, hospitals, schools, churches, pagodas, tuberculosis sanatoria and leprosaria— these are destroyed *and* specially targeted.

Fragmentation bombs, steel pellet bombs, napalm, white phosphorus and magnesium bombs are used to terrorise and massacre the peasants of North Vietnam. That is their sole purpose.

For any person capable of human impulse, for any man with a shred of intellectual probity, for any with the faintest murmur of moral feeling—this supreme atrocity is hateful. The cynical men who discourse in the newspapers about the extent of civilian damage as opposed to military targets are men who lack honor. They compare with Germans who argued as to the extent to which Jews polluted the Aryan race when these Germans discussed the gas chambers.

What is our proper response to this criminal barbarism? It is simple and compelling. We must call for an end to the aggression and for the victory of the Vietnamese people in their struggle for national independence. We must document the full record of the U.S. war of annihilation and expose the motive nestling behind the power. This is the task of the War Crimes Tribunal. The evidence from the U.S. Government's own acknowledged deeds is overwhelming—every bit as overwhelming as the evidence of Nazi atrocity...

The cost to the American people of this cruel war of aggression is very high. The country is being brutalised. The U.S. soldier fights for conquest on behalf of high finance. The Vietnamese fight for survival, for national independence, for land reform, for social justice. The whole people are against the U.S. war and even the Pentagon must acknowledge that American casualties exceed 1,000 a week, killed and wounded. This figure is lower than the truth for the U.S. Government always lies about this war to the American people. Yet it is high, very high.

Considering that only a small proportion of the U.S. forces are engaged in front line battle, this is an enormous percentage of men lost. A generation is scheduled by Johnson for slaughter. A whole nation is subjected to inhuman war involving torture and experimental weapons.

All of you know this. I appeal to you to move beyond decrying war in the abstract. Support the victims of this aggression. Support the Tribunal in its effort to present the evidence overwhelmingly. Fix the responsibility where it belongs. Do not always permit the argument to center on the assumptions of the aggressor. Remember that the Vietnamese are being asked to countenance mass murder on their soil by a foreign invader. They are denied the right to retaliate. Not one city in the U.S. is under threat from Vietnam. Even the Seventh Fleet and the air bases in the very south of their own country are immune from Vietnamese attack. Why? What permits the U.S. to massacre at will and declare their own bases and fleets immune from reprisal? There is a clear necessity for all of us. We must forget vague formulas which enable us to avoid supporting the victims of aggression. We must stop looking for others to take responsibility. The United Nations is not the arena. South Vietnam and the United States are the arenas of struggle.

It is in Vietnam and in America that this aggression must be defeated. Demand an end to the U.S. aggression *now*. The troops should come home *now*. The crimes should be exposed and denounced *now*. The Vietnamese should have our solidarity and unflinching support *now*. The American people should be told their Government is waging an aggressive and imperialist war *now*. This is the task of the American movement as it is the challenge to our War Crimes Tribunal. This spring the people of America should be mobilised to stop the destruction of Vietnam. Let us join in a clear struggle to the end *now*.[36]

The War Crimes Tribunal concluded its Stockholm session on May 10. To ensure a fair and open hearing the Tribunal had renewed its invitation to officials of the U.S. Government to appear at any time during the session to answer the charges and evidence adduced; but the only response elicited came indirectly through the American press who were informed by Dean Rusk, the secretary of state, that he had no intention of "playing games with a 94 year old Briton."[37]

Adjourning their proceedings until the sitting of the second session due to be held at Roskilde, Denmark from 20 November to 1 December 1967 the Tribunal announced its findings. Basing its verdict on an examination of evidence presented by Tribunal members and investigators, American military personnel and Vietnamese victims, the Tribunal declared on 10 May 1967:

1. Has the government of the United States committed acts of aggression against Vietnam under the terms of international law?

YES. (Unanimously)

2. Has there been, and if so, on what scale, bombardment of purely civilian targets, for example, hospitals, schools, medical establishments, dams etc.?

YES. (Unanimously)

We find the government and armed forces of the United States are guilty of the deliberate, systematic and large scale bombardment of civilian targets, including civilian populations, dwellings, villages, dams, dykes, medical establishments, leper colonies, schools, churches, pagodas, historical and cultural monuments.

We also find unanimously, with one abstention, that the government of the United States of America is guilty of repeated violations of the sovereignty, neutrality and territorial integrity of Cambodia, that it is guilty of attacks against the civilian population of a certain number of Cambodian towns and villages.

3. Have the governments of Australia, New Zealand and South Korea been accomplices of the United States in the aggression against Vietnam in violation of international law?

YES. (Unanimously)

The question also arises as to whether or not the governments of Thailand and other countries have become accomplices to acts of aggression or other crimes against Vietnam and its populations. We have not been able to study this question during the present session. We intend to examine at the next session, legal aspects of the problem and to seek proofs of any incriminating facts.[38]

In his closing address read to the Stockholm session Russell, in insisting that "wherever men struggle against suffering we must be their voice," declared that the Tribunal "has been subject to abuse from people who have much to hide."[39]

Russell's 95th birthday shortly after the Stockholm session brought good wishes, as well as messages of support for the Tribunal, from many Americans. Corliss Lamont "on behalf of the Emergency Civil Liberties Committee" conveyed "greetings and congratulations for May 18" and continued: "All fighters for freedom in the United States are most grateful to you for the example you have set for civil libertarians."[40]

Extending his birthday greetings, Rudolf Carnap, the renowned philosopher, wished Russell "many years of intensive life and fruitful activity, especially in your admirable efforts for the cause of peace."[41] He informed Russell of the impact of the Tribunal at his University.

October 1967 witnessed the most intensive demonstrations to date on the Vietnam War. In his message to the "International Mobilisation" of October 21 and 22, Russell stated:

It is fitting that demonstrations take place today in many parts of the world. Those who demonstrate in Washington and London, in Norway and in New Zealand, do so in order to confront a single foe, just as guerillas in South America and the partisans of Vietnam oppose the same cruel power. A worldwide pattern of aggression requires international resistance. It is a hopeful sign that after more than two decades of American intervention in the affairs of small nations, humanity has begun to take note.[42]

The second session of the Tribunal opened in Roskilde, Denmark, on November 20 to consider the outstanding questions. As with the first session considerable time was scheduled for hearing witnesses, especially Americans and Vietnamese who had participated or been victims of the conflict in Vietnam. The session concluded on December 2 and announced its verdict:

The International War Crimes Tribunal does as a result of deliberations render its verdict as follows:

Is the Government of Thailand guilty of complicity in the aggression committed by the United States Government against Vietnam?

YES. (Unanimously)

Is the Government of the Philippines guilty of complicity in the aggression committed by the United States Government against Vietnam?

YES. (Unanimously)

Is the Government of Japan guilty of complicity in the aggression committed by the United States Government against Vietnam?

YES, by 8 votes to 3.

(The three Tribunal members who voted against agree that the Japanese Government gives considerable aid to the Government of the United States, but do not agree on its complicity in the crime of aggression.)

Has the United States Government committed aggression against the people of Laos, according to the definition provided by international law?

YES. (Unanimously)

Have the armed forces of the United States used or experimented with weapons prohibited by the laws of war?

YES. (Unanimously)

Have prisoners of war captured by the armed forces of the United States been subjected to treatment prohibited by the laws of war?

YES. (Unanimously)

Have the armed forces of the United States subjected the civilian population to inhuman treatment prohibited by international law?

YES. (Unanimously)

Is the United States Government guilty of genocide against the people of Vietnam?

YES. (Unanimously)[43]

The Tribunal was an inspiration both to the Vietnamese victims of American aggression and to the international protest movement. In a message to a vast assembly in Trafalgar Square, London, on 17 March 1968, Russell declared:

The United States of America is floundering towards the complete defeat of all its declared objectives in Vietnam. The Vietnamese people, with a minimum of help from the outside world, have once again thwarted their colonial masters. This striking achievement gives new hope to the world. It opens the way to the collapse of the systematic

> "In America, black people are forced to live in ghettos unfit for human beings and are systematically deprived of their share in the nation's enormous wealth. Abroad, the war in Vietnam is fought brutally against people whom Lyndon Johnson has described as 'yellow dwarfs with pocket knives.'"

exploitation of the majority of the world's peoples by a small, wealthy elite in the West.[44]

Linked with America's growing crisis in Vietnam, violent repression of black Americans had reached unprecedented heights. On 4 April 1968 Martin Luther King, who had become increasingly outspoken on the issue of Vietnam, was assassinated. In a statement on the following day Russell paid tribute to King's "remarkable personal courage."[45]

Russell elaborated on King's assassination in a message to a commemorative meeting in London:

Dr. Martin Luther King was a courageous man who was assassinated because of his active opposition to American racism. This racism expresses itself forcibly both in America and abroad. In America, black people are forced to live in ghettos unfit for human beings and are systematically deprived of their share in the nation's enormous wealth. Abroad, the war in Vietnam is fought brutally against a people whom Lyndon Johnson has described as "yellow dwarfs with pocket knives..."[46]

One of the main targets of the heightened repression of blacks in America was the militant Black Panther party. Russell recorded his protest against this in a statement of 18 April 1969:

The police authorities in California are practicing political persecution of the Black Panther Party. The demand of that Party and the peace and freedom movement for independent observers to be stationed in the Black Ghettos of California has my entire approval, as it will help protect Black people from unjustified attacks by police and national guard occupation troops, and to protect the right to organise political movements such as the Black Panther Party. The disgraceful killing of Bobby Hutton, and the shooting and jailing of Huey P. Newton and Eldridge Cleaver, make it clear that the alternative is further brutality.[47]

The total failure of U.S. policy in Vietnam, exemplified by the victories of the National Liberation Front in the South; the determined resistance of the North to the bombings; the massive increase of American casualities and the general unpopularity of the war at home and abroad, caused Johnson to announce his decision to "abdicate" the presidency. In a comment for the *Washington Post* on the consequent line-up of candidates for presidential office, Russell stated on 20 May 1969:

> To those who wish to dismantle the American empire, create full employment, destroy the ghettos and respect black rights, the major candidates are irrelevant combinations of rhetoric and personal ambition. Humphrey is totally discredited after four years as Johnson's cipher.
>
> Robert Kennedy's cynical, calculating ambition is unequalled. His embarrassment at the failure in Vietnam does not conceal his complete orthodoxy on foreign policy. McCarthy, the least unattractive major candidate failed to develop an articulate or frontal attack on Johnson's Vietnam policy and, like Kennedy, would leave all the major assumptions of foreign policy unchanged. Nixon would probably be the most dangerous man in office.[48]

Another result of the collapse of American strategy in Vietnam was their agreement to participate in peace talks with the Vietnamese in Paris. Russell put this development into focus in a message to an international conference on Vietnam held in Sweden at the end of 1968:

> The war in Vietnam has now reached a crucial stage which it is important for the anti-war movement throughout the world to recognize and interpret with understanding. The rulers of the United States of America have at last recognized that, despite all their technological superiority, they cannot defeat the Vietnamese people and they have utterly failed to buy the allegiance of any substantial section of the people in South Vietnam. As is usual in such colonial wars, the United States is now trying to find some political and diplomatic means to achieve what it has failed to win on the battlefield. Within this strategy, we may expect to see in the coming months the representatives of the National Liberation Front and of the Government of the Democratic Republic of Vietnam subjected to the most extraordinary pressures to abandon those demands which are legitimately theirs, the failure to satisfy which will inevitably involve years of protracted warfare...[49]

While Russell was greatly heartened by the victories of the Vietnamese people, another event which gave him great pleasure, early in 1969, was the release from prison, after eighteen years, of Morton Sobell. Russell, who had continued to campaign throughout the sixties on Sobell's behalf, sent him and his wife a simply worded cable offering his "warmest greetings to you both on your reunion."[50]

President Nixon, who had replaced Johnson in January 1969, continued his predecessor's Vietnam policy. In June 1969, it was revealed that there were 539,000 U.S. troops in Vietnam. Despite this enormous commitment, U.S. and Saigon troops continued to suffer heavy defeats and after a meeting between Nixon and President Thieu of South Vietnam, it was announced that the U.S. would commence a gradual withdrawal of American forces from Vietnam.

In November 1969 in the wake of huge demonstrations by millions of Americans against the Vietnam War, it was revealed that U.S. troops had been involved in the massacre of civilians in South Vietnam. Revelations about a massacre at My Lai were quickly followed by disclosures of other atrocities. Although American officialdom had attempted to ignore the War Crimes Tribunal there is no doubt that its proceedings, seen in the light of these latest revelations, were a severe embarrassment to the U.S. administration.

By this stage, Russell's age and failing health were preventing him from playing as energetic a role as he would otherwise have wished. However, a tribute to his unflagging spirit is that he was campaigning to the last. On December 1 Russell sent an open letter to U Thant, excerpts from which appeared in the *New York Times* on 2 December 1969:

I am sending you this open letter at a time when the peoples of the western world are learning at last something of the barbarous character of the war against the people of Vietnam. Former members of the U.S. forces in Vietnam are coming forward daily with new evidence of torture and genocide. It is clear that we have heard only the beginning of these reports. When they were investigated by the International War Crimes Tribunal in 1967, they were greeted with considerable ridicule or indifference, but the record of the Tribunal's proceedings is today vindicated.

Now the magnitude of the horror is unfolding, and a new duty presents itself.

It has been reported widely that the Pentagon is considering the establishment, with the support of the White House , of its own War Crimes Commission. The result of this would be a foregone conclusion. Scapegoats would be found whilst the greatest culprits, the architects of the policy, and the true scale of the crimes would be ignored. A narrow definition of war crimes would be adopted which overlooked the indiscriminate use of napalm and fragmentation bombs.

I am asking you, therefore, to use the full authority of your high office to propose the creation of an International War Crimes Commission to hear all the relevant evidence and to pronounce solemnly upon it. It is within your power to help stamp out war crimes, and I earnestly beg you to seize this opportunity on behalf of all mankind.[51]

One of Russell's very last public acts was a statement on the war in Vietnam, published after his death on February 2, in the March 1970 issue of *Ramparts* magazine.[52] The article continued a theme he had pursued consistently throughout his long association with America, to challenge all attitudes and actions he believed inimical to the interests of the American people. Noting that reaction to the massacre revelations had been "more rapid and sharp in Western Europe than in the United States," Russell warned:

The entire American people are now on trial. If there is not a massive moral revulsion at what is being done in their names to the people of Vietnam, there may be little hope for the future of America. Having lost the will to continue the slaughter is not enough; the people of America must now repudiate their civil and military leaders.

Footnotes

1. See below, pp. 394-8.
2. Not published.
3. Unidentifiable clipping.
4. B. Russell, *Autobiography*, Vol. III (London, 1969) p. 169; (New York, 1969) p. 242
5. See below, pp. 399-402.
6. Published in *World Outlook,* July 1966; reprinted in B. Russell, *War Crimes in Vietnam* (London, 1967); (Monthly Review Press, New York, 1967).
7. Published in *Vietnam Solidarity Bulletin,* July 1966; reprinted in B. Russell, *War Crimes in Vietnam,* p. 113-114.
8. Not published.
9. Published in *National Guardian,* 17 September 1966 as "An Invitation to Lyndon Johnson."
10. B. Russell, *Autobiography*, Vol. III, p. 171; p. 245.
11. Not published.
12. Published in *World Outlook,* 24 February 1967.
13. B. Russell, *Autobiography*, Vol. III, p. 168; p. 241.
14. *Ibid.*

14. *Ibid.*

15. Not published.

16. See below, pp. 403-5.

17. B. Russell, *Autobiography*, Vol. III, p. 216; p. 320.

18. Published in *World Outlook*, 24 February 1967.

19. B. Russell, *Autobiography*, Vol III. pp. 217-18; p. 323.

20. *Ibid.*, pp. 218; p. 324.

21. *Mr. Wilson Speaks 'Frankly and Fearlessly' on Vietnam to Bertrand Russell* (Bertrand Russell Peace Foundation, 1968), p. 17.

22. *Ibid.*

23. *Ibid.*, p. 18.

24. *Ibid.*, pp. 19-21.

25. *Ibid.*, p. 23.

26. John Duffett (editor) *Against the Crime of Silence,* Proceedings of the Russell International War Crimes Tribunal (O'Hare Books, New York, 1968) pp. 27-28.

27. *Ibid.*, pp. 49-51.

28. 4 April 1967.

29. 24 October 1966.

30. 19 February 1967.

31. George Allen and Unwin Ltd., London.

32. B. Russell, *Autobiography*, Vol III, p. 168; p. 240.

33. *Ibid.*, p. 163; p. 234.

34. *Ibid.*

35. *Ibid.*,p. 171; p. 245.

36. Published in *Foundation Bulletin*, 15 April 1967.

37. Ken Coates, Peter Limqueco, Peter Weiss (Eds.) *Prevent the Crime of Silence,* Reports from the sessions of the International War Crimes Tribunal founded by Bertrand Russell (Allen Lane, the Penguin Press, London, 1971) p. 10.

38. John Duffett, *op. cit.*, p. 309.

39. *Ibid.*, pp. 310-12.

40. Corliss Lamont to Bertrand Russell, 12 May 1967.

41. Rudolf Carnap to Bertrand Russell, 14 May 1967.

42. Published in *London Bulletin* No. 3, October 1967.

43. John Duffett, *op. cit.*, pp. 649-50; excerpts appeared in *The Times* of 2 December 1967 as "Genocide Finding by Russell Tribunal."

44. Published in *World Outlook*, 19 April 1967, as "Bertrand Russell sees complete defeat for U.S. in Vietnam."

45. Published in *London Bulletin*, Summer 1968.

46. Message dated 3 May 1968; *Ibid.*

47. Not published.

48. Not published.

49. Coates, Limqueco, Weiss, *op. cit.*, p. 380.

50. Undated January 1969.

51. Coates, Limqueco, Weiss, *op. cit.*, p. 348.

52. See below, pp. 408-9.

Illustrations

1. Russell at his press conference in New York on 15 November 1950.

2. Russell with a group of students at Princeton University shortly after receiving news of his Nobel Prize for literature for 1950.

3. Russell's article criticizing the demand to "indoctrinate American youth for American democracy" in *Des Moines Sunday Register*, 25 November 1951

4. An illustration by Carl Rose accompanying Russell's article "The American Way (A Briton Says) Is Dour" in the *NYTM* of 15 June 1952.

5. Russell and the former Edith Finch leaving the Chelsea Registry office after their marriage on 15 December 1952.

6. Russell caricatured by Carl Rose in the 16 April 1953 edition of the *New York Times Magazine*.

7. Pickets outside the United Kingdom Mission to the United Nations in New York, 13 September 1961, protest at the imprisonment of Russell and his wife.

8. Russell in 1961 by Albert Hirschfield in *The World of Hirschfield* (Abrams, New York, 1969).

9. Russell with Morton Sobell's wife Helen who had visited him on 11 February 1962 while touring Europe to enlist support for the release of her husband.

10. Russell's portrait which appeared on the cover of the 20 August 1962 issue of *Newsweek*. Russell was also featured in the "cover story" as a man who "has devoted his last years to the quaint belief that man has a future on this planet of ours."

11. An illustration to "Time: The Weekly Fiction Magazine," a compilation of comments on *Time* by celebrities invited by and published in *FACT*, January-February 1964. Russell contributed the following statement: "I consider *Time* to be scurrilous and I know, with respect to my own work, utterly shameless in its willingness to distort. I cannot give you specific instances, because I have long ago discontinued attending to it. However, I do recall the remark of Zachariah Chafee upon being given an award by the Luce publications. He said: 'I note that I have been attended by the Luce publications. You know the ones I mean; the one for those who cannot read and the other for those who cannot think.' "

12. Martin Luther King's increasing attention to the Vietnam War prompted a columnist to warn that King was "in danger of becoming the Bertrand Russell of the United States."

13. The Russell's demonstrate outside the House of Commons 30 June 1965.

14. Russell by Norman Rockwell on the cover of the May 1967 issue of *Ramparts* magazine.

15. Russell and the War Crimes Tribunal caricatured by *The Times*, 1967.

16. Russell caricatured by David Levine 1967 and 1968.

17. A cartoon which accompanied a review of Russell's autobiography Vol. III in the *Washington Post* of 11 November 1969.

1

Bertrand Russell Tweaks the State of Indiana

(Reprinted from the Manchester, England, Guardian.)

The Indiana state superintendent of schools said:

Indoctrination has never been in great repute among educators in the United States. American schools have not followed the plan used in many countries of indoctrinating youth regarding a particular form of government. Boys and girls of Hitler's Germany, Mussolini's Italy, Franco's Spain, Stalin's Russia, Tito's Yugoslavia, and other totalitarian nations have for many years been educated by a program of indoctrination. Education in these countries has definitely sought to teach the young people that their particular form of government is the best and that all other forms of government are weak, evil, and corrupt. In particular, democracy has been attacked.

It now appears necessary for the schools in the United States to indoctrinate American youth for American democracy. We need to do this for self-protection, in order to combat the influences both at home and abroad that are trying to undermine our form of government.

Bertrand Russell replies:

I learn that in a certain important state of the Union, the education authorities have become impressed with the importance of defending the sacred institutions of the United States against the sinister machinations of those who are defending the sacred institutions of other countries.

I learn, from a document circulated to teachers in this state, that while in other countries education has "definitely sought to teach the young people that their particular form of government is the best," this is a proof of the inferiority of these other countries, since it is the form of government adopted by the United States that is the best.

I learn also from this document that "in any case necessary for the schools in the United States to indoctrinate American youth for American Democracy"; that is to say, since indoctrinating the youth is an evil, and since it is practiced elsewhere, it must also be practiced in the United States.

"We need to do this for self-protection," the document continues; that is to say, we must surrender everything that makes defense worth while before the defense begins.

Boys and girls, we are told, "should for-credit definitions and descriptions used by foreign governments of such words as social revolution, Communism, Fascism, Totalitarianism, police state, dictatorship, welfare state, bureaucracy, conservatism, liberals, capitalism, socialism, communal enterprise, and propaganda."

Social Revolution.

We are not told what definitions of these words are to be substituted. Perhaps I could assist those who drew up this interesting document.

"Social revolution," to begin with, clearly does not include what happened in America in 1776, for that was good whereas "social revolution" is bad.

Nor does "social revolution" include the overthrow of Hitler, for that also was good, it does include the failure to overthrow the

Democratic administration in the United States, and it does, of course, include the overthrow of Churchill in England in 1945.

Perhaps we may define "social revolution" as any political movement anywhere which is displeasing to the Republican party.

* * *

"Communism" is another of these words which are used dishonestly by the efforts population of Europe. Every honest man (honest men are only to be found in America) knows that Mr. Acheson is a Communist, that Mr. Attlee is a Communist, and that Communism is in catching that anybody whose sexual comes once just a Communist at a party is likely to be infected.

There are sophists in England who are particularly dangerous, since they pretend that "Communism" can be distinguished from democratic socialism, whereas Americans know that there can be no true democracy when plutocrats are in any degree curbed.

Fascism.

"Fascism" is a difficult word. During the late war we all knew what it meant. It meant the system of government employed in Germany and in Italy until the fall of Mussolini. But now that it is necessary to use Germans and Italians against the Russians, the word "fascism" has become one which prudent people will avoid.

It is true that during the late war we thought that we were fighting to defeat "fascism," but we now learn that "fascism" is disliked by Moscow, and we conclude that it cannot be wholly evil.

* * *

"Totalitarianism" is another of these slippery words. At one time we thought that Franco's regime was "totalitarian," but since we have realized the strategic importance of the line of Pyrenees, we have discovered that Franco is one of the bulwarks of moral values against the rising sea of atheism and materialism.

Police State.

"Police state." In Germany under Hitler, and in Russia under Stalin, nobody ventured upon a political remark without first looking behind the door to make sure that no one was listening. This used to be considered a mark of the "police state." It is no longer, for when I last visited America I found the same state of things there, and yet, as we all know, America is not a "police state."

It is true that Senator McCarthy's emissaries and his allies in the FBI are perpetually snooping, and that if by some misfortune you were to quote with approval some remark by Jefferson you would probably lose your job and perhaps find yourself behind bars.

But this, of course, is done in defense of liberty, and therefore does not make America a "police state."

* * *

"Welfare state" is a phrase against which every true American should be on his guard. We all know that England is a "welfare state," and that this proves that England is wholly unwell-basedly opposed to Moscow.

Capitalism.

Any new word which, according to this document, is wrongly defined by the wicked foreigners is the word "capitalism." Americans all know what this word means. I cannot help allowing free play to the Benevolent Impulse of those great and good men who have made vast fortunes by serving the sub-

for. There are people, incredible as it may seem, who suspect that sometimes (though of course rarely) fortunes are made by conduct which does not promote the general welfare. They think that perhaps the extermination of half the population of the Belgian Congo in order to enrich that great philanthropist King Leopold II was the sort of thing which ought not to be allowed, even if it can only be prevented by an interference with free enterprise.

* * *

The last of the words which this document considers that foreigners misinterpret is the word "propaganda." I am surprised at this, for I have found throughout the world a complete and absolute unanimity in the meaning assigned to the word "propaganda." "Propaganda" means always and everywhere, advocacy of opinions not held by the speaker.

The education authorities of the state in question will, I am sure, agree that the indoctrination which they advocate is not "propaganda." It is not "propaganda" because it is teaching doctrine with which they agree.

Democracy?

The document continues: "It is essential in America that we teach our young people that American democracy is the best government in the world." I know it must seem

incredible, but there actually are people, not in asylums, who question this.

I cannot remember any occasion in England when the leading elected representatives of the sovereign people had to be sent to prison as common thieves, as happened in Indiana some 20 years ago. Any Englishman going to America at the present time has the strange experience of a population subjected to a reign of terror, and always obliged to think twice before giving utterance to any serious conviction.

English people hold the clearly subversive opinion that a teacher should not be deprived of his post, merely on the ground that he has published a well-documented investigation of some facts inconvenient to certain rich men.

Yet this is part of the system which in America is called "democracy." The word "democracy" was not ambiguous until recently. It used to mean government by elected representatives of the people. Now it has lost this signification. In Russia it means government by a military tyranny; in America it means government by a plutocracy, or, at any rate, government in which the plutocracy is uncurbed.

It is perhaps regrettable that Americans who have no education and no knowledge of the world should be allowed to antagonize intelligent opinions in countries as unfriendly opposed to Communism as the United States itself.

"SAY, WHAT EVER HAPPENED TO 'FREEDOM FROM FEAR'?"
—*From the Washington, D. C. Post.*

Associated Press Photo

6

7

141 Bertrand Russell. 1961

8

Newsweek

AUGUST 20, 1962

Bertrand Russell

10

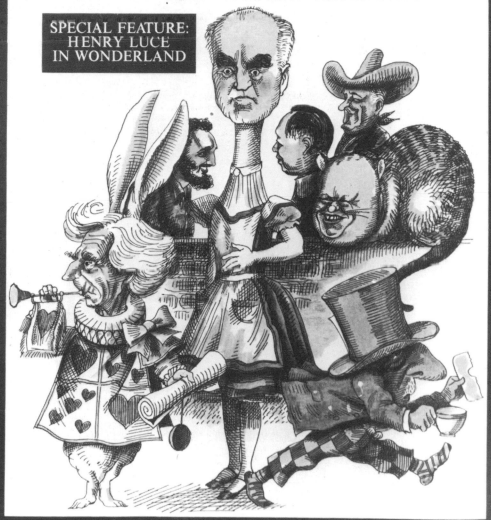

TIME

THE WEEKLY FICTION MAGAZINE

SPECIAL FEATURE:
HENRY LUCE
IN WONDERLAND

11

12

Los Angeles Times

As a public service, The Times presents on this page columnists whose opinions reflect those of our diverse readership, not necessarily those of The Times itself.

★ FRIDAY MORNING, AUGUST 20, 1965 Part II—5

Martin Luther King Could Share Bertrand Russell's Pitiable Fate

BY MAX FREEDMAN

Unless he watches himself very carefully, the Rev. Martin Luther King is in danger of becoming the Bertrand Russell of the United States. Like Lord Russell, he is in danger of putting off greatness and becoming a bore, an intruder where he has no business, and a busybody causing great mischief. Dr. King has created these risks for himself by his decision to use the prestige won in his campaign for civil rights for the purposes of conciliation in Vietnam.

If this decision concerned only Dr. King personally, it would be a small matter, whether it was right or wrong. But it may cause serious trouble for the whole civil rights movement.

★

The analogy with Lord Bertrand Russell is pertinent and instructive.

Like Dr. King, Bertrand Russell is a pacifist. He went to jail in the First World War in protest against England's part in that struggle. It took the brutal challenge of Hitler and Mussolini to teach him the limitations of pacifism. Then with the coming of the nuclear age he became the foremost and most irresponsible advocate of nuclear disarmament in Britain. He dwindled into a pitiable spectacle, a philosopher of distinction babbling erratic nonsense as a senile and garrulous old man.

Dr. King faces three dangers as a self-appointed apostle of peace.

In the first place, he may misrepresent the civil rights movement by his efforts to end the struggle in Vietnam. The people who support that movement have not agreed on common views on foreign policy. Who gave Dr. King a mandate to speak for them

on Vietnam? He is using his personal prestige for a new cause in which he has no general authority to pose as a national leader. On these grave issues of peace and war he speaks only for the small cluster of his immediate followers and for those who share his pacifist views.

Secondly, Dr. King may find his prestige abused by the Communists to the detriment of American interests. The Communists are always looking for a famous name with which to confuse and divide American opinion. Russia has frequently used Bertrand Russell in that way to advance its disarmament aims. North Vietnam and China may use Dr. King in a similar way to further their own plans and ambitions.

In short, the worst danger may come if Dr. King's letters are answered by the Communist rulers in Hanoi and Peking. Then the rest of us will have to be on vigilant watch to see

King

that Dr. King does not become an unwitting and unwilling instrument of Communist propaganda. If he does fall into that trap, he must endure swift and merciless exposure.

Thirdly, Dr. King is bringing the philosophy of pacifism to a test it cannot pass. In this country the non-violent movement has

had the conscience of America overwhelmingly on its side in its search for Negro rights. Does Dr. King think the Communists will feel a similar surge of conscience as he pleads the cause of peace? Unless he is far wiser in foreign affairs than any of us have reason to expect, Dr. King may find that it is not pacifism but communism that has carried the day.

Dr. King, as a private citizen, is escaping the restraints of the Logan Act by the technical plea that he is not entering into actual negotiations with foreign governments. He is simply offering his good offices as a distinguished citizen — to hasten that movement to the conference table which is one of the announced aims of American policy. This is delicate and doubtful ground. Dr. King had better watch his step lest he break the rule that only the President, or those speaking for the President, can conduct relations with foreign powers.

★

Since he won the Nobel Peace Prize, something tragic and unexpected has happened to Dr. King. He has become pompous and dull. Not so long ago he was a supreme orator. Now he can scarcely utter a simple sentence without intoning it as an exercise in solemn declamation. Is he casting about for a role in Vietnam because the civil rights struggle is no longer adequate to his own estimate of his talents? That is the kind of arrogance which fate soon punishes.

If Dr. King is looking for some real challenges, he does not have to look very far; he does not have to thrust himself into Vietnam.

13

Ramparts

14

WAR
CRIMES
TRIBUNAL

15

BERTRAND RUSSELL

16

PART TWO
The Articles

What American Could Do With the Atomic Bomb

Published as "Humanity's Last Chance"
Cavalcade, 20 October 1945

America has at this moment, and for a few years to come, an opportunity such as has never hitherto come to any nation throughout the whole history of the world. If the opportunity is used to the full, the peace of the world will be secure for a very long time; if not, it is likely that, during the lifetime of the present generation, all large cities in every part of the world will be wiped out, and the organisation upon which civilized life has come to depend will be destroyed. During the next two or three years the president and congress of the United States can decide this alternative either way; after that time, if the chance is missed, the worse alternative will be a virtual certainty.

Let us first get clear as to the facts. At present, the United States alone possesses finished atomic bombs; the United States, Canada and Great Britain, alone know the details of the process by which they have been manufactured. But since the difficult theoretical principles involved are well known to men of science throughout the world, every nation which chooses to spend the money will soon be in a position to make its own bombs. For the moment, a supply of uranium is necessary, and presumably every country which posseses uranium will place an embargo on its export (except from Canada to the United States). This places a temporary limitation on the countries that can manufacture the bomb, but it is to be expected that uranium will not long remain indispensable. Before many years have passed, every considerable country will be in a position to launch a surprise attack, in the style of Pearl Harbour, on any other country at any moment. And the measure of the damage to be expected must not be judged by the two bombs dropped on the Japanese; it is pretty certain that the destructiveness of atomic bombs will increase enormously as a result of further research and experimentation. Short of drastic action immediately, the outlook for the world is one of utter and unrelieved gloom.

There is much evidence that the United States Government, as well as many important citizens, is aware of the gravity of the issue, and anxious to act wisely in the interest of mankind. But such a change in habits of thought is called for that it is to be feared that the necessary mental adjustments may not be made quickly enough.

The first mistake to be avoided is that of trusting to agreements, as was done in the case of the Kellog Pact. No agreement will be observed by a number of powers throughout a period of years unless the penalties of infringing it are severe, obvious and certain. It would be utterly futile to negotiate a general treaty forbidding the use of atomic bombs, unless any power disregard-

311

ing such a treaty knew that it would be met by a force of atomic bombs exceeding its own. It has been suggested that the secret of the atomic bomb should be revealed to the United Nations. Such action, by itself, would be merely mischievous, since the various governments would all learn the secret, and would, in some cases at least, set to work making their own bombs. The United Nations would need to be a much stronger and tighter organization than it is before it could wisely be entrusted with such a source of national power in the several nations.

There is the same objection to the proposal, frequently made, that the secret should be revealed to Russia without previously securing effective guarantees of genuine cooperation on the part of the Soviet Government. The interests of Russia and the United States are bound to conflict, probably before long. We must all hope that every such conflict will be settled amicably, but if it concerns some matter which both sides regard as vital—say the oil of the Middle East or the trade of China—there is always the possibility that war may result, unless it is clear in advance, to both parties, which side will be the victor. At present, owing to the atomic bomb, it is clear that the United States would be the victor, and therefore war is unlikely while America retains this advantage. To tell Russia how to make atomic bombs would shorten the period of American supremacy, and might therefore, contrary to everybody's intention, hasten the advent of another world war. Whatever measures are to be taken to prevent another world war must be taken during the brief period of American supremacy, and must be enforced by a vigorous use of that supremacy, which should be used, not to secure special advantages for the United States, but to compel the world to adopt a system making great wars improbable.

There are certain liberal ideals—self-determination, liberty, justice, and so on—which are of great importance, and to be preserved in so far as it is at all possible. But at the present point in the history of mankind there are other things that are, for the moment, of even greater importance. If the inmates of a lunatic asylum were to succeed in breaking out, and were to set to work to let loose a store of poison gas sufficient to exterminate a whole large city, the authorities would not observe any pedantic adherence to general principles in frustrating their insane frenzy. In the present state of the world, those governments and individuals who are willing to promote a war are like such liberated madmen, but a thousand times more dangerous. I make, however, one exception to the condemnation of wars in the near future; a powerful group of nations, engaged in establishing an international military government of the world, may be compelled to resort to war if it finds somewhere an opposition which cannot be peacefully overcome, but which can be defeated without a completely exhausting struggle. Even in this case a war will not be justified unless the international government to be established is to have certain merits. I should, for my part, prefer all the chaos and destruction of a war conducted by means of the atomic bomb to the universal domination of a government having the evil characteristics of the Nazis. I think a world government supremely important, and I do not expect to see it established without an element of compulsion. But I should think too high a price was being paid if the world government had not that degree of respect for freedom and kindliness that has been characteristic of the Western democracies. Even if force be a necessary means, part of the purpose in using force must be to establish a system in which force will play a smaller part than it does at present.

The establishment of an international government possessed of a monopoly of armed force is the only way by which the peace of the world can be preserved. In view of the potentialities of the atomic bomb, it is more important to establish a world government than it is to make sure that it will be a perfect government from the standpoint of liberal principles. I would rather see the United States conquer the whole world and rule it by force than see a prolongation of the present multiplicity of independent Great Powers. But I think the United States could use its preponderance more effectively by a policy less illiberal than that of conquest.

The United States should forthwith invite the formation of a Confederation of nations, open to any government which would agree to certain terms (excluding Germany and Japan for the present). The terms should be as follows:

1. The members of the Confederation should bind themselves to abstain from aggression, and to resist jointly any aggression against one of their members, whether by a member of the Confederation or by an outside power. A court should be established with the duty of pronouncing quickly whether aggression had occurred in any given case.

2. There should be a permanent body, on which every member of the Confederation should be represented, which should have the duty of deciding disputes between members of the Confederation. Any member of the Confederation resisting such a decision should be deemed an aggressor. The same body should decide the policy of the Confederation as a whole, in the event of a dispute between a member of the Confederation and an outside Power.

3. The Confederation should possess a powerful armed force, to which each member should contribute on a basis determined in relation to both population and resources. To this armed force should be entrusted the existing stock of atomic bombs, all existing knowledge as to their manufacture, and a right to claim the necessary raw materials from any region within the territory of the Confederation. At the same time there should be an agreed drastic limitation of purely national armaments.

4. Each separate member of the Confederation should renounce the right to manufacture atomic bombs, which should be vested solely in the Confederation as a whole and its armed force. Sufficient inspectors should be appointed to insure observance of this provision, and any obstacle put in the way of their work should constitute an aggressive act.

If such a body were formed under the leadership of the United States, and with the understanding that powers remaining outside would be viewed with suspicion entailing economic disadvantages, it is pretty certain that within a very short time, it would be joined by a great majority of eligible powers. The powers concerning which there would be most doubt would be the USSR and its satellites. The USSR, we should hope, would also join, but it might refuse, if only from unwillingness to admit foreign supervision by inspectors of its armaments and munition works. But against such a bloc even the USSR would be powerless, at any rate while the United States still retained the lead as regards the atomic bomb, which would now be a lead of the Confederation. There might be a period of hesitation followed by acquiescence, but if the USSR did not give way and join the Confederation, after there had been time for mature consideration, the conditions for a justifiable war, which I enumerated a moment ago, would all be fulfilled. A *casus belli* would not be difficult to find. Either the voluntary adherence of Russia, or its defeat in war, would render the Confederation invincible, since any war that might occur would be quickly ended by a few atomic bombs.

I am afraid that what I have been suggesting, in the form in which I have suggested it, is Utopian, since it would involve the voluntary surrender of absolute sovereignty on the part of the United States. What is perhaps possible is something less desirable and less effective, but still capable of making world wars less probable. The United States might retain for the present its monopoly of the atomic bomb, but undertake to protect against aggression any Powers willing to enter into an alliance with it and to abstain from manufacturing their own atomic bombs. In this way, without surrender of sovereignty, the United States could become the leader in a bloc which would be jointly irresistible. The risk of being called upon actually to fight in defence of any power in the bloc would be negligible, since not even Russia would dare to attack it. In this way America could in all likelihood secure both her own peace and the peace of the world, at a cost immeasurably less than that of another war.

I know that a powerful section of opinion in the United States still believes, in spite of two examples to the contrary, that American can remain at peace when great wars break out elsewhere, by the simple process of declaring herself neutral. Neither the first world war not the second would have occurred if it had been known in advance that America would take part. In each case it was the fear of being involved that caused America to be involved, since, but for this fear, neither war would have taken place. I hope that the fallacy of attempting neutrality has now been fairly generally realized by the leaders of American public opinion, and that the new immense power for good or ill conferred by the atomic bomb will be used wisely, and with no undue shrinking from the responsiblities which this power confers. If so, the outlook for the world will be less gloomy than it has sometimes seemed in recent months.

The American Mentality: Don't Let's Be Beastly to the Yankees

News Review, 15 September 1949

America and Britain are faced with a problem. Unless they can co-operate, they are doomed; but bickering is so much pleasanter than co-operation that neither party is sure of being willing to purchase safety at so high a cost. Appeals by statesmen for mutual understanding fall on deaf ears, because, in each country, there is a profound popular conviction of one's own rightnesss and the other side's wickedness or folly.

We all know what the average man in this country feels and thinks. It is something like this: Britain had to face over two years of war while America was still neutral; but for our courage and stubbornness, Hitler would have been victorious. But in the process all our resources were used up; we emerged destitute, the United States emerged richer than ever. As a result of our greater loyalty to the common cause and our genuine belief in liberty, we have lost the best part of our Empire, and are compelled to accept grudging charity with such pretence of humble gratitude as we can manage to produce. And it is bad manners to mention that if the Americans would lower their tariffs we could soon end our troubles by our own efforts.

To the average American the whole thing looks very different. He starts from a deep-seated suspicion of Britain, derived largely from what he has been taught in school. He knows about the American War of Independence and about the war of 1812—the only two wars fought by Americans against a European power until 1917. It must be admitted that our record in those two wars was by no means creditable. If you try to persuade the average American that George III is dead, he does not effectively believe you. He knows that until the last few years our Empire was the largest in the world, and he is persuaded that we held it by brutal exercise of military power. He still believes that Canada is governed from Downing Street. He knows that we have a King and aristocracy, which makes him unshakeably convinced that our government is not democratic. He thinks that in the war we showed the grossest incompetence; not infrequently he knows that the Japanese conquered Singapore, but does not know that they conquered the Philippines.

Other causes of hostility reinforce these. Two very powerful groups—the Irish and the Jews—hate us with a fanatical hatred which is astonishing to most English people who come in contact with it. The most popular newspapers are vehemently anti-English. I frequently had occasion to see the *Chicago Tribune* during the war, and no reader could have guessed from its pages that America was not allied with Germany. In 1918 I was put in prison for some mild criticism of America, but throughout the late war important American newspapers, with complete impunity, said every day things ten times as damaging about England.

There was just one group that was friendly to us; it was the group of rich Conservatives, who disliked democracy, had no objection to imperialism, and from snobbery had a partiality for titles. This group loved Churchill, and turned against us when we came to have a Socialist Government. But nine-tenths of the American hostility to us ante-dates our adoption of Socialism.

Owing to skillful propaganda, appealing to the widespread hostility to Socialism which exists even among trade unionists in the United States, the average American has at present two contradictory beliefs about us. On the one hand, he is persuaded that wage-earners are pampered, and live comfortably on very little work. On the other hand, he is firmly convinced that owing to Socialism (not owing to the war), the country is heading for ruin, and everybody is on the verge of starvation. Kind friends in America frequently send me parcels of food, under the impression that I have not enough to eat to preserve health and vigour. I am deeply grateful for their friendly concern, but I feel bound to let them know that the newspapers have misled them as to our condition.

The ignorance of elementary economics in America is a perpetual surprise to educated Britons. It is very generally believed that it is possible for a nation to sell without buying, and that, if it does so, it will become rich. While America was a debtor nation, this belief did not do much harm. But since the rest of the world has come to be in America's debt, the results have been highly embarrassing, After the first world war we owed money to the United States. They did not want to be paid in goods, and prevented our doing so by prohibitive tariffs. While it was physically possible, we paid in gold, but this could not go on after America had acquired a virtual monopoly of the world's gold. We were therefore compelled to repudiate, which roused intense moral indignation in the breasts of virtuous Americans. They never realised that they had made it arithmetically impossible for the debt to be paid.

The same sort of situation, but on a larger scale, has now arisen again. An unjust cynic might interpret American policy by saying: If your customers are ruined, but you are determined to go on supplying them (on the ground that exports are desirable), there is nothing for it but to give away what cannot be sold. But it is irritating if the recipients of your charity pursue policies that you disapprove of; such behaviour is unseemly in dependants.

I have been speaking of average Americans, who have made no special study of the questions at issue. In the Administration there are many men who have a very sound understanding of the problems, and very wise opinions as to what ought to be done. Unfortunately for us, there is a great constitutional difference between Britain and the United States. In Britain, the Administration is virtually omnipotent so long as it remains in office, whereas in America Congress, though it cannot cause the Administration to fall, can insist upon altering or rejecting policies inaugurated by the President. Congress consists largely of men ignorant of Europe, or subservient to voters ignorant of Europe. The consequence is that the best brains in America are very often prevented from being effective by the pressure of uninformed popular prejudice. Prejudice especially takes the form of a rooted belief that Europeans are subtle and clever and wicked, whereas Americans are straightforward and gullible, and highly moral. Most Americans cannot believe that we are as stupid as we seem, and therefore the stupider we seem the more wily we are thought to be. Alas, this is seldom true.

It must be said that many English people make the opposite mistake, and think Americans stupid when in fact they are quite the reverse. There is a certain kind of "clever" talk which is practised in England, which often conceals from those who practise it their complete lack of any but verbal intelligence. Americans are much less proficient in this somewhat futile accomplishment, and are therefore apt to be despised by Englishmen who are really their inferiors. In the days when England had the kind of world-supremacy that America has now, English people, both in public and in private, not infrequently behaved with incredible insolence and contempt towards Americans. *Martin Chuzzlewit,* for instance, must have cost us many billions of dollars. This foolish contempt, which is wholly underserved, is not confined to the English, but exists equally in several countries of the Continent. At the time of Hiroshima, German atomic scientists were filled with incredulous amazement at the discovery that, where they had failed, American scientists had succeeded.

No good can come to us, or to the Americans, or to the world, from mutual recriminations and misunderstanding. The only people who can benefit are Russian Communists. Mutual understanding is of the utmost importance. There are two groups willing to wreck mankind for their respective "isms": on the one side, Communists and fellow-travelers, for whom America is the enemy; on the other side, the fanatical devotees of capitalism, who are willing to drive Britain into the arms of Russia rather than condone our very mild dose of Socialism. Fortunately, neither group is in power in either country. It should therefore be possible to cause the present disturbance to die down.

If we are to succeed in producing in America a better understanding of our situation and our policies, two things are vital; we must preserve courtesy, and we must preserve self-respect. The importance of courtesy is impossible to exaggerate, and I am afraid it is a quality in which we are very often lacking in our dealings with Americans. Many Americans, some of them very influential, have been turned into life-long enemies of England by British insolence. But when I speak of courtesy I do not mean subservience; I mean the kind of behaviour which is appropriate between gentlemen who regard each other as equals. We should make it clear that we are not to be treated as a subject nation; that it is for us, and no one else, to decide how much Socialism we will have; and that, if American help is regarded as giving a right to control our policy, we would rather starve.

The next thing that is important is to dispel American belief in our inefficiency. Most of us find bragging distasteful, and much prefer understatement. But this is not understood by Americans. We ought to employ writers and speakers to represent vividly and simply the problems with which we were faced during the war and at its close, the fatigue of a population which had endured six years of hardship, danger and grinding toil, and the truly heroic resolution involved in realising that peace was not the end, but demanded new efforts in a world grown drab and monotonous. We should point out the great liberality of our policy in India. We should lay stress on the fact that we produce very much more than in 1938. Finally we should point out that our policy has proved an effective antidote to communism, and contrast the tiny number of Communists in this country with the large number in France and Italy. I think if all this were done effectively and popularly throughout the United States, the beneficial effect would be enormous.

But if such emissaries are to be effective, they must be themselves actively aware of the immense merits that America has displayed in international affairs. At a time when all the great Powers of Europe were bent on plundering China, America held aloof. After the first World War, Wilson was certainly more enlightened than either Lloyd George or Clemenceau. Since the end of the second World War, America has proclaimed several resoundingly wise and magnanimous policies. I have in mind especially Marshall Aid, the Atlantic Pact, and the offer to internationalise atomic energy. America, in my opinion, has proved to be the best of the Powers in the years since 1945. If we remember this, as we ought to do, we shall not feel tempted to adopt the self-righteous tone that makes cordial agreement impossible. And cordial agreement is indispensable if we are to bring our troubles to a happy issue.

Political and Cultural Influence of U.S.A.

The Listener, 8 December 1949

America is affecting Europe in so many ways, and at so many different levels, that it is difficult to know where to begin, or what kind of influence to regard as the more important. How can we compare, and how bring within the compass of one discourse, such disparate matters as the effect of Mr. Justice Holmes on the mind of Mr. Laski? I cannot answer such a question. I will only say, to begin with, that Europeans with pretensions to culture are too apt to remember Hollywood with a sniff, and forget the respect due to such men as Holmes, who was, after all, equally a product of America. I will try to rectify this one-sidedness by dwelling chiefly upon the importance of America in the world of ideas.

What America stood for in the minds of Europeans of the early nineteenth century was, in many ways, the exact opposite of what America stands for at the present day. From 1776 to the death of Lincoln, America was the Mecca of radicals, the only large country where democracy was successfully practiced. Now, America has become the bulwark of capitalism, the main hope of those who dread the advancing tide of socialism and communism, and the chief promise of stability amid the kaleidoscopic transformations that bewilder the puzzled inhabitants of Europe and Asia. I once lectured in New York in a building called the "Hall of Liberty," erected by German radicals who fled from their native country after the failure of the Revolution of 1848. Their portraits hung on the walls, and among them was the father of Heinz of the 57 varieties. The contrast between what father hoped of America and what the son made of it (and out of it) typified the change of which I am speaking.

It must be said that the admiration felt for America by the radicals of a hundred years ago was not always well founded. When Cobden, after his triumph in 1846, was presented by his admirers with a considerable sum of money, he invested it all in the Illinois Central Railroad because of his belief in the United States. The railroad went bankrupt, and he lost every penny. It went bankrupt, not for lack of profitable business, and not for lack of skill in the management. Quite the contrary. Bankruptcy was the recognized method of transferring money from simple-minded shareholders to astute directors. But Cobden never grasped this aspect of American big business. And yet to this day Americans believe themselves so naive as to be liable to be twisted round the little finger of any European who will take the trouble to bamboozle them.

Throughout the period when radicals inordinately admired America, conservatives still more inordinately despised it. The Duchess of Cambridge, at a garden party, examined my mother's skirts, saying in a loud voice: "I want to see if they are dirty, because I hear you only associate with dirty radicals and dirty Americans." Lord Salisbury, the Victorian Prime Minister, saw fit to remind President Cleveland that we owned more of the American continent than the United States did—which displeased Canada almost as much as it displeased the United States. But the days for such insults are past. They depended upon naval supremacy, and when we lost that we had to mend our manners. The change in the attitude to America of European left-wing opinion is more due to a change in Europe than to a change in America. America in the time of Jefferson believed in democracy and free enterprise, and America believes in them still. Cobden believed in them, and therefore admired America, but left-wing Europeans, nowadays, are Socialists or Communists, and find in America the chief obstacle to the realisation of their hopes. There is also another reason for the change of sentiment: people of a rebellious disposition are temperamentally compelled to be against the rich and powerful, and America is more rich and powerful than any other nation. If you praise Sweden to a Communist, he may think you misguided, but will not call you a lackey of capitalism, because Sweden is not great and strong; but if you praise America, there is no limit to the subversive and moral iniquity of which he will suspect you. In the time of Byron and Shelley, both of whom praised America, it was otherwise. America could not threaten anyone, and they imagined it a country of simple farmers imbued with all the virtues of the early Romans. It must be said, however, that Childe Harold never went there.

Although America is opposed to socialism, it would be a mistake to think of the country as unprogressive. Since 1933 immense strides have been taken in social legislation. And in industrial technique—which most Americans think more important than politics—the United States remains the least wedded to tradition and the most receptive to innovations of all the industrial countries with the possible exception of Russia, about which knowledge is unobtainable. In the world of ideas, also, there is a readiness for novelty which is usually absent in Europe. Anyone who has attempted to present a new philosophy to Oxford and the Sorbonne and the universities of America will have been struck by the greater readiness of the Americans to think along unfamiliar lines. And if one could present a new philosophy to Moscow without being liquidated, one would find Russians less open to new ideas than even the most hidebound old dons in our older universities. All these are facts which left-wing opponents of America fail to recognize.

In international affairs the record of America compares very favourably with that of other Great Powers. There have been, it is true, two short periods of imperialism, one connected with the Mexican war of 1846, the other with the Spanish-American war of 1898, but in each case a change of policy came very soon. In China, where the record of Britain, France, Germany and Russia is shameful, that of the United States has always been generous and liberal. No territorial concessions were ever demanded, and the Boxer indemnity money was spent on Chinese education. Since 1945, American policy, both as regards control of atomic power and as regards the Marshall Plan, has been generous and far-sighted. Western union, economic and political, which America urges, is obviously to the interest of Western Europe; in fact, American authorities have shown more awareness of what Western Europe needs than Western Europe itself has shown. True, the United States ought to lower its tariff. But it took Britain thirty-one years after Waterloo to realise a similar need and it would be unreasonable to expect America to change its traditional policy overnight.

I come now to the main question: How far has the American outlook on life and the world influenced Europe, and how far is it likely to do so? And first of all: What is the distinctively European outlook? Traditionally, the European outlook may be said to be derived from astronomy. When Abraham watched his flocks by night, he observed the stars in their courses: they moved with a majestic regularity utterly remote from human control. When the Lord answered Job out of the whirlwind, He said: "Canst thou bind the sweet influence of Pleiades, or loose the bands of Orion?" The reply was in the negative. Even more relevant is the question: "Knowest thou the ordinances of heaven? Canst thou set the dominion thereof in the earth?" To which Job answered: "Behold, I am vile; what shall I answer thee; I will lay my hand upon my mouth." The conclusion is that man is a feeble creature, to whom only submission and worship are becoming. Pride is insolence, and belief in human power is impiety.

The Greek outlook was similar in this respect. Above even the gods, Necessity or Fate held inexorable sway. The most unforgivable and most swiftly punished of sins was *hubris*, which consisted in the self-assertion of human beings against cosmic laws. This, equally, was a natural outcome of contemplation of the stars. The Christian religion, Christian art, and Christian literature are deeply impregnated with this spirit of humility. And even among those Europeans who think that they have forgotten religion, it is natural to feel that it is for man to adapt himself to his environment rather than to adapt his environment to himself. Where life is hard, and the medieval tradition is still strong, as in most parts of Europe, this outlook on life still dominates philosophy, literature and the feelings of ordinary men and women. In America hardly a trace of this outlook survives. True, the old pious formulas are repeated on Sundays, and are thought, by those who repeat them, to be still believed. But they have lost their grip: they have become only Sunday truths, and during the rest of the week other views prevail. Why bother with the stars? We never see them, because our street lighting is too bright, and in any case they do not have that influence upon human affairs that astrology ascribed to them.

Religion is regarded as a useful influence in human affairs, but its super-human aspects are forgotten. There is truth in the jest about the newspaper which praised an eminent divine for "the finest prayer ever addressed to a Boston audience." In a modern great city, the works of God are much less noticeable than the works of man. If Job had been reincarnated as an inhabitant of New York, and had been twitted, as the original Job was, with the great size of Leviathan and Behemoth, he would have been unimpressed, and would have replied: "Gee, they ain't half as big as a skyscraper." And as for adaptation to the environment, how lazy and old-fashioned! Compare New York with

321

Manhattan Island as it was when the first white settlers arrived. Is this adaptation of man to his environment? No, it is adaptation of the environment to man. Man is lord of the earth: what he wants, he can get by energy and intelligence. The Soviet Government, using an American invention, boasts that it can remove mountains, but not by faith. True, the heavenly bodies remain, but why bother about them? And if, some day, we get tired of the moon, we shall find ways of disintegrating it by radio-active projectiles. To all intents and purposes, God is an adjunct of man, help in church work and in procuring victory in man-made wars. The Power that humbled Job out of the whirlwind no longer finds an echo in American mentality.

This attitude to life and the world is inspired by triumphant industrialism, and makes its appeal outside America wherever conditions resemble those in the United States. The country which has a philosophy most similar to that of the United States is Soviet Russia. There, also, there is optimism and energy, there is almost boundless belief in human power, there is determination to regard nature as providing opportunities rather than obstacles. But in Soviet Russia something remains of ancient piety, imported from the Old Testament by way of Karl Marx. In heaven the new synthetic god, Dialectical Materialism, and here below his vice regent Stalin, still demand mystical reverence, since it is man's destiny, willy-nilly, to work out the behests of this strange Hegelian-Hebraic Deity. But perhaps this lingering remnant of earlier philosophies will only survive as long as Russia remains poor; given prosperity, the new religion might lose influence in Russia as completely as the old religion has in the United States.

From the highest flights of philosophy to the silliest movie, the distinctive feature of American thought and feeling is a determination to have done with the notion of "fact." We used to think it a good thing if our beliefs were "true," and we imagined that "truth" consisted in correspondence with "fact." If you believe (say) that Edinburgh is north of London, you believe truly, because of a geographical fact which is quite independent of your belief. And so we thought it our duty to recognise "facts," even if they were unpleasant. Not so, says pragmatism, which is the typical American philosophy: there are no "facts" that have to be passively acknowledged, and "truth" is a mistaken concept. Dewey, the leading philosopher of America, replaces "truth" by "warranted assertibility." This is arrived at, not by merely observing the environment, but by an interaction with it which continues until it has been so modified as to become acceptable to us. For passive "truth" he substitutes active "inquiry," which, he says, "is concerned with objective transformations of objective subject-matter."

"Inquiry," according to this view, is like extracting a metal from the ore, or turning raw cotton into cloth. The raw material offered to our sense is not assimilable, and we put it through a process until, like an invalid food, it becomes easy to digest. A belief only has "warranted assertibility" when the consequences of holding the belief are satisfactory. Some governments have not been slow to realise that the police can decide what beliefs shall have "satisfactory" consequences. In old days, a belief might be "true" even if the government frowned upon it; now, it cannot have "warranted assertibility" if

> "When we see an American film, we know beforehand that virtue will be rewarded, that crime will be shown not to pay, and that the heroine, always faultlessly dressed in spite of incredible tribulations, will emerge happily to life-long bliss with the hero."

the police object to it—unless those who hold it are strong enough to promote a successful revolution. The political consequences of such a philosophy have been worked out with ruthless logic in George Orwell's book *Nineteen Eighty-Four*. But none of his gloomy forecasts will have "warranted assertibility" if they turn out to be true, for anyone who adheres to them after they have been realised will be liquidated, and therefore the consequences of adhering to them will not be "satisfactory."

The artistic consequences of the refusal to admit "facts" are equally bad. From pragmatism to the movies is not such a far cry as might be thought. I believe almost every European would agree that the English, the French, the Germans, and the Russians of some twenty years ago, all produced artistically better movies than those emanating from Hollywood. When we see an American film, we know beforehand that virtue will be rewarded, that crime will be shown not to pay, and that the heroine, always faultlessly dressed in spite of incredible tribulations, will emerge happily to life-long bliss with the hero. If you object: "But this is a sugary fairy-tale only fit for children," producers and American public alike will be simply puzzled, since the object is not to produce something that corresponds to fact, but something that makes you happy by corresponding to day-dreams. It is natural that, by contrast, some of the best American novelists are savage, cynical, and pessimistic. I wish they had as large a public as is enjoyed by the movies—though, if they had, they would no doubt become less savage and less cynical.

The lack of aesthetic sense produced by an excessive preoccupation with utility shows also in the matter of speech. Educated people throughout Europe, and peasants on the Continent and in Scotland and Ireland, have a certain beauty of diction: language is not merely a means of communication, but a vehicle for expressing the emotions of joy or sorrow, love or hate, that are the material of poetry. Words, many of them, have beauty: they have a history, and we are, each in our own day, responsible for handing on an unimpaired tradition in diction and enunciation. It is rare to find this feeling among Americans. If you make your meaning clear, what more can be desired? Accordingly their vocabulary is small, and sounds which should be distinguished are blurred. The only good thing about the American language is the slang. Fortunately it is just this that the English are most disposed to copy. I console myself with the reflection that French, now such a beautiful language, was in origin the argot of uneducated Roman soldiers. Perhaps in 1500 years Americans will become equally admirable.

But I have been dwelling too much upon what seems to me regrettable in the American outlook. There is another side, and one which it is very important that Europe should appreciate. The American outlook is the result of inhabiting a large country, not yet over-populated, with immense natural resources, and with greater wealth and less poverty than any of the old countries of Europe and Asia. A young American can be adventurous without folly; he does not need, to nearly the same extent as a European, to force himself into acquiescence with a narrow groove and a career that can be foreseen with dreary accuracy. The hopefulness and enterprise that circumstances permit increase the success that is achieved beyond what would be possible for men of a different temperament. Obstacles, it is felt, exist to be overcome, and therefore they are overcome. All this is admirable. It existed in Elizabethan England, and to a lesser degree in Victorian England. It is now lost to us, but I hope not forever. A little more of this American spirit would do us far more good than any amount of austerity unrelieved by hope.

Britain, and Western Europe generally, has new and very difficult problems to face. When we are lectured by optimistic Americans we are apt to feel the kind of annoyance that a suffering patient feels with a doctor whose bedside manner is unduly cheerful; we cannot resist the reflection that it is easy to be cheerful about other people's troubles. But we shall not solve them without a certain buoyancy of spirit, of which, at the moment, America and Russia share the monopoly. Austerity is unavoidable at present, but it should resemble the frugality of a young man determined to succeed, not the parsimony of an old man who fears to lose the last remnant of his former fortune. Fear has led us to lay too much emphasis on safety, and too little on enterprise. Without risk nothing can be achieved. In this respect I welcome the impact of America, and I only wish that Western Europe were more receptive.

A great deal of nonsense is talked about American so-called "materialism" and what its detractors call "bathroom civilisation." I do not think Americans are in any degree more "materialistic," in the popular sense of that word, than people of other nations. We think they worship the "almighty dollar" because they succeed in getting it. But a needy aristocrat or a French peasant will do things for the sake of money that shock every American. Very few Americans marry for mercenary motives. A willingness to sacrifice income for idealistic reasons is at least as common in America as in England. I think the belief that Americans are fonder of money than we are is mainly inspired by envy. It is true that, where there is no recognized aristocracy, wealth is the chief means of winning general respect. But where aristocracy has prevailed, individual aristocrats have been respected because aristocrats were rich. Now that this is no longer true in Europe, American standards, as regards snobbery, are rapidly coming to be accepted. As for "bathroom civilisation," it is altogether to the good, unless it is thought to be all-sufficient. Every traveller owes a debt of gratitude to American tourists for the improvement in hotels that has been brought about by their grumbling. The love of "gadgets," for which we are inclined to make fun of Americans, ought not to be decried. An American middle-class housewife, compelled, like an English housewife, to do her own cooking, does it with far less labour than is required in most English kitchens. The habit of keeping food in the refrigerator is wholly to be commended from the point of view of health. The more we copy America in these respects the better.

It is not only in utilitarian ways that the best Americans are admirable. What could be less utilitarian than the study of extra-galactic nebulae? Yet here far and away the best work has been done in America. True, the reason is that America has the best telescopes, and has them because there are very rich men in America who think this a good way of spending some of their money. But they would not think so if they and their public were as earthbound as is often supposed by Europeans.

There is one aspect of American life which I have not yet touched on, and which I think wholly undesirable—I mean, the tyranny of the herd. Eccentricity is frowned upon, and unusual opinions bring social penalties upon those who hold them. At the present day, people suspected of the slightest sympathy with communism are exposed to a kind of ostracism which would be absurd if it were not tragic. Atomic physicists maintain that the inquisition instigated by Congress is seriously impeding important work. After the first world war, there was a terrible persecution of Radicals; the case of Sacco and Vanzetti made the most stir, but there were many others only slightly less shocking. The guilt lies with the general public, which is intolerant to a degree that must astonish any Englishman. It has nothing to do with industrialism; indeed it is worst in purely rural communities. It is not a new thing: it was noted by Tocqueville in his book on American democracy; it was rampant in the time of Washington; and it goes back to the early Puritan colonies of the seventeenth century. It is, I think, the worst feature of America. I earnestly hope that fear of Russia will not cause us to imitate it.

The shift in world power, which is largely, though not wholly, the result of the two wars, is bound to bring with it, as such shifts always do, cultural changes of great importance. From the sixteenth century onward, Europe increasingly dominated the world, from a cultural no less than a military point of view. Now that domination is lost; the inheritance is divided between Russia and America. The culture of America is closely akin to our own, and adaptation can be easy and painless. The culture of Russia, on the other hand, is profoundly alien: partly Byzantine, partly Mongol, only quite superficially European. Only appalling suffering could force us into the Russian mould. It is therefore the part of wisdom to facilitate co-operation with America, cultural as well as political and economic.

In some respects, it must be admitted, adoption of American standards, in so far as it occurs, is likely to be harmful. Aesthetic standards, except in architecture, will probably be lowered. There will be less respect for art and learning, and more for the forceful "executive." The movement towards socialism will be retarded—but whether that is to be regarded as a gain or a loss is a controversial question. On the other side, however, are to be set gains which far outweigh possible losses. Our continued existence as free nations is only capable of being maintained by co-operation with America. Our tired and disillusioned communities, which, as independent separate entities, would be condemned to live on memories under the oppression of poverty and danger, can, in conjunction with America, recover a status less different from that to which they have been accustomed in recent centuries. Above all things, European culture, if it is to remain vital, needs hope and imaginative vision. These things are common in America, as they were in Victorian England. If we can recover them by contact with Americans, there is every possibility of a future no less glorious and no less happy than our past.

Why America is Losing Her Allies

The Wichita Beacon, 5 February 1951

The tragic misunderstanding which has been developing between the United States and the rest of the free world is due to a conflict between different moral principles, sincerely held on both sides. It is just because these moral principles are sincerely held, that adjustment is so difficult. The United States stands for the principle of international law enforcement. I cannot say too strongly how wholeheartedly I agree with this principle. I think it is the ultimate solution of the world's troubles, and if it were wholly applicable in the present situation I should agree completely with the United States' policy.

But unfortunately there are other principles which in the existing situation have an equal claim to respect. In the first place, there is the purely legal question: "Did not the United Nations forfeit their claim to legality when they crossed the 38th parallel?" In the second place, there is the question of the rights of the Chinese Communist government. Outside America, the opinion is held that the Chinese Communist government has the same right to recognition as the Soviet government has. We do not like either, but that is neither here nor there. People could be imagined who might not like the existing government of the United States, but that would give them no right to say that the government of the United States should not have legal recognition. A government should be recognized when, in fact, it has authority in the country concerned, and whether other governments like it or dislike it is totally irrelevant. Then there is the question of Formosa. By the Cairo Declaration, China is to have Formosa. But now, it appears that America will not consent to any United Nations decision about Formosa, if it conflicts with American strategic interests.

The American attitude on these subjects appears to the rest of the Free World immoral. What shocks them even more is the suggestion which has been made by various influential Americans, that if India persists in opposition to America, the financial assistance which India has been led to expect shall not be forthcoming, with the result that some millions of the inhabitants of India will die of hunger. This is a form of blackmail which some people who are not American, and possibly even some Americans, think not wholly admirable.

So far I have been speaking of moral issues. There are also more practical issues. If there is to be a war with Russia, it would be as well to win the war. It can hardly be hoped that the war will be won if American policy has been such as to alienate all non-American powers. India, Pakistan, and the Arab States have been somewhat hesitant, having had experience of Western imperialism

327

and being as yet not sufferers from the imperialism of Moscow. India and the Mohammedan world were being won for our side by British policy, and are being lost by American policy.

The United States, I think by mistake, and through lack of knowledge or information, has appeared to a large part of the non-Communist world as the inheritor of British imperialism, and as more of a warmonger than the Soviet Republic. This is infinitely regrettable, and I am sure does not represent the feelings of the average American citizen. But when Americans are inclined to regard Western Europe as a traitor to the great ideals for which America stands, I think they should remember that to many in Western Europe, it seems equally apparent that it is America which is being the traitor. Both, I am sure, are mistaken. Both America and Britain are guided in their foreign policy by high ideals. It will be a disaster not only to ourselves but to mankind if in this conflict of ideals they cannot find a middle course in which what is best in the ideals of both can be preserved. By all means let us be firm against aggression, as America desires. But let us at the same time admit what is just in the claims of China to Formosa and to membership in the United Nations, not from motives of appeasement, but solely because the claims are just.

I know that many people in America, misled, I think, by lack of knowledge or information, imagine that opinion in England is less hostile to communism than in America. This is not the case. We differ from America not in the desire to combat communism, but in our estimate of the best way of doing so. We think that a method which alienates possible allies, and chooses a disputable issue, is not so wise as one which, after making all concessions that justice can demand, finds itself faced with an indubitable aggression against which the free world can be united without hesitation. It may be that no such aggression will occur; in that case a great war can be avoided. But if it does occur, the chances of swift victory are very much greater than they are if the present policy of America is pursued.

For these reasons, those who dislike communism — and I yield to none in my horror of the Communist regime—if they are not blinded by hysteria, consider that the policy recommended by the British government in favor of negotiation with China, is to be preferred to the American policy of outright condemnation of China, not only on grounds of expediency, but also on moral grounds. Americans must not hope that British opinion, where it differs from the prevailing opinion in America, will admit either that it is less opposed to communism, or that it is inspired by less lofty moral ideals.

Are These Moral Codes Out of Date?

A Review of *The Folklore of Sex* by Albert Ellis
Evening Standard, London 22 May 1951

Morality in America is dominated by the censor to a degree which the unsophisticated inhabitants of the Old World may find puzzling. The definition of virtue is geometrical and is laid down precisely in codes that govern the cinematographic industry. Kisses must not last more than a certain number of yards and must be confined to the face.

It might be thought that while such codes might determine what can be shown in public they could not hope to have much influence on private life. This, however, would be a complete mistake. They do not, of course, decide what people do in private, but they do decide what, perhaps unconsciously, they consider it right to do. The consequence is that almost the whole nation believes itself abandoned to sinful practices. This has two consequences: on the one hand, since the accepted standards of morals is an impossible one, everybody in moments of depression or intoxication is persuaded he is a miserable sinner; on the other hand, prohibitions have an aphrodisiac effect. I have never coveted my neighbor's ox, but when I remember I must not, I am almost tempted to do so.

A new book by Mr. Albert Ellis may be confidently recommended to any European who is contemplating a journey to the United States. He will find in it vast stores of information far more useful than anything contained in Baedeker and if he studies the work diligently he may be able to behave in such a manner as to increase the American contribution to the expenses of European rearmament.

In America, largely I think because of the prohibitions that still govern the official pronouncements of the law, the police and the clergy, sex fills the thoughts of men and women more than in any other country known to me. Almost all advertisements, no matter what the product concerned, are carefully designed to titillate sexual feelings. The things that writers of cheap fiction permit themselves to say are such as to bring a blush to the cheek of any hard-boiled Frenchman. And even in the most hair-raising passages there is a sickly sentimentality which inclines any person of taste to enter a monastery at once.

I have known Americans before, during, and after prohibition. During prohibition most Americans thought about liquor morning, noon, and night, and other subjects had to be content with odd crannies of their minds.

"It is a curious phenomenon that a country which leads the world in mechanised technique still lingers in the 17th Century in matters of thought."

Prohibition in regard to liquor is at an end but in matters of sex the censorship is perennial and the mental effects are very similar to those which were produced by prohibition. One is compelled to suppose that conventional moralists are not very good psychologists since the steps that they take secure results exactly opposite to those they profess to desire. The attitude about sex in America is part of a more general attitude. Americans for the most part are unable to face reality except in a mood of cynicism. One finds this, for example, in politics. They have a set of ideal rules which they imagine that a virtuous politician would obey, but the rules are such as would cause any man to be out of politics in a week. Consequently, it is recognized that no politician can be virtuous according to the nominal code. It follows, so at least the average American concludes, that a politician cannot be justly blamed whatever crimes he may commit. It does not seem to occur to anyone that a moral code, if it is to serve a useful purpose, should not be something totally divorced from practical life, but something which real live people in actual situations may be able to follow.

There would be much less confusion than there is now in American thought and feeling if this view of moral codes were generally adopted both in matters of politics and in questions of sex.

Mr. Ellis's point of view throughout is wise and enlightened. He points out that capitalist enterprise views sex as a commodity which may be profitably sold for public consumption. This is true of advertisements not only in America, but also in England. In America, however, owing to the fact that advertisers have more money to spend, the evil is much greater in degree. He points out that a "cultural lag permits many highly illogical, inconsistent and immature sex views to linger on decades and centuries beyond their original usefulness and logical applicability to human affairs." It is a curious phenomenon that a country which leads the world in mechanised technique still lingers in the 17th century in matters of thought. It is earnestly to be hoped that the superiority of America in armed force will not be employed in destroying what is best in the outlook of the Old World.

There is in America, and to a lesser degree in England, a three fold division in what people say and think on moral questions. There is first of all the official code handed down from the past which cannot be publicly flouted without severe penalties, social if not legal. There is next what people's own reflections have led them to believe consciously. This, in many people, perhaps in most, is much less strict than the traditional code. But thirdly, beneath what people consciously think, there is still the unconscious effect of early upbringing which is usually in line with the old conventions. The result is a turmoil in the mind and a lack of consistency in action. As Mr. Ellis puts it:

...sexual discomfort and inconvenience, even when basic sex needs are partly satisfied, motivate millions of Americans to act differently than they think and unconsciously to think differently than they consciously permit themselves to think they think.

If modern men are to have mental health they must learn honesty in thought and feeling, even when honesty compels some departure from the precepts that they imbibed in infancy.

Democracy and the Teachers: Using Beelzebub to Cast Out Satan

Manchester Guardian, 30 October 1951 reprinted as
"Bertrand Russell Tweaks the State of Indiana"
Des Moines Sunday Register, 25 November 1951

I learn that in a certain important State of the Union the Education Authorities have become impressed with the importance of defining the sacred institutions of the United States against the sinister machinations of those who are defending the sacred institutions of other countries.

I learn, from a document circulated to teachers in this State, that while in other countries education has "definitely sought to teach the young people that their particular form of government is the best," this is a proof of the inferiority of these other countries, since it is the form of government adopted by the United States that is the best, and therefore to teach the excellence of this government in the United States is not at all the same thing as to teach the excellence of other forms of government elsewhere.

I learn also from this document that "it now appears necessary for the schools in the United States to indoctrinate American youth for American Democracy"; that is to say, since indoctrinating the youth is an evil, and since it is practised elsewhere, it must also be practised in the United States. "We need to do this for self-protection," the document continues; that is to say, we must surrender everything that makes defence worth while before the defence begins.

Boys and girls, we are told, "should discredit definitions and descriptions used by foreign governments of such words as Social Revolution, Communism, Fascism, Totalitarianism, Police State, Dictatorship, Welfare State, Bureaucracy, Conservatives, Liberals, Capitalism, Socialism, Communal Enterprise, and Propaganda." We are told what definitions of these words are to be substituted. Perhaps I could assist those who drew up this interesting document.

"Social Revolution," to begin with, clearly does not include what happened in America in 1776, for that was good, whereas "Social Revolution" is bad. Nor does "Social Revolution" include the overthow of Hitler, for that also was good. It does include the failure to overthrow the Democratic Administration in the United States, and it does, of course, include the overthrow of Churchill in England in 1945. Perhaps we may define "Social Revolution" as any political movement anywhere which is displeasing to the Republican Party.

"Communism" is another of these words which are used dishonestly by the effete populations of Europe. Every honest man (honest men are to be found

> "It is true that during the late war we thought that we were fighting to defeat 'Fascism,' but now we learn that 'Fascism' is disliked by Moscow, and we conclude that it cannot be wholly evil."

only in America) knows that Mr. Acheson is a Communist, that Mr. Atlee is a Communist, and that communism is so catching that anybody whose second cousin once met a Communist at a party is likely to be infected. There are sophists in England who are particularly dangerous, since they pretend that "communism" can be distinguished from democratic socialism, whereas Americans know that there can be no true democracy where plutocrats are in any degree curbed, and that the present government of England, although elected by popular vote, is a bureaucracy rapidly tending towards totalitarianism.

"Fascism" is a difficult word. During the late war, we all knew what it meant. It meant the system of government employed in Germany and in Italy until the fall of Mussolini. But now that it is necessary to use Germans and Italians against the Russians, the word "Fascism" has become one which prudent people will avoid. It is true that during the late war we thought that we were fighting to defeat "Fascism," but we now learn that "Fascism" is disliked by Moscow, and we conclude that it cannot be wholly evil.

"Totalitarianism" is another of these slippery words. At one time we thought that Franco's regime was "totalitarian," but since we have realised the strategic importance of the line of the Pyrenees we have discovered that Franco is one of the bulwarks of moral values against the rising sea of atheism and materialism.

"Police State." In Germany under Hitler, and in Russia under Stalin, nobody ventured upon a political remark without first looking behind the door to make sure that no one was listening. This used to be considered a mark of the "Police State." It is so no longer, for when I last visited America, I found the same state of things there, and yet, as we all know, America is not a "Police State." It is true that Senator McCarthy's emissaries and his allies in the F.B.I. are perpetually snooping, and that if by some misfortune you were to quote with approval some remark by Jefferson, you would probably lose your job, and perhaps find yourself behind bars, but this, of course, is done in defence of liberty, and therefore does not make America a "Police State."

"Welfare State" is a phrase against which every true American should be on his guard. We all know that England is a "Welfare State," and that this proves that England is only half-heartedly opposed to Moscow. America is not a "Welfare State." Some ill-conditioned persons might infer that it is an "Ill-fare State." Such persons must not be allowed to spread their poisonous doctrines.

Another word which, according to this document, is wrongly defined by the wicked foreigners is the word "Capitalism." Americans all know what this word means. It means allowing free play to the benevolent impulses of those great and good men who have made vast fortunes by serving the public. There

333

"...propaganda means, always and everywhere, advocacy of opinions not held by the speaker."

are people, incredible as it may seem, who suspect that sometimes (though of course rarely) fortunes are made by conduct which does not promote the general welfare. They think that perhaps the extermination of half the population of the Belgian Congo in order to enrich that great philanthropist, King Leopold II, was the sort of thing which ought not to be allowed, even if it can only be prevented by an interference with free enterprise.

The last of the words which this document considers that foreigners misinterpret is the word "propaganda." I am surprised at this, for I have found throughout the world a complete and absolute unanimity in the meaning assigned to the word "propaganda": "propaganda" means, always and everywhere, advocacy of opinions not held by the speaker. The Education Authorities of the State in question will, I am sure, agree that the indoctrination which they advocate is not "propaganda." It is not "propaganda" because it is teaching doctrines with which they agree. This is also the view taken in Russian schools. If one were to suggest that "propaganda," in so far as it is harmful, consists in indocrination by other than rational means, one would be liquidated in Russia, and regarded as a fellow-traveller in the United States. Perhaps on this basis these two great countries could reach an agreement.

The document continues: "It is essential in America that we teach our young people that American democracy is the best government in the world." I know it must seem incredible, but there actually are people, not in asylums, who question this. I cannot remember any occasion in England when the leading elected representatives of the sovereign people had to be sent to prison as common thieves, as happened in Indiana some thirty years ago. Any Englishman going to America at the present time has the strange experience of a population subjected to a reign of terror, and always obliged to think twice before giving utterance to any serious conviction. English people hold the clearly subversive opinion that a teacher should not be deprived of his post merely on the ground that he has published a well-documented investigation of some facts inconvenient to certain rich men. Yet this is part of the system which in America is called "democracy." The word "democracy" was not ambiguous until recently. It used to mean government by elected representatives of the people. Now it has lost this signification. In Russia, it means government by a military tyranny; in America, it means government by a plutocracy, or, at any rate, government in which the plutocracy is uncurbed.

It is perhaps regrettable that Americans who have no education and no knowledge of the world should be allowed to antagonize intelligent opinion in countries as unalterably opposed to communism as the United States itself.

The American Way
(A Briton Says) Is Dour

New York Times Magazine, 15 June 1952

It used to be said that English people take their pleasures sadly. No doubt this would still be true if they had any pleasures to take, but the price of alcohol and tobacco in my country has provided sufficient external causes for melancholy. I have sometimes thought that the habit of taking pleasures sadly has crossed the Atlantic, and I have wondered what it is that makes so many English-speaking people somber in their outlook in spite of good health and a good income.

In the course of my travels in America I have been impressed by a kind of fundamental malaise which seems to me extremely common and which poses difficult problems for the social reformer. Most social reformers have held the opinion that, if poverty were abolished and there were no more economic insecurity, the millennium would have arrived. But when I look at the faces of people in opulent cars, whether in your country or mine, I do not see that look of radiant happiness which the aforementioned social reformers had led me to expect. In nine cases out of ten, I see instead a look of boredom and discontent and an almost frantic longing for something that might tickle the jaded palate.

But it is not only the very rich who suffer in this way. Professional men very frequently feel hopelessly thwarted. There is something that they long to do or some public object that they long to work for. But if they were to indulge their wishes in these respects, they fear that they would lose their livelihood. Their wives are equally unsatisfied, for their neighbour, Mrs. So-and-So, has gone ahead more quickly, has a better car, a larger apartment and grander friends.

Life for almost everybody is a long competitive struggle where very few can win the race, and those who do not win are unhappy. On social occasions when it is *de rigueur* to seem cheerful, the necessary demeanor is stimulated by alcohol. But the gaiety does not ring true and anybody who has just one drink too many is apt to lapse into lachrymose melancholy.

One finds this sort of thing only among English-speaking people. A Frenchman while he is abusing the Government is as gay as a lark. So is an Italian while he is telling you how his neighbour has swindled him. Mexicans, when they are not actually starving or actually being murdered, sing and dance and enjoy sunshine and food and drink with a gusto which is very rare north of the Mexican frontier. When Andrew Jackson conquered Pensacola from the Spaniards, his wife looked out of the window and saw the population enjoying itself although it was Sunday. She pointed out the scandal to her husband, who decreed that cheerfulness must cease forthwith. And it did.

When I try to understand what it is that prevents so many Americans from being as happy as one might expect, it seems to me that there are two causes, of which one goes much deeper than the other. The one that goes least deep is the necessity for subservience in some large organization. If you are an energetic man with strong views as to the right way of doing the job with which you are concerned, you find yourself invariably under the orders of some big man at the top who is elderly, weary and cynical. Whenever you have a bright idea, the boss puts a stopper on it. The more energetic you are and the more vision you have, the more you will suffer from the impossibility of doing any of the things that you feel ought to be done. When you go home and moan to your wife, she tells you that you are a silly fellow and that if you became the proper sort of yes-man your income would soon be doubled. If you try divorce and remarriage it is very unlikely that there will be any change in this respect. And so you are condemned to gastric ulcers and premature old age.

It was not always so. When Dr. Johnson compiled his dictionary, he compiled it as he thought fit. When he felt like saying that oats is food for men in Scotland and horses in England, he said so. When he defined a fishing rod as a stick with a fish at one end and a fool at the other, there was nobody to point out to him that a remark of this sort would damage the sale of his great work among fishermen. But if, in the present day, you are (let us say) a contributor to an encyclopedia, there is an editorial policy which is solemn, wise and prudent, which allows no room for jokes, no place for personal preferences and no tolerance for idiosyncracies. Everything has to be flattened out except where the prejudices of the editor are concerned. To these you must conform, however little you may share them. And so you have to be content with dollars instead of creative satisfaction. And the dollars, alas, leave you sad.

This brings me to the major cause of unhappiness, which is that most people in America act not on impulse but on some principle, and that principles upon which people act are usually based upon a false psychology and a false ethic. There is a general theory as to what makes for happines and this theory is false. Life is conceived as a competitive struggle in which felicity consists in getting ahead of your neighbor. The joys which are not competitive are forgotten.

Now, I will not for a moment deny that getting ahead of your neighbor is delightful, but it is not the only delight of which human beings are capable. There are innumerable things which are not competitive. It is possible to enjoy food and drink without having to reflect that you have a better cook and a better wine merchant than your former friends whom you are learning to cold-shoulder. It is possible to be fond of your wife and your children without reflecting how much better she dresses than Mrs. So-and-So and how much better they are at athletics than the children of that old stick-in-the-mud Mr. Such-and-Such. There are those who can enjoy music without thinking how cultured the other ladies in their women's club will be thinking them. There are even people who can enjoy a fine day in spite of the fact that the sun shines on everybody. All these simple pleasures are destroyed as soon as competitiveness gets the upper hand.

But it is not only competitiveness that is the trouble. I could imagine a person who has turned against competitiveness and can only enjoy after conscious rejection of the competitive element. Such a person, seeing the sunshine in the morning, says to himself, "Yes, I may enjoy this and indeed I must, for it is a joy open to all." And however bored he may become with the sunshine he goes on persuading himself that he is enjoying it because he thinks he ought to.

"But," you will say, "are you maintaining that our actions ought not to be governed by moral principles? Are you suggesting that every whim and every impulse should be given free rein? Do you consider that if So-and-So's nose annoys you by being too long, that gives you a right to tweak it? "Sir," you will continue with indignation, "your doctrine is one which would uproot all the sources of morality and loosen all the bonds which hold society together. Only self-restraint, self-repression, iron self-control make it possible to endure the abominable beings among whom we have to live. No, sir! Better misery and gastric ulcers than such chaos as your doctrine would produce!"

I will admit at once that there is force in this objection. I have seen many noses that I should have liked to tweak, but never once have I yielded to the impulse. But this, like everything else, is a matter of degree. If you always yield to impulse, you are mad. If you never yield to impulse, you gradually dry up and very likely become mad to boot. In a life which is to be healthy and happy, impulse, though not allowed to run riot, must have sufficient scope to remain alive and to preserve that variety and diversity of interest which is natural to a human being. A life lived on a principle, no matter what, is too narrowly determined, too systematic and uniform, to be happy. However much you care about success, you should have times when you are merely enjoying life without a thought of subsequent gain. However proud you may be, as president of a women's club, of your impeccable culture, you should not be ashamed of reading a low-brow book if you want to. A life which is all principle is a life on rails. The rails may help toward rapid locomotion, but preclude the joy of wandering. Man spent some million years wandering before he invented rails, and his happiness still demands some reminiscence of the earlier ages of freedom.

Foreword to *Freedom Is As Freedom Does*

by Corliss Lamont (John Calder, London, 1956).

It is a pleasure to have the opportunity of introducing to the British public Mr. Corliss Lamont's book *Freedom Is As Freedom Does*. The book is an admirable epitome of the various forms of attack on personal liberty that have been taking place in America in recent years. So far as I am able to judge, Mr. Lamont is wholly reliable as to facts and he has shown good judgment in selecting from an enormous mass of material. Every friend of freedom ought to lay to heart what he has to say. This applies not only to Americans, since there is no country where liberty may not be endangered.

All countries (except perhaps Holland and Scandinavia) are liable to waves of hysteria, though the extent of the damage caused by such waves differs greatly in different places. France had such a wave in 1793 and, in a lesser degree, during the Dreyfus case. Germany had it in the worst possible form during the time of Hitler. Russia had it under Stalin. And America has had it three times, in 1798, in 1919-20, and since the outbreak of the Korean War. Let us not flatter ourselves that Britain is exempt. From the accession of Charles I until the Revolution of 1688, hysteria of all kinds—left wing, right wing, religious, and economic—was rife. In reading what has happened in America since 1950, I constantly feel as if I were reading about England under the Stuarts. Congressional Committees are the counterpart of the Star Chamber, and Senator McCarthy seems like a re-incarnation of Titus Oates who invented the Popish Plot. Nor is it necessary to go so far back. In the days of the French Revolution, when the mob sacked Dr. Priestley's house and the government employed spies and *agents provocateurs* to ferret out sympathisers with the Jacobins, England was not unlike what America has been lately. The younger Pitt, if he found himself now in Washington, would feel quite at home. I think it important that English readers should remember such facts and should not react to what is amiss in America by smug complacency. I think it also important to remember, in protesting against loss of liberty in America, that the loss in Russia is very much greater and that the defects of the American system afford no argument in favour of the Soviet dictatorship.

In spite of these provisos, I cannot deny that some of the facts about the anti-Communist hysteria in America are utterly amazing. Who would have guessed that the *Girl Scout Handbook*, a work intended to instruct what we should call Girl Guides in their duties, was savagely criticized because it praised the United States Public Health Service and spoke favourably of the United Nations, "the handiwork of that arch-traitor, Alger Hiss?" So severe

338

> "In reading what has happened in America since 1950, I constantly feel as if I were reading about England under the Stuarts."

was the censure that a correction had to be immediately issued omitting the offending matter.

Perhaps the most valuable chapter in Mr. Lamont's book is the one called "The Police State in the Making." The Federal Bureau of Investigation (FBI) has been steadily building up its power and spreading terror far and wide. It has 130 million finger-print cards and a system of indexing them of which it is enormously proud. Only a minority of the population do not appear in a police dossier. Members of the FBI join even mildly liberal organisations as spies and report any unguarded word. Anybody who goes so far as to support equal rights for coloured people, or to say a good word for the UN, is liable to be visited by officers of the FBI and threatened if not with prosecution, at least with black-listing and consequent inability to earn a living. When a sufficient state of terror has been produced by these means, the victim is informed that there is a way out: if he will denounce a sufficient number of his friends as Communists, he may obtain absolution.

As in ancient Rome and modern Russia, this system has produced its crop of professional informers, mostly men who once were Communists and who now denounce others at so much a head. These are generally men over whom the Government holds the threat of prosecution for perjury for having at some time denied they were ever Communists. They are safe so long as they continue to do the dirty work demanded of them, but woe betide them if they repent. One of them, Matusow, after securing the conviction of a number of innocent people, went before a Federal judge and recanted. For this the judge said he would give him three years in prison. Matusow appealed, and the appeal has not yet been heard, so the ultimate issue, in this case, is still in doubt.

The police have, for many years, shown a complete disregard for the law and, so far as I can discover, no Federal policemen has ever been punished for breaking the law. The whole terrorist system would break down if one simple reform were adopted: namely, that criminals should be punished even if they are policemen.

The evils of the system have not failed to be condemned by some who cannot be accused of subversive opinions. This is true especially of the Federal judiciary. For example, as Mr. Lamont relates, the Federal Court of Appeals in San Francisco objected to the Government's "system of secret informers, whisperers and tale-bearers" and went on to say: "It is not amiss to bear in mind whether or not we must look forward to a day when substantially everyone will have to contemplate the possibility that his neighbours are being encouraged to make reports to the FBI about what he says, what he reads and what meetings he attends." On the whole, however, such protests from "respectable" citizens are distressingly rare. The persecution of minority opinion, even when not obviously connected with communism, is a thing which has not been imposed from above, but suits the temper of most men and receives enthusiastic support from juries.

> "Who would have guessed that the *Girl Scout Handbook*, a work intended to instruct what we should call Girl Guides in their duties, was savagely criticised because it praised the United States Public Health Service and spoke favourably of the United Nations...?"

At first sight, it seems curious that a great and powerful country like the United States, which contains only a handful of Communists, should allow itself to get into such a state of fright. One might have expected that national pride would prevent any thing so abject, but such a view would be one which could only be suggested by a false psychology. We are all of us a mixture of good and bad impulses, and it is almost always the bad impulses that prevail in an excited crowd. There is in most men an impulse to persecute whatever is felt to be "different." There is also a hatred of any claim to superiority, which makes the stupid many hostile to the intelligent few. A motive such as fear of communism affords what seems a decent moral excuse for a combination of the herd against everything in any way exceptional. This is a recurrent phenomenon in human history. Whenever it occurs, its results are horrible. There is some reason to hope that Russia is past the worst in this respect. When McCarthy fell into disfavour, it seemed as if persecution in the United States might diminish. So far, the improvement has been less than one might have hoped. But improvement has begun, and it would be no excess of optimism to think that it will continue, and reach a point where men of intelligence and humane minds can once more breathe an atmosphere of freedom. If this comes about, books such as Mr. Lamont's will have served an immensely important purpose.

Justice or Injustice?

Professor Malcolm P. Sharp has performed a great public service by his book *Was Justice Done?* which examines the Rosenberg-Sobell case from the point of view of the evidence presented and its credibility or the reverse. The case is one of those arousing such strong passions on the one side or on the other that few people have the intellectual self-control required for a calm appraisal. Professor Sharp has this self-control. He is not and has never been a Communist. He is a man trained in the estimation of evidence and in the legal relevance of facts. He was concerned in the last stages of the Rosenberg case, but only because, as a lawyer, he came to the conclusion that justice was not being done. Like most people, he had been inclined to accept the verdict of the Court, and it was reluctantly that he was compelled to change this opinion. I have not found in his book any evidence of bias on his part. So far as I am able to judge, he gives due weight to all the evidence that was offered; and when he rejects or questions any piece of evidence, he does so either on grounds of internal inconsistency or because the witness concerned had powerful motives for departing from the truth. His book is as admirable in form as it is in substance, and in both respects deserves the highest praise.

It may be thought an impertinence for one who is not an American to find fault with a decision of the American Courts. As to this, I should wish to say that every country, and indeed every social group, is liable, from time to time, to an attack of mass hysteria. England had such an attack at the time of the Popish Plot and was on the verge of it in the early months of 1918. France had two very fierce attacks of mass hysteria, the first in 1793, and the second at the time of the Dreyfus case, but, at the end of the second, recovered sanity and brought Dreyfus back from Devil's Island. The Rosenbergs cannot be brought back.

Such attacks are apt to occur whenever a community is exposed to intense fear, and are apt to take completely irrational forms, as, for example, when the Japanese punished Koreans for the Tokyo earthquake. Mass hysteria is one of the most disastrous of human propensities and, unfortunately, it is not confined to this or that nation. In regretting and combatting any one of its manifestations, it is important to remember that no one nation is specially prone to this form of irrational behaviour.

In reading Professor Sharp's record, if one is not caught in the web of terror that enmeshed police and judge and jury and witnesses, all alike, the inability of the participants to form calm judgments is quite undeniable. It

341

seems to be an accepted maxim that a known perjurer is always to be believed if he says what the police wish him to say; but if he says anything else, one may remember his addiction to perjury. It seems to be also an accepted maxim that, if a man known to have committed a crime makes a statement, after having been told by the police that if he makes it he will escape punishment or have a light sentence, what he says, under the influence of such pressure, is bound to be gospel truth. When, on the other hand, the Rosenbergs, down to the very day of their execution, were told that their lives would be spared if they would incriminate others, and when they totally refused to do so, this is not regarded as evidence of courageous innocence, but as a shocking example of Communist cunning.

The conviction of the Rosenbergs depended mainly upon the evidence of the Greenglasses. Greenglass was Mrs. Rosenberg's brother and modelled his conduct upon that of Cain. As one critic quoted by Professor Sharp justly states: "The story of David Greenglass in so obviously false in so many material respects that he is entitled to no credence; a dog should not be put to death upon the strength of his testimony" (p. 94, quoting Mr. Stephen A. Love of the Chicago Bar, in a speech of 3 May 1953). If his testimony is accepted, he was as liable to the death penalty as the Rosenbergs were; but in view of his denunciation of them, he received only a fifteen-year sentence and Mrs. Greenglass was not indicted. Professor Sharp deals at length, and very convincingly, with the console table which derived its importance from the fact that it throws doubt upon the Greenglasses' veracity and from the circumstance that new facts about it were discovered shortly before the Rosenbergs' execution and were made the basis of an application for a new trial. This application was hastily rejected on frivolous grounds after the judge had refused to see the console table which the defence asserted to be the one in question.

Judge Kaufman injected prejudice into the proceedings by attributing to the Rosenbergs all the misfortunes of the Korean War. He seems to have thought, as most non-scientific Americans apparently did, that there was something which could be called the "secret" of the bomb, which was thought of as analogous to a magic formula in medieval necromancy. He led the jury to believe that the Rosenbergs has given this "secret" to the Russians and had thereby emboldened them to cause the North Korean invasion of South Korea. This whole conception is quite wide of the mark. There was very much less that was secret about the atom bomb after Hiroshima that was popularly supposed.

There are curious inconsistencies, which do not seem to have struck those who were concerned in the trial. For example, witnesses stated with great emphasis that a Communist spy in telephoning would seldom give his real name, but would substitute a code name that had been assigned to him. Nevertheless, great play is made with the assertion that somebody who telephoned gave his name as "Julius," and therefore must have been Rosenberg.

The evidence against Sobell, who got a thirty-year sentence, was even more flimsy than the evidence against the Rosenbergs. Judge Kaufman directed the jury that, if they did not believe the testimony of Elitcher, they must acquit Sobell. Elitcher had stated on oath that he had never been a

Communist, which the police knew to be false. He therefore knew himself to be liable to prosecution for perjury. He denounced Sobell, who had been his best friend, and he has never been prosecuted.

It is commonly alleged by those who consider that the guilt of the Rosenbergs and Sobell was established that the case was reviewed by the Supreme Court. This is not so. The Supreme Court was asked to review the case, but refused.

Apart from the question of whether the verdicts were right, there is something utterly horrifying about the indecent haste shown by all the authorities in the last stages of the case. The application for a new trial on the basis of new evidence was rejected before there had been time to examine the new evidence. Legal proceedings did not terminate until two o'clock on 19 June 1953.

An appeal to the President for clemency cannot be made until the legal proceedings are concluded. Counsel for the Rosenbergs endeavoured to place an appeal for clemency before the President. They met with every kind of obstacle from red tape and do not know to this day what final consideration was given to the case by the President. The execution had been fixed for eleven p.m. on that same day, but when it was pointed out that this would be on the Jewish Sabbath, the time of execution was advanced to be just before sunset on that same day. Up to the last moment, the Rosenbergs knew they could escape the death penalty by breaking the Ninth Commandment. They refused, and died. Those who had not refused survived.

Sobell, unlike the Rosenbergs, though he refused to bear false witness, is still alive and can still be helped. He is in Alcatraz prison, which is supposed to be for recalcitrant criminals, though the only way in which he has shown himself recalcitrant is in his refusal to denounce others as his accomplices in the crimes which he has not committed. It may still be hoped that there are enough people in the United States who hold that a man should not be punished for a crime unless there is convincing evidence that he has committed it to secure by means of agitation that Sobell is granted a new trial. I cannot believe that in the somewhat calmer atmosphere of the present time he would again be convicted.

Professor Urey contributes to the book an introduction which is valuable not only because of the scientific accuracy of his judgement but also because, as a distinguished nuclear physicist, he is in a better position than most others to judge as to what was possible in the way of espionage. He deserves very high praise as one of the first non-Communists to question the justice of the verdicts.

The miscarriage of justice, as I firmly believe it to have been, in the Rosenberg-Sobell case is analogous to such cases as the Sacco-Vanzetti case and, as I remarked before, the Dreyfus case. One is driven to ask: is there anything that can be done to prevent innocent people from unjustly suffering in times of national excitement? At such times, judge and jury alike are incapable of calm judgement. The crimes alleged are so heinous that some of the horror of the crime spills over on the accused before he has been proved guilty. Witnesses who take the unpopular side incur odium and are liable to be dismissed from their employment; whereas those who take the popular side are acclaimed as heroes.

The case of Matusow is interesting in this connection. By his own account, he hired himself out to commit perjury for money. But after a time he repented and said that he had been guilty of perjury. As soon as repentance led him to give up perjury, he was prosecuted for perjury. People who have been Communists and have ceased to be so have a lucrative and popular career before them if they are willing to invent stories that the police like to hear; but, if not, they suffer all the disabilities to which ordinary ex-Communists are exposed.

I am not a lawyer and I do not know on what principles lawyers decide as to the credibility of witnesses; but from the point of view of common sense, it seems to me that if a man who is known to have committed perjury will derive great advantages if he says A and suffer severe penalities if he says B, one cannot feel quite sure that he is speaking the truth when he says A. And, speaking still from a layman's point of view, I should have thought that, if you are not quite sure, you ought not to inflict the death penalty. It is commonly said by those who derive comfort from soothing platitudes that it is better that ninety-nine guilty men should escape than that one innocent man should be punished. More or less inadvertently, we have allowed our institutions to develop so as to favour the exact opposite of this result. To prove guilt, we have a vast public machine of policemen and detectives and public prosecutors, all supported by public money; whereas the proof of innocence is left to private people at their own expense and without any of the facilities that belong to the police. People have not realised adequately that what happens in court has required long preparation and great skill in deciding how to present the material. All this preparatory work is arranged on the assumption that the public has an interest in proving guilt but not in proving innocence.

It is customary among Western nations to speak with horror of the Police State, quoting the two awful examples of Nazi Germany and Soviet Russia. The examples are truly awful. When the Russians were engaged in acquiring power over the countries that became satellites, it was always the control of the police that they sought first. We do not wish the police forces in our countries to have the kind of power that they have in Communist countries, but I think we are not always sufficiently careful to avoid steps in that direction. It is not the business of the police to insure justice. That is, or should be, the business of the courts. It is the business of the police to secure convictions, and unless their virtue is almost superhuman, they will not invariably be careful to insure that it is only against the guilty, that they seek convictions. A state of affairs easily arises where those who belong to some unpopular party or who for some reason are opposed to the government come to feel terror in the thought that the police may at any moment accuse them of some crime and, even if they are lucky enough to be acquitted, they probably suffer financial ruin owing to the suspicion which has fallen upon them. Where this happens, there is no true freedom; and it is pretty sure to happen wherever police power is unchecked. The police in Western nations have not shown themselves very adept at catching genuine political offenders. When there were bomb outrages at the end of the First World War, none of the perpetrators were caught, but two innocent men were put to death and another innocent man, after being sentenced to death, had his punishment commuted to penal servitude for life. This caused the ignorant public to believe in the efficiency of the police. Professor Sharp's book deals with a more recent example of the same pattern. I hope it may awaken the public to the realisation that to be accused is not necessarily to be guilty.

Thermonuclear War:
Battle of Experts

New Republic, 3 April 1961

Two armament experts, one American, the other Russian, have lately set forth statements of policy: in the case of the Russian, clearly official; in the case of the American, such as some authorities are recommending to the Kennedy Administration. While reading their pronouncements, I imagined myself a member of one of the newly emancipated nations and I was consistently disquieted by the thoughts which the two pronouncements were likely to generate in such a reader.

The American is Herman Kahn, whose large book, *On Thermonuclear War* deserves study. I should like to say that there are things in his book with which I find myself in agreement. For example, he holds that neutrality on the part of the Western Powers is reasonable, since they add nothing to America's strength and cannot be effectively protected by America. He also expresses approval of the British Labour Party's proposal of a non-nuclear club of which Britain should be a member, supplemented, as it was not in Mr. Gaitskell's proposal, by cessation of membership of NATO. But, when it comes to what America should do, I can find almost nothing that seems to me compatible with rationality. Mr. Kahn admits that there are objective reasons for thinking that a thermonuclear war may occur, and he does not, so far as I have been able to discover, favor any U.S. policy which would make such a war less probable. He points out that conflicts analogous to the present cold war conflict are hardly ever settled amicably and he states explicty that there are not improbable circumstances in which a nuclear war would be "rational."

He concedes that we cannot tell what would happen in such a war and that the world would perhaps never recover, but he makes somewhat unconvincing attempts to persuade the reader that war would not be as catastrophic as many of us think. He believes that the genetic effects will only produce 10 million defective children, and he believes that the number of deaths in a thermonuclear war can be immensely reduced by the provision of shelters in cities, on which he urges the U.S. government to spend $30 billion. Given this amount of expenditure, he offers us somewhat pallid consolation: he says that, if the U.S. can get through the first three months and adequately decontaminate the workers, there will be a reasonable chance of survival, but he is not at all confident that these conditions will be fulfilled. He attempts to arrive at arithmetical estimates of the degree of damage which the U.S. government ought to find, what he amusingly calls, "acceptable." His limits, however, are somewhat wide and vague. He says that 200 million deaths would be "acceptable," but not 2 billion. Now and again, he surprisingly lapses into sentimentality—for example, when he says it might be right for America to fight to the last man, but not to the last woman and child. He does not pretend that a hot war would be advocated as a defense of freedom. He says that during and immediately after a thermonuclear war, "all remaining sources would be commandered and shared without owner-identity in collective misery (one might say 'disaster socialism')." He says that after such a war, "life is going to be stark, elemental, brutal, filthy and miserable."

In one place, he suggests recovery in 10,000 years; in another, he suggests recovery in 10 years. He nowhere discusses what will happen if his more optimistic prophecies come true. It is surely obvious, though Mr. Kahn does not say so, that if America persists in the attitudes that will have produced the first thermonuclear war, recovery will only lead to preparations for another. If a second thermonuclear war is to be avoided, it will have to be by the adoption of policies which might just as well be adopted now. If, on the other hand, those who agree with Mr. Kahn remain in control, thermonuclear wars will succeed each other until there is nobody left to fight them. This is a bleak and a cheerless outlook, but it is the best that Mr. Kahn can offer us even by stretching optimism to the very limits of credibility. Nowhere in this long book does he consider the possibility which would prevent a thermonulcear war by the ending of the cold war. The more or less tacit assumption upon which his whole discussion is based is that Russia will launch a surprise attack upon the U.S. at any moment when it seems likely that such an attack might lead to victory. He does not produce any evidence pointing to such a conclusion, and, in fact, as I shall argue shortly, all the evidence is to the contrary.

Major General Talenski, in an article called "The Character of Modern War" (first published in *International Affairs*, Moscow, 1960), expresses Soviet official policy in a way intended to appeal to Russian public opinion. He is quite astonishingly different from Mr. Kahn in his outlook and hopes. Fifteen thousand bombs, he estimates, would "destroy everything living and non-living in the territory of Europe, including mountains, forests and tundra." But, if mountains, forests and tundra are allowed to survive, and only the destruction of human life is aimed at, a much smaller number of bombs would suffice. He estimates that to wipe out the U.S. (excepting Alaska) from the face of the earth would require about 850 H-bombs. In more densely populated countries, a few tens of H-bombs would suffice. All these estimates are based upon statements either made by Western authorities or accepted by them. He points out that radioactive fallout will threaten not only belligerents, but all human beings; and he concludes, "not to see the danger of a nuclear rocket war is harmful, but to see and underestimate it is criminal." Assuming, as patriotism compels him to do, that the West would be more completely defeated than the East, he still holds that a war would not be justified. To justify it, he says, "would be a harmful and anti-humanitarian point of view."

Major General Talenski does not seek ways of making such awful destruction "acceptable," but, rather, looks to disarmament agreements to remove from the world the threat of thermonuclear war. "War in the military-technical sense has outlived itself as a weapon of policy." We must, he concludes, "struggle even more stubbornly and consistently for the destruction of all armaments, for the exclusion of war from the life of human society, for peace in the whole world."

I do not think that the candid reader can doubt General Talenski's sincerity or fail to see that his arguments aim at persuading Russians and Chinese. Further, I think we should all acknowledge that the West will be fortunate if the East accepts his advice, provided that the West, or rather those who have power in the West, are persuaded that peace is preferable to the results of thermonuclear war. The danger to mankind, while Russian policy remains what it is now, comes primarily not from Communist countries, but from the military authorities of the U.S. (This is perhaps a temporary situation, since Khrushchev may fall.) For American policy is doing what it can to persuade Russians that Khrushchev's hopes for peaceful coexistence are vain. We must hope that these efforts will fail, but, as things are, the hope can not be a very confident one.

To anybody not obsessed by either Communist or anti-Communist fanaticism, it must be obvious that the antagonism which has produced the cold war and the imminent danger of a hot war is not only insane and criminal, but quite simply, silly. The interests of both East and West can only be furthered by genuine and wholehearted acceptance of the principle of coexistence. Both East and West are spending vast sums on armaments, and the West, if not the East, is proposing to increase these sums indefinitely. The only "good" that either side can derive from these armaments is injury to the "enemy." Not the faintest benefit to itself is any degree possible, and with every advance in technique the disaster to be expected in a nuclear war is increased. Each side excuses itself by maintaining that the other side wants world domination by military conquest rather than by peaceful propaganda.

It is true that Russian and Chinese Communists often express the hope that, in time, the whole world will become convinced of the benefits of communism, not in the shape of Russian domination, but the ordinary process of internal politics. This hope is exactly analogous to the hope of Christian missionaries that their preaching will in time convert the whole world to Christianity. I cannot see that either of these hopes has any rational basis. There is, it is true, a fanatical opinion which is not uncommon in the West. This is the opinion that the end of Man would be a smaller evil than the universal acceptance of communism, and that, on this ground, methods of mass extermination are desirable. But if this view continues to govern U.S. policy the outlook for the world is black.

So firmly is it believed by dominant opinion in the West that Communists intend to conquer the world and will succeed if not opposed by military force, that anyone who allows himself to suggest means by which the death before the end of the present century of all members of Western countries can be avoided is regarded as a traitor. It seems that the Soviet government has become aware that Communist countries have more to fear from the hostility between East and West than from the peaceful survival of capitalist countries. There are those in the West who have realise the correlative truth that Western countries could be far happier if they lived in amity with the Communist world than they can ever be while the present hostility continues. But, unfortunately, the military authorities are able whenever they choose to cause a crisis which will prevent a relaxation of tension. They proved their power in the U-2 incident, and I fear they may give us many new proofs that they can prevent any whisper of sanity from influencing policy.

But for the destructive character of modern armaments, there is nothing new in this situation. Christianity and Islam believed for a thousand years that peaceful coexistence was impossible. At the end of a millenium of war, both sides realized that it had been a millenium of folly. Unfortunately, modern weapons have made it impossible for the human race to survive a thousand years of war. We now have to learn more quickly, or perish. Russia is learning. Will the United States learn in time? Or will Mr. Kahn and his friends put an end to the human species? No one knows.

The Imminent Danger of
Nuclear War

There are facts about the world in which we live that people would rather not know. Newspapers are loathe to disseminate these facts and Governments do their best to play down the facts or to supress them. It is a curious thing that people give their allegiance to policies but refuse to listen to description of these policies which make the assumptions on which they are based explicit.

Let us try to be impartial at looking at the nature of international conduct by the great powers today. When I do this I come to the conclusion that the standards of behavior held by nazism and fascism have become general and accepted. People are shocked by such a statement yet they support even worse things today. The world was supposed to react with horror to the doctrine of extermination. War was thought to require certain rules. Among these rules were the avoidance of torture, respect of prisoners and their "rights," and the avoidance of civilian targets. One was expected to concentrate on military objectives and not to slaughter entire civilian populations in a manner reminiscent of Genghis Khan. War was thought to have a realizable political end and although all such conflict resulted in atrocity, the scale was never extended to include entire masses of defenseless people. The Nazis exterminated millions of civilians and were felt to be more wicked than any comparable organised body of men. The bombings of Tokyo and Hamburg, each of which killed more people than the bombings of Hiroshima and Nagasaki brought something new. These cities contained civilian populations and were without particular military significance. The object of dropping napalm jelly-gasoline upon Tokyo was to so demoralise the population through extermination of great sections of it as to effect the defeat of the enemy. This was the theory of mass extermination, it was because of this sort of human behavior that the war against fascism was supposedly being fought.

Consider, therefore, what we are prepared to support today. All the great powers, East and West, have adopted a national policy of genocide. They believe in mass murder, the indiscriminate extermination of entire populations whether belligerent or not. This is the explicit consequence of national policy. It is proudly proclaimed. The military language is the common parlance of our time. We speak of overkill, kill-ratio and mega-corpse. It is because the moral corruption and cultural degeneration of our world have advanced to this degree that the governments in question not only propose this horror but have the support of their people in doing so. Each government makes victim the children of its country because of the acceptance of the Fascist belief in mass

350

> "All the great powers, East and West, have adopted a national policy of genocide. They believe in mass murder, the indiscriminate extermination of entire populations whether belligerent or not. This is the explicit consequence of national policy."

extermination. The testing of nuclear weapons condemned millions of people to death due to bone cancer, blood cancer, genetic and somatic damage. They are still dying in Hiroshima and Nagasaki. With what right do the governments poison the atmosphere which is the atmosphere of all the people's on earth? What would the governments of East and West have said if Indians and Pakistanis had poisoned the atmosphere of the planet and the lives of millions of children yet unborn in the course of their dispute over Kashmir?

The one lesson that the people in the East and in the West do not grasp is that it is not sufficient to point to the evil of others for that is often a reflection of one's own actions. How can normal men speak of mega-corpses?

I should wish people to be more aware, also, of the imminence of the annihilation they support. Rocket bases all over the planet await a moment's notice before they are to be fired. Radar cannot distinguish natural phenomena from missiles. The faintest error in judgement will result in the final catastrophe. With every day that passes this probability increases. Just as there are a certain number of accidents with airplanes and automobiles, so with missiles and radar, with human judgement and with electrical circuits, a fatal error will occur. To those who say not, there is a wealth of evidence to show. We have often been within a hair's breadth of the end. There are, after all, over 50,000 scheduled and unscheduled flights within the air space of NORAD *in every twenty-four hours*. Over 2000 originate from overseas each day. They have to be detected and identified each day. Meteorites and space vehicles fill the air. The computers now attached to radar must give reactions to such signals in micro-seconds. If a response should come from a computer, life on our planet ends. Every thirty seconds the NORAD apparatus must be rechecked. All this affects airplanes. Rockets and missiles provide even more grave difficulty. Eight hundred such bases must be coordinated. The communications system at one center equals that of a city of 30,000. How can it be sufficiently emphasised that we live from day to day and from moment to moment on the edge of total catastrophe?

Let us consider also the truth about the stockpiles of weapons of mass murder. Professor Linus Pauling has ascertained the stockpile of nuclear weapons in the possession of the United States to be 240,000 megatons as of mid-1963. The Soviet Union has approximately 80,000 megatons stockpiled. It is now possible to add 20,000 superbombs (fission-fusion-fission bombs) to American stockpiles *each year*. This is an annual addition of 400,000 megatons. What do these figures mean? It might be better to put it in the form of a parable: How many years are one million days? One hundred? Fifty? Fifteen? One million days is approximately 3,000 years. But the nuclear stockpile is three hundred thousand million tons of TNT or three hundred thousand million times the explosive power of a V-2 rocket, the most powerful conventional weapon of World War II. Mankind has come this distance in eighteen years. Small wonder that people cannot grasp or understand imaginatively what we risk and what we would inflict upon ourselves. We are in 1963 further from 1945 than we were in 1945 from the pre-human period on earth. Perhaps this perspective will allow us to realize the mad folly of risking imminently the extermination of all life on our planet because of a silly struggle for power. Were Caesar, Herod, Pharaoh, either side in the religious wars sufficiently evil in the eyes of their opponents to have justified the elimination of all subsequent human life?

Sixteen hundred and eighty-five intercontinental American bombers carry over 84,000 million tons of TNT. This load of 84 megatons is sufficient to end all life in the Soviet Union eight times over. There are also missiles of all descriptions and submarines carrying even more megatonnage. The United States can obliterate the USSR 200 times and the USSR can return the compliment 140 times.

Finally, it should be understood that if all the explosives used in the entire duration of World War II were employed *every day* beginning tommorrow, it would take *146 years* to exhaust the stockpile of nuclear weapons.

This is the great enterprise to which man has given his talent, his energy and his resources. It is to this murderous idol that governments sacrifice their populations and to which peoples give their trust and hope of security.

While this carries on, two out of every three human beings alive, live at a level below subsistence. The arms race costs *$100,000 per hour*. It is not good enough to say "Yes, but the others are wicked." All who compete in mass murder and who allow this nightmare state of affairs to exist, let alone continue, are immensely wicked. It is wickedness beyond that conceived by biblical prophets.

As citizens of the West, there are certain facts about the Cold War and its advocates which it is our duty to know. The power, for example, of the military and of large industry in the United States is ominous. The Cordiner Report of 1958 placed the value of property owned outright by the American Department of Defense at 160 billion dollars. This does not include property leased to the Department or dependent upon buildings of the Department for its value. Outright ownership of this kind has reached thirty-two million acres within the United States.

Kennedy's budget for 1962 called for seventy cents out of every one hundred spent on past wars, the Cold War and preparations for future war. Military assets are three times as great as the combined assets of United States Steel, American Telephone and Telegraph (the largest U.S. corporation), Metropolitan Life Insurance, General Motors and Standard Oil. The personnel of the Department of Defense is triple the number of all the above mentioned corporations and their subsidiaries.

> "Finally, it should be understood that if all the explosives used in the entire duration of World War II were employed every day beginning tomorrow, it would take 146 years to exhaust the stockpile of nuclear weapons."

Military power and the power of big industry are joined through the interchangeability of their personnel and the billions of dollars provided by the one and fulfilled by the other in military and quasi-military contracts. In 1960, 21 billion dollars were spent on military goods alone and this was only part of the military budget for that year. Three other corporations—General Dynamics, Lockheed and Boeing—receive over one billion dollars in such contracts in one year. General Electric and North American Aviation secure over 900 million dollars.

These contracts are conferred at the discretion of public men recently executives in the very industries receiving such contracts. Military officers who champion a weapon produced by one corporation retire to its board of directors. There are over 1000 such retired officers above the rank of major in the one hundred vast corporations which divided among them sixteen billion dollars. This list includes 261 generals and flag-rank officers. General Dynamics has on its payroll 187 retired officers, 27 generals and admirals and a former Secretary of the Army. The 16 billion dollars were secured in one year.

Subcontracts from major war contractors spread to every part of the American economy and society. The Defense Department alone hires over three and one-half million people; and four million people work directly in defense industries.

In many cities, missile production provides over fifty percent of all manufacturing jobs. In San Diego, California, it is over eighty-three percent. In eight states, one out of three jobs are *directly* in defense industry. In Los Angeles more than fifty percent of all jobs depend on defense expenditures. Finally, in the United States of America as a whole, between one quarter and one third of all economic activity hinges upon military expenditure, and it is predicted that this will soon reach fifty percent of all economic activity.

The psychological, political and economic involvement in preparations for mass murder affect every food store and petrol station proprietor, every industrial worker, every politician—in fact the entire nation.

These terrifying facts are not secret or inaccessible to people. Mr. Fred J. Cook has set them out in full detail in his book *The Warfare State*. Other writers have documented the nature of those societies involved in the arms race and the Cold War. What has to be remembered by those of us who inhabit the West, is that it is in our names that these practices occur. Technicians who have access to rockets will, in a few seconds of any given day, make a decision to exterminate man. Consider, for example, the statements of military men who, along with General Speidel and General Heusinger, speak for the West:

The American Air Force Association policy statement declared: "Freedom must bury communism or be buried by communism. Complete eradication of the Soviet system must be our national goal, our obligation to all free people, our promise of hope to all who are not free."

It is a curious hope that is being promised, since it can only be realised in heaven. The only promise the West can hope to fulfill in these terms is the promise to turn Eastern populations into corpses. The noble patriots who make this announcement omit to mention that Western populations also will be exterminated. The Air Force Association continues:

We are determined to back our words with action even at the risk of war. We seek not merely to preserve our freedoms but to extend them. Soviet aims are both evil and implacable. The people are willing to work toward, and fight for if necessary, the elimination of communism from the world scene. Let the issue be joined.

This ferocious document, which amounts to a sentence of death on the human race, does not consist of the idle vaporings of acknowledged cranks. It represents the enormous economic power of the armament industry. Let anyone with any illusions of the implications of this reflect on the statement of Admiral Arthur W. Radford, formerly Chief of Staff: "I demand total victory over the Communist system—not stalemate."

General Nathan Twining said that if it were not for politicians, he would settle the war in one afternoon by bombing Soviet Russia; and General Orvil A. Anderson has declared that he would be happy to bomb Russia: "Just give me the order to do it."

These men speak for power. Military technology and decision making are in their hands. What, then, can be done? It is said there is no use in seeking disarmament agreements with the Soviet Union because the Soviets will not agree to inspection or control along with disarmament. This is widely believed in America and is repeated continuously in the American press and by commentators like James Reston. It is stated untruly that the Soviets reject any inspection until the whole process of disarmament is complete.

The position of the Russians is as follows: If the West agrees to the *principle* of general disarmament the Russians call for internationally recruited teams to be placed in every country *before any measures* of disarmament are begun. If general disarmament were agreed to, the Soviets have stated that they would permit:

a) Thousands of United Nations inspectors on Soviet soil before any reduction of armaments is started.

b) Those inspectors could control on the spot: the disbanding of 60 percent of Russian manpower, 100 percent of the means of delivery of missiles and all other carriers.

It is vital, then, for man's survival that we cease to regard each other as devils, cease to lie about each other, cease to suppress the truth and begin to disemminate facts and work for survival of our kind while time permits.

The Myth of American Freedom

The Minority of One, May 1963

The active presence of freedom in America is vanishingly small. Words and slogans are used for long periods after they have been emptied of content by events. Those who know within themselves that to challenge their society fundamentally is a dangerous thing to do deceive themselves by clinging to such hollow slogans until they have been sufficiently corrupted to have lost interest in them. The next step for the absence of vital life is for the conceptions to be acknowledged as something desirable anyway. "National interest" is the replacement term most preferred.

I consider that there are three large developments in American society which have made talk of freedom and individual liberty empty talk which satisfies the diminished consciences of those who want to believe that they are motivated by these values at the same time that they embrace a society which despises freedom and individual liberty.

These three developments are: 1) Overt and unabashed police-state techniques; 2) the evolution of institutional life incompatible with freedom and liberty, and 3) the power struggle between two authoritarian giants, America and Russia, which has introduced the concomitant threat of annihilation for mankind. These three developments act upon and reinforce one another.

Since the end of World War II, the way to political power in the United States has been characterised by the crudest persecution of dissident opinion. The object of this persecution has been to impose upon the United States an acceptance of capitalism and of the power of large industry. To further this end, any potential critics of such a power arrangement have been hunted down and declared subversive. One of the tragic aspects of this development has been the willingness on the part of liberals to swallow the dishonest assumptions, seek to dissociate themselves from those under attack, and to allow the perpetrators to establish their power and values as beyond question. Questions have been decided to be incompatible with patriotism.

"Subversives" are those who pose such questions. They are called Communists because it was also a purpose of men who hold American power to discredit alternatives to capitalism by equating support of a foreign power with domestic dissidence.

Communists were a convenience and all who retained an independent mind were obligated to denounce communism if they were to remain free and employed. Communism, however, was an issue created as a conscious hoax. The power of the Soviet Union was real and the power-conflict with the Soviet

Union was real. Espionage, as old as nation-states, was also real. None of these facts had any bearing on the use to which they were put by cynical addicts of power. Communists had no political significance within American life. It is not clear why it is illicit for Communists to play a role in the political life of a free country.

It was soon clear, however, that Communists would be hunted, for that enabled the hunters to accuse all with whom they had politcial differences of being this new form of devil, carefully cultivated as a domestic "menace."

The Federal Bureau of Investigation is a secret political police. It has frequently fabricated evidence to frame innocent people and any who dared suggest that this had been done were themselves subjected to the same treatment. The Justice Department undertook to pay for a posse of terrified perjurers who, upon losing this terror, found official lying a lucrative way to live. American political life centered in the late forties and fifties upon the intimidation of all men of integrity prepared to criticize their country.

Investigating committees have also used the paid informer and instructed liar. Many individuals have been jailed and many thousands more deprived of livelihood. The effect of this systematic and pervasive program of intimidation has been to eliminate political alternatives from the public discourse in the United States.

Opportunist politicians such as Joseph McCarthy and Richard Nixon patterned their careers on the national pastime of inquisiting men with independent minds. The press has entirely cooperated in this. The press, like all media of communication, is controlled by large economic interests. These very economic interests have nutured the attack upon civil liberty and the "concentration camp for the mind," which charaterises the United States of America.

The Justice Department assisted with loyalty boards, subversive lists, and prosecutions of individuals for their political views. The F.B.I. persisted in fabricating evidence and even the existence of Communists to be hunted in order to continue to drain public funds.

The case of Alger Hiss illustrated the proposed fate of all foolish enough to defy; and the F.B.I. constructed a typewriter to secure a false conviction.

The atmosphere of hysteria so sedulously cultivated by the press and the government of the United States was sufficient to murder the Rosenbergs who were accused of espionage on the evidence of a perjurer. Even the law under which they were tried was substituted for the one under which they were accused because the former carried the death penalty. The Rosenbergs were incapable of having copied the documents they were said to have copied because, as Einstein pointed out, they lacked the essential training necessary to have done that of which they were accused. The peacetime death penalty showed how far the persecutors would go in the United States and helped diminish the danger of intellectual independence.

Espionage, however, was only the guise, for political views of a radical

> "The important fact is that a free society would not be one in which a political view could constitute a danger to the holder.

kind would hardly be cultivated by an intended spy. The continued object was the man who disagreed. After a time, however, the persecution of dissidents (called ferreting out Communists) became a career in itself and more and more victims were necessary to feed the inquisition and its victim-hungry administrators.

The case of Morton Sobell, illegally kidnapped, convicted on non-existent evidence, sentenced to thirty years, is one of the more obvious examples of "freedom" in the United States.

The Attorney-General's list included today many hundreds of organizations which are declared subversive. The Feinberg Law of New York requires teachers to report on the political beliefs of their colleagues. Those who are friends or associates of political dissidents are themselves subject to and in danger of overt persecution,

The system of terror which I am describing and which, I am certain, is familiar to Americans, has worked in an informal way as devastating as its more exhibitionist aspect. Private industry does not employ the politically suspect. The right to travel is a consequence of holding dependable views. A great blackmailing industry emerged with journals such as "Red Channels," destroying careers by smearing men as Communists. The important fact is that a free society would not be one in which a political view could constitute a danger to the holder. Nor could someone be "smeared." Smears betray the absence of freedom.

The result of this pervasive and systematic terror has been that Americans first respond to political discussion by seeking to attach labels to ideas, the better to dismiss them without having to consider them.

It is not possible to have such an environment for fifteen years without profound effect. Americans prefer to say that the witch hunt was a passing phase of hysteria created by nasty men such as McCarthy. On the contrary, the persecution which America has witnessed and largely embraced was created by men of power to destroy political opposition. McCarthy was an excrescence upon this fact.

The second development to which I have referred earlier is an institutional one. The nature of a large industrial society is bureaucratic and impersonal. The individual is submerged in vast collective units. Individuals who are created for such institutions are without features marking independence of mind. Adlai Stevenson said:

> Technology, while adding daily to our physical ease, throws daily another loop of fine wire around our souls.

This statement is one full of insight. It reveals that the United States is as collectivized as the Soviet Union in the sense that both societies are characteristically large and are dominated by bureaucracies. The private or public character of these institutions does not determine the extent to which people are cogs. It is technology and size which do that. Ideology is largely irrelevent.

For this important reason, the persecution of men of independent mind is not the only source of tyranny in America. The daily lives of people are incompatible with freedom. They no longer have real control over decisions which affect them and this is a fundamental fact.

Part of this second development is the nature of power itself within American political life. The corporate community constitutes a private Government. Industries are interlocked and the economic and political life of the United States cannot seriously be separated. So it is with economic and political power. The corporate community finances both political parties, provides the millions necessary for both candidates in Senatorial elections, owns and controls the media of communication and, in effect, exercises the power of decision-making. For this reason formal political democracy in the United States is largely a sham and "freedom" is a convenient myth at the disposal of faceless bureaucrats. The overwhelming political power of the corporate community is private in character only insofar as there is no public awareness of its role, let alone knowledge of its decisions or control over them. The two political parties operate within this system and the formal political institutions—the Congress and the Executive—merely serve to administrate for the corporate community. After fifteen years of persecution, systematic conditioning and the eradication of political opposition, the American public accepts national interest as defined by corporate capitalism. For these elementary reasons, the political democracy of which Americans speak is, for me, largely without serious meaning.

Intimately related to these two developments which I have sought to describe has been the power struggle between the Soviet Union and the United States—the Cold War. The elimination of dissent was achieved by identifying dissent in the popular mind with support of the "enemy," the "devil," the inconceivably wicked Russians. The nice thing about this was that it also became impossible to question the power-struggle itself. Russia was the means of ending American radicalism and the means itself was sacred. I am utterly convinced that if the conflict with the Soviet Union had never existed a different menace would have been adopted for the purposes of political persecution.

Nonetheless, the struggle for power with Soviet Russia has enabled American politicians to sanctify every oppressive act in the name of national security and to label every appeal for freedom as sympathy for the Russians.

In the course of the struggle it has become apparent that neither side is concerned about anything except dominating the other. The Russians may proclaim hostility to Capitalism and the Americans to communism. Yet the two systems, under the very pressure of their own conflict, have become remarkably alike. The bureaucratic and impersonal character of these two countries has taken them in two very similar directions! Stalin, it was true, was exceptionally cruel. Since Stalin the cruelty has diminished apace with the growth of intolerance in America.

The United States has created and supported tyrannical regimes around the world. The sole criterion for support has been subservience to American military needs and willingness to allow the resources and peoples of the respective countries to be exploited by American industry. This pattern in America had made the question of freedom directly relevant to the unlikely hope of human survival. Unless it becomes possible not only to question in isolation the holders of American power, but to mobilize effective political oppositon to their power and their policy, survival is in doubt.

If friendship with the Soviet Union is treasonable, if the power of the military-industrial complex is unchallenged, if the insane struggle between the Soviet Union and the United States is not halted, then the absence of freedom will lead to the end of life on our planet.

I believe that until a radical analysis of this kind is made by Americans and acted upon, regardless of the consequences, we must all live through the sufferance of semiliterate paranoids with their fingers on buttons.

War and Atrocity in Vietnam

The war in Vietnam is eighteen years old. It began as a broad movement of resistance to the French under the leadership of Ho Chi Minh, a Communist. The French fought with ferocity against an unarmed peasantry. Using guerilla tactics, the Vietnamese drove the French out of the North of Vietnam and finally defeated them in the battle of Dien Bien Phu. The negotiations at Geneva led to the establishment of an international Commission, intended to stablize peace and watch over any attempt at foreign intervention.

Before developing what I wish to say about this subject, I should like to make clear that the facts in this article are taken from daily papers and similar sources. Many are taken from bulletins of committees concerned with Vietnam. Some are from reports of the South Vietnam Liberation Red Cross and others from a very interesting book by Wilfred G. Burchett called *The Fugitive War*. Many of the facts have passed unscathed through the crucible of American denial. Many of them have been accepted even by the American authorities. All of them, I have good reason to believe, are incontrovertible.

It is important to realize that, since the French were defeated finally at Dien Bien Phu in 1954, the war has been conducted surreptitiously under American direction. A substantial number of American forces began to be committed thereafter the French withdrawal and the Geneva talks. One of the most important aspects of this war has been that the United States pretended for many years that no such war was taking place and that the war which was not taking place was not being conducted by Americans. I have experienced some frustration in attempting to bring to light the fact that the war has been taking place and that Americans have been deeply involved in its conduct. At first, Western newspapers and even persons connected with the peace movement in the West held that there was no evidence of American direction of this war. The *New York Times* stated this several times. Finally, in the course of the controversy, it was allowed that American participation was solely in an advisory capacity. When it was alleged that chemicals were being employed by the United States forces in Vietnam, it was first denied and then alleged that the chemicals employed were used against American advice and wishes. It was then admitted that they were used under the direction of the United States, but it was said that chemicals were harmless to human beings and were intended solely for the purpose of clearing vegetation and foliage.

I brought to public attention impressive and documented evidence concerning the use of additional chemicals and asked for international investigation of these allegations and the evidence adduced to support them. I was informed by various Western newspapers that no observers had found harmful results through the use of these chemicals and that no condemnatory comment had been made by the international Control Commission.

It is odd that this is advanced on behalf of that Commission. The function of the Commission was to regulate and prevent intervention from the outside. The failure of this International Commission to make known its observations of American participation was in violation of its mandate and did not inspire confidence in its ability to detect chemicals where it failed adequately to detect armed forces, aircraft, military supplies and a full-scale war. I shall wish to return to these more contemporary aspects of the war in Vietnam. It is sufficient here to note that the extraordinary war which has been raging in Vietnam managed to elude the juridical commitments of the Geneva agreements. It encompassed repression and extermination without great hindrance on the part of the Control Commission set up at Geneva, escaped for some time the notice of the Western press and enjoyed restrained consideration by those nominally committed to opposition to the Cold War, small wars and wars of annihilation.

The history of French and Vietnamese relations, particularly in the North, is much the same as that of the United States and South Vietnam. At the time of the conclusion of the Second World War, a movement of rebellion began, acquired new strength and culminated in the Geneva decisions. Vietnam was to be partitioned for an interim period, with the North under the control of the forces of Ho Chi Minh, and the South under the control of pro-Western groups. It was agreed that there would be a general election throughout Vietnam, out of which unification and neutralization were expected to come. The Geneva Conferences of 1954 were designed to bring neutralization to all of Indo-China. The United States, though not a signatory to these agreements accepted them in name and professed them to be the basis of American policy in Indo-China.

In fact, the United States quickly decided that it was impossible to permit a general election, in view of what it considered to be "the disturbed state of the country." The United States began to intevene actively with arms, money and men and established in power a ruling oligarchy subservient to American interests. This direct foreign intervention destroyed the purpose of the Geneva agreements and was a test for the International Control Commission. Its failure to resist this violation steadfastly prepared the way for violence, the intrusion of the Cold War and the present threat to the peace of the world in Southeast Asia.

John Foster Dulles had urged the use of nuclear weapons at Dien Bien Phu. His desire to encompass the area in the Cold War led to the formation of the Southeast Asia Treaty Organization. The purpose of this body was to forestall neutrality and to forge a military alliance of anti-Communists. The United States favored Ngo Dinh Diem, a rich refugee from North Vietnam. He and his family, together with the Nhu family, represented a group of landowners and the Catholic hierarchy in Vietnam—a small, closely-knit circle. The Diem family installed officers and relatives in various provinces, who administered them virtually as private estates. Various religious sects and cults in Vietnam were subdued because they failed to prove sufficiently loyal to the Diem regime. The Diem and Nhu families were dependent upon American backing for their power. American policy aimed at keeping South Vietnam in the anti-Communist camp and at opposing all groups not subservient to that purpose. The "Vietcong"[1] were to be eradicated, despite the fact that they were neutralist. Diem's regime was one of terror and persecution. Ghastly tortures were inflicted upon the peasants. It is instructive that it has been possible for 350,000 people to be placed in camps as political prisoners and for the greater part of the rural population to be uprooted and put in cages without vigorous protest taking place. Part of the responsibility for this default lies with the supression of facts which, until the last two years, characterised Western reports about Vietnam. Part of the fault lies with the silence of peace groups, frightened to appear to be seen supporting "the Communist side" of things.

One case is related in *The Furtive War*. It is that of a young girl:

"One day," she says, "I came home and there two security agents waiting for me. I was taken to the town of Faifo and for months on end I was tortured very badly...Once I recovered consciousness and found I was stark naked, blood oozing from wounds all over my body. There were others in the cell. I heard a woman moaning, and in the half dark saw a woman in a pool of blood. She had been beaten into having a miscarriage. Then I made out an old man. An eye had been gouged out and he was dying. Alongside him was a thirteen-or-fourteen-year-old boy, also dead; a little further away, another dead youth with his head split open. They had thrown me there, hoping the sight of this would break me down."

Finally, she was covertly conveyed to North Vietnam. This story was subsequently confirmed by neutral enquirers. It is typical of many among the 350,000 political prisoners.

The vast majority of the peasants support the guerillas. It is estimated that 160,000 have died and as many as 700,000 have been maimed. In order to combat the support of the population, Diem and the Americans instituted what were called "strategic hamlets," into which the inhabitants of rural areas and existing villages were, in cruel circumstances, moved at a moments notice. "Strategic hamlets" were, in reality, prisons. Those who had been forcibly brought into them were unable to get out. These hamlets were surrounded by spikes, moats and barbed wire and were patrolled by guards with dogs. They have all the character of concentration camps. The *Observer* estimated that sixty-five percent of the rural population, or over seven million people, were inside these "hamlets" by mid-1963. Their establishment was the result of a decision on the part of the United States, publically set out by W.W. Rostow, an adviser of the State Department. He suggested that Vietnam should be used as an experimental area for the development of anti-guerilla techniques and weapons by the American forces.

The rural population was stuffed into the "strategic hamlets" so that they would be shut off from the guerilla forces, who depended for their food and manpower upon them. I wrote letters to the *Washington Post* and the *New York Times* in 1963 in which I sought to set out the full nature of this war, which I designated as a war of annihilation and atrocity. The *New York Times* vigorously denounced me for making such a charge.

The State Department denied that chemicals were used in Vietnam and the *New York Times* admitted editorially that weedkillers were used, but stated that napalm was not used by Americans but only by Vietnamese governmental forces. Madame Nhu stated: "If they don't like our chemicals why don't they get out of our jungles?" The *New York Times* failed to remember its own reports of 19 June 1962, which refer to the destruction of nearly 1400 villages by government forces. Napalm and chemicals were used in the course of this devastation. My charge of atrocity was based upon the ruthless use of chemicals and jelly-gasoline, the devastation of civilian populations, and the use of concentration camps.

In addition to uprooting the population and establishing the hamlets, the United States sent special helicopters which could fire small rockets and ammunition in excess of that used by any aircraft during the Second World War. The Americans, as mentioned earlier, professed that their soldiers and airmen in Vietnam were only there in an advisory capacity and were not responsible for Diem's doings. At the same time, they took great pains to conceal from the world the sort of things that were being done. The *New York Times*, in its editorial comments, illustrates this attempt.

In the course of the controversy in the pages of the *Observer*, I sought to bring to the attention of people facts which I had before me in the form of photographs and documents which gave particulars of villages, dates, individuals and specific chemicals, and use of toxic chemicals in Vietnam by American forces. I have evidence that over 1000 people were caused severe illness, characterised by vomiting, bleeding, paralysis and loss of sight and consciousness. Other evidence concerned the destruction of fruit trees, vegetables, cattle and domestic animals. Further evidence specified the use of toxic gas on densely populated areas. This evidence was provided by the South Vietnam Liberation Red Cross and in part by the Foreign Minister of North Vietnam. It has been offered to any international agency for impartial consideration. The replies to my setting out of this evidence were indicative of Western attitudes towards this war. Dennis Bloodworth, the Far Eastern Correspondent of the *Observer*, blandly stated that I was "apparently referring to the defoliation campaign known as 'Operation Ranchland'" and said that the weedkillers were popularly known in America and had been used widely without causing harm to animals or to humans. He contended that a propaganda campaign was being employed in which it was falsely stated that these chemicals had ill effects and suggested that I was assisting in a Communist propaganda campaign.

Let us now consider some of the statements that have appeared in the American and British press over the past two years. These statements will help indicate the nature of the war and the validity of the editorial protests which have peppered my appeals about the situation in Vietnam. With respect to the contention that Americans served only as advisers, it is worth looking at the

New York Times of 17 March 1962. It was stated that, after two Vietnamese pilots pulled out of formation and launched a full attack on Diem's palace, Americans were designated to accompany every Vietnamese pilot on a mission. The *Saturday Evening Post* of 23 March 1963 published a long report in which it contradicted the *New York Times'* statement that uniformed Americans were "solely advisers and trainers." The *Post's* report said: "Virtually all the fighting is done by U.S. troops." Richard Hughes in the *Sunday Times* of 13 January 1963, speaks of the "Washington fiction that no United States troops are involved in combat and that United States officers and trainers are on the scene merely to "advise, support and assist." The Americans are now operating more than 200 helicopters and scores of reconnaissance and troop transport planes in the combat areas. Probably half of all bombing and strafing missions of the South Vietnam Air Force are undertaken by Americans serving as pilots and co-pilots." It is illustrative, as well of the nature of this war to quote the *New York Times* and other American papers for the period 1962 to 1963. On 7 June 1962, the *New York Times* stated:

> Tactical air support is used extensively. It is difficult to ascertain whether the people who are being killed by napalm and fragmentation bombs are guerillas or merely farmers.

On 16 June 1962, the *New York Times* had stated:

> Though the government makes some effort to re-educate the captured guerillas, many are shot.

The *New York Times* had stated on 5 June 1962:

> Seven leprosy clinics were wiped out by mistake in bombing raids last fall.

The *Chicago Daily News* is more direct in its statement of 18 January 1963:

> The Government regards Vietcong hospitals as fair targets for ground or air attack. If Vietnamese commanders order an airstrike on a medical center, the planes bomb and strafe it, even when Americans are along as advisers or instructors. When asked if Americans officially condone these attacks, a U.S. military spokesman said: "There has not been a definite policy ruling for Vietnam." Planes of the Vietnamese Air Force are frequently piloted by Americans."

The *New York Times* which, editorially, overlooks its news reports (as when it reported the razing of 60 percent of the villages of the country) might have been advised to listen to the Voice of America on 6 January 1963. It was stated that during the year 1962 the *American* Air Force carried out 50,000 attacks on villages and upon virtually all the peasant population outside of the strategic hamlets. This report was confirmed by the United States Defense Department. Senator Michael Mansfield of Montana stated that there were American troops in every fighting action in Vietnam. Senator Mansfield referred to the action as "America's secret war." Areas in which heavy guerilla activity was reported were denuded of population and then virtually obliterated.

The *New York Times* managed to say on 21 October 1962:

> Americans and Vietnamese march together, fight together and die together, and it is hard to get much more involved than that.

The *New York Herald Tribune* of 23 November 1962 stated:

> The United States is deeply involved in the biggest secret war in its history. Never have so many U.S. military men been involved in a combat area without any formal program to inform the public about what is happening. It is a war fought without official public reports or with reports on the number of troops involved or the amount of money and equipment being poured in.

This war in which seven million people have been placed in internment camps, 160,000 killed, 700,000 tortured, 350,000 imprisoned—requiring 16,000 camps—was described by *The Nation* of 19 January 1963:

> It is a dirty, cruel war. As dirty and as cruel as the war waged by the French forces in Algeria, which so shocked the American conscience.

The Nation continued:

> The truth is that the United States Army some 10,000 miles from home, is fighting to bolster up an open and brutal dictatorship in an undeclared war that has never received the constitutional sanction of the United States Congress.

The concealment to which I referred has included the effects of what were euphemistically called "weedkillers." Dennis Bloodworth described how in April, 1963, South Vietnamese officials "rubbed defoliants on their hands and arms in the presence of foreign correspondents who had selected the canisters from which it should be drawn—and in one case drank some of it" (*Observer* 9 Febuary 1964).

It is interesting to examine these weedkillers and their effects. The *Times* of 16 May 1963, disclosed the death by pesticide of fifty-eight species and described fifty pesticides in widespread use as responsible for "acute poisoning" of animals and human beings. President Kennedy found it necessary to halt their use and to begin a formal investigation. It was stated in the United States that chemicals used there for purposes of defoliation and the killing of weeds resulted in California in 1,100 cases of serious illness and 150 deaths (*Reuter*, 16 May 1963). Dr. Jerome Weisner, the Chief Science Advisor to President Kennedy, designated unregulated use of these weedkillers as potentially "more dangerous than radioactive fallout." The actual use of those weedkillers has killed and caused serious illness in Britain, the United States and Scandinavia.

Napalm is a chemical which burns unremittingly and cannot be extinguished. The victims suppurate before terrified observers. The object of this weapon is to create hysteria and panic, as well·as annihilate. This weapon has been used on over 1400 villages. The United States has spent one million dollars daily on the war. The *Observer* of 8 September 1963 estimates that there has been an average number of 4000 casualties monthly. The Central Intelligence Agency has spent an estimated sum monthly of 250,000 dollars on private armies, espionage and intrigue, according to *The Times* of 10 September 1963.

This war was largely conducted under the nominal rule of Diem. Diem grew more and more reckless and was at last murdered in a coup which most agreed was engineered by the United States, after a number of eminent Buddhist priests had burned themselves to death. It is noteworthy that the military oligarchy which suceeded Diem complained that he was secretly attempting to negotiate with the North, but not, noticeably, that his tyranny was unpalatable to the population. The death of Diem brought no amelioration. He had been, in fact, only the tool of the Americans and the sole change brought by his death was that the Americans had open responsibility for whatever they had formerly blamed on Diem and for what was done under his regime.

The National Liberation front was formed on 20 December 1960, unifying the various elements of revolt against American domination.[8] By 1961, 10,000 Diem troops had deserted and joined the guerillas with their arms. Let us consider again the treatment accorded to this popular revolt. Homer Bigart described in the *New York Times* of January 30, March 27, March 29, April 1, April 4, April 20, May 10, June 24 and July 25, all in 1962, the following program:

> The rounding up of the entire rural population in strategic hamlets, the burning of all abandoned villages with the grain and possessions of the inhabitants and the "locking" of strategic villages behind barbed wire.

It is clear that the majority of the inhabitants wish their country to be neutral. This the American Government cannot tolerate. The euphemisms used for the military operations which have belatedly been acknowledged to be the full responsibility of the United States are instructive. "Operation Sunrise," "Pacification of the West" and "Morning Star" resulted, in the area attacked, in the destruction of all villages, fields, and crops. In 1962 alone, according to General Paul D. Hawkins, 30,000 peasants were killed. The *Christian Science Monitor* described the process on 8 March 1963:

> Since the army finds sullen villagers and does not know which are pro-Communist and which are merely dissatisfied with Saigon, and since the army must do its job, it shoots anyone seen running or looking dangerous. It often shoots wrong peasants. They are in the records of battle listed as Communists. Anyone killed is automatically a Vietcong.

On 25 January 1963 *Life* had photos of napalm bombings with the following caption: "Swooping down low across enemy infested land U.S. pilot instructors watch Vietnamese napalm strike. The object of the fire bombing is to sear all foliage and to flush the enemy into the open."

The *New York Times* also reported that U.S. advisors made a tally of guerilla corpses after each battle to make sure that Diem's troops were using American equipment to maximum advantage, so that they could display a good "bag" (*Militant*, 15 April 1963). In light of the evidence it is strange to find the *New York Times* saying on 8 April 1963:

> Napalm has been used by the South Vietnam Air Force and has certainly killed innocent people, as other weapons have done in all wars. *American* (my emphasis) advisors have opposed its employment on both moral and practical grounds against all except clearly defined military targets.

The definition appears to include sixty percent of the villages, hospitals and clinics and all peasants who run or look dangerous. This editorial reply contradicts the *New York Times'* own news reports about American use and insistence upon the use of napalm and other weapons on non-military areas.

Many people in the Pentagon are urging that the war should be extended to an invasion of North Vietnam. President Johnson has announced that those countries which are directing and supplying the (so-called) Communist guerillas in South Vietnam are playing a deeply dangerous game. A map in the *New York Times* of 1 April 1962, shows the forces of the Liberation Front in the far South around Saigon, and nowhere near the borders of Laos or North Vietnam. Both British and American reporters have stated that primitive guerilla weapons have been used by the "Vietcong," in addition to those plentiful supplies captured from the forces of the nominal government of South Vietnam. The London *Times* of February 24 has stated that it is now considered doubtful whether the Government of South Vietnam has any will to win the war. The *Observer* of 1 March 1964, quoted an American official as stating that the trouble lay in the fact that, while the United States wished to extend the war, the Vietnamese only wanted to end the war

The situation which faces those who have conducted this war is grave. Should the United States retire and allow victory to the NLF? Should America engage in naked war of conquest, which will clearly be seen as such, and attempt to establish again a Government dependent entirely upon alien armed force? This "enemy" controls nearly 70 percent of South Vietnam. The majority of the NLF was described as non-Communist by the former Premier Tran Van Huu in Paris, as reported in the *Observer*. The "Vietcong" official policy asks for a neutral and disengaged South Vietnam. Despite all the attempts on the part of the Western press to describe this war as one in which a helpless democratic people is under ruthless attack from an aggressive Communist neighbor, it is evident that the NLF is a popular front which has fought an appalling tyranny in South Vietnam and has been opposed by the United States at an incalculable cost to the population. Why is this non-Communist, neutralist, popular front so ruthlessly opposed? Even the Communist North has declared through Ho Chi Minh, that it wished to be unified with the South on terms of neutrality in the Cold War and independence of Russia, China and the West (*The Times* 5 November 1963).

The policy of the United States which has led to the prospect of an American invasion of North Vietnam will likely bring on Chinese involvement, with war with China as the result. The Soviet Union would then be drawn in. There are few parallels with the war in Vietnam. It has lasted nearly two decades; two Western industrial powers of overwhelming might have fought peasant guerillas in a manner reminiscent of the Japanese during the Second World War. Everything short of nuclear weapons has been employed. Atrocity has characterised the conduct of the war throughout its history. The Western press has hesitatingly discovered some of the facts about this war during the last two years. The Western peace movement has been conspicuously silent or restrained in its setting out of the truth about the war. The war has had no purpose. Its extension will bring direct conflict between the Cold War powers, with the possible destruction of mankind as the culmination of this folly. The tragedy in Vietnam indicates the extent to which it is possible to hide or disguise terrible crimes and it is time that people in the West raised their voices for an end to the bloodshed.

Footnotes

---

1. "Vietcong." The United States has sought to slur the guerilla movement by naming it the "Vietcong." "Vietcong" means "Vietnamese Commies." No group in South Vietnam refers to itself by that abbreviated name. Those who chose that name for the guerillas ignored something very important. They relied on the fact that in the USA the term "Communist" is enough to alarm the public and smear any movement, and never realized until too late what favorable connotations "Communist" has elsewhere. The U.S. has, by its own intended slander, reinforced the good image Communists have had in Southeast Asia through associating communism with movements for national liberation, and movements of the people for independence and social justice. It is ironic that when the U.S. realized its grave blunder, it sought to rectify the situation by renaming the liberators. As reported in the *New York Times* on 5 June 1962 the United States Information Agency sponsored a contest "for a new name for the Vietcong guerillas," admitting that it didn't think "communist is the type of name to inspire hatred among the country's illiterate masses." It offered a cash prize for a "colloquial peasant term implying disgust or ridicule." In South Vietnam, the only names which meet the test are "French" and "American."

2. National Liberation Front. In this common front, all those forces combined who had suffered and decided on armed self-defense. It constitutes an organization of many segments of the population. Communist and non-Communist alike were victims of Diem's regime; they united in self-defense. Much of the leadership comes from intellectuals, who felt the lack of freedom most severely; doctors, lawyers, and

university professors play prominent roles in the committees of the National Liberation Front. Many religious leaders were instrumental in the organizing of the Front. They represent the majority (Buddhists) and the minorities (some Roman Catholics and many ethnic minorities whose unique ways of life were intolerable to the bigot, Ngo Dinh Diem) of South Vietnam's worshippers. Small businessmen and even progressive landlords joined peasant farmers, fishermen, and workers to help form the Front against the common enemy and oppressor.

Free World Barbarism

A distressing aspect of world politics is the extent to which liberals and even Socialists have accepted the basic assumptions of the large and powerful forces behind the Cold War. The role of the United States as a perpetual intruder in the international affairs of other nations is taken as sacred. The right of the United States to interfere in countries, if the social and political policies of those countries are incompatible with private economic power, is happily accepted.

Instead of questioning how private, corporate capitalism and its overseas commitments have become identified with American national interests liberals and many socialists accept this sinister sleight of hand. It is the sleight of hand which has successfully eliminated the Left in American politics. The investments in the Congo are sacred. If they are threatened, then "freedom" is proclaimed to be in danger, and the U.S. government and its military arm are brought to bear. If a national uprising takes place in Vietnam, American intervention is called "response to external aggression"—as if America had the right to treat a country on the borders of China as a part of her national territory.

Dissent calls itself a quarterly of Socialist opinion. In the summer 1964 issue there are several statements in its editorial, "Last Chance in Vietnam," which are odd:

> Even U.S. military men no longer say the war in South Vietnam can be won. The question now is how to minimise losses....But if continuing the present policy means a hopeless attrition of the Vietnamese people, it must be stressed that simply for the U.S. to pull out of the country would mean something quite as inhuman. For it would then be a matter of months, at most, before the country was completely under Communist control and there would almost certainly follow a slaughter in the South of all those...who have fought against the Communists. To abandon these people now, after years and years of bitter civil war, would be an act of callousness.

This statement sums up the ignorance and confusion of many well-meaning Americans who choose not to know the true role of the United States in world affairs or the true facts about conflicts such as that in Vietnam. I am certain that until Americans on the Left challenge the right of the United

> "The right of the United States to interfere in countries, if the social and political policies of those countries are incompatible with private economic power, is happily accepted."

States to suppress national revolts, to overthrow governments and to equate sordid economic exploitation with national interest or the "defense of freedom," Goldwater and his fellows will reign, in effect if not in name. If, for example, it is thought legitimate to wage full-scale war against Vietnamese guerillas, then it is, indeed, half-hearted to stop at the seventeenth parallel—or the Chinese border.

It is not the tactic of a world army for counter-revolution which should be disputed by the American Left; it is the policy itself which should be challenged. If the usurpation of power in America by the military and the large industrialists is credited with national or democratic aims, then both American democracy and world peace are sacrificed by default.

Dissent is tragically wrong about Vietnam. I know of few wars fought more cruelly or more destructively, or with a greater display of naked cynicism, than the war waged by the United States against the peasant population of South Vietnam. It is a war which epitomises the indifference to individual freedom, national sovereignty and popular well-being—which is so characteristic of the world policy of the military and industrial groups controlling the United States.

My files contain material on the war in Vietnam which tells of horrible inhumanities. It is important to set it before Americans. An examination of the facts exposes several myths: 1) the National Liberation Front is a Communist organization; 2) the United States is defending the freedom and well-being of the populace; 3) the National Liberation Front is controlled from outside the country; 4) the United States is merely advising and assisting an indigenous government which is responsive to the people of South Vietnam; 5) the United States' calculated attacks on North Vietnam had been provoked by that country.

The Central Intelligence Agency acts as if it were an independent government and on many occasions it has called the tune in South Vietnam. There is not very much to choose between the Central Intelligence Agency and the more polished diplomats who proclaim their love of freedom in Washington and at the United Nations. I have in mind President Johnson and Ambassador Stevenson. These people are responsible for the tragedy in Vietnam.

Much of my data comes from a publication, *Sword of Free Vietnam*, which is the official organ of the Democratic Party of Vietnam, a virulently anti-Communist group composed of former officials and sympathisers of the South Vietnamese governments prior to that of the late Diem. The motto of this party (which I shall refer to hereafter as DPV) is "for the defeat of Communism in the interests of Free Men EVERYWHERE." Much of the data is incomplete as it was compiled up to late 1963. The scope of the tragedies is broader than partial figures can suggest. The accounts of brutality and suffering are conservative.

Sword of Free Vietnam quoted General Paul D. Harkins, Chief of U.S. military operations in Vietnam, as stating that in 1962 alone 40,000 Vietnamese were killed. A White Paper of the DPV, for 1963, put the number of dead by late 1962 at 100,000. By mid-1962 over 5,000,000 people had been put in camps designated by the DPV White Paper as "concentration camps" and so described in the report quoting the White Paper in the *Los Angeles Times* of 19 October 1962. The Student Peace Union Bulletin for April 1963 stated that by late 1962 as many as 45,000 students alone were kept in South Vietnam's concentration camps. The number of people interned by 1963 on Paulo-Condore Island was 300,000. The DPV White Paper placed the number of *anti-communist* nationalists held in internment camps at 100,000. Paulo-Condore Island and other camps for anti-Communist prisoners indicate the vast extent of oppression in South Vietnam.

The leader of the Buddhists in the National Liberation Front is the Venerable Thich Thien Hao. His estimates concerning the results of the war are: 160,000 dead by mid-1963; 700,000 tortured and maimed; 400,000 imprisoned; 31,000 raped; 3000 disembowelled with livers cut out while alive; 4000 burned alive; 1000 temples destroyed; 46 villages attacked with poisonous chemicals; 16,000 camps existing or under construction. By mid-1962 over half of South Vietnam's rural population was held in these "strategic hamlets" and by mid-1963 their number had risen to over 7,000,000. These camps are distinguished by spikes, moats, machine gun turrets, patrols and forced labour. The appelation "concentration camp" given by the DPV White Paper seems just. The DPV report for September 1963 has a particularly sobering fact: 40 percent of "enemy casualties" claimed by the government are those of guerrillas and 60 percent are those of peasants not involved in the military struggle.

It is revealing that by mid-1963 the secret police numbered 300,000. So huge an army of oppressors suggests the suffering which has been inflicted and if the excesses of each agent on each individual occasion were collated, we should have an adequate idea of the kind of "freedom" upheld by the United States in Vietnam.

The U.S. Government embarked on the programme of "strategic villages" under the Staley-Taylor plan. The declared intention was to separate guerrillas from the peasantry, depriving them of food, shelter and recruits. The DPV report for September 1963 also gave an account of life in the "strategic hamlet":

Strategic hamlets mean forced labour under 300,000 secret police. The program is planned for fifteen million people. It is the only conflict on record in which every means is employed to destroy one's own people. (It is)...more severe and brutal than all the French colonial period. (It included)...series of barbaric attacks on unarmed peasant villages with American arms and assistance...Three hundred thousand secret police committed numerous atrocities...Farm land and food sources (are) destroyed."

Time magazine of 17 May 1963 was quoted in *Sword of Vietnam* for July 1963:

Already 8,000,000 villagers—59 percent of South Vietnam's population—are living in the 6,000 hamlets so far completed. The basic elements of the government's battle plan is to resettle almost the entire rural population in 12,000 "strategic hamlets" with bamboo fences, barbed wire and armed militiamen.

A DPV report was quoted in a letter to the *Dallas Morning News* of 1 January 1963, in an appalling account of "resettlement":

Supposedly the purpose of the fortified villages is to keep the Vietcong out. But barbed wire denies entrance and exit. Vietnamese farmers are forced at gunpoint into these virtual concentration camps. Their homes, possessions and crops are burned....In the province of Kien-Tuong, seven villagers were led to the town square. Their stomachs were slashed, their livers extracted and put on display. These victims were women and children. In another village, a dozen mothers were decapitated before the eyes of compatriots. In still another village, expectant mothers were invited to the square by Government forces to be honoured. Their stomachs were ripped and unborn babies removed...

On 18 October 1962 DPV submitted a report to the International Control Commission. It specified among its complaints "decapitations, eviscerations and public displays of murdered women and children...685,000 people have been maimed by firearms or torture." These accounts and these data convey what Tran Van Tung, the leader of the DPV, felt when he stated during an interview on CBS, reported in the DPV Bulletin for September 1963:

It is certainly an ironic way to protect the peasant masses from communism—to herd them behind wire walls under police control to subject them to intensive indoctrination, to burn their villages. Poor as the Vietnamese are, they are not domestic animals.

The Federation of American Scientists quoted Defense Department sources on the subject of chemical and biological warfare. It concluded that chemical poisons are used by the United States in South Vietnam and that South Vietnam has been used as a proving ground for chemical and biological warfare.

The United States Government admits that defoliants and other chemicals have been used extensively and that they have caused the destruction of fruit trees, vegetables, cattle and domestic animals. The South Vietnam Liberation Red Cross has offered evidence to any international investigatory body showing that over 1000 people were caused severe illness accompanied by vomiting, bleeding, paralysis and loss of sight and consciousness. Other more deadly chemicals cited by the Liberation Red Cross are: white arsenic, arsenite sodium and aresenite calcium, lead manganese arsenates, DNP and DNC (which inflame and eat into human flesh), and calcic cyanamide (which caused leaves, flowers and fruit to fall, killed big cattle and seriously affected thousands of people). These chemicals were sprayed over densely populated areas of considerable size. Ma Thi Chu, representing the Vietnam Woman's Union and the National Liberation Front, told last year's World Congress of Women:

> During the period from January to March (1963), when chemicals were used against 46 villages, 20,000 people were affected, many of them women, children and old people. I have been on the spot. I have seen children with swollen faces and bodies covered with burns. I have met women blinded or suffering from sanguinolent diarrhoea. Many of them died afterwards. I have seen the luxuriant vegetation of the Mekong Delta devastated by chemicals. Our enemies have thus attacked all life, human, animal and vegetable.

The Baltimore Sun on 21 March 1964 carried an Associated Press dispatch from Saigon reporting calmly:

> We supply a phosphorous explosive fired from artillery and from fighter bombers which erupts in a white cloud, burning everything it touches.

I am reminded of the argument of the eminent Nazi that he did not kill a single Jew; he provided the lorries. On 22 March 1963, the *Washington Star* carried an Associated Press report which said, "the spectacle of children half-alive with napalm burns across their bodies was revolting to both Vietnamese and Americans." When U.S. journals brag of military exploits in Vietnam, it defies human imagination to visualise the horror involved. When, for example, the Voice of America transmitted a U.S. Defense Department report (6 January 1963) declaring that in 1962 alone the U.S. Air Force carried out 50,000 attacks on virtually the entire rural population outside of "strategic hamlets," how much suffering, destruction and brutality corresponded to these familiar words of war?

When the *Saturday Evening Post* declaims "virtually all of the fighting is done by U.S. troops," it becomes clear who bears the responsibility for the indiscriminate murder, arson and destruction inflicted on this devastated country. The *New York Times* unwittingly reports, on occasion, what it is at pains editorially to deny:

> Many of the "enemy" dead reported by the government to have been shot were ordinary peasants shot down because they fled from villages as troops entered. It is possible that some were Vietcong sympathizers, but others were running away because they did not want to be rounded up for military conscription or forced labour. (25 July 1962.)

Nguyen Thai Binh, an anti-Communist leader of DPV, cried out like Job:

> The people cannot follow the strange logic which decrees that they should be shot or imprisoned in the name of freedom. Offered the very finest facilities for forced labour, they rebel; installed in the newest concentra-

tion camps, they protest. Showered with napalm bombs, they are so ungrateful as to think in terms of a new government. The charred bodies of innocent women, children and peasants, lying in their fields; the bullet riddled corpses of Buddhist demonstrators....this is the South Vietnam of today.

In spite of the slaughter of their children, the peasants, incredible as it may seem, still dislike the Americans...These almost unbelievable atrocities have been committed by troops under American authority, an authority chosen by more than half the voters of America. Those who voted otherwise were, for the most part, demanding even harsher measures. In the name of freedom pregnant women were ripped open, and the electorate did not rebel. Every American who voted Republican or Democrat shares the guilt of these sanguinary deeds. America, the self-proclaimed champion of freedom to torture and kill women and children for the crime of wishing to go on living in their homes. Is it surprising that American proclamations are looked on coldly?

It is sometimes stated by U.S. authorities that the war in Vietnam is used as an opportunity to test weapons, men and anti-guerilla methods. The American Federation of Scientists' report shows this. The U.S. military did not hesitate to admit this. They often express their enthusiasm to the press. Reports appeared in *Look* magazine of 23 December 1963 and circulated throughout the American press:

The Army tested small-calibre ammunition as long ago as the 1920s but it was not until the recent combat experience in Vietnam that it really sat up and took notice. About 1000 AR-15s were sent out by the hush-hush Advanced Research Projects Agency in the Defense Department. A report has been issued marked Secret because of the gory pictures in it. The story of what happens to Vietcong guerrillas who get hit with the AR-15 is being kept under heavy wraps. But, aware that the enemy already knows what the AR-15 does, you can find an occasional returnee who will tell you what he saw:

"When I left out there it was *the* rifle. The effect is fantastic. I saw one guy hit in the arm. It spun him around and blew the arm right off. One got hit in the back and it blew his heart literally out of his body. A man hit in the buttocks lived for five minutes. All others died instantly. His wound would have been superficial with other bullets. The fellow had his head blown clean off—only the stump of the neck left."

The article is accompanied by a photograph of a five year old child with his arm shattered and in tatters. What words are appropriate for such barbarism of which the military are proud?

The National Liberation Front was founded in December 1960. It has a thirty-one member Central Committee headed by a non-Communist lawyer. Represented on the Central Committee are leading Buddhist priests, Catholic priests, Protestant clergy, small businessmen, professional groups and three anti-government parties. Few will challenge the estimate made in a report of the DPV in July 1963 that "seventy-five percent of the people in varying degrees, support the rebels who dominate ninety percent of the land." Many sources, including American sources, claim a higher proportion of rebel support. It is clear that the rebels of South Vietnam speak for the people of that country. Any other view is insupportable. Even General Paul D. Harkins stated, "The guerillas are not being reinforced or supplied systematically from North Vietnam, China or anyplace else. They depend for weapons primarily on whatever they can capture." (*Washington Post*, 6 March 1963 and *Free World Colussus* by David Horowitz.) On 10 December 1962, *Newsweek* quoted a U.S. captain as saying:

All the Communists (in South Vietnam) have is their dedication. If I was (sic) in their shoes, I'd be pretty sore at Hanoi for letting me down.

David Halberstam reported in the *New York Times* of 6 March 1964: "No capture of North Vietnamese in the South has come to light." These statements refute the official U.S. posture and also indicate the odds against which the rebels have fought. In assessing the information about this atrocious war it is instructive to note the coincidence of reports from the National Liberation Front and the Democratic Party of Vietnam, despite the political opposition between them. The reports in Western newspapers have appeared, it would seem, in spite of U.S. efforts to hide the true nature of the war. The Associated Press issued a dispatch from Washington on 5 May 1963:

A potentially explosive document in the hands of a House sub-Committee is reported to lay down administration guidance for restricting movement of correspondents covering the warfare in South Vietnam: 1) keep reporters away from areas where fighting is being done entirely or almost entirely by U.S. troops. 2) keep reporters away from any area which will show the failure to attract full allegiance of South Vietnamese people. (Quoted in DPV report for June 1963.)

When slogans about freedom are put aside some of the more basic purposes for this war emerge. The DPV report for September 1963 reveals: "A tremendous dope smuggling racket has seen the light of day. One of the key figures is Mme ...., wife of a prominent General!" It was also reported in the *New York Herald Tribune* of 3 February 1964 that: "General Khanh boasted he had ten million dollars and could flee to lead a life of ease if he wanted to." The most revealing article, however, was carried in *Aviation Week* for 6 April 1964:

An air cargo company, Air America, incorporated in Delaware, is currently the principal instrument for the extension of the war in Laos, Cambodia and North Vietnam. This company has some two hundred aircraft...used under charter...It is airlifting South Vietnamese Special Troops to various places...the return trip (carries) a load of opium for further transport to markets in the U.S. in a big Boeing aircraft. These aircraft are under the command of U.S. General Paul D. Harkins and the pilots are former U.S. military pilots.

A further consideration of this remarkable article can be found in the Asian affairs monthly *Eastern World* by Edgar P. Young, Commander, Royal Navy, retired.

I should wish at this point to consider the actual program of the National Liberation Front, if only in the hope that readers of *Dissent* will take note:

> To carry out without delay, real and broad democracy in which freedom of thought, expression, the press, organization, assembly, demonstrations, trade-unions and freedom to set up parties, political, social and professional organizations; freedom of movement, trade, religion, worship, corporal liberties which are to be guaranteed by law for the entire people without discrimination...(We shall) stop persecution, arrest, detention and harassment of partriots and of opposition, of individuals and parties. We shall cancel the barbarous prison regime, especially torture, penitence, brain-washing and ill treatment of prisoners.
>
> (We shall) refrain from setting up in South Vietnam any form of dictatorial regime, either nepotic and militaristic or set up by a group or party, and refrain from carrying out a mono-party or mono-religious policy, a policy or dictatorship in ideology, politics, religions and economy...
>
> (We wish) free general elections to elect organs and to form a national coalition government composed of representatives of all forces, parties, tendencies, and strata of the South Vietnamese people...a policy of neutrality (through which we) will not adhere to any military bloc, nor let any country station troops or establish bases in South Vietnam. We will accept aid from all countries, regardless of political regimes and establish friendly relations on an equal footing with all countries. We respect the sovereignty of all countries and form together with Cambodia and Laos what must be a neutral zone on the Indo-Chinese peninsula. Reunification will be realized step by step on a voluntary basis with due consideration for the characteristics of each zone, with equality and without annexation of one zone by the other.

Why do American journals pontificate about the "Vietcong" when they are so ignorant of the program set out above? Are they aware that Ho Chi Minh of North Vietnam declared his desire for "Neutrality for both North and South Vietnam and independence of Russia, China, and America....?" (*The Times*, 5 November 1963.) The U.S. Government, however, is in a gross violation of its own official declaration at the conclusion of the Geneva Conference of 21 July 1954:

> We take note of the agreeements and of paragraphs one to twelve inclusive of the final declaration...The U.S. will refrain from threat or use of force to disturb them...and would view any renewal of aggression with grave concern (and as) a threat to international peace and security.

This declaration by W. Bedell Smith established American support for the Geneva Conference Report providing for neutrality, elections and non-interference. But U.S. troops are the only foreign troops in Vietnam today. W.W. Rostow, director of the State Department's Policy Planning Board, advanced a plan known as "Plan Six" providing for a naval blockade and air raids against North Vietnam. Representative Melvin Laird stated in a committee of the U.S. House of Representatives that "the U.S. administration is preparing plans for a strike into North Vietnam." The Associated Press reported a combat force of fifty jet bombers training in the Philippines in preparation for bombing of targets in North Vietnam. The bombers are said to be furnished with intelligence data obtained by U-2 reconnaissance planes. During the Honolulu Conference of June 1964, attended by Secretaries Rusk and McNamara, it appears plans for air raids and sabotage against North Vietnam were discussed. I take these references from a letter which I received from the Foreign Minister of North Vietnam. They have been amply supported by independent sources, as well as American sources.

Substantiation for the contention that the United States has been deliberately provoking North Vietnam can be found in *Aviation Week* for 6 April 1964:

> War against the Communists has already erupted over the borders of South Vietnam with raids and infiltration moves as far north as China ....With U.S. backing in aircraft, weapons and money, an estimated fifty thousand elite South Vietnamese troops are being trained to take the offensive in over-the-border strikes at Communist supply centers and communication routes. Despite Defence Secretary McNamara's implication in Washington (March 26) that the decision has not yet been made to extend the war, it is known here that guerilla strikes against the Communists have been increasing since last summer.

Despite this disclosure of plans and preparations, when the aggression actually occurred, U.S. officials had no qualms about feigning utter surprise. *Aviation Week* goes on to discuss the specific preparations:

> Key factor in the current raids is the airlift provided by Air America, a U.S. cargo company (which) camouflages its U.S. Governmental sponsorship. U.S. military advisers here are optimistic that extending the war beyond the borders, plus a stable government in Saigon, will force the Communist insurgency to collapse in a year....Special forces—now one-tenth of the half million South Vietnamese under arms—are not connected with the formal military organization. They rely on Air America using numerous secret airstrips in South Vietnam and Thailand.
> ...Last fall, when U.S. officals decided it was impossible to win the war by confining it inside South Vietnamese borders, they began an expanded programme of training special forces at secret bases, emphasising techniques of operation beyond national borders.

To his credit, Senator Wayne Morse delivered a speech in the U.S. Senate on 14 April 1964. He said:

> We have already aided and abetted the extension of the war beyond the borders of South Vietnam. I am fearful that as the proof of that becomes clearly established—as I believe it can be—we may wake up some morning to find charges levelled against us in the United Nations....

There were many more disclosures of raids into North Vietnam which had already occurred and more reports of plans for more ambitious military ventures. James Cameron wrote in the London *Daily Herald* of 4 March 1964:

> W.W. Rostow's Plan Six provides initially for a naval blockade of Haiphong, the port of Hanoi. If Hanoi still refuses to call off support, the Northern ports should be bombarded from the sea, and finally U.S. strategic bombers should attack Hanoi itself, if necessary flying the South Vietnam flag.

In the vernacular of the State Department, whenever Hanoi was urged to call off its "support of the South Vietnamese insurgency," what is really meant is that Hanoi shoud apply pressure and sanctions to force the rebels to submit to the United States. On 10 April 1964, the *New York Times* reported that "Secretary of State Dean Rusk told SEATO nations the U.S. (was) absolutely committed to remain in South Vietnam and reiterated that the war may be brought to North Vietnam soon." On 13 April 1964, the *Wall Street Journal* reported that "U.S. planned South Vietnamese bombing attacks on the North may commence as soon as late May or early June."

After all these announcements, when the U.S. finally attacked, the American press, which for days and weeks had carried the announcements, pretended shock and amazement as if the United States had been an innocent victim of surprise attack. Senator Wayne Morse has been more honest and stated after a secret briefing by Dean Rusk: "An expanded war in Asia could only be won if we used nuclear weapons." The report of James Cameron bears this out: "The grim thing about Plan Six is that it has no end. If Hanoi must be bombed ...Shanghai must be bombed to stop Chinese help to North Vietnam..." American and British warnings are reflected in the memorandum sent to me and others by the Chinese Charge d'Affaires in London:

> On July 30, U.S. warships intruded into the Northern territorial waters of the Democratic Republic of Vietnam and shelled Hon Me and Hon Ngu islands. On August 1 and 2, U.S. airplanes bombed a border post and village of the Democratic Republic of Vietnam. The bombing of coastal towns of the Democratic Republic of Vietnam on August 5 was a premeditated move by U.S. imperialism to extend the war step by step...(Mr. Hsiung Hsiang-hui, 6 August 1964.)

The *Manchester Guardian* editorial of 11 August 1964, confirmed that the movement of the Seventh Fleet into the Gulf of Tonkin was calculated and directly related to naval attacks by the "South Vietnamese" Navy.

A new account is now emerging in Washington...The North Vietnamese islands of Hon Me and Hon Mgu had indeed been attacked from the sea, as Hanoi alleged, before the crisis blew up; this is now admitted in Washington. The attackers were South Vietnamese ships, not the Seventh Fleet; but that distinction may not seem so significant in Hanoi as in Saigon and...at that point the U.S. Destroyer *Maddox* sailed into the Gulf of Tonkin....

Nonetheless, as far as the U.S. press is concerned, all the warnings and admissions, the leakage of Plan Six, the formerly acknowledged preparations for extending the war by the U.S Government, are ignored in descriptions of the attacks on North Vietnam. The knowledge of editors and of reporters is not brought to bear on the situation; the editors and reporters instead bear false witness. American dissenters, liberals and socialists who identify with the official presentation of the events in Vietnam and who accept the interpretation of national interest set out by the military and the industrialists, may be asked if they consider the facts discussed in this article to comprise a model of the Free World? Can national interest be allowed to mask such barbarism, however interpreted? Is it not time for "national interest," the "Free World" and the professed principles of American dissenters to be scrutinized more closely? The time for protest is overdue. We may hope it is not too late and that this war of atrocity may be ended.

The Increase of American Violence

Published in truncated form as "The Ethos of Violence"
in *The Minority of One*, January 1965

Since the end of the Second World War, there has been in many parts of the world an increase of extra-legal violence. The supremacy of the Nazis in this respect was ended by their defeat, which, however, did not end their evil work. The spirit of violence has spread to other countries, more particularly to America. America has painted communism as so great an evil that any methods are thought fair in combatting it. America accuses communism of desiring the Empire of the world, and, under protection of this slogan, is seeking to accomplish exactly that of which she accuses her enemies. The methods employed are little known to the average American, partly owing to deliberate concealment, and partly to the reluctance of peaceable citizens to become aware of the foul actions perpetrated in their name. I will deal with this evil under four heads: first, the war in South Vietnam; second, internal violence in the United States; third, the murder of Kennedy; and fourth, the threat of Goldwater.

I

South Vietnam, until the end of the Second World War, was part of French Indo-China, but nationalism caused a general revolt throughout Indo-China and the French suffered decisive defeat at Dien Bien Phu in 1954. A congress at Geneva divided the region into several new, independent states. Vietnam was, for the moment, divided into two parts, North and South, but it was decreed that the two parts should come together after a general election which was to be held shortly. W. Bedell-Smith said on behalf of the United States at the conclusion of the Geneva Conference, "We take note of the agreements and of paragraphs 1 to 12 inclusive of the Final Declaration....The U.S. will refrain from threat or use of force to disturb them....and would view any renewal of aggression with grave concern (in violation of agreements, and threatening international peace and security)." A reactionary government, depending upon foreign support, came into existence in South Vietnam. America poured in troops in suport of the dictator Diem. With American aid he perpetrated a series of atrocities which led to a revolt and caused America to abandon him. However, the new government, which was a puppet of America, proved very little better than the Government of Diem. Ever since it came into power, it has, with the armed support of America, committed a series of atrocities which can hardly be paralleled in modern times. The horrors which have taken place in South Vietnam during the past years, wreaked by the two native Governments with the connivance of America and even by American officers and men, would take far more space than I have to detail them.

The peasants, who constitute a great majority of the population, abhor the Government and, when they can, join the guerilla army known as the Vietcong. To check this tendency on the part of the peasants, a large proportion of them have been moved from their homes and imprisoned in what are called "Strategic Villages." In these villages, they are compelled to forced labour under the supervision of three hundred thousand secret police. Barbaric attacks are made on unarmed villages with American arms and assistance. The Government forces, led by Americans, commit appalling atrocities. The country is mainly Buddhist, and a head of the Buddhist church, the Venerable Thich Thien Hao, in a recent survey, estimates that 160.000 peasants had died of the regime by the middle of 1963, and 700,000 had been tortured and maimed, 400,000 had been imprisoned, 31,000 raped, 3,000 disembowelled with livers cut out while alive, and 4,000 burnt alive. One thousand temples have been destroyed. Forty-six villages have been attacked with poison chemicals between January and March, 1964. These figures, given in a report of the National Liberation Front, conform to the report of the South Vietnam Liberation Red Cross, South Vietnamese Women's Union and the reports of the Democratic Party of Vietnam. The Federation of American Scientists has reported that chemical poisons are used by the United States in South Vietnam and that the United States is using Vietnam as an experimental area for testing chemicals and biological warfare. A report in *Look* (December 23, and in *True*, December 1963), a magazine which is not generally opposed to American policy, reports that the governmental forces in South Vietnam employ steel bullets, which had, until lately, been rejected as barbarous. Reporting an attack with steel bullets, the *True* reporter says: "I saw one guy hit in the arm. It spun him around and blew the arm right off. One got hit in the back and it blew his heart literally out of his body. A man hit in the buttocks lived for five minutes. All the others died instantly. His wound would have been superficial with other bullets."

The Democratic Party of Vietnam, which is a virulent anti-Communist party with the motto "For the defeat of communism in the interest of free men EVERYWHERE," reports: "Supposedly, the purpose of the fortified villages is to keep the Vietcong out. But the barbed wire denies entrance and exit. Vietnamese farmers are forced at gunpoint into these virtual concentration camps. Their homes, possessions and crops are burned....In the province of Kien-Tuong, seven villagers were led to the Town Square, Their stomachs were slashed, their livers extracted and put on display. These victims were women and children. In another village, a dozen mothers were decapitated before the eyes of compatriots. In still another village, expectant mothers were invited to the square by government forces to be honoured. Their stomachs were ripped and their unborn babies removed." Interestingly enough this report was published in a Dallas newspaper, the *Dallas Morning News*, 1 January 1963.

> "According to a report of the FBI recently published (...1964), there is in the United States a murder every hour and a rape every thirty-two minutes."

It was felt that such incidents should not be reported and on May 5 of this year, 1964, the Associated Press announced that "a potentially explosive document in the hands of a House subcommittee is reported to lay down Administration guidance for restricting movement of correspondents covering the warfare in South Vietnam: 1. Keep reporters away from areas where fighting is being done entirely or almost entirely by U.S. troops; 2. Keep reporters away from any area which will show the failure to attract full allegiance of South Vietnamese people."

The atrocities mentioned above are only a small sample of many similar accounts. They illustrate the kind of war that America is waging in South Vietnam and is likely to carry on elsewhere in Asia and seems to be pursuing in the Congo. Every American who has not protested shares the guilt of such barbarism just as much as the average German shared the guilt of Auschwitz. What makes the continuation of the war in Vietnam more astonishing and more horrifying is the existence of an obvious policy for ending it. It is only necessary to recall the Geneva Convention and permit the tormented region to enjoy what it wants—namely, neutrality. This policy has been urged in influential quarters, but in vain. It is difficult to resist the belief that those who order atrocities and those who execute them enjoy the abominations of which they are guilty. And among those who order those atrocities are American officials up to, and including, the President.

II

The violence of American politics is reflected in the lives of individuals, especially in the Western portion of the United States. According to a report of the FBI recently published (*Evening Standard*, 20 July 1964), there is in the United States a murder every hour and a rape every thirty-two minutes. Through conflict with Indians and with Negroes, and during the Revolution, the Civil and Mexican wars and the conquest of the West, and largely because of the continual influx of non-Americans who are not yet assimilated, as well as for a number of lesser reasons, a habit of lawlessness has grown up. The present alignment of Negroes and white men is the most dangerous and explosive particular problem now existing in the United States, and the most difficult to solve. I shall write little of it, however, since it is so well known in America and the interest in it is so widespread. It seems more useful in the limited space of an article to dwell upon some of the dangers and ferocities that appear to be less generally recognised.

Until lately, if a white man shot a negro in a Southern state, that was not considered murder, and the white man would, in all likelihood, escape punishment. This is now changing under the influence of Negro revolt. The Harlem riots began with the slaughter of a Negro boy by a white policeman.

But in many parts of the country, whatever the law may say, Negroes are considered outside the law, in practice if not in theory. A reckless attitude not only towards Negroes but towards other white men, has been common in the West since it was first settled, and even law courts show much less respect for justice than might have been expected. Waves of law-enforced lawlessness have recurred in America ever since Adams, the second President. In modern times, Sacco and Vanzetti were executed, although their innocence was obvious. Sobell was sentenced to thirty years in prison for being a friend of the Rosenbergs. The only other evidence against him was that of a known perjuror who was never tried. The Court of Appeals of the Second Circuit declared on 6 February 1963, that Sobell should be entitled to retrial. but they refused his retrial on the grounds that it was too late for him to demand it. The Court said, in effect, that the original trial had been unfair, but that thirteen years of imprisonment, most of it at Alcatraz, had gone by, so that it was too late to do anything about it. (Sobell Committee Notes, 1963). He is still in prison. The prevailing view in America seems to be that, if a man is a Communist, he has no rights and the Courts may convict him of any crime they choose. The prevalent myth of American freedom sometimes takes grotesque forms. Take, for example, the case of a draft resister named Russell Goddard, who was had up on 6 July 1964, in St. Louis for the offence of resisting the draft. Judge Roy W. Harper, by whom he was tried, remarked in sentencing him: "I am glad I live in a country where anyone can take the position you do. You enjoy your freedom here because of the blood, sweat, toil and tears given by millions." Having delivered this paeon on American Freedom he sentenced his victim to five years in gaol. No doubt the Judge continues to think that America is a free country.

The lack of freedom in America is supported by the belief that Communists are very wicked and very sly. Every man whose opinions are in any degree unusual is supposed to be a Communist and to be an enemy of mankind. This belief is held with a kind of religious fervour much like that of the Hebrews in the *Book of Joshua*. Jael slaughtered Sasera while he slept and, for this act, became a national heroine. It is that kind of spirit that is bred by anti-Communists in America.

The obtaining of firearms in America is surprisingly easy, as appeared from the assassination of President Kennedy. Senator Dodd, after this event, brought in a bill to make more stringent rules as to who should have a right to carry firearms, but he announced that his bill had been killed by the National Rifle Association, and, therefore, people continue to die that the Association's coffers may be filled. As the law stands, anybody can obtain a firearm by post. One of the consequences is a great frequency of accidents with firearms. (*Guardian*, 14 August 1964).

Human life seems to have lost its importance. Perhaps this is not to be wondered at, since children are brought up from very early years to admire violence as proof of courage. The police, the FBI, the military—all armed—are their heroes. It does not seem to be noted that very dangerous accidents happen, that games are played with firearms, and that the fetish of readiness to fight is designed to make the heroes themselves quite mad. A Japanese woman who, by

> "There are now, in short, autonomous armies within the United States, armed to the teeth to fight anyone who shows any tendency to differ with them politically."

mistake, strayed on to an American preserve in Tokyo, was shot dead by an American soldier (London *Times*, 22 July 1964). The London *Times* of July 30 reports: "A United States airman aged 22, accused of 'using a firearm to play quick-draw', was sentenced at a court martial at the United States air base at Wetherfield, Essex, yesterday to six months hard labour. He was Lloyd la Barron, airman second class, who was also reduced to the rank of airman and ordered to forfeit $20 a month for 6 months." The Court's findings are subject to confirmation.

"Airman L.L. Reid said that on April 21 he went to Post 13 where Air Policeman Barron was on duty. Reid, also an air policeman, said: 'Barron was sitting behind his desk when I walked in. He said 'Let's see how fast you are,' and stepped out from behind the desk and drew. I pulled out my weapon and there was a shot.' "

"Barron, who pleaded Not Guilty, said he had answered the telephone in Post 13. 'I put down the phone, and as I turned I said to Reid 'draw.' He did and I was hit. Barron said that he was wounded in the stomach. His own weapon was, so far as he could remember, on the desk. He did not wear it when cleaning the post."

There are facts about the organisation of American Base camps in Britain (whose motto is "Peace is our Profession") and no doubt elsewhere, which are much less known than they should be. *The New Statesman* on 17 February, 1961, published an article of mine in which the following account occurs. No source can be given for the account since the facts were given me by someone who had experienced the circumstances and was corroborated by others with firsthand experience, and obviously their names cannot be revealed. I wrote: "Who knows that within each of them (The American bases in Britain) there is a hard kernel consisting of the air men who can respond to an alert call, who are so highly trained that they can be in the air within a minute or two? This kernel is kept entirely isolated from the rest of the camp which is not admitted to it. It has its own mess, dormitories, libraries, cinemas, etc., and there are armed guards to prevent other Americans in the base camp from having access to it. Every month or two, everybody in it, including the Commander, is flown back to America and replaced by a new group. The men in this inner kernel are allowed almost no contact with the Americans in the base camp and no contact whatever with any of the inhabitants of the neighbourhood. It seems clear that the whole purpose is to keep the British in ignorance and to preserve, among the personnel of the kernel, that purely mechanical response to orders and propaganda for which the whole of their training is designed. Moreover, orders to this group do not come from the Commandant, but direct from Washington."

How many people know that the American government has been for years and still is distributing through the army guns and ammunition to civilians and is training the recipients in their use? In an article in *The Nation* 8 June 1964, Stanley Meisler writes: "At the end of 1963, the army was instructing 384,950 civilians in markmanship, a number exceeding a third of the total American soldiers under arms. Half of those trained were younger than 18. This program cost the government $620,000 in the last fiscal year." The article proceeds with its revealing and utterly appalling facts. I quote only some of them. "The army has put almost a half a million used guns in the hands of civilians during the last five years." He quotes Representative Henry B. Gonzales (Dallas, Texas) as saying in the *Congressional Record* of 26 May 1964 that the "Minutemen the fanatical, right-wing guerilla-type anti-Communist organization, was in part supported, subsidized and encouraged by the federal government through the civilian marksmanship program." Mr. Gonzales also quoted from a newsletter written by M.S. Riecke, Junior, founder of the Paul Revere Associated Yeomen (Pray) in which he urged members to join the National Rifle Association "...Stock up on rifles, shotguns, pistols...Join the Minutemen. Remember the Communists cannot subdue an armed citizenry." The NRA he quotes as saying: "The NRA must continue to take the lead in turning the tide of uninformed anti-firearms opinion."

There are now, in short, autonomous armies within the United States, armed to the teeth to fight anyone who shows any tendency to differ with them politically. There are private propaganda organs such as H.I. Hunt's radio program, "Life Line," that coming from Washington, reaches an audience of 5 million people in forty-five states. (Robert G. Sherrill, *The Nation*, 24 February 1964). There are societies such as the John Birch Society and the Ku Klux Klan whose methods are unmitigatedly cruel and almost entirely illegal—but not outlawed. The situation, even without counting what is done in relation to the Negro problem, appears to be one of tumultuous savagery, unprecedented anywhere in the world.

The result of these various circumstances has been the creation of a trigger-happy population in which violence is admired and mildness is regarded as a proof of cowardice, and in which hate is constantly inculcated. It is scarcely surprising that a country in this mood should produce men willing to murder its President.

III

America, as we have seen, was rent with dissension and violence and filled with private armies supporting the Right. It should not have been surprising that some of this violence took a political form. However, the august facade of American constitutionalism had been so well maintained that the world was stunned by the news of Kennedy's assassination. An attempt was made by the police of Dallas and by the FBI to fasten the guilt upon an obscure individual, Oswald, and to persuade the world that he acted as an individual without accomplices. Almost the whole of the Press supported this attempt, and it might have been successful but for the arduous work of a few public-spirited men, chief among whom was Mark Lane, who is a New York lawyer and politically liberal though far from left. President Johnson appointed a body which has come to be known as the Warren Commission whose business is supposed to be the making of a full report as to the circumstances connected with Kennedy's death. This report was held over for two months, presumably to find ways to combat Mark Lane's evidence, and, at the time of writing, has not yet appeared. What will be the tenor of the report, it is impossible to guess. Meantime, many people in Europe are supporting Mark Lane's work, as it is as important to us as to Americans to expose such flagrant illegality as seems to be being upheld by officials of the American Government. Many of these European supporters have been threatened with dire consequences to themselves or their families by the American Embassies in their various countries if they support Mark Lane.

Mark Lane's work soon made it obvious to all who were willing to read it that the authorities in Dallas had told a tissue of lies and that there was no reason to suppose Oswald guilty. In the normal course of events, this would no doubt have been brought out at Oswald's trial, but the police discovered a simple way of preventing such disclosures. While they were holding Oswald in custody, they admitted into the courtyard in which he was held a pal of theirs named Ruby with whom they were familiar as the owner of a strip-tease club. Ruby, professing to be overcome by moral indignation, drew his revolver and shot Oswald. The authorities breathed a sigh of relief and continued the work of blackening Oswald's memory. Those who were not convinced by Oswald's guilt however, persisted in the work of uncovering official lies. The best account of their investigations is in a book by Joachim Joesten called: *Oswald: Assassin or Fall Guy?* (Marzani & Munsell, New York, 1964). What I shall have to say about the murder of Kennedy is mainly drawn from this book.

Oswald was an obscure hanger-on to fringes of political work. He had been in Russia where he had posed as a Communist. On his return to America, it was stated that he had gone as a spy for the FBI, and it seems that this version was accepted by the authorities. When it was known that Kennedy was coming to Dallas, the police investigated everybody whom they considered in any degree suspicious, but Oswald was not among those whom they so regarded. There was a large building, the Dallas book store, in which, not by his own initiative, he was given a job. The route that Kennedy was to pursue in Dallas was published and did not pass near the book depository. At the last moment, the route was changed, and part of it came within rifle range of the book store. These preparations were such as to make Oswald's guilt seem plausible.

The further stages however, were muddles in the official account. There is a long argument as to where the bullet came from, and whether Kennedy's mortal wound was made by a bullet from in front or a bullet from behind. Mr. Joesten's conclusion is that there were either three or four bullets. If all came from the depository, there had to be four, but if there were three, one of them had to come from a near-by underpass. The vagueness of this conclusion is due to the extraordinary indefiniteness of the medical reports on Kennedy. Immediately after the assassination, the doctors who examined the corpse unanimously testified that the bullet came from in front, but, when the corpse was taken to Washington, the report from "a reliable source" of the Washington doctors findings was the the bullets came from behind. The whole story since the assassination is one of evidence tampered with and of witnesses held incommunicado and intimidated and prevented from telling what they had seen and knew.

One of the most remarkable pieces of evidence of police complicity was an announcement which was made by the Sheriff five minutes before Kennedy was shot. The Sheriff broadcast at the time a statement saying: "I don't know what's happened, take every available man from the jail and the office and go to the railroad yard off Elm near the triple underpass." How he came to know that something terrible was about to happen has not been explained. When the President was known to have been shot police were sent to the book store and investigated everybody there except Oswald. They were told that Oswald worked there. They let him go. They maintained that he went to a somewhat distant part of the city and murdered a policeman called Tippit. No reason was assigned for the crime, and no evidence was produced that Oswald was incriminated. In fact, there is every reason to believe that he was not. Moreover, the description of Oswald as the murderer of Tippit was circulated almost half an hour before Tippit was shot.

There are various other pieces of evidence tending to prove the innocence of Oswald, more especially that the paraffin test showed that he had not had a rifle against his cheek. The case, as a whole, is entirely unconvincing, and it is unbelievable that he would have been convicted if his case had been allowed to come to trial.

There is nothing incredible about the theory of Kennedy's assassination which brings in the Dallas police and the FBI or parts of it. Kennedy had powerful enemies, especially in the oil business. Newspapers in Dallas published shortly before his death expressed a vehement hatred of him. Institutions such as the FBI and the CIA feel themselves above the law and able to control the actions of the civil Government. These institutions have been allowed to grow because of the insane fear of communism. The danger of a Fascist dictatorship is real.

IV

America, as we have seen, is a country in ferment. There are a number of private armies and these are composed almost exclusively of fanatical reactionaries. The result is that irrational Americans are armed and rational Americans are not armed. The first consequence of the ferment was the assassination of Kennedy; the second, was the choice of Goldwater as Republican candidate for the Presidency. It is not certain what would be Goldwater's policy if elected, but the best indication is his acceptance speech at San Francisco. In this speech he rejected all attempts at accommodation with the Communists. He stated that hostility to communism. should be the basic policy of the United States, and should be pursued by the methods of brinkmanship. He believes or professes to believe, that Russia, if threatened, will give way and that communism can be exterminated without a world war. He holds that the Commander of NATO forces, and not the President of the United States, should have command of American nuclear weapons with freedom to use them whenever he pleases. The Commander-in-chief of NATO is at present an American and is likely to remain so. It is to be expected that he will be a supporter of Goldwater.

It is impossible to judge in advance whether Goldwater will be elected in the coming election or not. American opinion has been educated to accept a totally false opinion both of communism and of America. It is very largely believed in America that America stands for freedom, whereas communism stands for the hated tyranny of a minority. Both these beliefs are false, and until they are abandoned, it is difficult for America to play a rational part in world politics. Goldwater heads the irrational part of America. If he wins, the prospect is dark, and so it is if he personally loses but his policy is adopted by his opponents. So far, appearances suggest that the most likely outcome is the rejection of Goldwater and the adoption of his policy. This is what has recently been happening in North Vietnam. His professed love of freedom does not go so far as to make him tolerant of efforts to change the fanatical attitude of the main part of the population of America. Fanaticism and mob rule governed the San Francisco Convention. Such moods are easily spread and difficult to combat.

What are likely to be the consequences if Goldwater's policy prevailed? It is difficult to believe that the Communist countries will tamely submit to American bullying and to more of such provocations as the U-2 incident at the time of the summit meeting at Paris or the more recent and dangerous U-2 incident at the height of the Cuban crisis, since it will be evident that there is no limit to such bullying and provocation short of the complete end of all Communist Governments. Even if Khrushchev himself were personally prepared to yield, the Russian counterparts of Goldwater, of whom I suppose there must be some, would dethrone him and insist upon a more vigorous policy. The result would be nuclear war and the end of civilisation if not of man. This prospect is not pleasing to America's European allies and it is to be expected that Goldwater's policy will put an end to NATO. If his policy were to succeed, and the Communist countries were to submit, the first result would be a world-wide American military tyranny imposed in the name of freedom. Such a tyranny would not be stable and would break down into chaos within a few years.

One or other of these alternatives must result from Goldwaterism. Both are horrible and both are rejected by all men who are not maddened by anti-Communist propaganda.

America professes to be the leader of the "Free World," but is inefficient in this role owing to the horror of socialism. Take, for example, the speculations about the Harlem riots. Goldwaterism would condone the shooting of coloured boys by white policemen as a first step towards freedom. A more rational policy would be the spending of public money on pulling down Harlem and providing new and adequate accommodation for the Negro population. But this would be regarded as socialism. Planning by private organisations in their own interest is thought admirable, but planning to improve the lot of the very poor by Government action is thought socialistic, and therefore wicked. This makes the economic problems connected with disarmament insoluble. America's economic creed is a hundred years out of date, and this incapacitates America as leader of the "Free World."

The only cure for this is a radical change in education and in conditioning by official propaganda, advertising and comics, all of which tend to cause the young to admire indiscriminate shooting by officials and to feel contempt for those who are shocked. The policeman is made to seem brave while his victim is exhibited as a coward. All this is a part of the road towards the police state. The Government itself is equally a victim of cliches, and teaches, perhaps unintentionally, that all evils can only be ended by shooting or some other form of violence. America contains many eminent sociologists whose advice might cure many evils. But the Government is deaf to their advice. It continues to think and teach in cliches, confounding socialism and communism and regarding imprisonment of opponents as proof of freedom.

America is sick and her sickness endangers the whole world. Given America's immense power and resources, a cure must be found within the country of their origin. The first thing that is needed is an education teaching that hate must be avoided, that excellence does not consist in violence. To achieve this change of outlook is an immense task which America's "Radicals" must attempt to carry out. Whether the necessary heroism will be forthcoming, I do not know. We can only hope that it may be so.

The Negro Rising

The Minority of One, October 1965

I have read with a certain incomprehension reactions of many liberal and Negro leaders in the United States to the revolutionary uprising of the American Negroes in Los Angeles. Who can deny that the entire Negro population rose up as one against the conditions with which they have had to live for decades? It is instructive that those who place such emphasis on formal legislation involving voting rights (yet unimplemented) only discover the true situation of the American Negro when he takes to revolutionary action.

Los Angeles has placed its Negro population in slums where crowding and insanitary conditons are so appalling that there is no alternative but to seek the streets for air and release. The white police function as an occupying army keeping a helot class in order. Suppression of deprived people historically has inspired revolution, but when those people suffer humiliation and contempt on racial grounds the cruelty of the oppression is magnified and the uprising assumes a national character. The oppressed Negro nation is rising against its three hundred years subjection. Why should people not revolt against conditions wherein they are shot down or beaten to death in police cells? The density of populaton in the Negro section of Los Angeles is five times that of white people in Los Angeles. The incidence of disease is equally high. It is increasingly clear that American Negroes are discovering the unreformability of the system which oppresses them. It is not possible for the American military industrial system to depend upon exploitation and domination as in Vietnam and, also, to effect a revolutionary transformation of the conditions of the Negro within the United States. I suspect that only the American Negro is able to understand fully the nature of U.S. oppression in Vietnam, the Congo, the Dominican Republic or other areas of Latin America, Asia and Africa.

The President has decried what he calls violence and rioting. I had never before realised that the President was an advocate of non-violence. He is not an advocate of non-violence in Vietnam or in the Congo, nor when he encourages State police in their use of dogs, gas and bullets. It is only when the Negro, in desperation, defends himself by violent means against long-endured violent oppression that President Johnson, and those who think like him, discover their antipathy to violence.

What is to be done? The elementary step is the tearing down of every slum in the United States and the construction of new and adequate houses, schools, hospitals and cultural facilities in their place. Beyond this, professional train-

"The President has decried what he calls violence and rioting. I had never before realised that the President was an advocate of non-violence. He is not an advocate of non-violence in Vietnam or in the Congo, nor when he encourages State police in their use of dogs, gas and bullets. It is only when the Negro, in desperation, defends himself by violent means against long-endured violent oppression that President Johnson, and those who think like him, discover their antipathy to violence."

ing program and full educational opportunites should be made available, particularly to the oppressed sections of the United States. Such a program would require an end to military expansion and domination on the part of America. It could not be undertaken at the same time as a war of oppression in Southeast Aisa, nor could it be undertaken without a fundamental transformation of social and economic relations in the United States. Is it likely that large industry, its military partner and the intelligence agencies which guard this partnership will countenance the transformation of social relations in the United States or abandon their control over sixty per cent of the world's natural resources? It is unlikely, and no amount of reformist legislation would appear to have a chance of effecting such a transformation.

It is my hope, therefore, that the revolutionary mood which is taking hold of the oppressed Negro people will find an organised political expression and that sections of the white population, particularly the more deprived, will come to see the way they have been used. Such an alliance may, in time, change the United States. The absence of one will bring America to the threshold of overt Fascism, in which martial rule and terror will be needed. It will be necessary to continue the oppression of the Negro nation and those whites who suffer comparable conditions. The very least middle class and professional white people can do is to understand and support the Negro in his struggle. Such understanding and support must encompass Los Angeles.

Peace Through Resistance
To U.S. Imperialism

Throughout the world today increasing numbers of people concerned with peace and social justice are describing U.S. imperialism as the commom destroyer of peace and justice. To some, the expression "U.S. Imperialism" appears as a cliche because it is not part of their own experience. We in the West are the beneficiaries of imperialism. The spoils of exploitation are the means of our corruption. Because imperialism is not part of our experience we do not recognise the aptness of the description for the economic and political policies of what President Eisenhower termed "the military industrial complex." Let us consider briefly the nature of U.S. power.

Thirty-three hundred bases and vast mobile fleets, bearing missiles and nuclear bombers, are spread over our planet to protect the ownership and control by U.S. capitalism of 60 percent of the world's resources. Sixty percent of the world's resources are owned by the rulers of six percent of the world's population. The aggressiveness of this empire imposes on mankind an expenditure of 140,000 million dollars annually or 16 million dollars each hour. The current arms expenditure exceeds the entire national income of all developing countries. It exceeds the world's annual exports of all commodities. It exceeds the national incomes of Africa, Asia and Latin America. The U.S. military budget is nearly 60,000 million dollars per year. One Atlas missile costs thirty million dollars, or the equivalent of the total investment of nitrogen fertilizer plant with capacity of 70,000 tons per annum.

Consider this in terms of the United Kingdom only, to take the example of a prosperous country: one obsolete missile equals four universities, one TSR 2 equals five modern hospitals, one ground-to-air missile, equals 100,000 tractors.

During the past fourteen years the U.S. spent 4,000 million dollars to purchase farm surpluses. Millions of tons of wheat, oats, barley, maize, butter and cheese have been stored and poisoned to keep prices up in the world markets. Blue dye is poured into great mountains of butter and cheese to render them unusable. By 1960, 125 million tons of bread grain had been stored in the United States to rot—enough for every citizen of India for one year. Unimaginably vast quantities of foodstuffs are calculatedly destroyed by the rulers of U.S. capitalism, for no other purpose than the continuation of their profits and the retention of their power. Like vultures, the handful of the rich fatten on the poor, the exploited, the oppressed. A drop of 5 percent in the world price of staple exports of any country would, according to Dag Hammarskjold, wipe out all investments of the World Bank, of the United Nations and all other bilateral and other investments.

"The aggressiveness of this empire imposes on mankind an expenditure of 140,000 million dollars annually or 14 million dollars each hour. The current arms expenditure exceeds the entire national income of all developing countries."

These were the fears of Hammarskjold. What are the facts? In recent years prices have operated against poor countries not merely at 5 percent but at 40 percent. The industrial production of Western capitalism is consciously employed not only to perpetuate the hunger which exists in the world, but to increase it vastly for profit.

In South Africa, 10,000 children die annually from gastro-enteritis. The smallpox which haunts many countries could be eliminated at a cost of 500,000 dollars. Hundreds of millions who suffer from yaws could be cured by a fivepenny shot of penicillin. Five hundred million people have trachoma. Sixty per cent of the children of Africa suffer from protein deficiency diseases such as kwashiokor, beri-beri or pellagra. When U.S. capitalists hoard food and poison it they not only deprive the starving, but force the developing countries to buy food at high costs. The riches of the earth are destroyed, wasted, stolen by the few and used to murder the millions. 3,300 military bases are spread across the planet to prevent the peoples from destroying this evil system.

Let us examine the role of the war industry in the United States. The United States Defense Department owns property valued in 1954 at 160 billion dollars.

This value has almost doubled. The U.S. Defense Department is the world's largest organisation. The Pentagon owns millions of acres of land, including thirty-two million in the United States and over three million acres of land outright in foreign countries. The Pentagon building is so large that the Capitol, which contains the United States Government, could be swallowed in any one of the five main segments of the Pentagon. The 1962 budget involved fifty-three billion dollars for arms, exclusive of the military space program.

Thus, by 1962, sixty-three cents out of every dollar were spent on appropriations for arms and space. A further six cents were for army services, and more than 80 percent of interest payments were for military debts. Seventy-seven cents out of every hundred are spent on past wars, the Cold War and preparations for future war. The billions of dollars placed in the pockets of the U.S. military give the Pentagon economic power affecting every aspect of American life, and of the lives of mankind.

Military assets in the U.S. are three times as great as the combined assets of the great monopolies, greater than the assets of U.S. Steel, Metropolitan Life Insurance, American Telephone and Telegraph, General Motors and Standard Oil. The Defence Department employs three times the number of all these great world corporations.

This immense world concentration of power and wealth is directly linked to large scale capitalism in America. The billions of dollars in contracts are awarded by the Pentagon and filled by large industry.

In 1960, 21 billion dollars were spent on military goods. Ten capitalist corporations received 71 billion dollars, three received 1 billion each and two others 900 million dollars. In these corporations there are more than 1,400 retired officers of the army above the rank of major. This includes 261 Generals and flag rank officers.*

The largest company, General Dynamics, has 187 retired officers, 27 generals and admirals and the former Secretary of the Army on its payroll. American policy and the military bases serve a vast power complex inter-connected and interested in the perpetuation of the arms race for its own sake. This concentration of power spreads throughout the economy of the United States. Sub-contracts awarded by war contractors involve every city of any size. The jobs at stake involve millions of people.

Four million people work for the U.S. Defense Department alone. The payroll of twelve billion dollars is twice that of the U.S. automobile industry. A further four million people are employed directly in arms industries. Thus eight million people depend for their jobs on the military adventures of the U.S. rulers. Eight million jobs mean twenty-five million people in total.

Missile production accounts for eight-two per cent of all manufacturing jobs in six States, including California. In Los Angeles nearly 60 percent of jobs are directly or indirectly dependent on the arms race. Thus the United States as a whole devotes over fifty per cent of all its public expenditure to military spending.

This colossal investment is in exploiting and domination. Every food store and every petrol station in America requires, under capitalism, the perpetuation of war production.

This is the world system of imperialism. And the system also has a silent army: the Central Intelligence Agency. The CIA has a budget fifteen times the size of all diplomatic activity of the U.S. This vast agency purchases members of the army and police in countries all over the world. It draws up lists of popular leaders to be assassinated. It plots to start wars. It invades countries.

In Latin America, a band of reactionary generals, at the instigation of the Central Intelligence Agency and the U.S. Ambassador in Brazil, Mr. Lincoln Gordon, crushed the democratic government of Joao Goulart. In Argentina, American tanks smashed the civilian government of Arturo Fondisi, solely because this conservative spokesman for middle-class interests was insuffi-ciently subservient to U.S. capitalism. Brutal military putsches have been imposed upon Ecuador, Bolivia, Guatemala and Honduras. For decades, the United States armed and supported one of the most barbaric and savage rulers in modern times, namely, Trujillo. When Trujillo no longer served their interests they allowed him to suffer the fate of Ngo Dinh Diem, but the United States remained the enemy of the people of the Dominican Republic, as can be seen by the arrogant military intervention to crush the brave revolution of April, 1965.

*See report of the Herbert Investigating Committee of the House of Representatives in the U.S. *Congressional Quarterly.*

The fact that this naked aggression is condoned by the United Nations, and the ability of the United States to escape expulsion from the United Nations for its gross violation of the Charter, demonstrates that the United Nations has become a tool of American aggression of the kind displayed in the Dominican Republic. All my sympathy lies with the struggle of the people of the Dominican Republic, which continues at this very moment.

In the Congo, mercenary troops, acting for Belgian and American interests and shamelessly supported by the British Government, have killed indiscrimately every living villager in the path of the advancing mercenary armies. The dregs of American militarism have been used for this purpose: the mercenary soldiery of South Africa and of the Cuban counter-revolution.

In the Middle East, United States' and European oil interests force tyranny and poverty on the people. British imperialism, relying on the military and financial power of the United States, is showering the people of Aden with napalm and high explosives in an attempt to suppress the popular movement.

In Southern Africa, incalculable riches are taken out of the Copper Belt of Rhodesia and of South Africa and the Fascist states of Salazar and Vermoerd survive through NATO arms. In South-East Asia, 50,000 troops prop up the puppet state of Malaysia, and right-wing generals, with United States' money have taken control of Indonesia. Throughout the South China seas, every patriotic and radical force is gaoled and persecuted by the imperialist powers. The United States boasts of its intrigues in the Maghreb. It brazenly publishes its plans to subvert all nationalist governments.

This is a predatory imperialism and nowhere has it been more cruel and reckless than in Vietnam. Chemicals and gas, bacteriological weapons and phosphorus, napalm and razor bombs, disembowelment, dismemberment, forced labour, concentration camps, beheadings, elaborate torture—every species of cruelty—have been employed by American imperialism in Vietnam. Clinics, sanatoria, hospitals, schools, villages have been relentlessly saturated with fire bombs: and still the people of Vietnam resist, after twenty-five years of struggle against three great industrial powers.

The people of Vietnam are heroic, and their struggle is epic: a stirring and permanent reminder of the incredible spirit of which men are capable when they are dedicated to a noble ideal. Let us salute the people of Vietnam.

In the course of history there have been many cruel and rapacious empires and systems of imperialist exploitation, but none before have had the power at the disposal of United States' imperialists. This constitutes a world system of oppression, and represents the true threat to peace and the true source of the danger of world nuclear war.

I have supported peaceful co-existence, out of the conviction that conflict in a nuclear age can only be disastrous. This conviction was based on the hope that the United States could be persuaded to come to an agreement with the Socialist and Communist countries. It is now painfully clear that U.S. imperialism cannot be persuaded to end its aggression, its exploitation and its cruelty. In every part of the world the source of war and of suffering lies at the door of U.S. imperialism. Wherever there is hunger, wherever there is exploitative tyranny, wherever people are tortured and the masses left to rot under the weight of disease and starvation, the force which holds down the people stems from Washington.

Peaceful co-existence, therefore, cannot be achieved by requesting U.S. imperialism to behave better. Peace cannot be realised by placing hopes on the goodwill of those whose power depends on the continuation of such exploitation and on the ever-increasing scale of military production. The system which oppresses the people of the world is international, co-ordinated and powerful; but it is hateful and oppressive and in various ways resisted by the people of the world.

A united and co-ordinated resistance to this exploitation and domination must be forged. The popular struggle of oppressed people will remove the resources from the control of U.S. imperialism and, in so doing, strengthen the people of the United States itself, who are striving first to understand and second to overcome the cruel rulers who have usurped their revolution and their government. This, in my view, is the way to create a secure peace, rather than a tenuous and immoral acquiescence to U.S. domination, which can neither work nor be tolerated by humane men.

If the Soviet Union, in its desire for peace, which is commendable, seeks to gain favour with the United States by minimising or even opposing, the struggle for national liberation and socialism, neither peace nor justice will be achieved. U.S. imperialism has provided us with all the evidence to which we are entitled as to its nature and its practice. The peoples of the world bear witness to it.

War and oppression have a long history in human affairs. They cannot be overcome except through struggle. A world free of exploitation and foreign domination, a world of well-being for the masses of people of all continents, a world of peace and of fraternity, has to be fought for. This is the lesson U.S. imperialism teaches us. It is not a palatable lesson, but nothing will be accomplished by ignoring it.

The danger of nuclear war will not be averted through fear of United States' power. On the contrary, the more isolated the wielders of power in the United States become, in the face of world rejection of their values and resistance to their acts, the more likely we are to succeed in avoiding a nuclear holocaust. It is the illusion on the part of U.S. imperialism that it can accomplish an aim and defeat people by the use of such weapons that constitutes today the main source of nuclear danger. But when the people of Peru, Guatemala, Venezuela, Columbia, Vietnam, Thailand, the Congo, the Cameroons, the United States, Britain—all the people—demonstrate and struggle and resist, nuclear power is of no avail. Its possession will destroy its user. Let us join together to resist U.S. imperialism.

Broadcast on National Liberation
Front Radio to American Soldiers

24 May 1966

This is Bertrand Russell speaking to you on the radio of the forces of the National Liberation Front of South Vietnam. I am speaking to you American soldiers in order to explain how your Government has abused your rights in sending you to occupy a country whose people are united in their hatred of the United States as a foreign aggressor. It is not difficult to understand why it is that the Vietnamese hate Americans. The people of Vietnam have been fighting for twenty-five years to secure their independence. They first fought against the Japanese, who were very cruel, and later against the French who set up guillotines in villages throughout Vietnam and who beheaded those suspected of being opposed to foreign occupation. Not many of you may know that the United States Government financed more than 80 percent of the cost of the French war and supplied France with all modern weapons, in order to assist France in her evil task of killing and subduing the people of Vietnam.

When the United States first began to intervene militarily in South Vietnam, the pretence was made that the United States was merely helping a Government in Saigon put down a subversion from the outside. But you American soldiers have seen for yourselves what kind of governments have existed in Saigon. They are brutal, corrupt, dictatorial and completely despised by the people. Why is it that these governments have been able to continue, one after another, in Saigon, despite the fact that the students, women, the villagers, everyone risks life itself to overthrow them? The sole answer is that the United States is using its enormous military force to impose on the people of Vietnam puppet governments which do not represent them.

Let us now consider together why the U.S. Government does this. The excuse that they are protecting the Vietnamese against the "Vietcong" or the North Vietnamese can be seen by all of you to be the disgusting lie it is. Vietnam is one country. Even the Geneva Agreements acknowledge that it is one country. The North Vietnamese and the South Vietnamese are not merely the same people, but the wives and children of men living in the North are in the South and many of those who live in the South were born in the North. You may not know that between 1954 and 1960 more Vietnamese died than since 1960. Think hard about that. The "Vietcong" had not taken up arms until 1960, and yet more Vietnamese died in the six years before that time than since the National Liberation Front began to struggle. The reason is simple. The Government of Ngo Dinh Diem killed, tortured, imprisoned and mutilated hundreds of thousands of Vietnamese and was able to do this solely because of the military support and direction of the United States. Can any of you forget the brutality of Ngo Dinh Diem, which moved Buddhist priests to burn themselves in protest?

It ought to be clear that the National Liberation Front, which you know as the Vietcong, took up arms to defend their people against a tyranny more brutal than the Japanese occupation itself, for more died under Diem than under the Japanese. This is the responsibility of the United States Government.

The reason why you American soldiers are in Vietnam is to suppress the people of Vietnam, who are trying to free themselves from economic strangulation and foreign military rule. You are sent to protect the riches of a few men in the United States.

Do you know that the United States controls 60 percent of the resources of the world, but has only six percent of the world's population, and yet one out of three Americans live in poverty? Do you know that the United States has over 3,300 military bases in the world, almost all of which are used against the population of the country in which the bases exist? The U.S. rulers have built an economic empire which is being resisted from the Dominican Republic to the Congo, and especially in Vietnam.

Could you imagine yourself voting for Cao Ky? If a foreign power occupied the United States to steal American resources for itself and if a traitor government were established by force, would you feel it was your government? Worse than this, because the Vietnamese people are so determined and show such fantastic heroism that the greatest military power on earth has found it impossible to conquer them, you American soldiers are trained to use every modern weapon of war.

Your Air Force is flying 650 sorties a week in the North and the tonnages used in the South are higher than those used during the Second World War or the Korean War. You are using napalm, which burns everything it touches. You are using phosphorus, which eats like an acid into those who are in its path. You are using fragmentation bombs and "lazy dogs" which cut up in pieces and lacerate women and children in the villages hit without discrimination. You are using poison chemicals which cause blindness, affect the nervous system and paralyse. You are using poison gases which are listed in army manuals of World War II as poisons, and other gases which are so deadly that even soldiers with masks have been killed by their own gas.

When you return from battle ask yourself who are these people you are killing? How many women and children died at your hands today? What would you feel if these things were happening in the United States to your wives, parents and children? How can you bear the thought of what is taking place around you, day after day and week after week? I ask these questions of you because you bear the responsibility and within your hands lies the choice of whether this criminal war is to continue.

When Britain occupied North America in the eighteenth century, American farmers fought with pitchforks in their bare hands, although they were hungry and in rags. They fought for eight years and they defeated the British Empire in their own country. Do you know that in the United States today, 66 million people are living in poverty? Do you know that in the United States today the unemployed equal the population of thirty-five individual states?

You are being used to enrich the few industrialists whose profits depend on taking the natural resources from other countries, and this is why the world is rising against this brutal war waged by the United States Government. You know that the Geneva Convention outlaws gas, chemicals, torture and mutilation and you also know that American special forces are trained in techniques used at Auschwitz and other concentration camps.

Master-Sergeant Don Duncan has revealed the truth about films showing Nazi tortures which were used for instruction of American servicemen. And you yourselves know from your daily experience what happens to villagers suspected of being "Vietcong" and who are captured. You know also that the strategic hamlets are little more than concentration camps, where forced labour, torture and starvation occur. These things were the reason for the hatred the world had for the Nazis. These things led to the trials at Nuremburg, in which the Nazi leaders were hanged as war criminals. I know that most of you come to Vietnam not because you wished to but because you were sent. I know that most of you have been told that you were defending helpless people against a stronger neighbour. But you have been lied to and no one knows it better than you yourselves.

You must not think that you are alone, for throughout the United States people are opposing this war. When 100 thousand people in New York City alone, and tens of thousands meet in other cities across the United States, it should be clear that the American people have seen through this war and want it ended. Why else has the Government been unable even to make a declaration of war?

Have you been present when an officer has attached electrodes to the genitals of a woman or a child? Have you been one of those who, out of fear or nervousness, pulled the trigger on an automatic rifle, releasing so many hundreds of bullets in an instant that, before you knew what had happened, women and children lay dead before you?

Along with world famous figures, Nobel prizewinners, novelists, philosophers, mathematicians, I am forming a War Crimes Tribunal in order to pass judgment, in most solemn terms and with the most respected international figures, upon the crimes being committed by the United States Government against the people of Vietnam. I appeal to you to end your participation in this barbarous and criminal war of conquest. I appeal to you to inform the War Crimes Tribunal of the truth about this war and to place before it the evidence of your own eyes. I appeal to you as a human being to human beings. Remember your humanity and forget the rest. If you can do this you will perform a courageous service to mankind. If you cannot, you will allow your rulers to continue to degrade your country and cause its name to be hated by decent people the world over.

Join us, Americans, Englishmen, West Europeans, Latin Americans, Asians, Africans, people from every walk of life, in our determination to defeat those in the United States responsible for the suffering and horror which you American soldiers have seen and for which you have responsibility. Refuse to fight any longer in this unjust war. Demand to be transferred anywhere but Vietnam. Make known that you will make public your opposition to this war and the way in which it is fought. There are too many people ready to support you for reprisals to take place. It is no use postponing your decision. The moment of trial is always. Now is the appointed time.

Introduction to Pamphlet on Black Militancy 1967

It is too little known outside the United States that the American Negro is an oppressed minority not only as a people denied full status as citizens of a country, nor merely in the sense of a people deprived of their full civil liberties in comparison with the majority of the population. The American Negro is oppressed in the sense of an occupied nation. He is oppressed in the sense that people selected for hard labour or extermination are oppressed. The American Negro has been subject to murder at random for many generations. In the rural South, he has been without the right to legal recourse. The peonage system which evolved since the days of slavery reduced the rural Negro population to a terrorised peasant mass, subject to most forms of brutality and mutilation.

There are many ways of measuring the suffering of the black population of the United States. It may be measured in the hundreds of thousands who have died unknown or in circumstances of great suffering. It may be measured in the absence of health facilities or opportunities for education. It may be measured in an atmosphere of such hostility and terror that the blood pressure of Negro patients in hospitals is much higher than that of whites causing a higher percentage of Negroes to succumb under surgery. It may be measured in the psychological—traumatic—consequences for the young who grow up in a world of menacing contempt and hostility.

It is in this context that the Black struggle must be understood. Without such understanding of the experience of the Negro people in the United States, the basic and elementary demand of black power will be lost on white Americans, who have only the most remote, if guilty awareness of the conditions imposed on their Black victims.

In the cities across the United States, in Watts of Los Angeles, in Harlem of New York, in the South Side of Chicago, in Detroit, in Pittsburgh, in Philadelphia, in St Louis, in Atlanta, Georgia, in Birmingham, Alabama, in all the vast metropolitan areas of the United States the Black community is isolated in ghettos. It is underhoused, crowded, and lives in conditions where adequate sanitation is virtually unknown, save the efforts of the people themselves in seeking to overcome the appalling limitations of their environment. In these circumstances, the young Negro is without serious opportunity of employment except in menial occupations which exhaust him and reduce him to early old age and great susceptibility to disease. Unless he chooses to entertain the white community as a boxer or a singer or in some way an amuser and creator of leisure pastime—and always on terms of white acceptance—the young

"The idea that the most oppressed and the most victimised should not know the reasons which propel them into open revolt is itself a racist expression of ignorance and arrogance. The white community which professes not to grasp the reasons for the Negro rebellion is a community which chooses to deny the reality of the oppression it practices."

Negro in the United States has before him a life of menial labour. His conditions are likely to secure for him a prison sentence and an early experience of brutal violence at the hands of the police. The brutality is applied by white police who are, in effect, occupying armies of the Black ghettoes from one section of the United States to another. In these circumstances the restiveness of a people without hope is treated with new brutality giving rise to the Negro resistance.

If in any part of the world an oppressed people had risen up not for days but for weeks, not in one city but in most cities, not in part of the country, but throughout it, how would this phenomenon be understood by an honest observer? Would it be called a race riot, or would it be called a rebellion, a revolution? Where but in racist America and where, but in the racist Western Press, could the explosion of Negro resistance be understood as anything other than a long delayed uprising by an oppressed nation? How can we begin to grasp the meaning of the demand for black power if we have not yet understood the difference between a revolution and a riot of "unthinking" people. The idea that the most oppressed and the most victimised should not know the reasons which propel them into open revolt is itself a racist expression of ignorance and arrogance. The white community which professes not to grasp the reasons for the Negro rebellion is a community which chooses to deny the reality of oppression it practices. Such attempts to deny the obvious have never succeeded and, can have no result other than the deepening of consciousness amongst the oppressed and the extension of a revolutionary mood to every sector of the Black community.

In this pamphlet, the most articulate and able leader of the black American community since Malcolm X, whose tragic death denied the United States its most able revolutionary leader since the American Revolution, speaks for his people in tones and in terms which are analogous to those used by revolutionary and popular leaders throughout the world. The voice of Stokely Carmichael echoes that of Fidel Castro, or Nguyen Huu Tho of the National Liberation Front of South Vietnam, or Hugo Blanco of the oppressed peasantry of Peru, or Amilcar Cabral of the revolutionary Guinean nation. This voice is of a people no longer prepared to accept oppression and brutality as a normal part of their everyday lives.

The cases of Charles MacLaurin and Johnny Wilson exemplify the oppression experienced by American Negroes and the resistance they are preparing at great risk and considerable personal sacrifice. Charles MacLaurin has been tried in Greenville, Mississippi, without the right of legal defence. He has committed no more grave'breach of the farce that passes for law in the American South than that of playing ball in a public park marked "for whites only." As a result, MacLaurin was sentenced to six months imprisonment in the most harsh conditions.

Johnny Wilson, a young man of nineteen years, was arrested for the grave offence of disorderly conduct. He participated in a peaceful demonstration protesting against the war in Vietnam. Part of his punishment included treatment with toxic chemicals and incarceration in an isolation box, 7 feet long and 4 feet wide, without toilet facilities, ventilation or any other food but bread and water. The death sentence on Johnny Wilson was subsequently commuted to three years hard labour on a chain gang—a Georgia chain gang. It is instructive to remind non-American readers of this pamphlet that recently such a chain gang was exposed as having imposed such conditions on the inmates that they chopped off their own feet rather than endure more of the torment and labour imposed on them from early dawn until late at night.

What is the offence of nineteen-year-old Johnny Wilson? His first crime is his colour. His second and perhaps, even more grievous charge is, for American racists and oppressors, the most dangerous of all. Johnny Wilson has translated his own suffering into an awareness of the suffering endured by the people of Vietnam. This altered consciousness has made of him a man dangerous to the United States as it is ruled today. Johnny Wilson has contended that the United States is committing genocide in Vietnam. He accuses the U.S. of imposing a system of oppression such as he and his people have experienced for many generations in the United States. It is this relationship between the oppressed in Vietnam and the black oppressed in the United States which is most alarming to the men responsible for death and agony in most parts of the world today.

In publishing this pamphlet, we hope to show people that the struggle against American oppression in Vietnam and the struggle against the brutality on the part of black militants in the United States are part of the same international resistance to exploitation and aggression—a long, arduous and heroic battle to which all of us must commit ourselves.

The International War Crimes Tribunal and The Nature of the War in Vietnam

The International War Crimes Tribunal has been established because the United States is waging a war of atrocity in Vietnam. The reason for this war is that the United States controls 60 percent of the world's natural resources but contains only 6 percent of the world's population. For the purpose of protecting this empire the United States capitalists have had to create a great army and military machine, designed to destroy popular resistance to American economic control.

Several techniques have evolved in the course of the United States' efforts to eliminate social revolution in the world. The United States rulers are in the habit of saying that the modern form of aggression is internal subversion. By this they mean any demand for social change on the part of the dedicated and self-sacrificing leaders of oppressed people. In fact, the modern form of aggression is the installation of puppet regimes which protect the interests of a foreign power. The basic characteristic of these puppet regimes is that they function as the local guarantors of foreign investment and they crush brutally all political opponents who dare to challenge the quisling-like behaviour of these same puppets. When the forces of social revolution become too strong for the puppets to overcome they then call on United States rulers to use the great military machine created by the United States for the very purpose of destroying social revolution. If countries succeed in overthrowing corrupt puppet dictators subservient to foreign capitalists, then the United States uses the Central Intelligence Agency with vast sums of money who buy, kill or overthrow by coup d'etat the popular government which defies American power. The United States government is aware that the cost of this brutal exploitation is mass misery, starvation and disease, the primary features of countries in Asia, Africa and Latin America. The social forces installed or protected by the United States in these countries are not only incapable of solving the misery, starvation and disease but exist to perpetuate these evils.

There is only one way to remove starvation and disease in the poor countries: to overthrow the puppet regimes and create a revolution capable of withstanding American power. This is what has happened in Vietnam. This is why the United States has used every form of torture and experimental murder in its efforts to crush the Vietnamese revolution. The United States is behaving in Vietnam as Hitler behaved in Eastern Europe, and, essentially, for the same reasons. The United States recognizes that Vietnam is not only a heroic and momentus event in the history of human affairs, but a dangerous sign for

> "The United States rulers are in the habit of saying that the modern form of aggression is internal subversion. By this they mean any demand for social change on the part of dedicated and self-sacrificing leaders of oppressed people."

American power. It regards Vietnam in the way that Hitler regarded Spain. The Spanish revolution was capable of inspiring revolution in other European countries. The Nazis tried to crush this revolution with local fascists and also used Spain as a proving ground in which they could test inhuman weapons and experimental methods of mass murder. This is the deep significance of what the United States is doing in Vietnam.

In Vietnam the United States is testing toxic chemicals, poison gas, nerve gas, bacteriological devices, white phosphorus, napalm and fiendish fragmentation bombs; not only to destroy Vietnam but also to prepare for other struggles. The gas and napalm tested in Vietnam have already been introduced by the United States government in several Latin American countries. In Peru, Columbia, Venezuela and Bolivia, these weapons are now being used against peasant partisans who struggle for land reform, food and an end to police torture. The great meaning of Vietnam is that the world revolution is continuous and the world counter-revolution is barbarous. This is the essential lesson and those who try to ignore it, not only promote painful illusions but sacrifice whole generations of other peoples to agony and death.

It is customary to speak of aggression in terms of the violation of national frontiers by armed forces. This is aggression in the formal, conventional sense, convenient for the United Nations or the World Court or the Hague. The world prices operate against the poor countries and are created by the rich ones for the purpose of pauperising the nations of Africa, Asia and Latin America. Ten million people suffering from famine in India experience a form of aggression. Powerful states and ruling groups have created institutions such as the United Nations and the World Court but it is these same states and ruling groups which exploit cruelly the peoples of the world. This is why their institutions cannot echo the demands or the sufferings of the oppressed. This is why the only aggression recognised is the kind which is largely irrelevant to the oppressed peoples of the world. It is true that the United States had committed armed aggression against Vietnam causing the Vietnamese revolution. It is because the Vietnamese revolution has challenged the aggression of the exploiting countries that the United States has moved its armed forces into Vietnam.

The International War Crimes Tribunal will, I hope, encourage people throughout the world to look on world events in the ways I have described here. I hope that this Tribunal will remain in existence so that it may meet when necessary in the future in order to expose and condemn future war crimes which will be committed inevitably until the peoples of the world follow the example of Vietnam.

The Entire American People Are On Trial

Ramparts magazine, March 1970

Violence is not new to America. White men of European stock seized the lands of indigenous Indians with a ferocity which endured until our own times. The institution of slavery shaped the character of the nation and leaves its mark everywhere today. Countless "local" wars were mounted throughout the twentieth century to protect commercial interests abroad. Finally, the United States emerged at Hiroshima as the arbiter of world affairs and self-appointed policeman of the globe.

What is new in 1969 is that for the first time many affluent Americans are learning a very little of this disconcerting picture.

The revelations of atrocities by U.S. servicemen in Vietnam illustrates not isolated acts inadvertently committed by disciplined troops, but the general pattern of the war, for its character is genocidal. It has been fought from the air with napalm and fragmentation bombs, helicopter gunships and pellet bombs, the spraying of poisons on thousands of acres of crops and the use of enormous high explosive weapons. Civilian areas have been declared "free fire zones" and the policy has been one of mechanical slaughter. On the ground "search and destroy" missions have used gas in lethal quantities, the killing of prisoners, and systematic interrogation under electrical and other tortures.

Senator Kennedy has released figures given to him as chair of the Senate Refugees subcommittee. He says that there have been one million civilian casualties in South Vietnam alone since 1965, of which 300,000 have been killed. In the London *Times* of December 3 its Washington correspondent, Louis Heren, compares such slaughter to the Nazi record in Eastern Europe: "These terrible figures, proportionately perhaps comparable to the losses suffered by the Soviet Union in the Second World War." Two days earlier, the same newspaper's correspondent in Saigon, Fred Emery, reported: "What begins as a 'firefight' in a hamlet continues compulsively long after opposing fire has been surpressed. With such appalling fire discipline among all units in Vietnam, it is only exhaustion of ammunition that brings engagements to an end."

This is precisely the picture which emerged from the International War Crimes Tribunal in Scandinavia in 1967. The Tribunal heard from former U.S. servicemen of the dropping of Vietnamese prisoners from helicopters, the killing of prisoners under torture and the shooting on orders of those trying to be accepted as prisoners. All this and much more was known to tens of thousands of troops in Vietnam. The London *Times'* Saigon correspondent, describing the reactions to the recent revelations of Americans in Vietnam, commented: "...There is a strong undercurrent of knowledge and fear that 'there but for the grace of God, go I.' "

This is why the prosecution of isolated junior officers is quite inadequate. They are to be made scapegoats. The more wicked war criminals are the highest ranking military and civilian leaders, the architects of the whole genocidal policy. Have we so soon forgotten the regular White House breakfasts at which, Johnson boasted openly, he and McNamara and their closest colleagues selected the targets for the coming week?

This in turn is why it is ludicrous to suggest that an enquiry should be mounted by anyone associated with the Government or Armed Forces. The whole establishment stands condemned, including those more moderate politicians whose every utterances are still dictated by caution and petty ambition Goldberg's call for a commission of "concerned patriotic Americans" would be a sublime irrelevance were it not the very means whereby the whole horror would be hidden. Only a Pentagon enquiry could do worse.

Because I doubt whether any enquiry in the United States would be free from the most severe harassment, I have invited some fifteen heads of state around the world to press the UN Secretary General to establish an enquiry into war crimes in Vietnam.

Several American newspapers have observed that reaction to the massacre revelations has been much more rapid and sharp in Western Europe than in the United States. This is highly alarming. The entire American people are on trial. If there is not a massive moral revulsion at what is being done in their names to the people of Vietnam, there may be little hope for the future of America. Having lost the will to continue the slaughter is not enough; the people of America must now repudiate their civil and military leaders.

Index

417